2 Cor. 9:8
Paul Tassell
3/23/93

Happy Reading!

QUEST FOR FAITHFULNESS

QUEST FOR FAITHFULNESS

THE ACCOUNT OF A UNIQUE FELLOWSHIP OF CHURCHES

Paul N. Tassell

REGULAR BAPTIST PRESS
1300 North Meacham Road
Schaumburg, Illinois 60173–4888

Library of Congress Cataloging-in-Publication Data

Tassell, Paul N., 1934–
Quest for faithfulness: the account of a unique fellowship of churches / Paul N. Tassell.
p. cm.
Includes bibliographical references.
ISBN 0–87227–152–8
1. General Association of Regular Baptist Churches—History.
2. Baptist—United States—History. I. Title.
BX6389.33.T37 1991
286'.13—dc20

91–7930
CIP

Regular Baptist Press
Schaumburg, Illinois

Printed in U.S.A.

DEDICATION

To my brother, Rev. Albert B. Tassell, Jr.,
and all the other beloved men of God
who pastor the hundreds of churches
in fellowship with the General Association
of Regular Baptist Churches.

ACKNOWLEDGMENTS

We acknowledge with appreciation the quotations taken from the following sources:

At Dawn We Slept by G. W. Prange; copyright 1981. Used by permission of McGraw-Hill, Inc.

Taken from *Bible Questions Answered* by William L. Pettingill. Copyright © 1979 by the Zondervan Corporation. Used by permission.

From *THE ROCKEFELLERS: An American Dynasty* by Peter Collier and David Horowitz. Copyright © 1976 by Peter Collier and David Horowitz. Reprinted by permission of Henry Holt and Company, Inc.

CONTENTS

FOREWORD

It is a special privilege to introduce this account of the General Association of Regular Baptist Churches by my good friend and associate, Dr. Paul N. Tassell.

An appreciation of the people, principles and purposes of the General Association of Regular Baptists will surely ensue as you read of the formation, leadership, growth, struggles and victories during its sixty-year history.

My first contact with the people of this Fellowship came in the late '30s as my parents supported missionaries in Brazil. It continued as I went to Bible camp as a youth in the '40s, pastored in the '50s, served at Regular Baptist Press in the '60s, built our church buildings in the '70s, then returned to the Press in the late '80s. All this is simply to say that I have been where I could personally observe all the national representatives chosen to serve the Association. Each had a Biblical ministry and an exemplary conduct that provided stability through the decades. It is fitting that their messages and leadership are featured in this account.

More than five years of strenuous effort by Dr. Tassell have gone into the compilation of this account of our heritage. You will be encouraged and strengthened in the faith as you become aware of God's leading away from modernism and into freedom to serve Him in a Biblical manner.

— Vernon D. Miller, Litt. D.
Executive Editor
Regular Baptist Press
Schaumburg, Illinois

INTRODUCTION

(Must Reading!!)

The following pages are the story of the General Association of Regular Baptist Churches. It is not the history of GARBC-approved educational, missionary or service ministries. We do write about the agencies as they relate to the GARBC, but including definitive histories of the agencies was not the purpose of this book. It is not a history of the Regular Baptist Press, although someone needs to write one on that work sometime in the future.

Neither is this book a history of other religious groups or movements. We have limited our work to telling the story of the GARBC, and that was a big job! We give information about other movements as they affect our Association in one way or another. But the personalities and work of the GARBC are the primary reasons for this book.

There are many quotations in this book. In my research (which included the laborious and painstaking, albeit rewarding, work of reading through almost sixty years of the *Baptist Bulletin* and sixty years of Council of Fourteen/Eighteen minutes), I discovered that many Regular Baptists had said and written quite eloquently on a number of subjects. That work needs to be preserved for future students of the GARBC. The reader will also find long lists of names and churches from time to time throughout the book. I do not apologize for such lists, for I have good Biblical precedents in Numbers, First and Second Chronicles, Matthew and Luke for such lists. If you find such reading difficult, just skip it—but you will be the loser! I wanted this book to be about more people than just the notables and well-known leaders. The "troops in the trenches" or "the grass roots" or the "unnoticeables" as some are called are important to the history of the GARBC. With God, I am sure there are no "minor prophets." If you are doing God's work God's way and where He placed you, you are "major." As you read through the names and places, you may find yourself! You will surely find the name of someone you have known, and your heart will well up with emotion as your memory is stirred.

If any names are omitted that you, the reader, feel should have been included, you may be sure the omissions were unintentional. I tried to be as representative as possible in the selection of people listed.

God has given me the privilege of serving in the office of National Representative longer than any of my predecessors. I count this responsibility a sacred trust. This book is the result of a lifetime of study and ministry in the GARBC. Any shortcomings you may find in the book are my responsibility. But you had better believe the story of the GARBC is indeed a quest for faithfulness!

— *Paul N. Tassell*

THE PRE-ASSOCIATION YEARS

1

The Roaring Twenties! The 1920s were indeed roaring. It was a decadent and dazzling decade. Three presidents served in the White House during those years: wily Warren G. Harding, cool Calvin Coolidge and hapless Herbert Hoover. Harding's administration was rocked by the Teapot Dome scandal involving bribery and a maze of corruption. Harding died suddenly in 1923, and Coolidge succeeded him. After Coolidge's presidency, the crash of the stock market in 1929 spelled doom for President Hoover and the Republican Party.

In the world of sports the Roaring Twenties were marked by superstars whose achievements still awe serious sport fans. Jack Dempsey and Gene Tunney ruled the boxing world. The New York Yankees of 1927 have been acclaimed as the greatest baseball team ever. They were led by Babe Ruth and Lou Gehrig. Bobby Jones and Gene Sarazen were the headliners in golf. The Galloping Ghost, Harold "Red" Grange, starred as an all-American halfback at the University of Illinois and then as a professional with the Chicago Bears.

But even greater battles were being fought in other arenas. Those arenas were spiritual arenas. They were denominational arenas. Titanic struggles were under way in Methodist, Presbyterian and Baptist organizations. The battles were being waged between Bible-believing fundamentalists and Bible-denying liberals.

Our concern in this book has to do with the outcome of the long struggle within the Northern Baptist Convention. The Convention, officially established in 1907, had from its inception liberals entrenched in churches, seminaries and mission boards. It had no definitive doctrinal statement.

Fundamentalists in the Convention had attempted in the 1922 conference in Indianapolis to get a motion on the floor affirming the New Hampshire Confession of Faith as the doctrinal position of the Northern Baptist Convention. One clever liberal immediately offered a substitute motion that declared: "The Northern Baptist Convention affirms that the New Testament is the all-sufficient ground of our faith and practice, and we need no other statement." The Convention accepted that nonspecific, nondefinitive statement by a two-to-one margin.

One of the most formidable influences in the Convention was John D. Rockefeller, Jr. He exerted his presence and financial power in favor of the liberals early in the Convention's history. That influence never waned until his death in 1960.

In their monumental work, *The Rockefellers, An American Dynasty,* authors Peter Collier and David Horowitz tell us that John D. Rockefeller, Jr., became "the most important financier of liberal and ecumenical Protestantism and a rallying point in the demands for change inside the church."[1] Collier and Horowitz go on to say the following:

> In this cause he was as usual greatly influenced by friends and associates, including Charles Evans Hughes, a leading layman of the Fifth Avenue (now Park Avenue) Baptist Church, the Reverends Buttrick and Gates from the charitable trusts, John Mott and even Ivy Lee. All were partisans of modernism in the church, endorsing the "progressive" trends that were transforming the life of the country: the centralization of administrative units, the growth of scientific ideas and technology, the internationalization of American influence and power. They wanted the church to relate to these tendencies in a positive way, and thereby retain its effectiveness as a cohesive social force in American life. Arrayed against them were the fundamentalists, responsive to the small-town conservatism of rural America and clinging to the old doctrines and the old ways.[2]

Of course the "old doctrines and the old ways" had to do with doctrinal integrity, the preaching of the gospel and worldwide missionary outreach. Rockefeller was not interested in funding such Scriptural ventures. He did fund a study group to examine the effectiveness of missionary work. After a year of intensive work, mainly in India, China and Japan, the study group issued its report titled *Rethinking Missions.* Rockefeller was overjoyed to read the report "criticizing foreign missions in the underdeveloped world, recommending less preaching and doctrinalism, a more sympathetic attitude toward the indigenous cultures, greater emphasis on education, medicine, and agriculture, and a gradual transfer of responsibility for the missions into the hands of foreign nationals."[3]

Rethinking Missions appeared early in 1932 and certainly confirmed what Ketcham, Van Osdel, Van Gilder and other fundamentalists had been saying about the unscriptural policy of inclusivism being practiced on the mission fields of the world by liberal Northern Baptist missionaries. Back of it all was the financial force and personal power of John D. Rockefeller, Jr.

Nothing happened in the Roaring Twenties to symbolize the mating of money and modernism so dramatically as the flowering friendship between Rockefeller and the leading liberal of the United States, Dr. Harry Emerson Fosdick. Dr. Fosdick had created a storm while he was pastor of the Old First Presbyterian Church at 11th Street and Fifth Avenue in New York. He had belittled the fundamentals of the faith and had ultimately been forced to resign as pastor.

> The confrontation was continued in the General Assembly. The fundamentalists, led by William Jennings Bryan, tried to excommunicate Fosdick, charging that he was guilty of heresy in casting doubt on the virgin birth. Fosdick was aided in his parliamentary victory over the Bryan forces by a young attorney who had become a leading layman in the church and who felt strongly about this question. His name was John Foster Dulles.[4]

After his resignation from the Old First Presbyterian Church, Fosdick was offered the pastorate of the Park Avenue Baptist Church by a one-man pulpit committee named John D. Rockefeller, Jr. Fosdick was reluctant to accept the offer for two major reasons: (1) the ostentatiously wealthy Park Avenue building and location; (2) the requirement for immersion for church membership.

In the end, the Park Avenue congregation removed the two final obstacles that had stood in the way of Fosdick's taking the job when it relaxed its insistence on baptism by immersion and agreed to move to a less swank area. After Junior [John D. Rockefeller, Jr., that is!] provided $26 million toward the construction of a new interdenominational church on Riverside Drive in Morningside Heights, Fosdick agreed to accept the calling, which was now the most influential pastorate in the country and the one that would be largely responsible for the victory of the Protestant liberals.[5]

Rockefeller not only greatly influenced his own local church and the missionary policy of the Northern Baptist Convention, he also had great and unbiblical influence on Convention seminaries. He poured millions of dollars into the University of Chicago Divinity School and the Rochester Theological Seminary. Those schools and other lesser-known liberal institutions connected with the Convention have sent a steady stream of liberal pastors and missionaries into the churches and mission fields of what we now call American Baptist Churches in the U.S.A.

It is no wonder that fundamentalists within the Convention during the Roaring Twenties had to take a stand against the rising tide of unbelief and infidelity. Fosdick and Rockefeller represented thousands of apostate clergymen and laymen in the Convention. To remain in such a convention and not protest and try to reverse the situation was an impossibility. What, but what could be done?

End Notes

1. Peter Collier and David Horowitz, *The Rockefellers: An American Dynasty* (New York: Holt, Rinehart and Winston, 1976), p. 152. Used by permission of Henry Holt and Company, Inc.

2. Ibid.

3. Ibid., pp. 151, 152.

4. Ibid., p. 153.

5. Ibid.

2

Bible-believing men in the Northern Baptist Convention decided to organize themselves in such a way as to make their influence and voice more effective. The result? The first conference of the Baptist Bible Union (BBU) was held at Kansas City, Missouri, May 10–15, 1923. Some of the original leaders were A. C. Dixon, Robert T. Ketcham, Ralph Neighbour, Sr., J. Frank Norris, William Pettingill, W. B. Riley, T. T. Shields and O. W. Van Osdel.

The BBU met each year just ahead of the NBC annual convention meetings. The BBU meetings were actually Bible conferences for the purposes of strengthening believers and standing for the faith once delivered to the saints. In 1923 the Southern Baptist Convention met in Kansas City on May 16–23. The Northern Baptist Convention convened May 23–29 in Atlantic City, New Jersey. The Baptist Bible Union elected T. T. Shields as its president. He was the honored pastor of the Jarvis Street Baptist Church in Toronto, Ontario, Canada. Elected vice presidents were W. B. Riley and J. Frank Norris. Riley was pastor of First Baptist Church in Minneapolis, Minnesota. Norris pastored the First Baptist Church in Fort Worth, Texas. The vice presidents were surely a study in contrasts! Riley was a scholarly, dignified statesman, while Norris was the ever flamboyant, dramatic preacher-evangelist. The three officers must have had some interesting meetings!

But could they preach! And so could the men who spoke at the annual meetings of the BBU. Dr. Merle R. Hull wrote: "Those Baptist Bible Union meetings surely produced some of the greatest preaching of this century."[1] Stirred by that great pulpit ministry, the fundamentalists would go to the NBC annual meeting each year determined to rectify the Convention and outvote the unbelievers. But each year they would sadly and soundly go down to defeat to the larger and better organized modernistic Convention leaders.

Wrote Dr. Hull:

> The Baptist Bible Union reached its peak in 1926. From then on it declined in numbers and interest. The notoriety attached to one of the prominent personalities, J. Frank Norris, did nothing to help the cause. Nor did the fiasco at Des Moines University, a school sponsored by the Union, forced to close because of student riots against the president and the board of trustees.[2]

Nevertheless, the BBU continued to limp along for another six years valiantly endeavoring to stem the tide of Baptist unbelief, inclusivism and rationalism. The liberals were firmly entrenched in leadership positions that totally controlled the convention finances, schools and missionary endeavors.

Harry G. Hamilton, pastor of the First Baptist Church of Buffalo, New York, and the first elected president of the new GARBC, had the following to say about the Baptist Bible Union.

> They were Revelationists as opposed to Rationalists.
> They were Creationists as opposed to Evolutionists.
> They were Trinitarians as opposed to Unitarians.
> They were Regenerationists as opposed to Reformationists.
>
> All this the General Association of Regular Baptists heartily endorse. However, the years that have passed have revealed some needed changes in the plan of organization along the following lines.
>
> 1. The Baptist Bible Union was an organization of individuals more than it was a union of churches and Baptists have no constituted authority apart from the church bearing that name.
>
> 2. It was an organization determined to do its work within the existing Northern Baptist Convention and to cultivate the churches until every Baptist church was made aware of the peril that threatened it. It is now believed that any attempt to promote the program of Christianity while in association with Modernism is contrary to the teaching of Scripture. Therefore, the cause of true Christianity can best be advanced by the establishment of a new association for those who desire to be true to our Glorious Lord and to the historic principles of Baptists.
>
> 3. The Union was organized to preserve the denomination, but the socalled denomination with its overlordship foisted upon the churches "The

Inclusive Policy" which meant that our schools and colleges were permitted to propagate infidelity under the guise of Modernism and these ministers and missionaries, as graduates of these schools, were sent forth to spread this heresy together with others who went forth to spread the Gospel.[3]

Thus the weaknesses of the Baptist Bible Union came steadily, certainly and clearly into focus. Toward the end of 1928 three Ohio pastors, who were to figure largely in the GARBC of the future, were slowly but surely coming to separatist convictions. They were Rev. Earle G. Griffith, pastor of Emmanuel Baptist Church, Toledo, Ohio; Rev. Robert T. Ketcham, pastor of First Baptist Church, Elyria Ohio; and Rev. H. O. Van Gilder, Sr., pastor of Central Baptist Church, Columbus, Ohio. Dr. Ketcham said, "We had no idea of separation at first, but the longer the controversy raged and the more hopeless it became to correct it, gradually we got the idea that if we can't clean the leaven out of our house, then we must leave the house."[4]

Therefore, in 1928, at the Central Baptist Church in Columbus, the Ohio Association of Independent Baptist Churches was formed. The year 1928 was the last good year for Herbert Hoover politically, but it was just the beginning of good and godly things for Ohio Regular Baptists. The eyes and hearts of northern Baptists were starting to see their orders in the form of 2 Corinthians 6:14–18:

> Be ye not unequally yoked together with unbelievers: for what fellowship hath righteousness with unrighteousness? and what communion hath light with darkness? and what concord hath Christ with Belial? or what part hath he that believeth with an infidel? And what agreement hath the temple of God with idols? for ye are the temple of the living God; as God hath said, I will dwell in them, and walk in them; and I will be their God, and they shall be my people. Wherefore come out from among them, and be ye separate, saith the Lord, and touch not the unclean thing; and I will receive you, and will be a Father unto you, and ye shall be my sons and daughters, saith the Lord Almighty.

The decade that had begun as "the Roaring Twenties" ended as "the whimpering twenties" as the stock market crashed and the Great Depression set in. Shock, disbelief and despair permeated and pervaded society at every stratum. For the unregenerate, glee turned to glumness, happiness to hopelessness, riches to rags and optimism to pessimism. What a time for the true church and true believers to witness! What a time for a new Association of Bible-believing, Christ-honoring, gospel-preaching, missionary-minded people to launch a new movement for God, in the power of God and for the people of God!

Not only were matters disheartening economically as the '20s drew to a close, but the takeover of the large denominations by a liberalism that offered no supernaturalism, no gospel and no authoritative Bible had left the populace with no real relationship to a personal God. In his book, *A Preface to Morals,* Walter Lippmann said with incisive insight:

> Churchmen, like Dr. Fosdick, can make no such claim [a claim of authority] about their message. They reject revelation. They reject the authority of any church to speak directly for God. They reject the literal inspiration of the Bible. They reject altogether many parts of the Bible as not only uninspired, but false and misleading. They do not believe in God as a lawgiver, judge, father and spectator of human life. When they say that this or that message in the Bible is "permanently valid," they mean only that in their judgment, according to their reading of human experience, it is a well-tested truth. To say this is not merely to deny that the Bible is authoritative in astronomy and biology; it is to deny equally that it is authoritative as to what is good and bad for men. The Bible thus becomes no more than a revered collection of hypotheses which each man may reject or accept in the light of his own knowledge.[5]

Can you imagine a Robert T. Ketcham or a Harry G. Hamilton or an Earle G. Griffith or an H. O. Van Gilder working in the same denomination with a Harry Emerson Fosdick? Neither can I! Nineteen thirty-two, here we come!

End Notes

1. Merle R. Hull, *What A Fellowship!* (Schaumburg, IL: Regular Baptist Press, 1981), p. 14.

2. Ibid.

3. *The Bulletin* (June 1933), pp. 1, 2.

4. J. Murray Murdoch, *Portrait of Obedience* (Schaumburg, IL: Regular Baptist Press, 1979), p. 110.

5. Walter Lippmann, *A Preface to Morals* (New York: The Macmillan Co., 1929), pp. 46, 47.

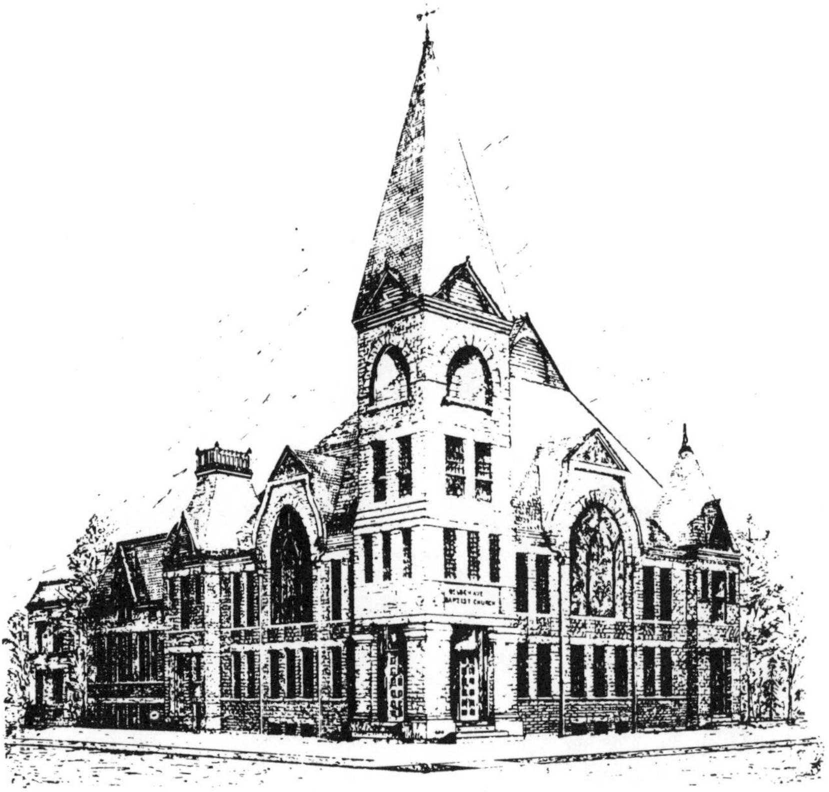

Belden Avenue Baptist Church, Chicago

The Formative Years

1932–1944

3

Nineteen thirty-two was a great year for Franklin Roosevelt. He was elected to the United States presidency in a major landslide. He garnered 22,821,857 votes to Herbert Hoover's 15,761,841 votes. The electoral college tally was 472 to 59 in favor of Roosevelt. Clearly the American public wanted the "new deal" promised by FDR.

Bible-believing Baptists also got a "new deal" in 1932. It all began when 34 messengers from 22 local churches met at the Belden Avenue Baptist Church in Chicago, Illinois, for what turned out to be the last meeting of the Baptist Bible Union and the first meeting of the General Association of Regular Baptist Churches. Total separation from the Northern Baptist Convention was the clear requirement for fellowship in the new Association. Unqualified and unswerving loyalty to the Bible as the inerrant, infallible, inspired, authoritative Word of God was basic to all 34 of those original GARBC messengers. They agreed with Walter Lippmann's words:

> Something quite fundamental is left out of the modernist creeds. At least something which has hitherto been quite fundamental is left out. That something is the most abiding of all the experiences of religion, namely, the conviction that the religion comes from God. Suppose it were true, which it plainly is not, that Dr. Fosdick by his process of selection and decoding has retained "precisely the thing at which the Bible was driving." Still he would be without the thing on which popular religion has been founded. For the Bible to our ancestors was not simply, as he implies, a book of wisdom. It was a book of wisdom backed by the power of God Himself. That is not an inconsiderable difference. It is all the difference there is between a pious resolution and a moral law. The Bible, as men formerly accepted it, contained wisdom *certified* by the powers that govern the universe. It did not merely contain many well-tested truths, similar in kind to those which are to be found in Plato, Aristotle, Montaigne and Bernard Shaw. It contained truths which

could not be doubted because they had been spoken by God through His prophets and His Son. They could not be wrong. But once it is allowed that each man may select from the Bible as he sees fit, judging each passage by his own notions of what is "abiding," you have stripped the Scriptures of their authority to command men's confidence and to compel their obedience. The Scriptures may still inspire respect. But they are disarmed.[1]

The May 1932 meeting was chaired by Dr. Howard C. Fulton, pastor of the Belden Avenue Baptist Church. During the conference he preached a ringing message titled "What Regular Old Fashioned Baptists Stand For." The questions Fulton asked in that message are still powerful and valid:

How can we cooperate with and support those who deny the great verities of the historic Baptist faith; those who say the Bible is not the inspired Word of God but a man-made book; those who say that Jesus Christ is not the virgin born Son of God and God the Son, but the illegitimate son of Joseph and Mary, born out of wedlock, or the product of evolution; those who say that the death of Jesus Christ was exemplary and not expiatory; those who say that Jesus Christ did not rise bodily from the dead and is not coming back personally into this world of men?[2]

Such potent, probing, pricking, powerful preaching has been the hallmark of our GARBC annual conferences.

The name given to the fledgling Association is significant. The Food and Drug Administration has made us aware of how crucially important it is to have bottles or cans correctly labeled. Our label tells an accurate story.

GENERAL: The word general was chosen to denote geographic scope. We were coming out of the "northern" convention, but we did not desire to limit ourselves to the North or South or East or West. According to our GARBC constitution our geographic scope includes "the North American continent, the United States and her territorial possessions."[3] At this writing we have 1,582 churches in 45 states and 3 provinces of Canada. We do not have churches in Alabama, Mississippi, North Dakota, South Carolina and Vermont. The states with the most GARBC churches are Michigan with 226, Ohio with 196, New York with 148, Indiana with 124, California with 114 and Iowa with 110.

ASSOCIATION: We are not another convention. We are a voluntary fellowship of independent Baptist churches working together for common causes with common convictions. The following paragraphs are taken from *The New Directory for Baptist Churches* by Dr. Edward T. Hiscox, and they properly define an association.

1. The term *Association* is used in *two* distinct and quite dissimilar senses. . . .

First, the organized body which meets annually for the transaction of business, is called the *Association.* This body corporate consists of *pastors* and *messengers,* as its constituent elements and active *members.* It has its constitution, by-laws, its order of business, meets and adjourns. . . . *Second,* in a somewhat vague and ideal sense all the associated churches, and the geographical limits over which they are scattered, are called the *Association.* . . .

2. An Association—the organized body that meets for business—is *not* composed of churches, but of individuals, the pastors and messengers. It is a common way of speaking, but a very loose and misleading way, to say it is composed of churches. This arises from a misapprehension, and perpetuates a misunderstanding. A Baptist Church cannot be a member of any other body whatever. It would violate its sacred charter, and lose its identity as the body of Christ, to attempt such a union. And if many churches should enter into organic relations, and constitute an ecclesiastical confederation, the local churches would be absorbed, losing largely their individuality and their independence. Also, in that case, the confederate body would possess legislative and judicial control over the separate congregations. This is the actual *status* of most Christian denominations. But our polity and our traditions repudiate both the inference and the hypothesis on which it rests.

3. But it may be asked, How is it, if churches are not *members* of the body, that the Associations uniformly receive new churches to their number, or dismiss or drop churches from it? The reply is this: Churches are not received to *membership,* though such expressions are often, and indeed ordinarily used; but they are received to *fellowship* and *cooperation;* which fact is evinced by their pastors and messengers being admitted to *membership,* thus composing its constituent elements.

4. An Association is not a *representative* body, in the ordinary acceptation of that term. A Baptist Church cannot appoint persons with delegated authority to act for it, so as to bind it by their action. It cannot transfer its authority and responsibility to any person, or persons whatever. It can appoint persons as committees to perform service for it, and report their doings. If it be still insisted, for the sake of terms, that the churches do meet in the Association, by their representatives, the pastors and messengers, the reply must be—such is not the case, and cannot be, either actually or constructively for a Baptist Church cannot be *represented* by delegates [who are]

authorized to act for it in any other organization whatever.

5. An Association is a *voluntary* society formed and maintained for mutual help among the churches associated, and for the religious welfare of the field it occupies. It is of human, not of divine authority; it grows out of the sympathies of Christian fellowship, and the need of mutual help. No Church is under obligation to affiliate with it; and any connected Church can withdraw cooperation, at any time, for any reasons which seem to itself sufficient, without prejudice to either its evangelical or its denominational reputation and standing. But while it continues associated, it must abide by the rules and regulations, mutually agreed upon, by which the body is governed.

6. Because an Association is not a representative body, and because a Church cannot be represented in any other organization, and because a Church cannot, even if it would, alienate, or transfer its powers and responsibilities to any man, or body of men, *therefore* an Association cannot legislate for the churches, exercise any authority over them, or bind them in any way by its own action. Whatever is done while in session, is of authority only to those who do it. . . .

7. The fact that the messengers are appointed by their respective churches argues nothing as to their being invested with delegated power. This appointment is made at the request of the Association, and according to its constitutional provisions, as the most convenient and equitable method of constituting the body, not because the appointment carries any ecclesiastical authority with it. . . .

8. An Association is an *independent* body, not subject to the authority or control of the churches any more than the churches are subject to its authority and control. It frames its own constitution, makes its own by-laws, elects its own officers, and manages its own business, without dictation from any one. Within its own sphere of action it is just as independent as a Church is within its sphere of action."[4]

REGULAR: When we say we are "regular" Baptists, we automatically imply there are some "irregular" Baptists! When Northern Baptist Convention leaders and seminary professors and leading preachers like Harry Emerson Fosdick denied the inerrancy of the Bible and scoffed at the Virgin Birth and denied the necessity for the substitutionary death of Christ and other fundamentals of the faith, they became irregular.

The term "regular" was not new. The Ohio Baptist fundamentalists organized themselves as the Union of Regular Baptist Churches on October 31, 1928. They later changed their name to the Ohio Association of Regular Baptist Churches. Other Baptist groups used the name "Regular" as far back as the nineteenth century.

Regular Baptists are genuine, true, real, bona fide Baptists. We are not interdenominationalists or Methodists or Presbyterians or Episcopalians—we are Baptists, regular true-blue "real McCoy," "sure-thing" Baptists!

BAPTISTS: Although the word in our name is in the singular, let us look at the plural of the word. The word spelled plurally has eight letters, and each letter stands for a Baptist distinctive.

Biblical authority. In a truly Baptist church if the Bible says it, that settles it. If the Baptist pastor is preaching the Word of God faithfully and accurately and it rubs your fur the wrong way, you don't fire the preacher. You turn around so your fur goes the right way! True Baptists do not believe in saying, "I know the Bible says that, *but* . . ." As someone once said, "When you start butting God, you'll find out He has bigger horns than you do." Seriously, genuine Baptists look at the Bible as their final rule of faith and practice.

Autonomy of the local church. A Baptist local church is a sovereign, independent, autonomous body. It calls its own pastor, elects its own officers, decides its own budget and chooses its own educational, missionary and service agencies. For example, our six approved missionary agencies have about two thousand missionaries. It is obvious that one local church cannot support all two thousand of them; so they decide whom they will support and for how much. There are no denominational dictators who interfere in the least with the local churches in fellowship with the GARBC.

Priesthood of every believer. Peter called believers "a royal priesthood" (1 Pet. 2:9). John wrote that Christ has "made us kings and priests unto God and his Father" (Rev. 1:6). Every believer has direct access to God through the shed blood of our High Priest, Jesus Christ. We don't need to go through Saint Jude or Saint Elmo or Saint Joseph or Saint Mary. "For there is one God, and one mediator between God and men, the man Christ Jesus" (1 Tim. 2:5). Since every believer is a priest, we Baptists believe in congregational church government. We do not believe in "elder rule" or "deacon rule" or "trustee rule" but in congregational rule.

Two church ordinances. First, we believe in believer's baptism by single immersion. Someone may ask, "What difference does the mode or method of baptism make?" The answer is simple: *The mode is the message.* New Testament baptism is for one purpose—to picture the believer's identification with Christ in His death, burial and resurrection. Only single immersion in water shows that identification. When you bury someone, you immerse that person in the soil. You don't sprinkle dirt on him, you *bury* him. And you don't bury him headfirst three times! Only single immersion properly identifies the believer with Christ's death, burial and resurrection.

Second, we believe in the Lord's Supper. There are three major interpretations of the Lord's Supper in Christendom. First, there is the Roman Catholic view of *transubstantiation.* This view holds that when the Roman Catholic priest blesses the wafer, it literally turns into the flesh of Christ. When the priest blesses the cup, it literally turns into the blood of Christ. Such a view truly makes participants cannibals and vampires. Transubstantiation is *magic,* and Baptists do not believe in magic. Second, there is the Lutheran view of *consubstantiation.* Luther taught that when the priest or pastor blesses the bread and wine, the presence of Christ mysteriously and wondrously combines with the bread and wine. Luther moved from magic to *mystery,* but Baptists do not accept that either. We believe the Lord's Table to be *memorial.* Jesus said, "This do in remembrance of me" (Luke 22:19). Baptists believe that a ceremony must meet three qualifications in order to be classified as a New Testament ordinance. First, it must be commanded by Christ in the New Testament Gospels. Second, it must have been practiced by the churches in the book of Acts. Third, it must be taught somewhere in the epistles. Only believer's baptism and the Lord's Supper meet this threefold qualification.

Individual soul liberty. Dr. Paul R. Jackson said it well:

> Soul liberty is the implementation of the truth that we must "obey God rather than men" (Acts 5:29). Every man must give answer to God individually, and therefore no other man, and no church, can act as his conscience now. He has the right to interpret the Scripture for himself and the responsibility to answer to God for the way in which he does so. He has, as a believer, the Holy Spirit to guide and enable him, apart from any other ministry of man or of the church.[5]

Separation of church and state. We do not believe any church should rule over the state. When Roman Catholic popes became more powerful than European kings and exerted civil authority, the results were devastating for both the so-called Church and the civil states involved. And when the secular rulers have used the church or churches as instruments to subjugate people to their wicked ends, such as Adolph Hitler and others have done throughout history, the results have also been terrible. The words of our Lord are timelessly relevant here: "Render therefore unto Caesar the things which are Caesar's; and unto God the things that are God's" (Matt. 22:21).

Two church officers: pastors and deacons. We do not believe in popes and archbishops. We believe the terms "elder," "pastor" and "bishop" to be interchangeable terms applying to the same person who is most often referred to as "pastor." The term "deacon" simply means a servant of others. The pastor is the undershepherd who is assisted by the deacons. Their qualifications and responsibilities are clearly outlined in 1 Timothy 3:1–13.

Saved church membership. No doubt one of the contributing factors to the downfall of the major Protestant denominations has been the practices of infant baptism followed by confirmation at approximately age twelve with no concern for individual salvation through personal faith in the crucified, buried, risen, ascended Lord Jesus Christ. Wrote Dr. Jackson:

> Nothing will more rapidly corrupt the doctrine and ministry of a church than an unregenerate group within it. They do not have the spiritual discernment to divide between truth and error. Neither do they have a spiritual hunger after truth nor a burden to proclaim a pure, Biblical message. Human reason soon displaces divine revelation, and expediency displaces the commandments of God.[6]

Thus we are the General Association of Regular BAPTIST . . . ; yes, there is one more very important word. . . .

CHURCHES: The GARBC was from its very beginning an association of churches. The makeup of the Association consisted of voting messengers sent by the churches to the annual conference. Only members in good standing of Regular Baptist churches could qualify as legitimate members of the Association. A non-church member could not be a card-carrying GARBC'er! The Association is a fellowship of local churches, not pastors. And every church is equal to every other church in its voting privileges. Big churches do not have more voting "clout" than little churches any more than a 250-pound man should have more votes than a 100-pound lady just because he is 150 pounds bigger.

THE NAME: General Association of Regular Baptist Churches. In Chicago in May of 1932 the new Association numbered only 22 churches. Sixty years later that number is almost 1,600 local churches. But what else happened at Belden Avenue Baptist Church in 1932 after the messengers chose the name?

End Notes

1. Walter Lippmann, *A Preface to Morals* (New York: The Macmillan Co., 1929), pp. 47, 48.

2. Howard Fulton, "What Old-Fashioned Baptists Stand For," *Baptist Bulletin* (May 1988), p. 22.

3. GARBC Constitution, Literature Item 1.

4. Edward T. Hiscox, *The New Directory for Baptist Churches* (Philadelphia: The Judson Press, 1894), pp. 332–336.

5. Paul R. Jackson, *The Doctrine and Administration of the Church* (Schaumburg, IL: Regular Baptist Press, 1980), p. 138.

6. Ibid., p. 142.

4

Leadership. How important it is! From its very beginning the General Association of Regular Baptist Churches was blessed by godly and wise leadership. Those early GARBC leaders had learned by bitter experience that denominational dictatorship was counterproductive in the Lord's work. Their desire was for happy, humble and holy cooperation, not arrogant coercion on the part of their leaders.

As the messengers at that first conference prayerfully sought the face of God, they were led to choose Rev. Harry G. Hamilton, pastor of the First Baptist Church of Buffalo, New York, as their first president. First vice president was Rev. Earle G. Griffith, who had just moved from the Emmanuel Baptist Church of Toledo, Ohio, to the pastorate of the Bethel Baptist Church in Erie, Pennsylvania. Six more vice presidents were T. W. Wood from California, Leo Sandgren from Minnesota, C. E. Wood from Michigan, M. E. Hawkins from Indiana, A. G. Annette from Iowa and Howard C. Fulton from Illinois. The secretary-treasurer was John Muntz from Forrestville, New York.

The first issue of the official Associational magazine was published in January of 1933. It was called *The Bulletin.* On page 2 Dr. O. W. Van Osdel, pastor of the Wealthy Street Baptist Church in Grand Rapids, Michigan, is quoted as saying:

> It is not necessary for anyone to get the impression that the General Association of Regular Baptists is something new. Regular Baptists have always stood for the defense of their independence, and have formed Associations and Conventions whenever it seemed to be for the good of the cause, and now that there are hundreds of churches throughout the country unwilling longer to endure the overlordship of the Northern Baptist oligarchy and the inclusive policy, it is in order, according to Baptist usage, for these churches to associate themselves together in this fellowship so that

they may carry forward their missionary undertakings and defend the principles for which Baptists have always stood. Modernism, and churches with an open membership, and all sorts of unscriptural beliefs, are not for one moment to be tolerated in Regular Baptist Churches.[1]

The first *Bulletin* also carried some items of news. Rev. Howard Keithley, later to be a great force for God in Michigan Regular Baptist circles, reported that his church, the Calvary Baptist Church of Buffalo, had withdrawn from the Northern Baptist Convention. Robert T. Ketcham had closed out 1932 by finishing his ministry at First Baptist Church in Elyria, Ohio, and beginning his new work as pastor of the Central Baptist Church in Gary, Indiana. Dr. Howard C. Fulton of the Belden Avenue Baptist Church in Chicago reported a Sunday School attendance average of 471 with a goal of 500 for the new year. Rev. Leo Sandgren reported the seventy-fifth anniversary of First Baptist Church in Austin, Minnesota, and finished his report with words that gladden the heart of a treasurer—"Voted to put the Association on our budget." Rev. Harry G. Hamilton announced a January Bible conference featuring Dr. James M. Gray, Dr. Henry Ostrom and Dr. Harry A. Ironside. Clearly the churches of the new Association were virile, victorious and valiant testimonies for God in a nation sorely in need of such dynamic and determined local churches.

At the May 1933 annual conference in Buffalo, the outgoing president, Harry G. Hamilton, gave "the president's message" titled "Why the General Association of Regular Baptists?" He said:

Therefore, it is proposed that the General Association of Regular Baptists—

FIRST—Become an Association of Baptist Churches to maintain a testimony to the supernaturalism of Christianity as opposed to the anti-supernaturalism of modernism.

SECOND—It is an organization determined to do its work independent of, and separate from, the Northern Baptist Convention and all its auxiliaries.

THIRD—It does not in any way propose to preserve a denominational order, but rather to re-affirm the truths of Scripture historically believed by Baptists and expressed by the Baptist Confessions of faith of London 1689 or the New Hampshire Confession of Faith or the Philadelphia Confession of faith or the Baptist Bible Union Confession of faith or any such which enunciates the same truths though in other words.

FOURTH—It is an organization designed to promote a Missionary spirit amongst Baptist Churches for the spread of the Gospel in all the world, and to contend earnestly for the faith once for all delivered to the Saints.

FIFTH—It also proposes to assist churches secure safe, sound and satisfactory pastors for the proclamation of the Gospel and the work of the ministry. And to assist churches in needy places as much as in them is.[2]

President Hamilton's heavy emphasis on doctrine and missionary enterprise was especially noteworthy. On December 18, 1932, Dr. I. M. Haldeman, famous pastor of the First Baptist Church in New York City, preached a great sermon on modernism and fundamentalism. The thrust of that message is epitomized in the following words:

Modernism is the opposite and the antagonist of Doctrine. The supreme aim of Modernism is to deny, discount, overthrow and completely destroy the doctrinal side of Christianity. . . . MODERNISM IS NOT CHRISTIANITY. It has no more right to the name of Christ than a counterfeit dollar bill would have to bear the name and imprint of the United States Treasury.[3]

The coming to power of Adolph Hitler in 1933 and the rise of an imperialistic Japan would both have a serious impact upon those who would endeavor to evangelize the world. Nevertheless, Regular Baptists determined to make the GARBC a missionary-oriented Association. At the initial meeting of the Association in Chicago, May 15–18, 1932, a missionary committee was appointed. The chairman was Earle G. Griffith. Working with him were Howard Fulton of Chicago and Clyde E. Wood of Grand Rapids. They were instructed to seek out missionary societies interested in working with the GARBC. Three responded and were recommended to the messengers at the 1933 conference. They were the Lithuanian Missionary Association with headquarters in Chicago; the General Council of Cooperative Baptist Missions of North America (later to become Baptist Mid-Missions) with headquarters in Mishawaka, Indiana, M. E. Hawkins, director; and the Inter-State Evangelistic Association with headquarters in Rochester, New York, Rev. Harold Strathearn, director. Another missionary society was heartily recommended to the GARBC by Rev. David Otis Fuller of Atlantic City, New Jersey, who said:

The Association of Baptists for Evangelism in the Orient, Inc. [later to become ABWE] has been standing the past five years without one hint of compromise for the great fundamentals of the "faith once for all delivered to the saints." This is true not only of its missionaries on the field, but those also on the Executive Committee here at home. It was founded in much prayer and power of the Holy Spirit. . . . We feel it is needed at this very moment and we are confident that the Lord has "reserved yet seven thousand who have not bowed the knee to Baal."[4]

The 1933 conference in Buffalo elected Earle G. Griffith GARBC president. Robert T. Ketcham was chosen as first vice president. John Muntz was retained as secretary-treasurer. In the August 1933 issue of *The Bulletin* a provocative item appeared on page 2 titled "How to Promote Modernism." The anonymous but competent author wrote:

Modernism is that form of blasphemy which substitutes human reason for Divine Revelation, that says what we think is more important than what God says.

WE SUPPORT IT by continuing in a denominational organization which acknowledges that its policy is "inclusive."

WE SUPPORT IT by sending our sons and daughters to college where modernism is taught and accepted as truth.

WE SUPPORT IT by continuing in the membership of a church whose pastor is a modernist.

WE SUPPORT IT when we give our money to a denomination or a religious organization to send out missionaries to the foreign field who are modernists.

WE SUPPORT IT when we promote the interests of a denominational paper whose aim is to aid in the furtherance of an "inclusive policy."

WE SUPPORT IT when we welcome a modernist to the fellowship of our home. See II John 10:11 [sic].[5]

Strong words, but just as true today as when they were penned.

Disappointments. In the midst of the happy singing and warm fellowship that pervaded the first two GARBC conferences, there was also keen disappointment. Disappointment in men like W. B. Riley. Dr. Riley was pastor of the prestigious First Baptist Church in Minneapolis, Minnesota, from 1897 to 1943. His long pastorate in the Northern Baptist Convention paralleled that of the Southern Baptist Convention pastor, Dr. George W. Truett, who pastored the First Baptist Church of Dallas, Texas, from 1899 to 1944. Dr. Riley was a great disappointment to GARBC leaders because he refused to separate from the Convention. Not until the year of his death in 1947 at the age of 86 did

Riley finally separate from the Convention. The First Baptist Church of Minneapolis never did come out. We will never know, of course, how many preachers and churches were influenced to stay in the Convention because of Riley's failure to separate, but the number no doubt was considerable.

Another disappointment was William Ward Ayer, who preceded R. T. Ketcham as pastor of the Central Baptist Church in Gary, Indiana, from 1927 to 1932. After serving as pastor of the Philpott Tabernacle in Hamilton, Ontario, Canada, Dr. Ayer went on to pastor the large and influential Calvary Baptist Church in New York City. He ministered there from 1936 to 1949 and never did lead the church out of the Northern Baptist Convention. He, like Riley, was a great preacher and a fundamentalist, but he did not embrace the separatist movement as embodied in the GARBC.

Jasper C. Massee was 61 years of age when the GARBC was formed in 1932. J. C., as he was popularly known, had been a great beacon light of hope for Convention fundamentalists in the Roaring Twenties. He pastored the Tremont Temple from 1922 to 1929, and under his dynamic leadership the church grew to more than 4,000 members. But Massee fiercely fought the Baptist Bible Union and later opposed the formation of the GARBC. His influence was a factor, no doubt, in the failure of other Bible preachers to come out of the apostate Convention.

Although younger men like Ketcham (who was only 43 years old in 1932) were deeply disappointed in the shortsightedness of older men like Riley and Massee, the GARBC leaders pressed on in the confidence they were obeying the Word of God and had the blessing of God upon them. The quest for faithfulness had its rocky rides, but no one ever said following Jesus would always be easy.

End Notes

1. *The Bulletin* (January 1933), p. 2.
2. *The Bulletin* (June 1933), p. 2.
3. *The Bulletin* (March 1933), p. 1.
4. *The Bulletin* (April 1933), p. 3.
5. "How to Promote Modernism," *The Bulletin* (August 1933), p. 2.

5

The decade of the 1930s was politically and socially revolutionary in the United States of America. In 1933 Prohibition ended. Billy Sunday, whose fiery preaching against alcohol had helped bring about Prohibition, died in 1935. In 1933 President Roosevelt named Frances Perkins secretary of labor, the first woman ever appointed to a Cabinet position. On March 6, 1933, Roosevelt ordered all banks closed in the United States. Congress passed the Social Security Act in August of 1935. Aviation was beginning to flourish, but Will Rogers lost his life in a plane crash in Alaska in 1935, and Amelia Earhart was lost in the Pacific Ocean near Howland Island on July 2, 1937. In 1936 Roosevelt was elected to a second term by an unprecedented landslide over Alfred Landon. Roosevelt's electoral college margin was 523 to 8. His popular vote victory was 27,751,597 to 16,679,583. Riding the crest of his popularity, Roosevelt tried to pack the Supreme Court by adding six more judges to the nine-man court. Congress soundly rejected the move. However, Roosevelt's modernistic political philosophy and federal dollars began to permeate and pervade every segment of American society.

What was going on in the Northern Baptist Convention of the 1930s was a microcosm of what was taking place in the country as a whole. The modernistic theology of Harry Emerson Fosdick and the money of John D. Rockefeller, Jr., were turning the Convention into a hotbed of religious infidelity and its mission program into a glorified socialism. But just as Roosevelt had his conservative opponents, so the Convention was opposed and exposed by a band of faithful, fervent, fearless and fruitful fundamentalists whose GARBC was making an impact for God and the Bible.

Dr. Robert T. Ketcham was elected president of the General

Association of Regular Baptist Churches in May of 1934. He was reelected in 1935, again in 1936 and yet again in 1937. At the annual conference in Waterloo, Iowa, in 1938, Dr. Ketcham recommended a new organizational structure that would do away with the convention-type makeup, which provided for a president, vice president, secretary-treasurer and state vice presidents. Dr. Ketcham's proposal was enthusiastically accepted by the executive committee, and the messengers later passed it unanimously. In presenting the new structure, Dr. Ketcham said the following:

> There has been widespread criticism that this organization is a one-man outfit. While this is not true and could not be true, due to the method of election which we have always constitutionally observed, whereby the members of the nominating committee are selected by the individual churches themselves, (each church naming one of its messengers to serve on such a committee prior to the annual gathering)—yet the general public still regards the president of this organization—whoever he may be, as the director and controller of all its activities; and the acts of the president in the public mind have become the acts of the Association; and his statements, however definitely personal they may be, are attributed to be the considered and collective thought of the entire Association.
>
> While this should not be, it never-the-less exists and will continue to exist regardless of who is made president of the Association, as long as the public is unable to differentiate between the personal views of the president of the Association and the stated policies of the Association itself. Hence the Executive Committee feels that if the constitution of the Association is changed to eliminate the lifting up of one man to the headship of the organization as president, and instead provides for the establishment of a properly elected council of fourteen men, independently nominated by the individual churches prior to the convening of any annual gathering of the Association, that the public will begin to realize what we have long contended, namely, that there are no big men in the General Association but only many little men with a big God.[1]

The first Council of Fourteen was duly elected in the 1938 meeting. They were as follows: Earle G. Griffith of Johnson City, New York, chairman; A. G. Annette of Plainfield, Illinois; P. B. Chenault of Waterloo, Iowa; David Otis Fuller of Grand Rapids, Michigan; Raymond F. Hamilton of Gary, Indiana; Robert T. Ketcham of Gary, Indiana; W. A. Matthews of Los Angeles, California; David Gillespie of Elkhart, Indiana; Ralph W. Neighbour of Elyria, Ohio; J. Irving Reese of Ithaca,

New York; Leo Sandgren of Austin, Minnesota; E. C. Shute of Decatur, Illinois; Heber O. Van Gilder of Portsmouth, Ohio; and Leroy Wortman of Bunker Hill, Illinois. The Council organized itself into various committees such as Publications, Program, Missionary, Education and Evangelism Committees. The men were chosen for two-year terms so that for the first Council seven were elected for only one year. The Council has through the years met twice a year, once in December and again the week before the annual conference. The Council chairman also serves as moderator for all the sessions of the conference. The Council secretary is in charge of tabulating nominations from the churches and supervising the actual election process at the conference. Dr. Ketcham's hope that the GARBC would not become a "one-man show" had been realized.

The Association has wisely avoided the ownership and control of educational, missionary and benevolent agencies. According to the GARBC Constitution, "It shall be the policy of the Association to abstain from the creation and/or control of educational, missionary and other benevolent agencies" (Article VII, Section I). Instead of ownership and control, the Council "approves" agencies. Approval simply means certain agencies that have requested such approval have met the requirements set down in the Constitution and are worthy of the careful and prayerful consideration of the churches. Such commendation does *not* carry with it any coercion whatsoever. Neither is the Council or the Association saying that "approved agencies" are perfect in every respect. And all that is required for approval is a majority vote of the messengers at an annual conference.

In the 1930s no social agency was approved, but three mission agencies (earlier mentioned) were. In 1935 two schools were approved. The first was Los Angeles Baptist Theological Seminary, founded in 1927 and presided over by William A. Matthews. Years later this school became Northwest Baptist Seminary of Tacoma, Washington. The other school that gained approval had been founded in 1932. Dr. Richard Murphy, president, and Dr. Emery H. Bancroft, dean, were the key leaders in this fledgling institution known then as Baptist Bible Seminary in Johnson City, New York. The school is now located in Clarks Summit, Pennsylvania, and is called Baptist Bible College and Seminary of Pennsylvania.

The local churches in fellowship with the GARBC in the 1930s were vigorous centers of spiritual light and life. Many were pastored by some of the strongest Bible expositors of their time. The Association had started with 22 churches in 1932. In 1937 the number had grown to 76. By 1938 that number had climbed to 105. In 1939 there were 125. At the annual conference in 1940 in Erie, Pennsylvania, the total had reached 143. Merle R. Hull wrote:

> Not an astounding increase from the original 22, but substantial and satisfying. Those were years of struggle and stress as church after church voted to leave the apostasy of the Northern Convention and affiliate with the Regular Baptist movement. Some were involved in court cases as the Convention sought to claim properties. And separatists all across the country prayed about such battles, then rejoiced together when God gave victories.[2]

One of the strongest churches in fellowship with the young GARBC was the Wealthy Street Baptist Church in Grand Rapids, Michigan. The church was led by Pastor O. W. Van Osdel from 1909 to 1935. Dr. Van Osdel was a staunch and unwavering defender of the faith and was one of the driving forces behind the founding of the GARBC. He went Home to be with the Lord on January 1, 1935. Always an outspoken champion of Biblical fundamentalism, Dr. Osdel declared:

> There is nothing, viewed from the intellectual standpoint, or from the Christian standpoint, that is slower, more out-of-date, and completely behind the times than that which people are pleased to call Modernism. An unbeliever is not modern. Every objection that men called Modernists raise against the Bible, against the supernatural, against the virgin birth and the deity of Christ, is old, so old that it is bald and toothless, and ought to have been in the grave long ago. In the second century Celsus wrote against Christianity and its author all that is brought to the front as modern objections of today. Celsus could as well have made a shorter Bible or a short Bible as the University of Chicago. While these men are posing as scholars and up to date, they are simply making an exhibit of their ignorance and their brainlessness, and are severely antiquated and behind the times. The Bible is new, the Bible lives. It is exactly adapted to the human need of the present decade.[3]

Dr. Van Osdel was followed in the Wealthy Street pastorate by Dr. David Otis Fuller, who served the congregation for the next 40 years. Dr. Fuller served as editor of the *Baptist Bulletin* from 1935 to 1938. Under his editorial leadership the magazine grew from 8 to 16 pages.

Another strong church through the years has been the First Baptist Church of Johnson City, New York. On December 20, 1935, Dr. Earle G. Griffith succeeded Dr. Harold T. Commons as pastor of that strategic church. Dr. Commons was an extremely busy man. He was serving as president of Baptist Bible Seminary in Johnson City while at the same time serving as president of the Association of Baptists for Evangelism in the Orient, which later (as we have already noted) took the name of Association of Baptists for World Evangelism. Dr. Commons served as its president for about 40 years. Dr. Griffith eventually became president of Baptist Bible Seminary. Both men had extremely heavy schedules, and they were extremely gifted as preachers and administrators.

Still another strong church in those early days was the Walnut Street Baptist Church in Waterloo, Iowa. Under the dynamic leadership of Pastor P. B. Chenault, Walnut Street voted out of the Northern Baptist Convention and the Iowa State Baptist Convention in 1936. Just three years later, on April 1, 1939, Dr. Chenault was killed in an automobile accident. Reporting on Chenault's death, Dr. Ketcham wrote:

> Pastor Chenault had just closed a ten day meeting with Dr. John R. Rice in his Baptist Tabernacle at Dallas, Texas. Together with his wife, and baby daughter, Virginia, two years of age, he had started on the homeward trip leaving Dallas shortly after midnight. About thirty miles out of Dallas, Pastor Chenault's machine was crowded off the road by another car, the driver of which was intoxicated. . . .
>
> Pastor Chenault's car was thrown off the highway on the opposite side into a deep ditch and a pile of rocks. Pastor Chenault was thrown 75 feet, striking his head amidst the rocks, and was killed instantly. . . .
>
> Between 2800 and 3000 people were packed into the Walnut Street Church to pay their last tribute to this beloved brother in the Lord. More than fifty young people dedicated their lives to full-time Christian service at the close of the service, and twenty-five unsaved confessed the Lord Jesus Christ as Saviour and Lord as the invitation was extended.[4]

At the time of his death, Pastor Chenault was serving on the Council of Fourteen as chairman of the Missionary Committee. He was one of the great young men (he was 35 at the time of his death) of the early GARBC, and we should not allow men like him to be forgotten. He helped to make Walnut Street Baptist Church a great soul-winning church. Robert T. Ketcham succeeded Chenault as pastor.

Belden Avenue Baptist Church in Chicago continued to be a fortress of faith. The fourth annual conference of the GARBC was hosted by Dr. Howard Fulton and the Belden congregation during the week of May 25, 1936. Speakers at these meetings included T. T. Shields of Toronto, Ontario, Canada; Dr. Ford Porter; J. Frank Norris; Louis Entzminger; and Earle G. Griffith. The song leader was Harlie Stevick of Elyria, Ohio. Dr. Ketcham opened the conference with a stirring message on the problems of Christian youth in a modern world and how Christ could meet all their needs in the face of all the problems. Dr. Fulton preached with conviction and pastored with compassion. When he led his church out of the Convention, the story was published in the *Chicago Tribune!* His mighty influence for the Bible and the gospel and the Faith is lasting and eternally productive.

In 1934 Frank L. Smith was pastor of the Emmanuel Baptist Church in Toledo, Ohio. A young couple in their twenties started to attend Emmanuel with their little boy. They were Albert and Bessie Tassell; their little boy's name was Albert, Jr. On July 20, 1934, Al and Bessie welcomed another boy into their home. He was born at home in a second-story bedroom. His name was Paul Tassell, and Grandmother Tassell said he was going to be a preacher.

End Notes

1. "Truly a Glorious Fellowship," *Baptist Bulletin* (May–June 1938), pp. 3, 4.

2. Merle R. Hull, *What A Fellowship!* (Schaumburg, IL: Regular Baptist Press), 1981, p. 27.

3. "The Regular Baptist Meeting at Gary, Indiana," *Baptist Bulletin* (June 1934), p. 3.

4. R. T. Ketcham, "P. B. Chenault—At Home with the Lord," *Baptist Bulletin* (May 1939), p. 3.

6

The year 1940 was a troubled one for planet earth. On March 15, 1939, Hitler's German troops had invaded Prague and swallowed up Czechoslovakia. The Germans had then overcome Poland on September 1, 1939. In April, May and June of 1940 Hitler conquered Denmark, Norway, Holland and Belgium. Meanwhile, Japan occupied large areas of China and occupied Indochina in September of 1940. To complicate matters even more, Russia took East Poland in September 1939, attacked Finland in November 1939 and conquered the Baltic states in July 1940. Before all the conflicts ended, 45 million people would lose their lives in World War II.

In November 1940, Franklin Delano Roosevelt won an unprecedented third term as president. He defeated Wendell Willkie 449 to 82 in the electoral college tally and won by a popular vote landslide of 27,243,466 to 22,304,755. But events around the world did not allow political leaders the luxury of gloating over the winning of elections. On June 3, 1940, Congress approved the sale of surplus war material to Britain. President Roosevelt, sensing the impending worsening of international relationships, ordered the first peacetime draft in United States history on September 14, 1940. On the religious scene, liberal church leaders, who had preached for twenty years that man was getting better and better, were increasingly chagrined as the ominous world scene turned from tense to ugly to murderous. Their unbiblical optimism was stripped of its arrogant facade, and mankind again showed how wicked is the sinful nature.

In 1941, Dr. Shailer Matthews died at the age of 78. He had taught systematic theology and New Testament at the University of Chicago from 1894 to 1933. Shailer Matthews did as much as any man to corrupt the Northern Baptist Convention. He was one of the founding fathers of the Convention in 1907, and his classrooms were think tanks of modernistic infidelity. Hundreds of men went from his classrooms into Convention pastorates, college professorships and foreign mission fields. They carried with them the false teachings learned at the feet of Shailer Matthews. His 39 years of teaching Baptist leaders poisoned the Convention incalculably. What an incredible influence for infidelity! Unfortunately, his death was not the end of his apostate influence.

Another influential man died in 1941, but his influence had been for Biblical fidelity. Courtland Myers pastored the strategic Tremont Temple in Boston from 1909 to 1921. During those twelve years he thundered against the unbelief in the Convention. He was retired by the time the GARBC came into existence in 1932, but when he died at the age of 77, he left a legacy of true and faithful ministry.

Perhaps these two men, Matthews and Myers, epitomize the opposite sides of the conflict that had raged within the Convention for so many years until the clean break came in 1932. The conflict was not limited to the Convention, however, for the same battle between conservatives and liberals was being waged in other denominations, in world politics and on the great university campuses.

> Countless silent, unseen forces are incessantly at work in history's "majestic sweep," "innumerable waves," "slow rhythms," "surging forces"—call them what you will—those small yet numerous incidents which are often little more than scratches on history's slate, those elusive intangibles that alter men's thinking and actions; all in their way so illogical, yet so relative and relevant, and virtually impossible to deal with adequately. How does one accurately separate cause from effect, fact from fiction, moment from momentum, or determine the influence of time, place and circumstance on any given event? It is impossible for the historian to read the whole record of the past, which invariably is incomplete. And to write that record? Ah, that is where, to paraphrase Voltaire, history plays tricks on the dead. By his nature the historian must be selective, choosing this or that fact, event, circumstance, example, or quotation which he considers relevant to his subject.[1]

Bible-believing Christians know, of course, that back of that maze of multitudinous details and seemingly unrelated events is the omnipotent, omniscient, omnipresent, sovereign God "Who worketh all things after the counsel of his own will" (Eph. 1:11). We also know that "the steps of a good man are ordered by the LORD: and he delighteth in his way" (Ps. 37:23). Woven into the background and history of the

GARBC, therefore, are hundreds of personalities whose names are not as well-known as Shailer Matthews and Courtland Myers, but all of them are known to God and help to make up the whole story. No faithful service goes unrewarded, and no influence for infidelity and apostasy goes unpunished.

On December 7, 1941, at 7:55 A.M., Japan attacked Pearl Harbor, Hawaii. Nineteen American ships were damaged or sunk, and 2,300 American men were killed. During the 1940 presidential election campaign, Roosevelt had said: "I hate war. War destroys individuals and whole generations. It throws civilization into the dark ages." But on December 8, 1941, the United States officially declared war on Japan. On December 11, the United States also declared war on Germany and Italy. The next four years would be a global nightmare that would certainly affect all of the Regular Baptist churches in the United States and all of their missionary ministries around the world.

While well-known political leaders were making headlines and the events of war were riveting the attention of the masses to their radio newscasts, the work of God continued steadily and faithfully. On February 2, 1941, William E. Kuhnle began his three-decade ministry as pastor of the Garfield Avenue Baptist Church in Milwaukee, Wisconsin. Kuhnle went to Milwaukee after a ministry of four years as assistant pastor at the Walnut Street Baptist Church in Waterloo, Iowa. Pastor Kuhnle succeeded Dr. Frederick W. Kamm, who had served the Milwaukee church for 25 years. Dr. Kamm had led the church out of the Northern Baptist Convention and into the GARBC.

During May 18–25, 1941, Dr. Oswald J. Smith, pastor of the People's Tabernacle in Toronto, Ontario, held a tremendously fruitful series of evangelistic meetings at the Wealthy Street Baptist Church in Grand Rapids.

On January 9, 1941, the Campus Baptist Church of Ames, Iowa, led by Pastor Robert M. Arthur, voted to affiliate with the GARBC. Campus Baptist Church is adjacent to Iowa State University and has had a fruitful ministry to university students for more than 50 years. The First Baptist Church of Ames is still in the Convention and totally given over to religious liberalism.

In Tacoma, Washington, Temple Baptist Church, pastored by Robert L. Powell, celebrated its seventh anniversary with a special series of meetings beginning February 23, 1941, and featuring Dr. John Scroggie, an eminent British preacher. Forrest Johnson of

Everett, Washington, spoke at the anniversary banquet attended by 360 people. Temple Baptist Church was formed when a large group of believers left the First Baptist Church of Tacoma because of Scriptural convictions that made it impossible to stay in a church that was satisfied to remain in the apostate Convention.

In January of 1941 Baptist Bible Institute of Grand Rapids was organized and opened for classes with more than 200 students. The school was housed in the facilities of the Wealthy Street Baptist Church, and 12 area pastors served as instructors. Forty-three churches from seven different denominations were represented in the original student body. Also during January 21–26, First Baptist Church of Lapeer, Michigan, had productive evangelistic meetings led by Raymond F. Hamilton. D. Walter Davis, pastor of the growing Lapeer church, reported 40 new members had been added to the church during the previous four months of 1940. While Pastor Hamilton was away, his pulpit in Pana, Illinois, was filled by the well-known radio preacher, John D. Jess. In March of '41 Anthony Zeoli held two weeks of revival meetings at Central Baptist Church in Gary, Indiana, and many accepted Christ as Savior during those fifteen days! (Whatever happened to "protracted" meetings?)

The ninth annual conference of the GARBC was held at the First Baptist Church of Pontiac, Michigan. Dr. H. H. Savage was the host pastor. The regular church auditorium was too small for the crowds that ran 1,700 in attendance for the evening sessions, so the meetings were moved a block away to the tabernacle property owned by the church. During the May 12–15, 1941, conference several accepted Christ as Savior, and four young men gave themselves for full-time Christian service. Rev. J. Irving Reese was moderator for the conference, and Harlie G. Stevick the energetic song leader. Special music was provided by the Carolina Gospel Quartet!! Speakers for the evening sessions were Dr. Harold T. Strathearn, president of the Interstate Evangelistic Association of New York; Dr. David Otis Fuller of Grand Rapids, Michigan; Dr. Robert T. Ketcham of Waterloo, Iowa; and Dr. H. O. Van Gilder of Portsmouth, Ohio.

Just a month before the GARBC conference, the Regular Baptist Churches of California held their annual meeting at the Calvary Baptist Tabernacle in Los Angeles where Carl M. Sweazy was pastor. The new officers for the California fellowship were Pastor J. C. Derfelt, moderator; Pastor Paul R. Jackson (a future national representative), vice moderator; and Pastor Samuel Post, secretary-treasurer.

Moody Day services were held on April 6 of '41 at the Garfield Avenue Baptist Church, with Moody president, Dr. Will H. Houghton, speaking. Pastor Kuhnle reported that the Milwaukee church was working toward a goal of five hundred in Sunday School.

The great interest of Regular Baptists in Bible study was evident by the number of Bible institutes being organized across the country. The Christian Workers Bible Institute was held in the First Baptist Church of Elyria, Ohio, with 114 registrations for the first week.

One of the more innovative preachers in the GARBC of 1941 was Ford Porter. He pastored the Berean Missionary Baptist Church in Indianapolis, Indiana, had a half-hour radio broadcast every Sunday morning, and during the summers canvassed the surrounding communities with his specially equipped gospel trailer preaching to whoever would listen. He also wrote a gospel tract that has become the most-distributed tract in history. It is titled "God's Simple Plan of Salvation."

As the war clouds began to gather, R. F. Hamilton in the July 1941 issue of the *Baptist Bulletin* quoted Heinrich Heine, one of Germany's greatest writers of the nineteenth century:

> "It is the greatest merit of Christianity to have assuaged the joy of the German in brutal bellicosity, but when one day the cross of Christ is broken, the savagery of the old warriors, the wild berserk wrath, will break forth anew in all the barbaric fury of which our Nordic poets tell in song and saga. . . . Then will the storm god arise. . . . It will come one day and you will hear an explosion such as never occurred in the history of the world."[2]

In September 1941, Rev. Arthur Williams became pastor of the world-famous First Baptist Church of New York City. Little could Pastor Williams have known what a great ministry God was going to give him during the war years when thousands of military personnel would visit New York. About the same time as Williams moved to New York, the Baptist Bible Institute of Buffalo began its third year of operation under the leadership of Harry G. Hamilton, Frank A. Waaser, Kenneth A. Muck, Clarence B. Hayden and Milton G. Arnold, all of whom pastored churches in and around Buffalo and all of whom ministered effectively for many years within the ranks of the GARBC.

A great autumn evangelistic campaign was held at the Berean Baptist Church in Grand Rapids. Pastor Howard Keithley had prepared thoroughly for the meetings, and Evangelist John R. Rice preached with spiritual power resulting in many people coming to Christ as Savior. Many people were introduced to Dr. Rice's paper, *The Sword of the Lord.* Also active in evangelistic work was R. T. Ketcham's brother, Rev. Harry E. Ketcham. During the first two years of the 1940s Harry preached in many meetings covering Minnesota, Iowa, Pennsylvania and New Jersey. Pastors always commented on how much Harry preached with a "pastor's heart." Another "traveling preacher" who ministered among GARBC churches in the '30s and '40s was the pastor of Moody Memorial Church in Chicago, Dr. Harry A. Ironside. He had an especially blessed series of meetings with First Baptist Church of Elyria, Ohio, in November of 1941. Still another powerful itinerant preacher, John Carrara, held a two-week evangelistic campaign at the Riverside Baptist Church in Decatur, Illinois, pastored by Rev. J. M. Carlson.

The eventful year of 1941 came to its climax for First Baptist Church in New York City with a special week of meetings to commemorate the fiftieth anniversary of the laying of the cornerstone of the present edifice. The meetings, alas, began on December 7. The much-beloved Bible expositor, Dr. William L. Pettingill, was the speaker for the week.

Dr. Harold T. Commons, longtime and now retired president of the Association of Baptists for World Evangelism, told how the war affected ABWE missionaries in the Philippines:

> When Manila fell to the Japanese, our missionaries in Manila were all rounded up, registered, questioned, and temporarily released to their homes—all except Mr. Bomm. Since he was our field treasurer and business agent, the Japanese considered him our responsible official or head man. All the leaders of the various religious groups were summoned before the Japanese military commandant and required to sign a pledge of cooperation. The representatives of His Imperial Majesty, Emperor Hirohito, were establishing a "new order for greater Asia," which they said would bring peace and prosperity to all, but which really meant subservience to Japan. All who signed were released. Those who did not sign were put in a prison camp at Santo Tomas University. The amazing thing is that most of the religious leaders signed. Mr. Bomm and three or four others refused to sign and were jailed. None of our other missionaries were required to sign, only the head man of each group. Mr. Bomm was separated from his wife and never set foot outside the Santo Tomas internment camp for the duration, which was a little over three years.
>
> As time went on, Mrs. Bomm was suspected by the Japanese of

subversive activity in aiding the Filipino Underground Resistance Movement. She was arrested and confined for several weeks in the infamous Spanish dungeon of Fort Santiago. There, in solitary confinement, she was subjected to all kinds of abuse. The Japanese never convicted her of anything, and eventually released her in pitiable condition. Her husband hardly knew her the first time he saw her. Fortunately, none of our other missionaries were subjected to such inhumane treatment. We honor Ed and Marian Bomm for their courage and stamina and salute them for standing steadfastly for what was right.[3]

The war made all missionary activity unusually difficult. Travel on the seas and in the air was greatly restricted. Gasoline was rationed. Many nations had to put all of their raw materials into the war effort; it was a matter of national survival. Moreover, Germany and Japan and their allies were certainly not favorable to Bible-preaching Christians. Many young men came home from foreign battlefields to train for missionary service and to return to those countries in order to evangelize them. We are reminded again of Psalm 76:10: "Surely the wrath of man shall praise thee: the remainder of wrath shalt thou restrain."

In the May 1942 issue of the *Baptist Bulletin* Robert T. Ketcham highlighted developments in the interdenominational field of fundamentalism. The Federal Council of Churches of Christ had been for many years the ecumenical voice of liberal Protestantism. The Northern Baptist Convention was part of the Federal Council. Ketcham wrote:

> For many years we have been painfully aware of the fact that the Federal Council of Churches of Christ in America was casting its cold and blighting shadow across the pathway of the great denominational conventions in which there were both Modernists and Fundamentalists. Modernists enough to permit the Federal Council with all of its near communism (if not outright communism), its near immoral sex literature (if not outright immoral), and its downright denial of the fundamentals of the Christian faith, to find a large place in their financial budgets and cooperative fellowship; Fundamentalists enough to have done something definite and drastic about it all, but who never did. . . .
>
> While thousands were discussing the need of a Fundamental organization to be the exact opposite of the Federal Council as to Christian emphasis, it was like the weather, everybody discussing it and nobody doing anything about it. Finally two Christian groups in the East, namely the Bible Protestant Church and the Bible Presbyterian Church under the leadership of Dr. Carl

McIntire of Collingswood, New Jersey, got together and really did something about it. In 1941 they organized *The American Council of Christian Churches.* They have been doing business now for the better part of a year. Already a third denominational body has united in the Council and at least four other church bodies have taken preliminary action, looking forward to definite affiliation. In addition to this, individuals from seventeen other denominations have expressed their approval of the American Council of Christian Churches by associating themselves as individuals with the Council.

The American Council during its existence has already made itself felt in Washington, working particularly in the realm of the radio, chaplains, and other important fields.[4]

At the GARBC annual conference of 1942, the Association voted to participate actively with the American Council. However, to protect and maintain the sovereignty and autonomy of each GARBC local church, the Association informed the ACCC that each GARBC church would have to vote individually to participate with the interdenominational organization. In the October 1942 issue of the *Baptist Bulletin* Dr. Ketcham told his readers: "Why the General Association of Regular Baptists Declared Itself in Fellowship With the American Council of Christian Churches (rather than the widely-publicized National Association of Evangelicals for United Action).[5]

He went on to say the ACCC (1) openly opposes the Federal Council, whereas the NAE refuses to take a definite stand against the modernistic Federal Council; (2) restricts membership to those churches (and individuals) who have repudiated the Federal Council, whereas the NAE includes in its membership many churches still related to the Federal Council (through their denominational affiliations); (3) was organized and in operation *seven months before* the NAE met at St. Louis to consider the advisability of organizing, whereas the NAE was organized *seven months after* the ACCC was in the field; and (4) was organized to provide a *united evangelical front against the Federal Council* and other apostate organizations, whereas the NAE was organized *in definite opposition to the American Council's* repudiation of the Federal Council. Once again, separation from apostasy was a must for Regular Baptists. In the November 1942 *Baptist Bulletin* Dr. Ketcham summarized the whole matter:

Again we would call attention to the inescapable fact that the issue is not *persons, leadership, or little groups.* The issue is *organized opposition to the*

Federal Council of Churches of Christ in America. The National Association says that as an organization they *will not* oppose the Federal Council. The American Council says that as an organization it *will* oppose the Federal Council. Membership in either one of these groups should be determined *solely on that issue.* If a church, association, or denomination wants an outspoken testimony in behalf of the Gospel of Jesus Christ and the propagation of such by a new emphasis upon evangelism and missions *plus* an outspoken testimony against the modernistic control, by the Federal Council, of public religious thought through radio and chaplains, then they should declare themselves in fellowship with the American Council.

If on the other hand a church, association or denomination wants no *organized voice* raised in opposition to the iniquitous control by the Federal Council, but wants to continue quietly and peaceably within the associations and denominations controlled by the Federal Council, then by all means they should declare themselves in fellowship with the National Association of Evangelicals.

The issue is clear![6]

End Notes

1. Donald M. Goldstein and Katherine V. Dillon in Preface to *At Dawn We Slept, The Untold Story of Pearl Harbor* by G. W. Prange (New York: McGraw-Hill, Inc., 1981), p. xvi.

2. R. F. Hamilton, "Gleanings," *Baptist Bulletin* (July 1941), p. 22.

3. Harold T. Commons, *Heritage and Harvest* (Cherry Hill, NJ: Association of Baptists for World Evangelism, 1981), pp. 57, 58.

4. R. T. Ketcham, ed., "Shadow of the Federal Council," *Baptist Bulletin* (May 1942), p. 1.

5. R. T. Ketcham, ed., "Why the General Association . . .," *Baptist Bulletin* (October 1942), p. 1.

6. R. T. Ketcham, ed., "Facing the Facts," *Baptist Bulletin* (November 1942), p. 8.

7

Missionaries to the military! Merle Hull wrote:

> It was during World War II that the General Association of Regular Baptist Churches first began to provide chaplains for the nation's military forces. From what seemed a small beginning, a great burden and ministry have developed in serving military personnel and their dependents.
>
> Initially it was necessary to endorse chaplain candidates through the Chaplaincy Commission of the American Council of Christian Churches. This proved unsatisfactory because of unavoidable delays and the difficulty of keeping in touch with the chaplains. (No criticism of the ACCC; just a statement of fact.) Thus the GARBC applied to the Armed Forces Chaplain's Board to constitute its own Chaplaincy Commission. Such approval would enable the Association to provide the necessary ecclesiastical endorsement for our chaplain applicants and would also give recognition before the Department of Defense.[1]

The first GARBC chaplain, Rev. Vernon Bliss, later became registrar at Faith Baptist Bible College and served in that capacity until his retirement. The best-known Regular Baptist chaplain to serve in World War II was Dr. David Otis Fuller. While he was away from Wealthy Street Baptist Church, Dr. Paul R. Jackson served as interim in that Grand Rapids church. But when Regular Baptists think of the chaplaincy, their minds automatically turn to Dr. William E. Kuhnle, who served as chairman of the GARBC Chaplaincy Committee for almost 30 years. Dr. Kuhnle pastored the Garfield Baptist Church in Milwaukee, Wisconsin, for 29 years. From there he came to the GARBC home office and served for ten years as assistant to the national representative (from 1969 to 1979). He was elected to the Council of Fourteen many times and was the program director for the

Association's radio outreach, *Living Reality.* He was president of the board of Shepherds, a ministry that began at his Milwaukee church. He was on the executive committee of the Association of Baptists for World Evangelism and on the board of administrators of the Baptist Builders' Club. But no ministry was any dearer to Dr. Kuhnle than the work of our military chaplains. When he went Home on September 6, 1981, at the age of 71, the *National Chaplaincy Letter,* published in Washington, D.C., noted his passing with regret and affection. His ministry to the chaplains had been warm, witty and winsome. He was respected by all of the denominational endorsers and was loved and admired by the GARBC chaplains. He was known in Washington, D.C. as a man of integrity, humor and compassion.

Dr. Kuhnle was succeeded by Chaplain (COL) E. D. Ellison III, USAF (Retired). He is affectionately referred to by the chaplains as "Doc." Colonel Ellison has continued the work of the GARBC Chaplaincy Commission with the same grace and competence that marked Dr. Kuhnle's tenure. All of us who have worked with "Doc" during the past decade have appreciated his insistence on quality and his uncompromising leadership in our behalf in Washington, D.C. The Chaplain's Hour and the Chaplain's Luncheon are two of the most cherished hours of every annual conference.

In December of 1989, Mrs. Tassell and I had the privilege of visiting Captain Jerry D. Moritz of the United States Navy in Honolulu, Hawaii. At the time, Jerry was senior chaplain over the entire Pacific area. We were thrilled as he briefed us on the great work God was doing through him and our other chaplains. It is doubtful if many preachers have as large a parish as Moritz. John Wesley used to say "the world is my parish," but the military parish served by Moritz and his men included millions of square miles of Pacific Ocean expanse. My wife and I were fascinated as we talked over dinner with Chaplain and Mrs. Moritz about their many adventures in their years in the chaplaincy. When Jerry volunteered for combat duty in Vietnam in 1970, he was ordered to report to the First Marine Division positioned just 20 miles northwest of Da Nang. In the words of John Newton, "through many dangers, toils and snares" he safely came. Those dangers and snares sometimes included snipers and land mines. "But," said Jerry, "I wouldn't trade those meetings with the men up on those ridges and hillsides for the fanciest cathedrals in the world."

Throughout World War II, the Korean War and the Vietnam War

plus many other places and assignments our chaplains have served with valor, vigor and virtue. They have exhibited courage beyond the call of duty. They have been instrumental in the evangelization of thousands upon thousands of military personnel.

Chaplain (COL) Chester R. Steffey of the United States Army gave his testimony:

Regarding personal evangelism, I think this is upon all our hearts and ultimately this is the reason why God calls us to serve in this particular mission field. Several months ago it was my privilege to lead a general in the United States Army to a saving knowledge of the Lord Jesus Christ. He was a man who had serious problems and he was unable to deal with those problems. He was a religious man, very respectful of the things of God, in some ways very similar to Cornelius in the book of Acts. He believed there was a God; he believed the things concerning the Lord Jesus Christ. But he had no personal relationship with the Savior. As he shared his heart with me and the problem and the anxiety and the ravages of sin in his life, it was my privilege to share the Word of God with him and the claims of Jesus Christ. Therefore, on a rainy afternoon in the quietness of my office, we both knelt down on our knees beside a couch, and that man invited Christ to be his personal Savior; asked the Lord Jesus to come into his heart. It's a wonderful thing to be able to witness that. This man is growing in the Lord.

Now you think you know nothing about him. But some of you do know about him, for it is the same man who was given the responsibility for the military mission to all the Cuban refugees at Fort Chaffee, Arkansas. This is quite a test for a new believer in Jesus Christ because he has been undergoing serious pressures. There are very responsible kinds of things he has to do, and he's been publicly criticized in some of the news media as being responsible for permitting those riots to take place. May I assure you that this man, even if he were not a Christian, is a responsible, capable and dedicated officer. And as a new babe in Christ, he is now a committed Christian officer and needs our prayers.

Another area of responsibility and privilege is that of my staff work. I am a three-corps artillery staff chaplain and have the supervisory responsibility for some seventeen or eighteen chaplains. That's a permanent requirement, and in addition to that, for the remainder of the summer I am the acting post chaplain at Fort Sill and have the responsibility of supervising some thirty-four chaplains. I also have collateral duties. I share these things with you to show you where God places your missionaries, some of the things that are on us, and to help you pray for us knowledgeably and intelligently. I also have the responsibility for all the religious coverage for the Cuban refugees at Fort

Chaffee. This last requirement has been a special blessing. There's been some criticism, I realize, on the part of our citizens about whether we should let those refugees into our country. I personally believe it is the morally right thing to do. But, also, I want to assure you that among those refugees there are many born-again Christians, and they have at last escaped Castro's tyranny and oppression. One Baptist minister imprisoned for some twenty-five years is now free. My responsibility to those nineteen thousand Cubans is to insure that every one of them has the privilege of hearing the gospel of Jesus Christ. God is saving people there and people are coming to know Christ; so we can rejoice in that.

The third and final area that I want to share is that of personal preaching and teaching ministry. Since March it's been my privilege to conduct a home Bible class for the commanding general in his home in Fort Sill, Oklahoma. Fort Sill is the artillery center for the United States Army. Everything that concerns the guns and the missiles is found at Fort Sill. Therefore, the commanding general at Fort Sill is responsible to the American Army for the status of our artillery and army missile programs. This man and his wife are committed believers in Christ. A few months ago, because of the busyness of their schedule, they asked me if I could find time, which I did, to be on call to conduct private Bible studies one evening a week in their home. It's been my privilege to do this.

Well, God has given us men through the military of great authority who are believers; committed Christians in Christ. And, therefore, much rests on them, and a lot rests upon us as their chaplains to minister to their spiritual needs. I would solicit your prayers for these two generals I have mentioned; I solicit your prayers for us as chaplains. The Scripture says, "Without me," meaning the Lord Jesus Christ, "ye can do nothing," and it is so true. So, pray for us.[2]

Our chaplaincy committee during World War II was chaired by Dr. Clarence E. Mason, Jr. The chaplains were as follows: Fremont L. Blackman, Vernon R. Bliss, Roy H. Boldt, C. Douglas Burt, Alfred P. Conant, Milton L. Dowden, David Otis Fuller, William V. Goldie, Arlin M. Halvorsen, Clarence R. Nida, Karl B. Smith, C. Allen Taff, Frank L. Waaser and Arnold C. Westphal.

As of the printing of this book, Colonel Ellison continues as a member of the Task Force and National Conference on Ministry to the Armed Forces and the Endorsers Conference for Veterans Administration Chaplaincy and was elected as an officer in the Military Chaplains Association in Washington, D.C. He holds regular meetings with the Chiefs of Chaplains of the U.S. Army, the U.S. Navy, the U.S. Air Force and the director of the Veterans Administration. In his report to the GARBC at the June 1990 annual conference, Colonel Ellison said:

> The events in Europe this past year have impacted the entire world politically, sociologically, religiously and militarily. The shock waves are still clashing with the status quo. As a result the Department of Defense continues in a state of suspended projection in armament, ordinance, and personnel while Congress debates. Nevertheless, a quality force continues to present an imperative goal. Realistically, however, there must be a reduction in forces.
>
> Regular Baptist chaplains consistently uphold enviable standards and records in ministry and service. It is, however, becoming increasingly difficult for conservative/nonliturgical chaplains to survive in the competitive environment of the Armed Forces. This past year, for example, your chairman interceded in a number of cases of discrimination and harassment. Incidents in the Pacific required intervention and conferences with chaplains, their superiors and commanding officers. . . . It is increasingly evident that constant surveillance is imperative at [the] Post/Base operational level and in [the] Washington, D.C. policy level on behalf of our chaplains. All services are having "selection-out" boards to remove chaplains from active duty. If our chaplains do not survive, they cannot minister.[3]

At the June 1990 Council of Eighteen meeting, Colonel Ellison requested and received unanimously from the Council the following "Statement on Joint Services." It reads as follows.

> Since the inception of the General Association of Regular Baptist Churches, a basic doctrinal position has been separation from participation in any joint worship or special services. In our pluralistic society, the GARBC fully recognizes and respects the distinctives, privileges and prerogatives of other faith groups. For example, the GARBC acknowledges the legal right of ordained females, who have been endorsed by their specific faith group, to serve as chaplains in the Armed Forces. However, the GARBC does not permit the ordination or endorsement of females to the ministry in the chaplaincy.
>
> Consequently, for our Armed chaplains to jointly participate in worship services would be denominational compromise. We therefore respectfully request that chaplains endorsed by the Regular Baptist Churches not be required to jointly participate with other male or female chaplains in any worship or special services.[4]

End Notes

1. Merle R. Hull, *What a Fellowship!* (Schaumburg, IL: Regular Baptist Press, 1981), p. 51.

2. Ibid., pp. 52, 53.

3. "Report of the Chaplaincy Committee," by Col. E. D. Ellison, Chairman, in *GARBC Annual Report* (Schaumburg, IL: Regular Baptist Press, 1990), p. 13.

4. "Council of Eighteen Minutes," Niagara Falls, New York, June 1990. (Typewritten.)

8

The war years were traumatic times both abroad and at home. A race riot in Detroit, Michigan, left 34 dead and 700 injured on June 21, 1943. A similar riot in the Harlem section of New York left six dead and many wounded. In 1942 the federal government forcibly displaced 110,000 Japanese–Americans, including 75,000 United States citizens. They were moved from the West Coast to detention camps where they were held for the next three years. In the political realm, President Franklin D. Roosevelt sought and won a fourth term by soundly defeating Thomas E. Dewey in the November 1944 elections. Roosevelt received 25,602,505 votes to Dewey's 22,006,278 votes. The electoral college margin was 432 to 99. Roosevelt died suddenly at Warm Springs, Georgia, on April 12, 1945, at the age of 63. He was succeeded by Harry Truman.

The first nuclear chain reaction was produced at the University of Chicago under the supervision of physicists Arthur Compton and Enrico Fermi on December 2, 1942. The first atomic bomb was exploded at Alamogordo, New Mexico, on July 16, 1945. On May 7, 1945, Germany unconditionally surrendered to the United States and her allies. President Truman ordered the atomic bomb dropped on Hiroshima, Japan, on August 6, 1945, and on Nagasaki, Japan, on August 9. Japan then unconditionally surrendered on August 15. General Douglas MacArthur took over supervision of Japan on September 9.

During the war years Regular Baptist churches continued to flourish. While the United States and her allies were fighting the fascist forces around the world, Bible-believing, Christ-honoring churches were fighting the good fight of faith. One of the most heartening trends in the young GARBC in the '30s and '40s was the growing number of young men and women who were surrendering their lives for full-time Christian service. These young people were not "draft dodgers." They were sincerely dedicated to entering Christian schools where they could be trained to serve Christ.

As we pick up our story of the churches in the GARBC, we must note with joy some ordinations of men whose names longtime Regular Baptists will recognize readily. On June 30, 1942, twin brothers, Carl and Kenneth Elgena, were ordained by the Thompson, Pennsylvania, Free Baptist Church. In November of 1942 the Hough Avenue Baptist Church of Cleveland, Ohio, formally ordained Alvin G. Ross and Joseph L. Gavitt. In that same month J. Lester Williams was ordained by the First Baptist Church of Plainfield, Illinois. Also in that month the Burton Avenue Baptist Church in Waterloo, Iowa, ordained Kenneth Larrabee and Sargeant Lusthoff to the gospel ministry. That November was surely the month for ordinations! Before it was over, the Calvary Baptist Church of Clinton, Indiana, ordained Herman Pendleton; and Herbert Orman was set apart to the ministry by the Tabernacle Baptist Church of Ithaca, New York.

In 1942 the First Baptist Church of Atlantic City, New Jersey, purchased a five-story building to be used by the church as a Christian center for military personnel. Pastor Coulson Shepherd said:

> There are upwards of thirty thousand soldiers in the "Basic Training Center Army Air Forces Technical Training Command" housed in the hotels of our city, and over one thousand Coast Guardsmen in the radio school two blocks from our corner. Within two blocks radius of this corner, there are well over twelve thousand service men housed, so our building is really the most strategically located in the city for the work. Most of the men are here for ten days to two weeks.[1]

Thank God for a church with such vision! Clarence E. Mason, Jr., the pastor of the Chelsea Baptist Church, the other Regular Baptist church in Atlantic City, spoke at the 1942 November Bible conference of the Southeastern Bible School in Birmingham, Alabama. Pastor Phil Halvorsen reported a blessed series of meetings with Henry H. Savage at the Brunswick Baptist Church in Gary, Indiana, in January 1943. Rev. Adam Lutzweiller, a talented musician and gifted preacher, held a special series of meetings at Pastor R. L. Matthews' Calvary Baptist Church in Norwich, New York. In Elyria, Ohio, the year 1942 closed with a Bible conference at First Baptist Church conducted by Dr. William Pettingill. Pastor Walter Davis of the First Baptist Church in Lapeer, Michigan, closed out his pastoral ministry there in January of 1943 in order to enter into an itinerant evangelistic work.

William E. Kuhnle conducted a week of meetings in November of '42 in the First Missionary Church of Detroit, where his father was pastor. Mrs. Edna Kuhnle provided special music. Pastor Wilbur Strader reported a splendid November revival meeting at the First Baptist Church of Bethalto, Illinois. The evangelist was Marion Beene. Dr. Wilbur M. Smith of the Moody Bible Institute delivered a fine message of encouragement at a mortgage-burning service for Belden Avenue Baptist Church in Chicago. Dr. Harry Rimmer preceded that day with a special two weeks of meetings October 4–18, 1942.

Dr. Robert T. Ketcham began 1943 as guest speaker for ten days at the Collingswood, New Jersey, Presbyterian Church pastored by Dr. Carl McIntire. Dr. Ketcham followed that series in January by two special engagements in February: a great rally for the Fundamental Young People of Greater Chicago in the Moody Memorial Church and the Founder's Week Conference at the Moody Bible Institute.

In California the Tabernacle Baptist Church of Los Angeles ordained H. Carroll Aagard, Lawrence Rogers Kelly and Henry E. Ziemer. The latter came into the GARBC fellowship from the Christian and Missionary Alliance with whom he had pastored in Los Angeles. Pastor G. Sherman Lemmon reported completion of an enlarged auditorium for First Baptist Church of Wilmington, California. The First Baptist Church of Hemet, California, started 1943 with a new pastor, Walter S. Risor. In Iowa, the Hagerman Baptist Church of Waterloo called Burchard G. Ham to be pastor. Rev. Robert Cook of First Baptist Church of LaSalle, Illinois, conducted meetings for Pastor John Rader and the First Baptist Church of Silvis, Illinois. In Indiana, the Hessville Baptist Church of Hammond ordained their pastor, Robert Johnson.

In Grand Rapids Dr. David Otis Fuller announced the launching of a brand-new ministry called "The Children's Bible Hour," a radio broadcast heard over a network of stations. Dr. Fuller served as chairman of the sponsoring committee, along with Merle W. Johnson of the Mel Trotter Rescue Mission, Donald G. Hescott of Calvary Gospel Center, Malcolm R. Cronk of Calvary Undenominational Church and Mrs. Ted Engstrom of the Swedish Covenant Church. Dr. Vance

Havner held a special series of meetings at First Baptist Church in LaSalle, Illinois, in January of 1943. At its annual business meeting in January the First Baptist Church of Patchogue, Long Island, New York, voted to sever all connections with the Northern Baptist Convention. James A. Ker, former missionary to Ceylon, India, then led the church to affiliate with the GARBC. In Buffalo, the First Baptist Church celebrated the eleventh anniversary of the ministry of Pastor Harry G. Hamilton, the first president of the GARBC.

On January 18, 1943, Pastor James T. Jeremiah of the Emmanuel Baptist Church in Toledo, Ohio, concluded his 235th broadcast over station WTOL. In February a radio rally was held at the church with Hall Dautel of Bethel Baptist Church in Erie, Pennsylvania, as speaker. Also conducting a fruitful radio ministry was Pastor Orville Yeager of the First Baptist Church of Princeton, Indiana. His network of stations reached from Nashville, Tennessee, to Chicago. Rev. A. Donald Moffat resigned his work at Fort Dix, New Jersey, to accept the pastorate of the Berean Baptist Church in Bunker Hill, Illinois. Rev. Clarence E. Sharer resigned the pastorate of the First Baptist Church of Monroe, Iowa, to accept the call of the Grove Avenue Baptist Church of Racine, Wisconsin. Rev. Walter Carvin, former pastor of Grove Avenue, had accepted a call to the Rhawnhurst Baptist Church in Philadelphia, Pennsylvania.

Some of the names that appear in the above paragraphs are not as well known as are the names of the early Associational leaders, but the Van Gilders and Ketchams and Fullers could not have had the success they did without the loyal support of the "grass roots." The GARBC was definitely a nationwide movement just a dozen years from its small beginning in 1932. The 1943 annual conference was held at the First Baptist Church in Johnson City, New York, pastored by Rev. Kenneth Kinney. The featured speakers at the '43 conference were Dr. Arthur Williams, pastor of the First Baptist Church in New York City; Rev. Hall Dautel pastor of the Bethel Baptist Church in Erie, Pennsylvania; Rev. A. D. Mohr, pastor of the Grandview Park Baptist Church in Des Moines, Iowa; and Dr. T. T. Shields, pastor of the Jarvis Street Baptist Church in Toronto, Ontario, from 1910 to 1955. Dr. Howard Jones led the music.

One of the highlights for fundamentalists in 1943 was a cross-country series of conferences held under the auspices of the American Council of Christian Churches. The three traveling conference speakers were Dr. Carl McIntire, ACCC president; Dr. Robert T. Ketcham, ACCC vice president; and Dr. H. McAllister Griffith, ACCC general secretary. The series began at the Church of the Open Door in Los Angeles, pastored by Dr. Louis Talbot. The itinerary included Trinity Methodist Church in Los Angeles, pastored by Dr. Bob Schuler; the Brethren Church of Long Beach, pastored by Dr. Louis S. Bauman; Temple Baptist Church of Tacoma, Washington, pastored by Robert Powell; and the Bible Presbyterian Church in Tacoma, pastored by Dr. Roy T. Brumbaugh. The conference messages pointed out the glaring differences between the Federal Council of Churches and the ACCC.

During the war years, the First Baptist Church of Hackensack, New Jersey, pastored by Dr. Harry C. Leach, was active in ministries to the many military personnel in the New York City area. They strongly supported with finances and workers the Soldiers' Gospel Center near Camp Shanks in north New Jersey.

On July 16 of '43, a new church was organized in Moscow, Idaho, under the leadership of missionary-pastor E. E. Bramblet. Grace Baptist Church was the first independent Baptist church in the state of Idaho. The University of Idaho is located in Moscow, and liberalism had gone unchallenged until the Grace Baptist Church began to preach the gospel and teach the Word in that needy, intellectually proud city.

On August 1 Fundamental Baptist Tabernacle of Pontiac, Illinois, extended a pastoral call to Robert L. Sumner, a recent graduate of Baptist Bible Seminary in Johnson City, New York. Pastor Sumner had been a member of the Calvary Baptist Church in Norwich, New York, pastored by Reginald L. Matthews. Also in the summer of '43 Milton Dowden resigned the pastorate of Merton Baptist Church in Wisconsin to become an army chaplain. At about the same time Rev. Orville Yeager concluded his pastorate with the First Baptist Church of Princeton, Indiana, in order to give full time to evangelistic and Bible conference work.

Good young men continued to be ordained to the gospel ministry in 1943. Some of them were Leymon Ketcham and Ralph Mucher by the First Baptist Church of Atlantic City, New Jersey; James W. Anderson by Emmanuel Baptist Church of Flint, Michigan; Floyd Darling by Hagerman Baptist Church of Waterloo, Iowa; Donald E. Douglass by Walnut Street Baptist Church of Waterloo, Iowa; Harley Eisentrager by the South Jefferson Baptist Church of South Jefferson,

New York; Emmanuel Woods, a converted Hebrew, by the Berean Baptist Church of Bunker Hill, Illinois; and Curtis Peterson by the First Baptist Church of Rochester, Minnesota.

The second annual Labor Day Bible Conference was held at the Wealthy Street Baptist Church and featured Dr. Wilbur M. Smith of Moody Bible Institute. Another great Bible conference was held October 4–14 at the First Baptist Church in Beech Grove, Indiana, pastored by Rev. F. C. Carlson. Featured speakers were Rev. D. B. Estep of the Calvary Baptist Church in Covington, Kentucky, and Rev. H. B. McClanahan of the Grace Baptist Church in Indianapolis. Other special conferences included Berean Missionary Baptist Church of Indianapolis with Carlyle Scott and Jimmy Johnson as speakers; First Baptist Church of Elyria, Ohio, with H. A. Ironside and Dan Gilbert as speakers; and Garfield Baptist Church of Milwaukee, Wisconsin, with Walter R. (Happy Mac) McDonald. All in all, 1943 was a great year for the churches of the GARBC.

End Note

1. R. F. Hamilton, ed., "Gleanings," *Baptist Bulletin* (January 1943), p. 16.

9

The General Association of Regular Baptist Churches has always been mightily missions-oriented. Our missionary orientation has never wavered. We have from the beginning purposed to preach the gospel to the uttermost part of the earth. Our Commander-in-Chief, Jesus Christ, clearly gave us our orders in what we call the Great Commission: "All power is given unto me in heaven and in earth. Go ye therefore, and teach all nations, baptizing them in the name of the Father, and of the Son, and of the Holy Ghost: teaching them to observe all things whatsoever I have commanded you: and, lo, I am with you alway, even unto the end of the world" (Matt. 28:18–20). Our mission is *not* educational or economical or ecological or environmental; our mission is *evangelistic.* We are called to make disciples. We are called to establish local churches. We are not called to preach a social gospel. We are called to preach redemption and reconciliation and regeneration through the crucified, buried, risen and ascended Lord Jesus Christ.

This does not mean that fundamentalists in general and Regular Baptists in particular do not have a social consciousness. Our well-trained missionaries have founded hospitals, established schools, built homes for orphans and trained national preachers and teachers all over the world. But we do not believe men are saved through economics or education. Men may have a better environment on the outside, but if their wicked hearts are unchanged on the inside, men will still be lost. Men need the Bread of Life, Jesus Christ, more than they need physical food. And they do need physical food—we do not deny that! Men need clothing for their physical bodies, but they need to be clothed in the righteousness of Christ even more. Men need physical healing, but they need spiritual healing a thousand times more. Man's major malady is sin, and only the Savior, Jesus Christ, can cure that cursed malady. Our missionaries have, therefore, carried on many-faceted ministries all over the world.

The GARBC missionary outreach has not been accomplished through a program of centralization whereby the Association created mission agencies, staffed them and controlled them. Rather, the Association has "approved" certain agencies already established. The agencies themselves are fully independent, autonomous, sovereign institutions that meet the GARBC constitutional requirements for "approval status." They are then recommended and commended to the churches by the Association as worthy of the financial support of the churches.

By 1943 nine agencies had been listed as approved by the GARBC. They are as follows: Association of Baptists for World Evangelism, then headquartered in Philadelphia; African Christian Mission (Independent Baptist), then headquartered at Paterson, New Jersey; General Council of Cooperating Baptist Missions (Mid-Missions), then headquartered at Mishawaka, Indiana; Mexican Gospel Mission (an Independent Baptist work), then headquartered at Phoenix, Arizona; Baptist Bible Society of Johnson City, New York; Interstate Evangelical Association (a Baptist fellowship) of New York City; Fellowship of Baptists for Home Missions, then headquartered in Elyria, Ohio; Columbia Basin Mission in Wenatchee, Washington; and Hiawatha Land Independent Baptist Missions of Escanaba, Michigan.

Through the years the nine have become five, with more than 1,800 missionaries girdling the globe. They are Association of Baptists for World Evangelism of Cherry Hill, New Jersey, Dr. Wendell Kempton, president; Baptist Mid-Missions of Cleveland, Ohio, Dr. Gary Anderson, president; Committee on Missionary Evangelism of Grand Rapids, Michigan, Rev. Douglas Beason, general director; Continental Baptist Missions of Comstock Park, Michigan, Rev. Charles Vermilyea, executive director; and Evangelical Baptist Missions of Kokomo, Indiana, Mr. David Marshall, general director.

It is not the purpose of the author to give detailed histories of the above-named mission agencies. Definitive histories have already been written for ABWE by Dr. Harold T. Commons and for Baptist Mid-Missions by Miss Polly Strong. Information and historical data may be easily obtained by contacting the agencies themselves. What the author would like to do in this chapter is give the reader some idea of what went on in the early pioneer days. This is possible because of the extensive amount of space given to missionary activity in the pages of the *Baptist Bulletin* in the first two decades of its existence. Most mission agencies now have their own official organs; so less space is now given to detailed letters and accounts from individual missionaries in the *Baptist Bulletin.* But we must not forget the names and exploits of those early pioneers.

The largest of our mission agencies is Baptist Mid-Missions. It was brought into being in 1920 by Rev. William Haas, a Bible-believing Baptist pastor in Ohio. He was convinced the Lord was calling him to Africa, but the Northern Baptist Convention refused to approve him and send him. He went anyway! From a tiny beginning Baptist Mid-Missions has grown to a ministry with almost one thousand missionaries serving around the world. Past presidents include Dr. M. E. Hawkins, Mr. George S. Milner, Dr. Allan Lewis and Dr. C. Raymond Buck.

One of the more adventuresome couples to go to French Equatorial Africa in the 1930s was Roy and Fern Hamman. Roy had the privilege of baptizing the first converts of the Disc Lip tribe. Writing on October 17, 1942, Hamman said:

> In August we had our first baptismal service and I wish you could have been there. On a Sunday morning we went down to the river, a few miles away, and gathered with our little crowd of some fifty. We had just begun to sing when we saw a line of nearly 200 native men and women coming our way. They had crossed the river farther upstream and were on the same side as we. They were from a remote section of this district and were on their way to the Government Poste with Shea nut oil to sell. I invited them all to sit on the bank with our people while I stood at the water's edge and told them the wonderful story of Salvation through the blood of our precious Lord Jesus. As we found out later, there were not more than one or two who had heard the name of Jesus before, much less the way of Salvation. They listened very attentively, and while we have not been privileged to see any results, who knows what may have happened during that meeting? There were two Sara-Kabbas and three Saras who followed their Lord in Baptism. They have all been living a consistent Christian life for at least two years, and two of them more than three years. Most of the people present had never seen a baptismal service, and as the account of it reached others who were not there, it caused them to ask many questions concerning the procedure. The Paramount chief of the whole tribe called in two of the believers the next day and questioned them all about it. This, of course, gave the latter a good opportunity to witness to

the big chief. . . . Other than the French Government Official, who comes up from Fort Archambault once a month, Fern and I haven't seen another white person in three months and it will be another month before we do.[1]

On December 20, 1935, Dr. Harold T. Commons wrote from Manila in the Philippines:

Romanism in these islands is nothing but pagan heathenism and idolatry. If space permitted I would like to tell you of some of the other heathen practices such as the "flagellantes" or those who on certain feast days scourge themselves until their backs are lacerated and the blood flows freely, all in a vain attempt to purify themselves and atone for their own sins.

Or I might tell you of the iniquitous system of masses for the dead, and the farming out of these masses by the bishops or priests, at a handsome profit to themselves, while the people are bled of their money, and the souls of the dead are most certainly not benefitted.

These and other superstitions of Romanism clothed in an outward garb and name of Christianity render our work here more difficult than that in purely pagan territory; but oh how much the real message of salvation by grace through faith in the finished work of Christ is needed in the midst of this darkness![2]

Dr. Commons, as president of ABWE for the next four decades, was pleased to see hundreds of churches established in the Philippines. For the past fifteen years, his successor, Dr. Wendell Kempton, has continued to see the work in the Philippines grow and glow for the Lord Jesus Christ.

Another pioneering couple, Lester and Martha Fogle, ministered at Fort Archambault, French Equatorial Africa. On October 24, 1937, they wrote:

Rev. P. F. Metzler baptized 32 in the river about one-half mile from our station. Among them was his daughter, Helen. Last Sunday we had meetings from sunrise to sunset, and we are planning a Sunday like this each month. Sunrise prayer meeting first; then Sunday School and church. In the afternoon, starting at 2:00 is the meeting for testimonies, scripture reading, songs, specials, quoting of scriptures and prayers. The meetings really proved to be a real blessing and many attended in every meeting. We wish we had time to write many of the testimonies out for you. One blind man walked twenty-five miles for the meetings.[3]

Another letter of testimony was written from Fort Archambault on October 22, 1937, by Paul F. Metzler:

The next morning we found the road mostly under water as we went on to the village of Sawea. Many places the push-men were unable to handle the push with the passenger, and many times I was forced to wade in the water over my knees. There were only about ten miles of this road, however, and before noon we had reached the village. This was my first visit to Sawea and I was astonished to find, here in the heart of the bush, a village of at least 500 houses. My visit was unannounced, but before long the rest-house was swept clean; wood, water, eggs and several chickens were brought to show a hearty welcome.

In the afternoon, the chief of the village came to pay his respects, and we spoke long to him concerning the Gospel. I had often wondered why it was that these people were so anxious for an evangelist. As I talked with the chief, I found that he had taken for a wife one of the daughters of the big chief Bezo. This woman was one of those who had heard the Gospel at Fort Archambault, had accepted Christ, and had learned to read the Word of God. "This woman is not like any other woman I have," said the chief. "She does not quarrel like the others; she does not drink the native wine; and she is constantly telling others about Jesus whom she calls her Saviour. Before I go on a trip she prays that God will take care of me, and I have come to trust more in her prayers than in the medicine that the witch doctors make. It is to learn more about her God that I have asked for an evangelist to come and stay with us and teach us His ways. . . ." Perhaps some of you are becoming discouraged in His service because you do not see results. The first years we were in this place, we did not realize results either, but the witness of this daughter of Bezo has put desire in the hearts of the people in Sawea to know more about God. Was not this one woman worth all the years of labor that we have spent giving forth the Gospel in this land? We did not know about this woman until just a few weeks ago. Perhaps somewhere there is someone living for Christ because of the testimony of your life. Some day up there you will know about it, and praise God you did not give up the fight.[4]

In an item in the February 1938 issue of the *Baptist Bulletin* we were told Manáos is situated on the Amazon River one thousand miles inland. The Rio Negro River joins the Amazon at this point. Six hundred miles up the Rio Negro, Mid-Missions had opened the first mission station ever to be located in that area. Mr. and Mrs. W. A. Ross were occupying that station. Mr. and Mrs. A. Donald Moffat and Mr. and Mrs. Garnet Trimble were at the Manáos base learning the language. This item went on:

In an earlier letter from the Moffats, they report interesting experiences with flying ants, scorpions, tarantulas, but their chief discomfort lies in the fact that their five thousand pounds of baggage is still lying in the customs house and they are unable to move the Brazilian officials one inch in getting it released. They have been in Manáos one month now, and are still living out of the two small suitcases which they took ashore.[5]

Temporary annoyances and eternal blessings! In March 1938, Mr. Walter Warfield and his wife, Mildred, arrived at Manáos to join the missionary force, making a total of four young couples to evangelize along the mighty Rio Negro.

In the July-August 1938 issue of the *Baptist Bulletin* the following information was given about what is now known as the Evangelical Baptist Missions, headquartered at Kokomo, Indiana:

The Africa Christian Missions is a regularly organized Independent Baptist Mission working among the Moslems in French West Africa in the Niger Colony with headquarters in the capital of the colony—Niamey—a cosmopolitan town with a population of about 20,000 people: Arabs, Berbers, Djermas, Hausas, Bambaras and Senagalese. This presents an endless opportunity to present the Gospel where it has never been heard before.

The Mission is working among a people who number about 250,000, and its influence reaches beyond the confines of these people to many of the Arabic speaking peoples inhabiting the southern border of the Sahara Desert in French West Africa.

The Mission had its inception in 1928 when a group of missionary minded business men, including some pastors, met in Paterson, New Jersey, to consider this area and these people, and sent Mr. and Mrs. Joseph McCaba as their first missionaries.[6]

ABWE, BMM and EBM are the original pioneering agencies approved by the GARBC. Through the years, however, other mission agencies were formed to establish churches here in the United States. The Fellowship of Baptists for Home Missions came into being in 1941, and Rev. J. Irving Reese was chosen as its first president. In 1947 Dr. Reese resigned as pastor of First Baptist Church in Elyria in order to give his full time to the mission's leadership. FBHM a few years ago merged with the Galilean Baptist Mission of Michigan to form the Baptist Mission of North America. BMNA had some serious financial difficulties and finally had to close down in the summer of 1990. Continental Baptist Missions was originally (1921) organized as Hiawatha Land Independent Baptist Missions by Rev. Arthur Glen. The Committee on Missionary Evangelism provides missionary evangelists who serve churches in the United States and also give time every year to foreign evangelistic efforts.

According to the 1990 reports, the GARBC-approved missionary agencies have a total of 1,895 missionaries on the field with 323 accepted candidates who are presently on deputation. Their total receipts for the year were $48,380,782. The Council of Eighteen Missionary Committee included the following statement in its 1990 report:

> The mission agencies listed in this report, some of which are older than the GARBC itself, have the honor of being approved by the Association and are grateful that the Association has considered them worthy of approval. Though approval is not ownership, nor does it carry with it the right to control, the Association and agencies sustain a meaningful relationship.
>
> Within the histories of each of these agencies a constituency of cooperating churches composed of GARBC churches and unaffiliated independent Baptist churches has developed.
>
> To interpret properly the mission personnel and financial figures of this report, remember that each mission agency is an autonomous, independent ministry with only a portion of its constituency being Regular Baptist churches. So in calculating totals and averages, Regular Baptist churches have provided only a portion of the income, veteran missionaries or new appointees of any given agency or in the totals of all the agencies.[7]

If the reader would like a more comprehensive treatment of GARBC-oriented missionary agencies and philosophy, see *The Missionary Emphasis of the General Association of Regular Baptist Churches* by William J. Hopewell, published by Regular Baptist Press in 1963; and *Missionary Administration in the Local Church* by R. L. Matthews, published by Regular Baptist Press in 1970. We close this chapter with the following statement from Dr. Matthews:

> Both at home and around the world, missions or evangelism is the business of the church. A careful consideration of God's will for us in the light of the Word has overwhelming evidence that He has called all of us to the task. Some may be called to go to the ends of the earth as was Paul. Today that

may involve such places as Southeast Asia, Japan, India, Africa or South America. Some He may call to go to "Samaria" as He did Philip. Samaria for you today may be Mexico, Canada or nearby islands. Some He may call to go to "Judaea." For us today Judaea could be a neighboring state or a rapidly developing suburban area. Still others He will call to go to "Jerusalem." Jerusalem is right where we live—the town, the city, the community where our local church is located. Let us yield ourselves to Him afresh that we may give a good account when we stand in His presence which may be very soon.

A faithful missionary who faced the knowledge that she had an incurable cancer expressed her burden of heart to her husband in these words: ". . . And if in God's wisdom He wants me to lay aside these few pounds of flesh in the land of my birth. . . . Darling, if God opens the door, go back to the people to whom God called us and whom we love so dearly."

May the Lord forgive us for our apathy when the command of God is so clear, the need of the world is so great, and some have been so willing to lay down their lives for the cause of Jesus Christ. In the very face of death they have pleaded with those who would continue to live to keep on serving the Lord in the outreach of missions until Jesus comes.

Let us be challenged by the words of our Savior: ". . . All power [authority] is given unto me in heaven and in earth" (Matt. 28:18); ". . . as my Father hath sent me, even so send I you" (John 20:21).[8]

End Notes

1. "Hamman Baptizes First Converts . . . ," *Baptist Bulletin* (March 1943), pp. 19, 20.

2. "President Commons Writes of Great Mission Work," *Baptist Bulletin* (March 1936), p. 12.

3. "Blessings at Fort Archambault," *Baptist Bulletin* (February 1938), p. 5.

4. "A Two Days' Journey Into the Bush," *Baptist Bulletin* (February 1938), p. 18.

5. "Manáos and the Joy (?) of Customs!" *Baptist Bulletin* (February 1938), p. 7.

6. "The Africa Christian Mission," *Baptist Bulletin* (July–August 1938), p. 15.

7. "Report of the Missionary Committee" in *GARBC Annual Report* (Schaumburg, IL: Regular Baptist Press, 1990), p. 14.

8. R. L. Matthews, *Missionary Administration in the Local Church* (Schaumburg, IL: Regular Baptist Press, 1970), pp. 116, 117.

H. O. Van Gilder

THE ERA OF H. O. VAN GILDER

1944–1948

10

By 1944 churches were leaving the Northern Baptist Convention in droves. At the GARBC annual conference in Johnson City, New York, in 1943, 72 churches were welcomed into the Fellowship. At the 1944 conference 42 more came in, making the total number of GARBC churches 296. The Council of Fourteen recognized the necessity for opening a "home office," *not* a "headquarters," and also of putting a man in that office to promote the work of the Association and provide counsel and encouragement to the local churches when asked. That man would not be an "executive secretary" but a "national representative." The Council wisely chose Chicago, Illinois, for the location of the home office, since Chicago was centrally located among our churches and also the nation's transportation hub. In 1944 that trans-lated into a railroad center; now it means O'Hare Airport, the world's busiest.

In May of 1944 at the annual conference in Grand Rapids the Council chose the first GARBC national representative. The Council of Fourteen for that historic action included H. O. Van Gilder, chairman; David Otis Fuller, secretary; Raymond F. Hamilton, treasurer; Arthur Annette; David Gillespie; Earle Griffith; William Headley; Robert T. Ketcham; Kenneth R. Kinney; Clarence Mason, Jr.; Robert L. Powell; J. Irving Reese and Robert L. Ryerse. Their choice—Dr. H. O. Van Gilder.

Heber Osborne Van Gilder was born March 26, 1897, in Fairmont, West Virginia. He married Belle Lynch in 1918. Dr. Van Gilder graduated from the Philadelphia Bible Institute in 1922. During his college years Van Gilder pastored the First Baptist Church in Perkasie, Pennsylvania. He left Perkasie to pastor the Central Baptist Church in Columbus, Ohio, from 1922 to 1931. Those were busy days for him as he studied Hebrew and Greek at Capitol Seminary in Columbus and also took some classes at Ohio State University. During his Columbus pastorate Van Gilder led his church out of the Northern Baptist Convention and also helped to create the Ohio Association of Independent Baptist Churches in 1927. In 1931 Van Gilder was called to the Temple Baptist Church in Portsmouth, Ohio, a pastorate he held until his call to the National Representative's office in 1944. In 1933 Eastern University in Philadelphia awarded Van Gilder a doctor of divinity degree.

Dr. Robert T. Ketcham introduced Dr. Van Gilder to the readers of the *Baptist Bulletin* with the following well-chosen words:

> It has been this editor's high privilege to know Dr. Van Gilder and to work intimately with him for the past twenty years. It was Dr. Van Gilder, along with Dr. Griffith, who was associated with us in founding and organizing what is now known as the Ohio Independent Association of Baptist Churches. Aside from the Grand Rapids Association founded by Dr. Van Osdel, the Ohio group was one of the first to really set an organized expression of the fel-lowship of churches which had withdrawn from the Northern Baptist Convention.
>
> It was in those days that we learned to know and love "Van." Not only to know and love him, but to trust him. We found in this man that delightful thing called "stability." One always knew where they would find Van Gilder. When one was looking for Van Gilder all they would need to do would be to find the right side of any issue and there they would find Van Gilder.
>
> Our association with Dr. Van Gilder during these twenty years has produced the conviction in our mind to which we have often given public expression that he is the outstanding Bible expository preacher in all our Fellowship—and a long way outside of it too! This outstanding pulpit ability of Dr. Van Gilder makes him a doubly valuable man for this position. He is open for engagements, for evangelistic meetings, Bible conferences, weekend missions and any kind of public ministry of the Word. This in addition to his ability to sit down in face to face, and heart to heart counsel with pastors and churches and boards, who have problems about which they wish advice, all adds up to the fact that the G.A.R.B.C. is presenting in Dr. Van Gilder a man whose ministry and message ought to mean much in the days ahead.[1]

And mean much he did! He set precedents and high standards for the office of National Representative that are appreciated to this day.

The new home office welcomed Dr. Van Gilder on September 1, 1944. That office was a three-room suite that rented for fifty dollars per month in the Ashland Building, 155 North Clark Street, Room 1112, Chicago 1, Illinois! The Ashland Building was across the street from the Sherman Hotel in the very center of the Loop in downtown Chicago.

Every national representative needs an above-average secretary, and the Council found one in the person of Miss Ruth Ryburn of Waterloo, Iowa. She had recently finished her work as a student at Baptist Bible Seminary in Johnson City, New York. She ultimately served every national representative, working in the home office from 1944 until her retirement in 1982. Dr. Merle R. Hull reported that Miss Ryburn's account of the beginnings of the home office is "both illuminating and amusing." Wrote Ryburn:

> I had heard of Dr. Van Gilder, but had never seen him. Nor had he ever seen me! However, we located each other at Union Station when I arrived in Chicago. We decided to set up operation. I would need a desk, chair, file and L. C. Smith typewriter (my favorite in those days). At a second-hand store we found all these items; they were delivered the next day to the office in the Ashland Building at 155 North Clark Street. [The Greyhound bus depot now occupies that corner.]
>
> After ordering the furniture, Dr. Van Gilder took me to the Chicago Hebrew Mission; he was a personal friend of the director. The Mission gave each of us a room and breakfast! The next day I found a room in the residence of an older couple on Chestnut Street near Moody Bible Institute—across from what is now the Torrey-Gray Auditorium.
>
> The first real day in the office, Dr. Van Gilder dictated a few letters, then left for speaking engagements. And I suddenly realized that except for the Lord, I was alone in the heart of Chicago. During the first few weeks no one came to the office—not even the mailman, because there was no mail! Finally he did begin to come, and I would engage him in conversation just to have someone to talk to! I discovered he was a Christian; in fact, a member of one of our churches! We had a phone in the office but it seldom rang because the pastors and churches had not yet realized they had a home office. They would still call the chairman of the Council.[2]

From such small beginnings has grown a ministry that numbers almost 50 full-time employees in the GARBC and Regular Baptist Press facilities. Dr. Van Gilder and Miss Ryburn were pioneers in their own right, and their ministries have left indelible imprints on the Association.

Van Gilder's keen mind and Scriptural savvy were more than

adequate to meet the challenges of liberal infidels like Harry Emerson Fosdick. From Fosdick's pen and pulpit had poured an avalanche of apostasy that had surely undermined the faith of Northern Baptists for decades. The titles of his books seemed innocent enough, but their contents were deadly to belief in Biblical inerrancy, Biblical infallibility and Biblical inspiration. His books included *The Meaning of Prayer* (1915), *The Meaning of Faith* (1917), *The Meaning of Service* (1920), *Christianity and Progress* (1922), *The Modern Use of the Bible* (1924), *As I See Religion* (1932) and *A Guide to Understanding the Bible* (1938). Those books were amazingly popular and were, therefore, reprinted again and again. Concerning the book *A Guide to Understanding the Bible,* J. L. Neve wrote:

> The book is important not for the originality of investigation but rather for the ease and lucidity of style with which the author presents the findings of critical Biblical scholarship. Fosdick traces the growth of six Biblical concepts: those of God, of man, of right and wrong, of suffering, of fellowship with God, and of immortality. The words about God in the Bible, he holds, are of minor importance. Jesus revealed God "not so much in the words He used about Him as in the life He lived with Him" (p. 42). It is doubtful whether the Biblical writers have reported with precision the words of Jesus. The essential thing is the new relation between God and man as exemplified in Jesus. Inspiration, he holds, fortunately has not been stereotyped and is not mechanical. The unfolding of ideas which the Bible presents is dual, he says; seen from one end, it is a "human achievement; seen from the other, a divine revelation."[3]

Such frontal assaults on the verbal-plenary inspiration of the Bible poured from Fosdick's tongue and tomes during his entire pastorate of Riverside Church in New York City from 1930 to 1948 and until his death at the age of 91 in 1969. How God-directed was the GARBC in having as its first national representative a stately, scholarly and Scriptural leader who was not intimidated by the pseudo-scholarship of men like Harry Emerson Fosdick and other Convention apostates.

End Notes

1. "National Representative," *Baptist Bulletin* (October 1944), p. 1.

2. Merle R. Hull, *What A Fellowship!* (Schaumburg, IL: Regular Baptist Press, 1981), pp. 29, 30.

3. J. L. Neve, *A History of Christian Thought,* vol. 2 (Philadelphia: The Muhlenberg Press, 1946), p. 322.

11

The January and February 1944 issues of the *Baptist Bulletin* reported the ordination services of seven young men who would have long and meritorious ministries within the ranks of the GARBC. Richard Crandall was ordained by the First Baptist Church of Johnson City, New York; Leon Wood by the Covey Hill Baptist Church in Paw Paw, Michigan; Joseph H. Bower by the Brunswick Baptist Church of Gary, Indiana; George O'Keefe and Austin Ireland by the First Baptist Church of Spartansburg, Pennsylvania; Warren H. Faber by the Calvary Baptist Church of Grand Rapids, Michigan; and John E. Allen by the Tabernacle Baptist Church of Ithaca, New York.

The January 1944 *Baptist Bulletin* also reported some news about some brave young women who were interned by the Japanese in the Philippines. Dr. Harold T. Commons wrote:

> Miss Woodworth is generally in good health, but tends to anemia. Miss Congleton has had various illnesses and is not too sturdy. A nose and throat infection caused loss of voice for a while and raised suspicion of a lung infection. However, she responded to treatment and seems to be coming along all right. There is no clinical evidence of such an infection. Miss Kemery needs special prayer. She has a low thyroid and a very low basal metabolism, with excessive fatigue and some temperature. She was responding to thyroid medicine by mouth, and X-ray examinations of the lungs showed no positive evidence of tuberculosis. Her condition is somewhat puzzling, but she is continuing to have the best of care, and there are fine missionary and medical facilities still available in Manila. Mrs. Bomm had a thyroid operation in Manila before the war, and while some results appeared beneficial, it is not entirely so. There has not been much change in Mrs. Bomm's health since the war [began], and she continues to carry on well, although she tires easily. . . . Last June, the entire Iloilo Internment Camp

was moved to Manila and merged with Santo Tomas. The Friederichsen family, Miss Parks and Miss Hinkley are now all at Santo Tomas. I have not yet acquired a detailed picture of what happened at Iloilo, but I do have this present information concerning the whereabouts and health of our Iloilo group. Dr. Daniels treated both Mrs. Friederichsen and Miss Parks at Santo Tomas, and the rest of them were well enough not to require medical attention. . . . Generally speaking, the Japanese treatment of Americans in the Philippines has been better than in China and in other places. The Japanese are apparently doing their best to curry favor with the Filipino people and their regime is, therefore, more lenient than we had dared hope.[1]

At the same time, Willard and Grace Stull with their son, Billy, were seeing God move in their work in Brazil. Grace Stull wrote:

The same day that our baggage arrived, a little bundle of heaven came to grace the home of Dynes and Maxine McCullough. Little Judith Marie is fat, rosy and good natured, and the very picture of her proud Daddy. We believe she has even inherited his beautiful tenor voice for at this very early age she sings a language all her own. Pray with us, that God will make her a real blessing not only to her parents but also in the work at Cruzeiro do Sul.[2]

Back in the United States, Rev. A. G. Annette, who had pastored the First Baptist Church in Plainfield, Illinois, for ten years, announced he was resigning to enter the field of full-time itinerant evangelism. He was succeeded at Plainfield by Rev. Charles F. Fields. Dr. Fields was the founder and first pastor of the Portage Park Baptist Church in Chicago when it began in the 1920s. Rev. Ralph W. Neighbour, formerly associated with the Interstate Evangelistic Association, was called to the Fort Wayne Gospel Temple, an outstanding gospel center founded by Rev. B. E. Rediger in 1928. Paul Rader, the internationally known evangelist and missionary leader, pastored there from November of 1934 to February of 1937. The auditorium seated 3,500, and the congregation supported an extensive radio ministry. For a number of years Ralph Neighbour pastored the First Baptist Church of Elyria, Ohio, and served on the GARBC Council of Fourteen.

In West Virginia, the West Virginia Association of Independent Baptist Churches was growing under the leadership of Kenneth Smelser, M. I. Amundson, Harry Babcock, Joe Gavit, E. V. Howell, Benjamin Green, James Shields, R. A. Blessing, Calvin Burton and R. T. Nordlund. In Des Moines, Iowa, Pastor A. D. Mohr announced that the morning worship services of the Grandview Park Baptist Church would be broadcast over two powerful radio stations. In Tacoma, Washington, Dr. Robert L. Powell and his congregation celebrated the tenth anniversary of Temple Baptist Church. In Pennsylvania, Rev. Hall Dautel, pastor of the Bethel Baptist Church in Erie, preached a special series of Sunday night sermons on subjects chosen by the congregation. In Montana, Rev. Ralph Werner began a thriving work in the Kalispell area. An adventuresome pioneer, Werner held meetings in mining and lumbering camps and saw his ministry grow through many years under the blessing of God. First Baptist Church in Columbia Falls, Montana, and Bethel Baptist Church of Kalispell are prospering works to this day. In New York, Rev. Kenneth Elgena reported the Great Valley Baptist Church had voted unanimously to sever all connections with the Northern Baptist Convention.

On the national scene, the fundamentalists still in the Convention were becoming more and more displeased with the missionary policies of the Convention Foreign Board. The unhappy conservatives, therefore, organized a new Conservative Mission Society. Commenting on that development in the April 1944 *Baptist Bulletin,* Dr. Ketcham said:

> Dr. Pierce and his colleagues in the formation of his new Conservative Mission Society are engaging in one of the most inconsistent moves conceivable. Their announced reason for breaking with the Foreign Board and setting up a Conservative Board is that the Foreign Board has become so modernistic that it is hopeless to work further for reform within it. To all of this we agree and have agreed for the past fifteen years, but there is something else that these Conservatives within the Convention are overlooking. Why do they insist upon a separation from the Foreign Board because of its modernism and still stay "within the framework" of the Northern Baptist Convention when it is equally modernistic? The only reason under heaven why a foreign board could become and continue to be modernistic is because the convention which controls it has become and continues to be modernistic. Why penalize the Foreign Board by separating from it and at the same time stay within the framework of everything else that is equally modernistic? If these conservative brethren feel called upon now to create a Conservative Baptist Mission Board, then why not obey God fully and create a Conservative Baptist Convention. We would gladly welcome these fundamental Baptists into the fold of the G.A.R.B.C. which saw this issue fifteen years ago and pioneered the way and set up just such a Baptist body. If these conservative

brethren do not like the G.A.R.B.C., then they should be consistent enough to organize one of their own. As regrettable as it would be to have another fundamental Baptist body organized, it would certainly be preferable to a continued alliance with that which denies every fundamental truth of the Baptist faith.[3]

The historical background of the Conservative movement is explained by Joseph M. Stowell:

With the forming of the Baptist Bible Union in 1923, the more militant Fundamentalists and the moderate Fundamentalists of the Convention Fundamental Fellowship (formed in 1920) had to a great degree parted ways. When the G.A.R.B. was born as a separatist movement in 1932, this breach became more severe. But in 1943, the Convention Fundamentalists became militant and formed the new Conservative Foreign Mission Society, which the Convention officialdom deeply resented.[4]

Dr. Ketcham's challenge of April 1944 did not go unheeded by some of the Conservative leaders, and while Dr. Van Gilder was in the National Representative's office, conservatives including Dr. R. S. Beal of Tucson, Arizona, and Dr. Albert Johnson of Portland, Oregon, expressed a cautious willingness to discuss the issues with the GARBC leaders.

The situation in the Northern Baptist Convention by 1944 resulted from decades of liberal teaching in the seminaries and unbiblical preaching from the pulpits. The Convention machinery was controlled by the modernists, and Bible-believing churches were leaving the Convention by the hundreds every year. According to NBC statisticians, in 1944 the NBC had 5,826 fewer churches than it had had in 1913. Also, there were almost 400 fewer missionaries on foreign fields in 1944 than were on the fields in 1913. The barrenness of infidelity was clear for all to see. While the NBC missionary force was shrinking, the GARBC-approved mission agencies were growing and prospering, even in the face of a global war.

At the annual conference of the GARBC in Grand Rapids in May of 1944 several resolutions were passed by the messengers, but one was particularly significant in light of the conservative movement within the Convention. The resolution is titled "Concerning Northern Baptist Convention Fundamentalists" and reads as follows:

We look with deep concern, and yet with fervent hope upon the movement which has formed a new missionary society in the Northern Baptist Convention. We believe that many of the brethren who are responsible for this stand for truth are faithful and loyal to the Book and, while we do not believe that such a movement within the Convention can ever clean up the Convention, yet we would be negligent were we to fail to recognize the earnest desire of these brethren to give a true testimony to the historic faith of Baptists.

We pray that they may soon see the wisdom of a clean cut break with evil, inevitably involved in a fellowship with the Northern Baptist Convention. We not only would rejoice to see these brethren take a glorious stand for truth and righteousness, but we would welcome the privilege of a larger fellowship of true Baptists who have the courage of their convictions and are willing to pay the price of breaking away from all machines which harbor and encourage heretical teachings.[5]

The GARBC was growing whether or not the conservatives affiliated with them, and the summer of 1944 saw the ordinations of six more outstanding young men. Rollie Baker was ordained by the First Baptist Church of Hamburg, New York; Ernest Ingling by the West Corners Baptist Church of Endicott, New York; Leland Brooker and Merle R. Hull by the First Baptist Church of East Branch, New York; and Robert L. Sumner by the Calvary Baptist Church of Norwich, New York. Quite a summer for New York! It was climaxed by the ordination of Kenneth Ohrstrom by the First Baptist Church of North Tonawanda, New York.

The summer of 1944 also saw the withdrawal from the Northern Baptist Convention of the historic First Baptist Church of New York City. This church, located at 79th Street and Broadway, had been pastored by the famous pulpiteer, Isaac Massey Haldeman, from 1884 until his death in 1933 at the age of 88. He was a great preacher on prophecy and was often referred to as "the dispensational pastor." It remained, however, for the strong leadership of Dr. Arthur Franklin Williams to bring the church to vote out of the Convention. The two-century-old church is still true to the Faith.

Dr. Van Gilder had many reasons for optimism as he moved to Chicago. In the November 1944 *Baptist Bulletin* he gave a brief report in the following words:

We began this ministry the first of September, and during that first month traveled nearly thirty-five hundred miles, preached eighteen times and interviewed a number of pastors, besides buying office equipment and getting the office functioning. . . .

. . . A word about the schedule ahead: November 12 to 19 we are to be with the Nottingham Baptist Church of Cleveland, Ohio, Rev. George A. Bates, pastor. Beginning Sunday night, November 19th with Rev. Walter Spieth, North Royalton, Ohio. December 8–11, Immanuel Baptist Church, Columbus, Rev. Ralph E. Hone, pastor.[6]

Thus it was that Dr. Van (as he was known affectionately) set sound precedents for the work of the national representative: preaching, counseling with pastors, consulting with pulpit committees, working with the Council, writing for the *Baptist Bulletin* and carrying on a voluminous correspondence with pastors, missionaries, educators, seminary students and whoever had questions about the Association and its workings and/or philosophy. And, of course, much, much traveling!

Another wonderful aspect of the national representative's ministry has to do with the godly and honorable men with whom he has the privilege of working. One of those blessed co-laborers for Dr. Van was Dr. Emery H. Bancroft, the beloved dean of the Baptist Bible Seminary in Johnson City, New York. During an elemental theology class on October 27 Bancroft suffered a cerebral thrombosis and steadily grew worse until he went Home to be with the Lord on November 11, 1944, at the age of 66.

Bancroft had served in the Spanish-American War and in bayonet practice in the Philippines received the injury that finally cost him his eyesight. In 1919 he began teaching theology. Thirteen years of that time were spent in the Practical Bible Training School, Bible School Park, New York, during which time he wrote his first work, *Christian Theology, Systematic and Biblical.* In 1932 Dr. Bancroft began his ministry with Baptist Bible Seminary as instructor and dean. That same year he published his second work, *Elemental Theology.* Hundreds of his students and thousands who have read his theological tomes will always be grateful for his input and insights.

The funeral service was held on November 15 at the First Baptist Church in Johnson City. Dr. Earle G. Griffith, president of Baptist Bible Seminary, conducted the service, assisted by his pastor Rev.

Kenneth R. Kinney, Rev. Kenneth Muck and Rev. Thomas G. Thomas. At the time of his father's death, Rev. Bernard N. Bancroft was an accepted missionary to the Philippines with ABWE.

Before 1944 ended four more young men were ordained formally to the ministry: G. Arthur Woolsey by the Central Baptist Church of Binghamton, New York; G. Louis Jones by the West Bainbridge (New York) Baptist Church; Clifford Miller by the First Baptist Church of Creston, Iowa; and Clarence D. Kennedy by the Castle Creek (New York) Baptist Church.

The year 1944 may have been an eventful year for Franklin D. Roosevelt, but it was eternally more so for Dr. H. O. Van Gilder.

End Notes

1. "To Relatives and Special Friends of Our Philippine Islands Missionaries," *Baptist Bulletin* (January 1944), pp. 9, 10.

2. "God's Highway in Brazil," *Baptist Bulletin* (January 1944), p. 11.

3. "The New Conservative Baptist Foreign Mission Society," *Baptist Bulletin* (April 1944), p. 2.

4. Joseph M. Stowell, *Background and History of the GARBC* (Hayward, CA: J. F. May Press, 1949), pp. 69, 70.

5. "Resolutions Adopted by General Association of Regular Baptists," *Baptist Bulletin* (June 1944), p. 14.

6. "Dr. Van Gilder Reporting," *Baptist Bulletin* (November 1944), pp. 8, 9.

12

As 1945 dawned upon a war-weary world, weary fundamentalists still within the Convention sought solutions to their problems. Dr. Van Gilder and Dr. Ketcham strongly urged the conservatives to come out from the NBC in obedience to clear Scriptural mandates to separate from apostasy. Dr. Ketcham suggested that if the Fundamental Fellowship conservatives would come out of the Convention, there ought to be a sincere attempt to get them together with the GARBC. According to Joseph M. Stowell:

> This approach the Council of Fourteen approved and confirmed. Later at their meeting in Los Angeles, California (December 1946), the Council sent a proposal to the Conservatives suggesting that both groups work toward a merger in 1950. A meeting was held in January, 1947, at the Stevens Hotel, Chicago, between the Council of Fourteen of the G.A.R.B. and the Committee of Fifteen of the Convention Conservatives. The ice was broken, suspicion was dissipated and a wonderful spirit of fellowship was established. Little was actually accomplished except that the Conservatives for the most part voiced the opinion that they were on the way out of the Convention and promised to adopt a resolution indicating the impossibility of continued cooperation with the Convention.[1]

Dr. Van Gilder penned a five-page editorial in the April 1947 *Baptist Bulletin* titled "Convention Conservatives—Can We Get Together?"

> Van Gilder's editorial also included correspondence that he had had with key fundamentalists within the Convention. It was the clear hope of the General Association of Regular Baptist Churches that a merger with Convention fundamentalists would effectuate one strong separatist organization to stand against modernism and liberalism.[2]

Perhaps the most incisive paragraph written by Van Gilder is the following one:

> We, of the General Association of Regular Baptist Churches, have made honest, earnest and prayerful efforts to meet our Conservative brethren more than half-way in the hope that the state of fundamentalism may not be made more tragic than it already is by needless multiplication of division among brethren. We tell the story here not because we are despairing or discouraged, but because we believe its telling will promote a better understanding and make a further contribution toward the achievement of the end in view. We have found many of the Conservative pastors to be "true blue," courageous and sincere, and we believe they will be as desirous as we to avoid anything which might serve to divide our Baptist forces further.[3]

The Regular Baptists, one with the spirit of Van Gilder's plea, planned their 1947 conference to convene in Atlantic City, New Jersey, just before the pre-Convention meetings of the Conservatives. When the two groups met, the GARBC Council of Fourteen and the Conservative Committee of Fifteen agreed to create a "Committee of Six" to explore plans of merging in the coming year. The plan was that each group was to select three from the other group to serve on the special committee. The Conservatives chose Dr. David Otis Fuller of Grand Rapids, Michigan; Rev. William Kuhnle of Milwaukee, Wisconsin; and Rev. J. Irving Reese of Elyria, Ohio. The Regular Baptists chose H. H. Savage of Pontiac, Michigan; Dr. R. S. Beal of Tucson, Arizona; and Dr. Albert Johnson of Portland, Oregon.

The special committee was unable, however, to reach agreement on the issue of separation.

> Regular Baptists insisted that any association with their organization be on the basis of absolute and total separation from the Northern Baptist Convention. Conservative Baptists, in contrast, were determined to accept any fundamental church regardless of its other affiliations. Hence, the Conservatives wanted to form an association which would permit dual membership in their organization and the Northern Baptist Convention.[4]

The hoped-for merger was dead.

During the 1947 GARBC conference Dr. Van Gilder received a copy of a letter written by Dr. W. B. Riley to the president of the

Northern Baptist Convention. We print the letter in its entirety because it is one of the most remarkable and in many ways one of the saddest epistles in Baptist history.

Rev. Edwin Dahlberg, D.D.
Northern Baptist Convention
152 Madison Avenue
New York 16, New York

My Dear Dr. Dahlberg:

I was truly sorry to be too ill to attend the meeting when you were here a few days since and consequently had to miss a visit with you. Your suggestion of further conferences on the subject of Minnesota's relationship to the Northern Baptist Convention involved what to me was a waste of time, inasmuch as more than two years ago I spent seven or eight mornings in such conferences to find no common ground upon which to proceed.

That fact provides the basis of this present communication. I write to you as my friend and former Minnesota co-laborer to ask that you present to the proper authorities my request for the cancellation of my life-membership in the Northern Baptist Convention, thereby saving your secretary his annual announcement to me of the Convention's assembly.

I shall not attend the Convention again in any capacity, since I can no further fellowship it [sic]. This is not in consequence of any personal pique. I came into the bounds of the Northern Convention January 1, 1887, and have been for sixty years a member of that body—first of the Anniversaries, and for forty years now of the Convention itself. In that time I expect I have attended something like fifty such meetings of the Convention, but always (with the exception of 1889 when the First Church of Lafayette, Indiana sent me to the Convention) I have gone at my own personal expense, thereby proving, I think, my interest in Convention affairs. The Convention has reciprocated by showing me every personal courtesy; and I confess that after five years of intermission in attendance when three years ago at Atlantic City I rose to speak for just a minute or two, I was very much impressed by and appreciated the fact that the entire Convention rose—doubtless in respect to my gray hair and my return to Convention assembly.

My reasons, therefore, for withdrawing at this time are several in number:

First, the Convention has gone into the hands of Modernists so largely that Conservatives seem to me to attend its sessions in vain. I am by unshaken convictions a Fundamentalist.

Second, I count any convention that is controlled by salaried servants, undemocratic; and on that account the Northern Convention is not, to me, either Biblical or Baptistic, as its balance of power is easily with these same multiplied people of convention salaries.

Third, the refusal of the Foreign Board to adopt and demand the Virgin Birth of Christ as a condition of foreign mission commission, together with the rejection of Judge Fickett's Resolution at the Convention a year ago at Grand Rapids, Michigan, constitute the Unitarian triumph with which I am not at all in sympathy.

Fourth, the illegal and immoral withholding of the entire quota due Minnesota from money given by our people for the common cause in which our state was to share is so remote from both the Northern Convention rules and regulations and our Minnesota constitution and bylaws, and the employment of a minority as a medium through which the Convention now works is so un-Baptistic and so undemocratic that I cannot conceive of Minnesota Baptists regarding themselves as under any circumstances further members of the Northern Convention assembly.

I have just finished reading the life of Mr. Crowell of Chicago by Dr. Day. I know of no more manly and Christian conduct than he evinced when he withdrew from the Presbyterian General Assembly, thereby proving both his loyalty to his Lord and his fidelity to the Holy Word of God.

I am no longer a young man, having seen my eighty-sixth birthday, and I should be ashamed to die in the fellowship that seemed to me un-Biblical, and consequently un-Baptistic.

John, in his second epistle, verses 9 to 11 writes, "Whosoever transgresseth, and abideth not in the doctrine of Christ, hath not God. He that abideth in the doctrine of Christ, he hath both the Father and the Son. If there come any unto you, and bring not this doctrine, receive him not into your house, neither bid him God speed: for he that biddeth him God speed is partaker of his evil deeds." I accept those words as divinely inspired.

Paul, writing to the Corinthians in the second epistle, sixth chapter, verse 14, says, "Be ye not unequally yoked together with unbelievers;" and in verse 17 he adds, "Wherefore come out from among them, and be ye separate, saith the Lord." Again I believe this to be divinely inspired direction; hence, my request. I am expecting, of course, that it will be granted willingly.

Respectfully yours,
Signed: W. B. Riley[5]

The gifted and gracious warrior from Minneapolis at last had concluded that the leaders who formed the GARBC had been right all along. The Convention was incurably apostate. The only course of action, Scripturally, for the fundamentalists still in the Convention was to follow Riley out of the Convention. "Better late than never," but one can only wonder what might have been had Riley joined the come-outers in 1932. Surely the Association would have started with far more churches, and its early strength would have been even greater and more productive. Surely many Minnesota churches would have followed Riley into the GARBC in 1932 had Riley chosen to cast his lot with the Regular Baptists. His vast influence would also have impacted many churches outside Minnesota. But, alas, he waited until the year of his death to leave the Convention, and the church he had pastored for more than 45 years stayed in the Convention. Instead of joining ranks with the GARBC,

> The Convention Fundamentalists organized in Milwaukee in May 1948 into the Conservative Baptist Association of America. This new organization, while separate from the Convention, will accept Convention churches into its fellowship. Meanwhile, the Fundamental Fellowship continues in the Convention under the name Conservative Baptist Fellowship of Northern Baptists.[6]

End Notes

1. Joseph M. Stowell, *Background and History of the GARBC* (Hayward, CA: J. F. May Press, 1949), p. 70.
2. J. Murray Murdoch, *Portrait of Obedience* (Schaumburg, IL: Regular Baptist Press, 1979), p. 217.
3. H. O. Van Gilder, "Convention Conservatives—Can We Get Together?" *Baptist Bulletin* (April 1947), p. 7.
4. Murdoch, p. 220.
5. Stowell, pp. 72–74.
6. Ibid., p. 71.

13

GARBC churches have been through the years "special meetings" churches. Evangelistic crusades, revival campaigns, missionary conferences and Bible conferences are held regularly in GARBC churches. Many churches have special meetings every fall and every spring. This was especially true during the decade of the 1940s when great preachers traveled among the churches stirring revival fires, winning souls, recruiting missionary candidates and teaching great pretribulational, premillennial, dispensational prophetic doctrines. Some of them were A. C. Gaebelein, Hyman J. Appelman, John Carrara, Keith L. Brooks, Fred Brown, Martin R. DeHaan, H. A. Ironside, Dan Gilbert, Vance Havner, William L. Pettingill, Carl Sweazy, John Linton and Paul Levin.

Regular Baptists cooperated in city-wide campaigns with men like Bob Jones, Sr., John R. Rice and Bill Rice. Meetings were well-planned, well-advertised and well-financed. Crowds came and churches grew.

In January 1945, newly appointed state missionary under the West Virginia Fundamental Baptist Home Mission Society, W. J. Richardson, held two weeks of evangelistic services for Pastor Robert L. Sumner and his congregation, the Tabernacle Baptist Church of Pontiac, Illinois. The Burton Avenue Baptist Church of Waterloo, Iowa, started the new year with its annual missionary conference led by Pastor Harvey Taylor. Farther west, the First Baptist Church of Ceres, California, pastored by Paul R. Jackson, began the year with three weeks of evangelistic meetings with Orville Yeager. Pastor Jackson reported many conversions. He also reported that two couples from the church were heading for the mission field of Africa: Rev. and Mrs. Harry Buerer and Rev. and Mrs. LaVerne Olson. Dr. Van Gilder started the year with nine days of meetings with the four GARBC churches in Flint, Michigan: Emmanuel, Grace, Riverdale and South, pastored respectively by Jack Bowen, Frank Hurley, Robert Titus and Ewing Walters.

In February the Calvary Baptist Church of Corning, New York, profited from a series of evangelistic meetings held by Evangelist Clayton Howard Gray. Rev. Leo Sandgren, pastor of the First Baptist Church of Austin, Minnesota, conducted a one-week evangelistic crusade at Walnut Street Baptist Church, Waterloo, Iowa, pastored by R. T. Ketcham. Faith Baptist Church of Saginaw, Michigan, and Ashman Avenue Baptist Church held a double ordination service to set apart to the ministry Edwin A. Dubois and Hugh Woodside.

Dr. Van Gilder began the month of March with special meetings at Jameson Baptist Church of Alton, Illinois, where his son, H. O. Van Gilder, Jr., was serving his first pastorate. Pastor Robert L. Ryerse reported that his congregation, Cherrydale Baptist Church in Arlington, Virginia, was led in a special Bible conference by Rev. Sale Harrison. Rev. Bert Turner of Detroit was mightily used of God in a youth crusade at First Baptist Church in Lapeer, Michigan. On the Saturday afternoon of the crusade, Pastor E. C. Shute led a "Christian Parade" through the streets of Lapeer. Two Sunday School buses headed the parade with 150 teenagers following, followed by a fine array of church members in automobiles with two more Sunday School buses bringing up the rear. More than 100 young people professed Christ as Savior during the crusade, while 35 teenagers publicly dedicated their lives to do God's will.

Pastor Carl Sweazy of the Los Angeles Calvary Baptist Tabernacle reported two great weeks of evangelistic meetings with Dr. W. P. Nicholson, an Irish preacher who had preached his way around the world twelve times! Evangelist Carlyle T. Scott held a month of tent meetings for Missionary Baptist Church of Michigan City, Indiana, pastored by Rev. Carl Brown. A formal ordination service was held at First Baptist Church of Brown City, Michigan, to set apart Donald Olsen to the gospel ministry. A prophetic Bible conference was held at the Brunswick Baptist Church in Gary, Indiana, pastored by P. R. Halvorsen. The prophetic teacher was Dr. Arthur E. Bloomfield of Angola, Indiana. Pastor David A. Wood of the First Baptist Church of Strathmore, California, reported a fruitful two weeks of revival meetings with Willard W. Riggs, vice president of the Phoenix Bible Institute of Arizona.

The month of May began for the Central Baptist Church in Aurora, Illinois, with a Bible conference featuring Pastor O. L. Masemore and Rev. Raymond F. Hamilton. The month of May was designated "Prove Me Month" at Garfield Avenue Baptist Church in Milwaukee, where Pastor William E. Kuhnle preached on stewardship throughout the month. Two weeks of meetings were held by Carl Sweazy at the Hagerman Baptist Church of Waterloo, Iowa, where B. G. Ham was pastor. The First Baptist Church of Petaluma, California, pastored by Fred R. Brock, was filled to capacity for a northern California youth rally. The exciting program included Don Allen, well-known piano artist; Kenneth Hansen, general secretary of the Christian Service Brigade; John Begley, chalk-talk artist; and Herbert Farrar, pastor of the Hayward First Baptist Church, speaker.

At the Berean Baptist Church in Grand Rapids, Michigan, Rev. Paul Friederichsen, a missionary to the Philippines under ABWE, was the featured speaker at a missionary rally. He told of his experiences over a period of three years in the Santo Tomas Prison Camp in Manila. Pastor Howard Keithley reported the congregation gave more than five hundred dollars to help pay medical expenses for Friederichsen and his family. Another missionary conference was held at the Tabernacle Baptist Church in Ithaca, New York, pastored by Joseph M. Stowell. Speakers were Rev. George Sinderson, recently returned from French Equatorial Africa; Rev. John Deroseta, who was headed for Africa; Rev. William Ross from the Amazon River Valley of South America; Miss Grace Bennett of Venezuela; and Miss Louise Lynip of the Philippines.

In September the First Baptist Church of New York City celebrated its 200th anniversary with special meetings held by Dr. H. A. Ironside. The church had begun in 1745 and, amazingly, its pastor, Dr. Arthur Franklin Williams, was only its eleventh pastor in 200 years! The church early in September voted to undertake the full support of Rev. and Mrs. Donald J. Hare, missionary appointees to Brazil under ABWE. Dr. H. O. Van Gilder had held a Bible conference in this historic church August 17–26.

Rev. Coulson Shepherd reported four weeks of summer Bible conferences in First Baptist Church of Atlantic City, New Jersey. The speakers were Dr. William L. Pettingill, Rev. Frank C. Torrey, Rev. Ralph H. Stoll and Dr. Max I. Reich. Also in New Jersey a series of evangelistic meetings were held at the First Baptist Church of Caldwell with Walter (Happy Mac) MacDonald as speaker. Rev. Thomas G. Thomas, pastor, reported excellent attendance and results.

In September John Carrara preached two weeks of soul-winning messages at the Seward Avenue Baptist Church in Topeka, Kansas, pastored by Gaylord S. Hamilton. Belden Avenue Baptist Church in Chicago heard Joseph Hakes of Winona Lake; E. C. Lasswell of Eldora, Iowa; S. Franklin Logsdon of London, Ontario; and Chester E. Tulga of Chicago. Belden continued to grow under the dynamic ministry of Howard Fulton.

The fall missionary conference of the First Baptist Church of Troy, Illinois, according to Pastor Harry O. Babcock, featured Robert Vaughn of Baptist Mid-Missions to French Equatorial Africa; Walter Warfield of Brazil; Milton Arnold, field representative for Mid-Missions; and Earl Anderson of the St. Louis Baptist Hebrew Mission.

One of the most special ministries of the war years was the Ship-A-Hoy Service Center in Geneva, New York. Joseph M. Stowell, one of the founders and directors of that work, reported at the end of the war that the Center had ministered to more than 145,000 service men and women from the Samson Naval Training Center. Many hundreds of them had accepted Christ as Savior.

Two special ordination services were held in Ohio. Douglas Beason was ordained by the Calvary Baptist Church of Bellefontaine, and Cleveland McDonald was ordained by the Avon Baptist Church.

The Temple Baptist Church of Tacoma, Washington, Dr. Robert Powell, pastor, cooperated in a city-wide evangelistic campaign that continued for three weeks with speaker Dr. Harry McCormick Lintz. In Roxana, Illinois, the Wes Auger Evangelistic Party conducted a series of special meetings at the First Baptist Church, pastored by Rev. Don Zeimer. The First Baptist Church of Hayward, California, was led in a week of evangelistic meetings by Rev. Cliff Barrows. Pastor Herbert Farrar reported that many young people in the community were reached for Christ. The Calvary Baptist Church of Ecorse, Michigan, had an unusual series of meetings in November. The pastor, Merle T. Huffmaster, did the preaching, and Rev. Adam L. Lutzweiler with his famous eight-foot "marimbaphone" was in charge of the musical program.

Also in November, Evangelist Paul Levin and blind singer Bob Findley held two weeks of meetings at Riverside Baptist Church in Decatur, Illinois, pastored by Rev. J. M. Carlson. All in all, 1945 was a busy but blessed year throughout the General Association of Regular Baptist Churches.

The year following the close of World War II was a challenging one for Regular Baptists who continued to war against the world, the flesh and the Devil. Dr. Van Gilder set the pace for 1946 with the following challenge to the churches:

> Now that the war is over and the service men are coming home, every one of our churches should be making some effort to reach these men with its ministry. Some who are members of our churches will find difficulty in fitting into the life of the church again. Some who left unsaved have received Christ while in the service and are returning without any church home. Some have suffered deep psychological wounds from the terrible experiences of combat, while others have succumbed to the temptations that have had a severe effect on their moral and spiritual lives. All need the ministry of the Word of God in the godly atmosphere of a spiritual church.[1]

While GARBC churches were busily engaged in answering the spiritual challenge set forth by Dr. Van Gilder, many other activities were making 1946 a memorable year. Dr. Earle G. Griffith resigned the presidency of Baptist Bible Seminary after ten years of fruitful growth. He took a position with the National Bible Institute of New York City. Succeeding Dr. Griffith was Paul R. Jackson.

During the year Rev. Milton Dowden, who served as a United States Army Chaplain from July of 1943 to January of 1946, was called to Walnut Street Baptist Church in Waterloo, Iowa, to be assistant to Pastor Robert T. Ketcham. Rev. Albert Rust, after a 17-year pastorate in the First Baptist Church of Corwith, Iowa, accepted a call to the First Baptist Church of Pana, Illinois. Rev. Wilbur Chapman Rooke resigned the pastorate of the South Baptist Church in Belvidere, Illinois, to become pastor of the Burton Avenue Baptist Church in Waterloo, Iowa. Dr. H. C. Thiessen accepted a call to the presidency of Los Angeles Baptist Seminary. Dr. Thiessen went to LABS from Wheaton College, where he had served since 1935 as chairman of the Department of Bible, Philosophy and Theology. Rev. Harry E. Ketcham was called to the pastorate of the First Baptist Church of Monroe, Iowa. He had earlier served as an itinerant evangelist and as acting pastor of Walnut Street Baptist Church in Waterloo, Iowa, while his brother,

Robert T. Ketcham, was in New York for six months for a cornea transplant.

Nineteen forty-six ordinations included William Pedersen by the Stanford Heights (New York) Baptist Church; Vincent Trimmer by the Calvary Baptist Church of Niagara Falls, New York; Robert Brooks by the Randall Memorial Baptist Church of Williamsville, New York; Lawrence Barney and Charles D. Miles by the Randolph Street Baptist Church of Charleston, West Virginia; Duane A. Lindsay by the Hope Baptist Church in Hope, Michigan; Arthur Larkin by the Tabernacle Baptist Church in Ithaca, New York; Robert F. Hurne by the First Baptist Church in Belfast, New York; David P. Wright by Haddon Heights (New Jersey) Baptist Church; Paul Leber by the Doylestown (Pennsylvania) Baptist Church; Merle Booth by the Prairie Flower Baptist Church of Washington, Iowa; and Everett Sterling by the Ridgewood Baptist Church of Joliet, Illinois.

Dr. Harry G. Hamilton terminated his pastorate of 15 years at First Baptist Church of Buffalo, New York, to become associated with Dr. J. Frank Norris in the work of the Bible Baptist Seminary at Fort Worth, Texas. Dr. Hamilton was the first editor of the *Baptist Bulletin* and the first president of the fledgling GARBC.

Rev. Douglas Christen resigned the pastorate of the United Tabernacle Baptist Church in West Endicott, New York, to become pastor of the Chelsea Baptist Church in Atlantic City, New Jersey. Rev. Leonard V. Fardon ended his ministry at Campus Baptist Church in Ames, Iowa, to take the pastorate of the First Baptist Church in New Hartford, Iowa. Rev. H. Clifford Bristow, chaplain in the Army from 1941 to 1945, assumed the pastorate of Tabernacle Baptist Church in Ithaca, New York. He had taken part in seven military campaigns—French Morocco, Tunisia, Sicily, Rome-Arno, Southern France, Rhineland and Central Europe—and was awarded the Bronze Star for meritorious service. Also returning from the chaplaincy was Rev. Charles Dear, Sr., to take up the pastorate of the Crescentville Baptist Church in Philadelphia, Pennsylvania.

Nineteen forty-six was a banner year for many ministries within the GARBC, but one pastorate deserves special mention. In December the First Baptist Church of Hackensack, New Jersey, celebrated the thirtieth anniversary of the coming of its pastor, Rev. Harry C. Leach. During Dr. Leach's 30 years the membership grew from 179 to 1,051. He received 1,625 new members into the church family, 921 coming by baptism. Between 1916 and 1946 the Sunday School grew from 125 to 1,201. During those three decades, 31 members went into full-time Christian service; the church as of 1946 supported 13 of its own missionaries, and 20 young people were in Bible school preparing for the ministry. In 1940 Dr. Leach led the church out of the Northern Baptist Convention and into the GARBC. In concluding the 30-year celebration, Dr. Leach said, "The secret of these achievements lies in the persistent emphasis that has been placed upon God's infallible Word, a loyal people and the manifest presence and power of a supernatural Savior in our midst!"

The new year began auspiciously for Norman Warner, a missionary in Saylor, Kentucky, under Baptist Mid-Missions. On January 3, the Park Avenue Baptist Church in Binghamton, New York, ordained Warner. Rev. Everett V. Osterhout, a former Mid-Missions missionary to South Texas, Mexico and Panama, began the new year by accepting the pastorate of the Pavilion (New York) Baptist Church.

At the home office, Dr. Van Gilder was carefully going over the correspondence between GARBC leaders and Conservative Baptist leaders. That correspondence had been initiated by Robert T. Ketcham in his joint letter in March of 1945 to Dr. R. S. Beal and Dr. Albert Johnson. Dr. Van Gilder had furthered the contacts by answering a February 1947 letter from Rev. Gabriel R. Guedj, pastor of the Baptist Temple in Brooklyn, New York. In a letter dated March 5, 1947, Dr. Van Gilder had said to Dr. Guedj:

> Truthfully, Dr. Guedj, if I believed that your present constituency had shaken down its convictions, clarified its thinking, and crystallized its structure, sufficiently to provide an adequate substitute for our own Association, I would not lift a hand to preserve our Association, but would encourage our churches to go along in the formation of the CBA. However, I think it will be two or three years, at least, before these things become true of your group. To allude to Dr. Clearwater's quip, based upon your own humorous statement, some of you may have to "shave in the evening" for four or five years. I believe that in the meantime, during the transitional period, the stabilizing influence and testimony of such a group as ours is needed. If our brethren get the idea that you Conservatives are attempting to "raid" our group, any real union may be delayed for years.[2]

All of the efforts put forth in Atlantic City in the month of May by both groups came to frustration and impasse. Positionally, the Conservatives would not give up their desire for dual affiliation. They insisted that churches should not have to give up affiliation with the NBC in order to be in fellowship with the CBA. The GARBC was, of course, adamant that total separation from the NBC was imperative before a church could be accepted into the GARBC. Practically, the CBA leaders never could completely accept the organizational structure of the GARBC, which called for a Council of Fourteen. Seemingly enamored with the traditional political structure of presidents, etc., etc., the Conservatives were not impressed with an organization where the leaders really were "servants to the churches." As Dr. Ketcham would say again and again through the years, "In the GARBC there are no big men. We are all little men serving a great God."

Interestingly, the 1946 GARBC annual conference at Atlantic City, although preoccupied somewhat with the CBA matter, turned out to be what many termed "the best GARBC conference ever." The speakers were Leo Sandgren, Gaylord S. Hamilton, F. W. Haberer, Forrest E. Johnson, Earl V. Willetts, R. L. Matthews, Thomas S. Field, R. T. Ketcham, Kenneth A. Muck, C. Allen Taff, Paul Jackson and Robert L. Powell. What a lineup of homerun hitters!

Dr. Van Gilder's visionary leadership was apparent as he challenged the GARBC in the June 1947 *Baptist Bulletin*. His words are just as needed today as they were 44 years ago. He wrote:

> We of the General Association of Regular Baptist Churches must awaken to the urgent need for more aggressive, sacrificial, intelligent response to home mission opportunities, or we shall deserve to have our candlestick removed from its place. Our home mission councils and agencies are struggling along on the most meager support, while great areas of the country are going without any evangelical testimony, and all too many such areas are being invaded and taken over by modernistic agencies, or by unscriptural sects. . . . Every reader of the *Bulletin* should talk to the Lord about this need; perhaps talk to his pastor about what his local church is doing for home missions, and write to approved Agencies for information as to their needs and plans.[3]

Amen, Dr. Van! The Association has through the years been goaded by similar challenges and ever must be. We now live in a nation of 240 million people, and the need for church planting is greater than ever.

End Notes

1. H. O. Van Gilder, "Editorial Comment," *Baptist Bulletin* (January 1946), p. 3.

2. H. O. Van Gilder, "Convention Conservatives—Can We Get Together?" *Baptist Bulletin* (April 1947), p. 7.

3. H. O. Van Gilder, "Editorial Comment," *Baptist Bulletin* (June 1947), p. 3.

14

As Dr. Van Gilder traveled throughout the states of California, Oregon and Washington, he became increasingly burdened for church planting in that great area of our country. On Tuesday afternoon of the 1948 annual GARBC conference in Wealthy Street Baptist Church in Grand Rapids, Dr. Van announced his resignation as national representative. He also announced his acceptance of the call to the presidency of Western Baptist Bible College in Oakland, California. He was also going to start a Regular Baptist church in Oakland. In tendering his resignation Dr. Van declared that in a seven-year period the three West Coast states had had a population increase averaging 555,954 annually, and that this represented a 40 percent increase of population in this area in contrast with an 8.9 percent increase for the entire United States. "It is," he said, "our intention to provide in this school a Bible training center that will supply in all this great western area, trained missionaries and pastors, and as rapidly as possible, to develop a Bible-centered College which will meet the need in our G.A.R.B. educational program for our entire constituency."[1]

During Dr. Van Gilder's 16 years as president of WBBC, the school and the California Association of Regular Baptist Churches grew greatly. He led in the move of the school from Oakland to larger facilities in El Cerrito in 1956. When Van Gilder resigned from WBBC in 1964, he returned to the pastorate, becoming pastor of the First Baptist Church in Los Gatos, California, from 1964 to 1970. In 1970 he returned to Ohio to enter itinerant Bible conference work. His wife, Belle, went to be with the Lord shortly after the return to Ohio. In 1971 he married Lola Peters. They called their Blanchester, Ohio, home "Vanhaven." Dr. Van Gilder authored three books: *Election and . . .*, *May A Believer Be Lost?* and *Divine Light on Divine Healing.* He went to Heaven one day before his ninetieth birthday, March 25, 1987.

The next chapter is Dr. Van Gilder's original, unabridged farewell address given at the annual conference in Grand Rapids in May of 1948.[2]

End Notes

1. H. O. Van Gilder, "Greatest Meeting in G.A.R.B. History," *Baptist Bulletin* (June 1948), p. 7.

2. H. O. Van Gilder, "Retrospect, Prospect and Principles," *Baptist Bulletin* (September 1948), pp. 4, 5.

15

RETROSPECT, PROSPECT AND PRINCIPLES

H. O. Van Gilder

Four years have passed since, here in this church, I was chosen by this Association to serve as its representative. These have been busy and turbulent years, years that have brought growth and multiplied problems to the Association, and that have brought to me an increased appreciation of the character and qualities of our pastors and churches, and a deep conviction as to the destiny of our movement.

I have been asked by the council to address you today at more length than I have employed for the brief reports I have made at the annual meetings heretofore. Accordingly, I shall speak of some features of our history, of some of the prospects which may be visualized as lying before us, and of some of the principles which I hold to be essential for our development: Retrospect, Prospect and Principles.

Retrospect

One of our Baptist distinctives, rated by some as the most significant, is our conception of the local church as a spiritual body composed of believers who have been regenerated by the Holy Spirit and who have borne testimony to their faith by means of New Testament Baptism.

Since apostolic times, there have doubtless been groups of believers at various times and places who have held this distinctive, as well as other New Testament truths with varying emphases. It is these groups which give some validity to the claims of some Baptist historians that they can trace our spiritual lineage back to Apostolic times. However, modern Baptist history dates from about 1640. Then, for the first time in modern days, the clear recognition of the church as a company of regenerated and immersed believers took definite and organized form with the Particular Baptists of London. Soon afterward, the General Baptists of England began to maintain that baptism is solely for believers and that nothing but immersion may be regarded as baptism.

Luther had seen the truth of justification by faith, but he had retained Infant sprinkling, and had put the government of the church in the hands of princes instead of the people. As Dr. A. H. Strong once said:

> The Puritan Fathers aimed at the establishment of Christ's sole authority, but they identified that authority with that of the State, and it needed a Roger Williams to teach them that there could be a church without a bishop, and a State without a king. But Baptists first in modern times furnish the example of a spiritual church organized after the New Testament model, self-governing and independent of the civil power, and expressing in both its ordinances the believer's communion with the death and resurrection of Christ (Mis. I, p. 4).

In 1640 the General Baptists of England claimed 20,000 members, and there were perhaps half that number of Particular Baptists. During the century from 1640 to 1740, Baptists did not greatly increase in numbers. That was the century of Charles II and of the Deists, a century of ethical and spiritual declension during which Baptists were severely persecuted. Macauley estimates that the population of England in 1640 was about 5 millions. In 1740 it was 9 millions, but Baptists had increased to not more than 50,000. Then came the Wesleyan revival and the missionary awakening under Andrew Fuller and William Carey, and by 1840 the Baptists of England had increased to at least 150,000. During the next thirty years, they increased by 93,395, numbering 243,395 by 1870. Then, in the next ten years, from 1870 to 1880, they gained more than 122,000 adherents.

At this point, a decline set in. The percentage of increase in the decade from 1870 to 1880 was 21%, in the next decade it dropped to 12%, and in the decade from 1890 to 1900 it decreased still further to a mere 10.7%!

How shall we explain this decline, and the drying up of the fountain? A moment's reflection on Baptist history in England will call to mind the fact that before the end of the Nineteenth Century Charles Haddon Spurgeon had quit the Baptist Union because of what he called "the downgrade movement" in theology. Modernism had not only set in among Baptists there, ***but had become so strongly entrenched that the great Spurgeon found himself helpless to combat it except by withdrawal!***

The blight that smote the Baptist testimony in England was not confined to that side of the Atlantic. Indeed, before the close of the century, the blight of a materialistic, evolutionary philosophy was upon everything. As Professor Norborg says, in the prelude to his "Varieties of Christian Experience,"

> The last generation thought it had a final answer to all problems of human life and universal life. It was thought to be an answer so accurate and rational that there would be no need of religion, mysticism or metaphysics. The nineteenth century died in a cocksure dogmatism so blindfolded that it mistook a materialistic chamber of horrors for a temple of a man-made millennium.

Nevertheless, during the last two decades of the nineteenth century, Baptists in this country continued to move under the impetus of an earlier faith and zeal. In 1880 there were but 100,000 Baptists here, but by 1900 they had increased to 4,181,686. While the population was increasing by 15%, Baptists increased by 40%.

Seven years later, the Northern Baptist Convention was organized.

A year prior to its organization, Dr. A. H. Strong published his Systematic Theology, in the preface of which he wrote:

> Under the influence of Ritschl and his Kantian relativism, many of our teachers and preachers have swung off into a practical denial of Christ's deity and of His atonement. We seem upon the verge of a second Unitarian defection that will break up churches and compel secessions in a worse manner than did that of Channing and Ware a century ago. American Christianity recovered from that disaster only by vigorously asserting the authority of Christ and the inspiration of the Scriptures. . . . Without a revival of this faith, our churches will become secularized, mission enterprises will die out, and the candlestick will be removed out of its place as it was with the seven churches of Asia, and as it has been with the apostate churches of New England.

That was published in 1906: "Many of our teachers and preachers have swung off into a practical denial of Christ's deity and atonement." Organized the next year without any creedal test or doctrinal standard, the Northern Baptist Convention was, *from the very outset,* a conglomerate mixture of believers and unbelievers. It was not long until the consequences against which Strong had warned began to be apparent, and you are aware of how the process of disintegration is continuing to this day.

In 1915 there were 13,000 churches in the Northern Baptist Convention. By 1945 that number had been reduced to 7,000.

In 1917 Dr. Strong made a report on a tour of the mission fields. He found conditions there which led him to utter a warning:

> The tendency in our missions to put the main stress upon physical and social agencies to the detriment of simple gospel preaching, is sure to be disappointing in its results. . . . I grieve over the minimizing of Christ's nature and claims that is current in our day, because I believe that it cuts the sinews of our Christian faith and destroys the chief dynamic in our missions.

The warning went unheeded, modernism continued its depredations in schools and missions, and the missionary dynamic was destroyed to such an extent that in a twenty-year period (from 1922 to 1942) the number of missionaries was reduced from 844 to 459, and missionary giving dropped from $9,900,000 to $3,672,000.

In 1909 a group of churches here in Grand Rapids withdrew from the old Grand Rapids Association, adopted a fundamental statement of belief, and took the name, Grand River Valley Association. This group chose to remain in the Michigan State Convention, but in 1920, under the leadership of Dr. O. W. Van Osdel, then pastor of Wealthy Street Church, the association changed its name to the Michigan Orthodox Baptist Association, and, as many of the churches had ceased supporting Convention projects, the Association was disfranchised by the Michigan Baptist Convention. Eight years later, in 1928, it changed its name to the Grand Rapids Association of Regular Baptist Churches.

That same year a group of pastors and laymen met in the church which I was then pastoring in Columbus, Ohio, and formed the Ohio Association of Independent Baptist Churches.

In May, 1932, at the eighth convocation of the Baptist Bible Union in the Belden Avenue Baptist Church, Chicago, 34 messengers registered from eight states. A committee was appointed to draft either a new constitution, or a revision of the B.B.U. constitution, to establish an Association of Churches in such a way that the new Association should be "the legal successor of the Baptist Bible Union of North America."

That was the birthday of the General Association of Regular Baptist Churches. The meeting the next year was held in the First Baptist Church of Buffalo, and the following year in the Central Baptist Church of Gary, Indiana. From that time to this present hour, the growth has been continuous and substantial. There were only about fifty churches that participated in the meeting in Buffalo in 1933, and today we number more than 470.

Having dwelt at such length on history, the limitations of time forbid more than a brief glance at Prospect and Principles.

Prospect

There is every prospect of continued growth through recruiting from the ranks of the Northern Baptist Convention. The uncompromising position which has characterized our Association from its beginning, its complete loyalty to the Word of God in theological belief and practical separation, will continue to commend our Association to other Baptist churches which come, in time, to recognize not only the theoretical validity, but the practical inevitability of our position in a world of increasing theological tensions. If we keep the faith, and proclaim it in a spirit free from rancor, bitterness, and Pharisaical self-righteousness, we shall prosper. The Northern Baptist Convention is breaking up because there is a growing awareness of apostasy in Convention circles, and a growing impatience with the coercive measures of Convention officials. In spite of the confusion represented in the multiplicity of organizations in Northern Baptist Convention territory—Roger Williams Fellowship, Northern Baptist Fellowship, Conservative Baptist Fellowship, Conservative Baptist Foreign Mission Society, Conservative Baptist Association, and any others that may have been organized since we last saw the list—there are certain to be among the churches quitting the Convention a percentage attracted to our Association.

There is another field of expansion and development which we have not cultivated to the extent we should. It is the field of missionary endeavor at home, and to this I am convinced we must apply ourselves with more vision and zeal, industry and determination than we have ever devoted to any project heretofore. It is in the establishment of our own churches that our greatest hopes must lie. It is in this manner that the current wave of materialism, infidelity, and delinquency can best be resisted. It is in this way, and only in this way, that the annual supply of preachers graduated from our schools can be assimilated and given useful, productive employment in an independent Baptist ministry. It is only in this way that the new communities resulting from the vast population moves of recent years can be provided with the distinctive testimony which God has committed to us. All over the United States new communities have arisen, many of them without any gospel testimony, and few with any ministry from Regular Baptists. Without minimizing the challenge presented by thousands of communities in the East and Middlewest, we confront the astounding fact of a population shift to the three West Coast states which has proceeded for the last seven years at the rate of 555,954 every year.

If we are to keep faith with the Lord, we must carry the faith to these multitudes, and it is here I believe our major emphasis in the immediate future should rest. It is much easier to interest our people in missions in any other part of the world than here at home. It unquestionably is more romantic to send missionaries to *India* than to help erect a building and provide adequate support for a pastor in *Indiana,* but unless we begin concentrating upon the establishment of a few more churches in Indiana, Idaho, Washington, Wyoming, and all the other states, our children may live to see the time when India and Africa will be sending missionaries to us.

If our prospects are envisioned as consisting chiefly of accretions from N.B.C. defections, we shall find ourselves increasingly involved in competition for organizational loyalty. But if we conceive of our prospects as lying chiefly in the realm of missionary expansion, we shall be more successful in avoiding the conflicts of competition and shall know increasingly the favor of the Lord, because of our loyalty to His command to evangelize.

This leads me to speak of certain [Principles].

Principles

The numerical strength of Baptists has always been proportionate to doctrinal fidelity, which is to say that God blesses in the measure to which we are true to His Word. The records of the past confirm this, and today in England, where the apostasy has been longest at work, there is one Baptist to every 123.7 persons; in Canada, one to every 81.9; in the Northern U.S., one to every 57.5, and in the South, one to every 4.8!

If we would prosper, we must be loyal to the Truth, and to be loyal to the Truth we must preach all of it, and live what we preach. Truth to be true must be the whole truth, and truth to be effective must be translated into life. One may tell the truth, and yet because he does not tell the whole truth, he tells a falsehood. In a Chicago restaurant recently, it was not until I had been served and was doing my best with the entree, that I realized that when the menu said "roast leg of spring lamb," it hadn't said *which* spring. . . . Error is sometimes propagated by those who never preach it, but who fail to preach *all* the truth—and sometimes by those who fail to live the truth they preach.

At this point in our development, it seems to me there is no principle more vital to the life of our Association than that expressed by Christ in Matthew 16:24–26; John 12:24, 25. It is the principle of life through death, that only as we lose our lives for Christ do we find them; that only as we die to sin, to the world, and to self, do we begin to live. This is the principle of discipleship, of the salvation of a *life.* Salvation of the soul is through the death of Christ, salvation of the life is through the death of self.

All through life I see a cross
Where sons of God yield up their breath;
There is no gain except through loss,
There is no life except through death!

This principle is applicable to groups of believers as well as to individuals who comprise the groups. It applies to local churches, to associations, and to the G.A.R.B.C. If we ignore this, live selfishly, seek to save our lives, to conserve our resources, to build our Association, we shall go the way of other ecclesiastical organizations. If we lay down our lives for Christ, are willing to spend and be spent, count not our lives dear unto ourselves, we shall *"find" life.*

Let us set our eyes on the ideal of lives laid down for Christ, of real missionary endeavor, and let us be prepared to make whatever adjustments may be necessary in our organizational structure the more effectively to achieve this ideal.

We are the General Association of Regular Baptist Churches. If our emphasis comes to rest upon the word *Association,* we shall become a Convention, regardless of what we may call ourselves. If it continues to rest upon the word *Churches,* we shall remain a fellowship. If we conceive it to be our duty, and our goal, to build an Association, we shall fail; if to build churches, we shall prosper. The one emphasis leads to a spirit of ecclesiasticism, the other to a spirit of evangelism.

Robert T. Ketcham

THE ERA OF ROBERT T. KETCHAM

1948—1960

16

Many thousands of people were shocked and dumbfounded when Harry Truman defeated Thomas E. Dewey in the presidential election of 1948. But no Regular Baptist was at all surprised when Robert Thomas Ketcham was elected GARBC national representative in May of 1948. The Council of Fourteen who chose him were Raymond F. Hamilton, chairman; David Otis Fuller, vice chairman; William E. Kuhnle, secretary-treasurer; William Headley; Paul R. Jackson; Robert Ketcham; Clarence Mason, Jr.; Robert L. Powell; J. Irving Reese; Leo Sandgren; Joseph M. Stowell; Carl Sweazy and Arthur F. Williams.

Robert T. Ketcham was born in Nelson, Pennsylvania, on July 12, 1889. He trusted Christ as his personal Savior on February 16, 1910, and two years later, without any college or seminary education, became pastor of the First Baptist Church in Roulette, Pennsylvania. In 1915 Ketcham became pastor of First Baptist Church of Brookville, Pennsylvania, and in 1919 he accepted the pastorate of First Baptist Church in Butler, Pennsylvania.

Ketcham had severe eye problems that finally led to two corneal transplants plus cataract surgery that left him with about 10 percent of normal vision. In 1920 his wife died leaving him with two daughters, six-year-old Lois and three-year-old Margaret. In 1923 Ketcham married Mary Smart, and they became the proud parents of Donn Ketcham in 1930.

He left Butler for the First Baptist Church of Niles, Ohio, where he pastored from 1923 to 1926. It was during his pastorate of First Baptist Church in Elyria, Ohio, from 1927 to 1932, that he helped to form the Ohio Association of Regular Baptist Churches. In 1932 he became pastor of Central Baptist Church in Gary, Indiana, where he ministered until 1939. While there Ketcham served as vice president of the new GARBC in 1933 and as president from 1934 to 1938 when the Council of Fourteen system was inaugurated. From 1939 to 1948 he was pastor of the Walnut Street Baptist Church in Waterloo, Iowa.

Dr. Ketcham accepted the call of the Association, and in his letter to the Council chairman he said:

> The task to which you have invited me is not an easy one. The road ahead is going to be increasingly difficult as the apostasy deepens and the pressure of this godless thing lays itself more and more heavily upon every single minister of the gospel, and every local church, and every organized group of believers. It is going to require increased wisdom and courage from God to find and follow the pathway of His will. It is going to require the best there is in every one of us to follow the pathway of separation which was written into our charter and constitution seventeen years ago, and at the same time to exercise the greatest measure of sympathetic understanding and helpfulness toward those who, while not yet having accepted our position on separation, are nevertheless honestly seeking to know God's will in the matter.[1]

The National Representative's office was indeed a heavy responsibility to undertake for a man almost 60 years of age with very little eyesight, but Robert T. Ketcham was without doubt God's man for the position.

Not long after Ketcham arrived in Chicago, the home office was moved from the Ashland Building to the Manhattan Building at 431 South Dearborn Street. As the building transition was made smoothly, so the transition from Dr. Van Gilder to Dr. Ketcham was made with no snags or snarls. In introducing Dr. Ketcham as the new editor of the *Baptist Bulletin* and the new national representative, Dr. Van Gilder said:

> It has been my privilege to number Dr. R. T. Ketcham among my close personal friends for more than twenty years. I have seen him think his way through intricate problems, and I have come to have a high regard for his judgment. I have seen him under attack by the enemy, and I have never had occasion to doubt his courage.
>
> No other person has had more influence in molding the character of our Association, and no one has been more outstanding among its successful pastors. His succession of pastorates during the years since I have known him has marked a continuous progress in achievement, from Niles, to Elyria,

to Gary, to Waterloo. And the numerical growth, spiritual development and financial strengthening of each of these churches bears tribute to his ability as a pastor.

In his new ministry he will need your prayers, your fellowship and understanding. His defective eyesight—which two corneal transplants have failed to improve—will be a handicap. When it comes to seeing issues, however, Dr. Ketcham can often see more with one defective eye than most of us can see with two good ones! He has often said, with apparent sincerity, that there are no big men among us, but only little men with a big God. Of course, bigness is purely relative, as a certain State Secretary was reminded once when a pulpit committee consulted him about a pastor. After talking things over for a few moments he said: "I suppose you want a big man; all churches seem to want 'big' men whether they are big churches or not."

"Well," replied the chairman of the committee after a moment's thought, "I don't reckon it matters a whole lot whether he's big or little, just so he's big enough to reach to heaven when he's on his knees!"

I think Dr. Ketcham qualifies there, too, but so can you—don't leave him all the "reaching" to do for himself; stand by him in prayer.[2]

End Notes

1. Merle R. Hull, *What a Fellowship!* (Schaumburg, IL: Regular Baptist Press, 1981), pp. 31, 32.

2. H. O. Van Gilder, "This Month with the Editor," *Baptist Bulletin* (September 1948), pp. 2, 24.

17

Nineteen forty-eight was surely an eventful year in the lives of Doctors Van Gilder and Ketcham. It was also a special year for a number of other men of God. On January 8 the Calvary Baptist Tabernacle of Los Angeles accepted the resignation of Carl Sweazy, its founder and pastor since 1937. Dr. Sweazy had organized the church after a five-week tent campaign. He was succeeded at Calvary by A. D. Mohr, who had resigned from Grandview Park Baptist Church in Des Moines, Iowa, after serving there from 1935 to 1948. On the other side of the country, Rev. Wilbur Strader began the new year by taking up his responsibilities as pastor of the Friendly Baptist Church in Rowley, Massachusetts.

Dedicated young men continued to devote themselves to the Lord's work as pastors and missionaries. The ordinations of men to the gospel ministry were not uncommon events in the lives of GARBC churches. Bruce Irving Rosenau was ordained by the Evangel Baptist Church of Wyandotte, Michigan; Raymond S. Overstreet by the Southeast Baptist Church in Los Angeles, California; William D. Hopper by the Paul Street Bible Church in Ottawa, Illinois; Samuel Greydanus by the Grace Baptist Church of Modesto, California; and James Mason by the Immanuel Baptist Church in Denver, Colorado.

On February 1, Rev. George A. Bates completed 11 fruitful years at Nottingham Baptist Church in Cleveland, Ohio, to become pastor of the Riverside Baptist Church in Decatur, Illinois. Pastor Bates was the founder of the Youth Church of the Air and was chairman of the Christ for Greater Cleveland Committee of 96 cooperating churches. He was one of the founders, a vice president, a trustee and an instructor in the Baptist Bible Institute of Cleveland, the forerunner of Cedarville College.

Dr. William L. Pettingill celebrated the fiftieth anniversary of his ordination to the gospel ministry in 1898 by accepting the call of the First Baptist Church of New York City to be its interim pastor. Dr. Pettingill was one of the consulting editors of the *Scofield Reference Bible.* He was for many years dean of the Philadelphia School of the Bible and pastor of the North Baptist Church in Wilmington, Delaware. He was a popular speaker among GARBC churches until his Homegoing.

As older men like Pettingill were coming to the end of their fruitful ministries, new men were taking their places. Donald Steinfort was ordained by the Grace Baptist Church of Corning, Iowa; Harold Hahnlen by the Hallstead Baptist Church in Hallstead, Pennsylvania; Roy T. Plank by the Unadilla Forks Baptist Church in New York; George P. Whitman by the Carmel Baptist Church in Mosiertown, Pennsylvania; Truman Robertson and Fermin Runas by the Belden Avenue Baptist Church in Chicago; and Alfred A. Anderson by the Grace Baptist Church of Saginaw, Michigan.

Rev. A. M. Veltman was called to the pastorate of the Grandview Park Baptist Church in Des Moines. He had established the Grace Baptist Church in Saginaw, Michigan, and was widely known as an excellent expository preacher. Rev. Carl Elgena, who would succeed Pastor Veltman in Grandview in 1954, in June of 1948 became pastor of the Spruce Street Baptist Church in Philadelphia.

Gerald Becker was ordained by the Custer Park Baptist Church of Illinois; Guy E. King by the Watersmeet (Michigan) Baptist Church; Alan Dillon by the Berean Baptist Church of Adrian, Michigan; Edward W. Morrow by the Calvary Baptist Church of Muskegon, Michigan; Raymond Frank Smith by the Tabernacle Baptist Church of Ithaca, New York; and Charles Vermilyea by the Carmel Avenue Baptist Church of Detroit, Michigan.

Rev. R. G. Nicholas, founder, pastor and builder of the Bible Baptist Church of Huntington Park, California, completed his six years of labor there to move to Vista, California, to establish and pastor the First Baptist Church.

In August a meeting of historic significance took place in the English Reformed Church of Amsterdam, the Netherlands. Delegates and observers from 31 countries assembled for the purpose of bringing into existence an International Council of Christian Churches, true to the fundamentals of Biblical, historic Christianity. Fifty-six church groups were represented in addition to twelve mission agencies and four educational institutions. The GARBC was represented by Paul R. Jackson, Raymond F. Hamilton, David Otis Fuller, Kenneth R. Kinney and Kenneth Muck. Rev. Carl McIntire, who had acted as chairman of the Congress, was chosen president of the ICCC. Raymond F. Hamilton was elected treasurer. Of course, each local church in the GARBC was free to declare itself in favor of the ICCC or to reject it.

Rev. Allan E. Lewis became pastor of the Nottingham Baptist Church in Cleveland. He had pastored the Randolph Street Baptist Church in Charleston, West Virginia, and during those four years he also served as president of the Fundamental Baptist Mission of Trinidad. He was born of missionary parents in Africa.

Pastor Howard Miller of the Calvary Baptist Church of Quincy, Illinois, reported a great harvest of souls following an evangelistic crusade led by Evangelist Paul Levin and blind singer Bob Findley.

When Dr. Ketcham came to the home office of the GARBC, there were five GARBC-approved schools: Baptist Bible Institute and School of Theology in Grand Rapids, Michigan; Western Baptist Bible College in Oakland, California; Baptist Bible Seminary in Johnson City, New York; Los Angeles Baptist Theological Seminary; and Baptist Bible Institute of Cleveland. Although the schools were relatively small, a good number of the missionaries and pastors coming into the churches and mission fields of the GARBC were coming from the approved schools.

Robert Luby was ordained by the Grace Baptist Church of Flint, Michigan; George Heaney by the First Baptist Church of Perkasie, Pennsylvania; Earl Muller by the Riverside Baptist Church of Decatur, Illinois; Irvin Stanton by the Brookside Baptist Temple of Cleveland, Ohio; John White and William Smith by the First Baptist Church of Patchogue, New York; Warren Rommel by the Notus (Idaho) Baptist Church; William Springsted by the Calvary Baptist Church of Everett, Washington; Lawrence Bong by the Waukon (Iowa) Baptist Church; Edward Stiner by the Grace Baptist Church of Omaha, Nebraska; Roy Lovegrove by the Hancock (Massachusetts) Baptist Church; William Harris by the Walnut Street Baptist Church of Waterloo, Iowa; Norman Bosworth by the First Baptist Church of Hobart, Indiana; Peter Kobe by the Evergreen Memorial Baptist Church of West Hobart, Indiana; Ernest Whitney by the Calvary Baptist Church of Bellefontaine, Ohio; Harold M. Richards by the Cazenovia Park Baptist Church of Buffalo, New York; and Homer George by the New Hyde Park Baptist Church in Long Island, New York.

Some of the above-mentioned men went on to pastor churches that were rather prominent. Others worked in remote places. But doing the will of God is the supreme matter, whether it leads to prominence or not. In a book like this, only brief mention may be made of men who served long and meritoriously. But God keeps the records!

Have you ever asked yourself what Abraham did during the 175 years of his life? What we read in the book of Genesis concerning Abraham's deeds would total only a few years, but he lived twice as long as most twentieth-century men. How little is said of 365-year-old Enoch or 950-year-old Noah! The biographical, Biblical data may be brief, but God sees the whole life—the complete ministry—and will reward accordingly.

Nineteen forty-eight was not without its problems both in the secular world and in the religious world. Communist Russia under Joseph Stalin's orders began a land blockade of Berlin's allied sectors on April 1. The blockade was finally lifted in 1949 after United States and British planes had flown 2,343,315 tons of food into the allied areas of the city. President Truman did not give up his responsibility to those people in Berlin just because of opposition. As we take the Bread of Life, Jesus Christ, to a lost and dying world, we, too, must continue our mission in the face of all enmity. It may be the liberalism of the Northern Baptist Convention or the paganism of Filipino Roman Catholicism or the fanaticism of Islam, but we must not quit. And the evidence is ample that Regular Baptists did not quit in the months of 1948. The Association continued to grow and glow for God.

18

In the latter part of 1947, Ivan M. Shreve, pastor of the First Baptist Church of North East, Pennsylvania, penned for his church a 27-page pamphlet titled *The Baptist Denomination: Who We Are, What We Are, Why We Are.* Shreve tried to convince his readers that Northern Baptists had not departed from the Faith. He conceded that some individuals in the Convention were liberal in their theology, but he insisted that the NBC generally was conservative in its theology. Shreve accused the GARBC of attacking the NBC on the basis of what was perhaps true in 1920, but he contended the Convention leaders had "cleaned up their act" over the following 25 years. The Convention executives liked the pamphlet so much they had it printed and distributed to all of the NBC churches.

Dr. Ketcham in 1949 wrote a powerful booklet called *The Answer* in order to reply to Shreve's contentions. Ketcham's booklet stirred up a real "storm" among Baptist leaders across the nation. Ketcham began his booklet with an incisive statement on "creeds." Wrote Ketcham:

> Mr. Shreve labors at several points in his paper to point out that Baptists are a "creedless" body of believers. This, of course, is the main theme song of the leaders of the Northern Baptist Convention itself. "Baptists have never had a creed" we are told. These leaders seem to forget that when they say that Baptists are a creedless body of believers they have instituted a head-on collision between two contradictory statements. Just how a group of people could be a *"creedless"* body of *"believers"* is a bit difficult to understand. If they are believers, then they believe something, and the moment they believe something, whatever it is they believe, constitutes for them, a creed. Webster says that the word "creed" means "any formula or confession of religious faith." Baptists have always been willing, until comparatively recent years in

the Northern Baptist Convention, to tell the world what they believed. In fact, so far as we know Baptist history, the Northern Baptist Convention is the first Baptist body that has ever refused to go on record in a declaration of what it believes. To our knowledge there is not a single, solitary Baptist body other than the Northern Baptist Convention but that has, on occasion, and sometimes more than one occasion, declared to the world, in detail, its doctrinal beliefs. The Northern Baptist Convention, however, has consistently refused to go on record from the very day it was organized. This refusal is significant. The late Dr. William B. Riley used to insist that William Rainey Harper, Shailer Matthews, John D. Rockefeller and others who were (some of them) moving geniuses back of the organization of the Northern Baptist Convention in 1907, deliberately planned that the Northern Baptist Convention should always be a creedless body. The originators of the Northern Baptist Convention deliberately set out to keep the Convention on a creedless basis in order that they might have an open door through which to process their modernistic students which they were producing in their already modernistic schools. . . .

Such renowned Baptist historians as Dr. W. J. McClothlin, in his Baptist Confession of Faith, says "Baptist confessions are almost numberless. . . . Baptists have preserved a remarkable doctrinal agreement." So the popular theme song of Convention leaders that Baptists have never had a creed will not stand up under the facts of history and definitions.[1]

Throughout the booklet Ketcham answered Shreve's defense of the alleged doctrinal purity of the NBC by quoting liberal NBC pastors, missionaries and convention leaders whose own statement revealed them to be classic infidels. Shreve's position was simply untenable.

One more example of Dr. Ketcham's penetrating, probing, pungent logic has to do with his response to Shreve's contention that no Unitarian church was in good standing in the NBC. Asked Ketcham:

And what shall we say concerning Mr. Shreve's statement that there is no Unitarian Church in good standing in the denomination, when we remember that in 1926 the Northern Baptist Convention was held in the grip of a debate for four hours and forty-five minutes as to whether we would retain in our fellowship the Riverside Church of New York City, of which Harry Emerson Fosdick was pastor? The Convention finally decided that Mr. Fosdick and his church should be retained in good standing by a vote of about three to one. We now quote from a letter written by Dr. Harry Emerson Fosdick in January of 1945. It was written to an inquiring individual from Peru, Indiana. Dr. Fosdick says: "Of course I do not believe in the virgin birth or in that old-fashioned substitutionary doctrine of the atonement, and I know of no intelligent person who does." When we remember that one of the cardinal doctrines of Unitarianism is the denial of the Virgin Birth and the making of Jesus into a purely human individual, then we cannot escape the conviction and the conclusion that Mr. Fosdick qualifies as a Unitarian, and since his church accepted his ministry, and stood by him one hundred percent in what he taught, then his church, regardless of the name over the door, is a Unitarian Church, and it is in good and regular standing in the Northern Baptist Convention.[2]

To respond in 1990 lingo: Is Dr. Ketcham's *The Answer* unanswerable or what?! The booklet sold by the thousands and went into several more printings. The Lord certainly used the booklet to open the eyes of many pastors and laymen in the Convention, and many came out of the NBC as a result.

In 1949 Dr. Ketcham was involved with a local church that was endeavoring to separate from the Northern Baptist Convention, the Pennsylvania Baptist State Convention, the Allegheny River Baptist Association and the Federal Council of the Churches of Christ in America. They were determined to separate from apostasy. Under the leadership of Pastor L. C. Wilcox, First Baptist Church of Smethport, Pennsylvania, voted by a large majority to sever relationships with the above-named associations. However, there were some knotty, extenuating circumstances! Let J. Murray Murdoch tell the story:

Several years prior to this action, the church had received some monies from the Convention. In 1913 the Pennsylvania Baptist State Convention had given them $500 for physical plant repairs. In so doing, the state convention demanded the deed to the property and continued to hold that deed through the years. When the church built a parsonage in 1940, the Pennsylvania Baptist State Convention "donated" $1,000 toward the project. . . . When the church voted to withdraw from the Convention, they had their attorney draft a letter, asking the state convention for a clear title to their church property. They agreed to return the donation of $1,000 which the Convention had given them in exchange for the clear title.[3]

According to Dr. Ketcham,

[The Pennsylvania Baptist State Convention] began a series of attempts to dig in behind the sovereign action of a sovereign church, and through the creation of dissension [sic] among its members, seek to undo the action of the church, and reverse the will of the church and the leadership of its pastor. . . . For nearly a year the Pennsylvania Baptist State Convention, through its officials, did everything in its power to disturb and break up the harmony and happy fellowship of a Baptist church, rather than to proceed to an orderly and honest settlement of the claims of the church.[4]

Wrote Murdoch:

In the context, L. C. Wilcox, pastor of the Smethport church, contacted Dr. Ketcham. Ketcham agreed to come to Smethport to confront Convention representative G. A. Gabelman. . . . Gabelman accepted, and the meeting was arranged for Monday, December 5, 1949.

On the appointed night, Ketcham and Gabelman met to confer prior to the public meeting. As a result of that confrontation, Gabelman and the men that accompanied him refused to appear in the public meeting. With the congregation of the Smethport church waiting, the Convention representatives walked away. Following their departure, Dr. Ketcham, accompanied by Pastor Wilcox and Dean Banta (who had been appointed moderator) entered the auditorium to face approximately four hundred people who had been waiting forty-five minutes for the meeting to begin.[5]

Mr. Banta explained that Pastor Wilcox had agreed to let the State Convention men say anything they wanted to say and discuss anything they wanted to discuss on the condition they would first listen to Dr. Ketcham's documented disclosures of modernism in the Convention. The Convention men refused that condition and walked out. Ketcham then went on to deliver his whole message! The Convention people in Pennsylvania put out a 24-page booklet called *The Truth about the Smethport Church—An Unmasking of Charges Made by R. T. Ketcham.* Ketcham refuted the charges in a pamphlet titled *A Reply to the So-called 'Unmasking' of Charges in the Case of the First Regular Baptist Church of Smethport, Pennsylvania.* Dr. Murdoch concluded: "After refuting the charges made by his opponents, Ketcham closed his reply by posing a series of eighteen questions for the Convention group to answer. There is no record of any answers ever being given."[6]

Ketcham's first year as national representative certainly was not dull!

End Notes

1. Robert T. Ketcham, *The Answer* (Chicago: General Association of Regular Baptist Churches, 1949), pp. 3, 4.
2. Ibid., p. 23.
3. J. Murray Murdoch, *Portrait of Obedience* (Schaumburg, IL: Regular Baptist Press, 1979), pp. 227, 228.
4. R. T. Ketcham, *When A State Convention Secretary Walked Out* (Hayward, CA: J. F. May Press, n.d.), p. 2.
5. Murdoch, pp. 228, 229.
6. Ibid., p. 232.

19

Like Van Gilder before him and the three national representatives after him,

Ketcham's travels brought him into contact with pastors from churches of all sizes. Bob Ketcham had a pastor's heart, and he loved to fellowship with other servants of God. He had pastored large and small congregations and was familiar with both situations. He knew the ministry could be very lonely at times. One of the major burdens of his heart was to provide counsel and encouragement for others in the ministry. Literally hundreds of pastors through the years benefited from his practical wisdom and his fellowship.[1]

Dr. Ketcham followed closely and with great interest the pastoral changes among the GARBC churches. Nineteen forty-nine was a busy year for such moves.

Rev. Peter Ypma resigned the First Baptist Church of Vassar, Michigan, in order to become pastor of the Second Baptist Church of Grand Rapids. Wilbur C. Rooke, formerly pastor of Burton Avenue Baptist Church in Waterloo, Iowa, accepted the call of Randolph Street Baptist Church in Charleston, West Virginia. R. J. Hansen resigned the pastorate of the Lighthouse Baptist Church of Rockford, Illinois, to become president of the Trinity Bible Seminary of Atlanta, Georgia. Dr. Harry Leach retired after having served the First Baptist Church of Hackensack, New Jersey, for 32 years. H. Don Schleicher accepted a call to pastor the Faith Baptist Church of Saginaw, Michigan. The First Baptist Church of Merton, Wisconsin, called Clayton J. Bates to its pastorate. While serving on the faculty of Los Angeles Baptist Theological Seminary, Alfred Dodds pastored the First Baptist Church of Graham. Merle T. Huffmaster, pastor of the Onaway and Tower Baptist churches in Michigan, resigned in order to work with the staff of the "Sermons from Science" films produced by the Moody Institute of Science.

Leslie Thomas resigned the pastorate of the Hagerman Baptist Church in Waterloo, Iowa, in order to assume the pastorate of the First Baptist Church in Creston, Iowa. Charles Vermilyea left the assistant pastor's position at Carmel Avenue Baptist Church in Detroit to become senior pastor of First Baptist Church in Weston, Michigan. Herbert W. Orman accepted a call to the Silvis Heights Baptist Church in East Moline, Illinois. Cyril George Collison left First Baptist Church of Galion, Ohio, to become pastor of Chelsea Baptist Church in Atlantic City, New Jersey. George Whitman left First Baptist Church of Mosiertown, Pennsylvania, to become pastor of First Baptist Church in Edinboro, Pennsylvania. Calvary Baptist Church of Anderson, Indiana, called Norman Bosworth, newly graduated from Moody, to its pastorate.

Lawrence Williams resigned the Melvindale (Michigan) Baptist Church to become pastor of the Baptist church at Silver Lake, Wisconsin. J. M. Carlson resigned from the People's Church of Montreal, Canada, to become the pastor of the Cherrydale Baptist Church in Arlington, Virginia. R. C. Johnson left First Baptist Church of Perry, Iowa, to become pastor of Central Baptist Church of East Chicago, Indiana. Rev. Henry Murdoch was called to the First Baptist Church of Lock Haven, Pennsylvania. Rev. William Ford resigned the pastorate of the First Regular Baptist Church of Bellefontaine, Ohio, to pastor the Hessville Baptist Church of Hammond, Indiana. Frank M. Thatcher left the First Baptist Church of Holland, Michigan, to be pastor of Woodward Avenue Baptist Church in Grand Rapids. James Shields left First Baptist Church in Meadow Bridge, West Virginia, to become pastor of Jameson Baptist Church in Alton, Illinois.

Frank M. Peterson resigned as pastor of Grace Baptist Church of Corwith, Iowa, to become pastor of First Baptist Church of Polson, Montana. M. Donald Currey was called to Calvary Baptist Church in Ypsilanti, Michigan. Allan N. Williams left the First Baptist Church of Luverne, Minnesota, to pastor the First Baptist Church of Safford, Arizona.

Arthur W. Christmann accepted the call of the Monterey Baptist Church in Beaver Dams, New York. William R. Rice was called to the First Baptist Church of Melvindale, Michigan. Harry Sabin resigned from Beverly Bible Church of Michigan City, Indiana, to become pastor of First Baptist Church in Streator, Illinois. Allan Vine was called to First Baptist Church of Oglesby, Illinois. The First Baptist Church of Bloomfield, Iowa, called Clay Deaver of Broken Bow, Nebraska, to its pastorate to succeed J. Lester Williams, who was called to First Baptist Church in Guthrie Center, Iowa. The Temple Baptist Church in Tacoma, Washington, called J. Newland Pfaff, missionary appointee to China, as assistant pastor to Dr. R. L. Powell until such a time as Pfaff could leave for the field.

Rev. Martin Orman became pastor of First Baptist Church of Holland, Michigan. He was a veteran of World War II and had seen active duty in Africa and Europe. Prior to his military service he had been associated with Evangelist Phil Ward.

Rev. R. E. Moss, pastor of the First Baptist Church of Grand Haven, Michigan, for 24 years, retired from the active pastorate. Pastor Moss was in the ministry for 40 years. Before becoming a Baptist, he was elected moderator of the Wisconsin Presbytery on two different occasions and once vice-moderator of the Illinois Synod in the United Presbyterian denomination. He came into the GARBC by conviction. During his long pastorate in Grand Haven many young people went out from his church to full-time Christian service.

Loyal H. Marx ended a nine-year ministry at the American Baptist Church of Forest City, Iowa, to become pastor of the First Baptist Church in Waverly, Iowa. Francis A. Crown left the Winifred (Kansas) Baptist Church to become pastor of the Calvary Baptist Church of Phillipsburg, Kansas. Melvin O. Welch left Camden Baptist Church of Oberlin, Ohio, to be the pastor of First Baptist Church of Findlay, Ohio. Herbert C. Johnson resigned the pastorate of Berean Baptist Church in Bunker Hill, Illinois, to become pastor of the Missionary Baptist Church of Michigan City, Indiana. Lloyd Morris left the Bethel Baptist Church in Jamestown, New York, to become pastor of the Tabernacle Baptist Church in Baltimore, Maryland.

Donald B. Stowell resigned the pastorate of the Calvary Baptist Church in Los Angeles in order to plant a new Regular Baptist church in El Centro, California. James Westcott was formally ordained by the church of which he was the pastor, Goodwill Baptist Church of Laurel, Virginia. William Howard Green resigned the pastorate of the Central Baptist Church of Columbus, Ohio, and accepted a call to the First Baptist Church of Gallipolis, Ohio. Guy Dillon left the Dover Baptist Church of Tustin, Michigan, to pastor the Independent Baptist Church of Rogers City, Michigan. Earl Brown went to the pastorate of Berean Baptist Church in Bunker Hill, Illinois, from the Hosford Park Baptist Church in Gary, Indiana. Milton Davis left the Saugerties (New York) Baptist Church to become pastor of the First Baptist Church of Phoenicia, New York.

Theodore Glick left the Monterey Baptist Church of Beaver Dams, New York, to pastor the Mehoopany (Pennsylvania) Baptist Church. Harry E. Ketcham left the First Baptist Church of Monroe, Iowa, to pastor the Hagerman Baptist Church of Waterloo, Iowa. Wilfred Booth resigned the Birchardville (Pennsylvania) Baptist Church to pastor the First Baptist Church of Galion, Ohio.

The chairman of the Council of Fourteen (1949), Joseph M. Stowell, resigned the pastorate of the First Baptist Church in Bay City, Michigan, to become pastor of the First Baptist Church of Hackensack, New Jersey.

Dr. Charles F. Fields, pastor of the First Baptist Church in Plainfield, Illinois, for six years, retired after 42 years of service in the gospel ministry. He was the first president of the Illinois Christian Fundamentals Association and was active in the Illinois Association of Regular Baptist Churches.

Richard A. Elvee pastored the Calvary Baptist Church in Muskegon, Michigan, for four years and resigned to accept the pastorate of the 127-year-old First Baptist Church of Buffalo, New York. Norman Edwards left the Brookside Baptist Temple in Cleveland, Ohio, to pastor the First Baptist Church of Wenatchee, Washington. H. C. Short succeeded E. C. Lasswell as pastor of First Baptist Church of Eldora, Iowa. Pastor Lasswell accepted the call to the pastorate of First Baptist Church of Monroe, Iowa. C. D. Miles left the Evansville Baptist Church to pastor the Grace Baptist Church of Troy, Ohio. Joseph H. Troup accepted a call to Camden Baptist Church in Kipton, Ohio. Alvin G. Ross left the Taylor Center Baptist Church of Inkster, Michigan, to pastor the Blessed Hope Baptist Church of Springfield, Ohio.

John Schimmel accepted a call to the pastorate of Eighth Avenue Baptist Church in Sacramento, California. Lawrence Bong resigned the Waukon (Iowa) Baptist Church to become pastor of First Baptist Church of Perry, Iowa. Gene Stevens left Highland Parkside Baptist Church in Joliet, Illinois, to pastor the Grace Baptist Church in Corwith, Iowa. J. L. Patten, president of the Omaha Bible Institute, accepted the call of the Temple Baptist Church in Omaha to serve as interim pastor. He continued to lead the Institute.

James T. Jeremiah finished 11 fruitful years at Emmanuel Baptist Church in Toledo, Ohio, to become the pastor of Emmanuel Baptist Church in Dayton, Ohio, on January 1, 1950.

Robert L. Titus resigned the pastorate of Riverdale Baptist Church in Flint, Michigan, to become pastor of Immanuel Baptist Church in Columbus, Ohio.

All of the above pastoral changes were accomplished without the aid of archbishops, general superintendents or denominational dictators. Each local church in the GARBC is free to call its own pastor under the terms it deems fair and acceptable. As churches unite in prayer, as pulpit committees lean upon the Holy Spirit and His Word for guidance and as men of God are contacted and burdened by the Holy Spirit for certain ministries, then, and only then, are God's men confidently led to the churches of God's choosing and God's people are happy.

End Note

1. J. Murray Murdoch, *A Portrait of Obedience* (Schaumburg, IL: Regular Baptist Press, 1979), p. 237.

Merle R. Hull

20

In January of 1950 the work of the GARBC had grown to such an extent that the home office was moved from the third floor of the Manhattan Building to the twelfth floor. The office area was exactly doubled by doing so. Besides handling the heavy correspondence of the National Representative's office, Ruth Ryburn had been trying to keep up with the work of the *Baptist Bulletin* subscription list. Since the subscription family had grown to more than 6,000, it became necessary to relieve Ruth Ryburn of that responsibility. Miss Lucylle Powers, for nine years the church secretary at the Walnut Street Baptist Church in Waterloo, Iowa, was called to the home office to take over the work of the *Bulletin.* She was already familiar with the details since she had handled it in the Walnut church office when Dr. Ketcham was editor of the magazine while pastoring the Waterloo church. Miss Ryburn was able to turn her full attention to the increasing work load of the GARBC itself.

Yes, the GARBC was growing, and the annual conference in Buffalo, New York, in May of 1950 was truly a watershed meeting. In reporting on that conference Rev. Kenneth Good said:

> Undoubtedly the most important item of business was the adoption of a resolution by the conference to secure the services of a man (or men) to be added to the staff in the Chicago office for the publication of Bible School literature. This, and other literary efforts, will create a vast, new opportunity for forward strides of our fellowship.
>
> To date we are handicapped by the fact that our churches do not have proper literature for their Bible Schools. Local churches are hampered by the fact that all available quarterlies are either Interdenominational, or fragmentary as they relate to the Bible, or both. There is a great need for a thoroughly Scriptural, Baptistic, and Separationist literature for our Bible schools, and

this we voted to create, and will do as soon as the Lord indicates His selection of personnel.[1]

In referring to that historic piece of associational business to create our own Sunday School literature, Dr. Ketcham wrote:

Another one of our "holy causes" is the preparation of a great Sunday School literature that will be second to none in this country for the use of our G.A.R.B. churches and for all other Baptist churches who desire a real Baptist Sunday School lesson system of the very highest type.[2]

The farsighted Council of Fourteen who voted for this enormous adventure were as follows: Joseph M. Stowell, chairman; Paul R. Jackson, vice chairman; William E. Kuhnle, treasurer; Robert L. Ryerse, secretary; George A. Bates; Kenneth F. Dodson; Raymond F. Hamilton; James Thomas Jeremiah; Howard A. Keithley; Kenneth Kinney; Donald J. MacKay; Clarence E. Mason, Jr.; Robert L. Powell and Arthur Franklin Williams. These men, along with R. T. Ketcham, were surely led of the Lord in founding Regular Baptist Press.

Dr. Merle Robert Hull wrote about those early days:

As far back as the 1930s the Association considered the possibility of producing Sunday school literature, but nothing materialized at that time. A decade later the project again came up for discussion. Undenominational materials were available which were true to fundamental doctrines. Yet they avoided Scripture teaching on certain subjects and issues. In the conviction that Sunday school literature should include "all the counsel of God," the Council of Fourteen directed that such a program should begin.

And thus was born . . . Regular Baptist Press!

Heading the new effort was Larry Ward, whose roots were in Calvary Baptist Church of Norwich, New York. With a native resourcefulness, aided by a background of editorial experience, Ward was an ideal choice. Though his later associations took him outside Regular Baptist circles, Ward must be credited with a remarkable piece of work in launching a Sunday school publications program from a standing start and with severely limited finances. He was given invaluable assistance by Ruth Herriman, who served faithfully as Managing Editor for twenty-eight years until her death in 1979.

The first manuals were offered to the churches in the fall of 1952. What a pleasant surprise for everyone when sales exceeded expectations so much it was necessary to go back on the press for additional copies!

Initially the entire operation was based in Hayward, California. In 1954 printing was shifted to Ohio, and the Customer Service office established there. But the situation proved impractical. With the editorial office in California, Customer Service in Ohio and the Association home office in Chicago, effective communication and coordination were extremely difficult. Thus in 1955 all offices were consolidated in Chicago. When Ward chose to remain in California, Merle R. Hull was named Executive Editor.[3]

Merle R. Hull was born in 1921. He graduated from Baptist Bible Seminary in Johnson City, New York, in 1942. During his college days he sang in a quartet whose other members were Carl Elgena, Ray Poludniak and Kenneth Elgena. The four of them traveled extensively with BBC president Earle G. Griffith. After pastorates in Marshalltown and Muscatine, Iowa, and Flint, Michigan, Dr. Hull was asked by Dr. Ketcham to join the Regular Baptist team. After a short time in Dayton, Ohio, Merle and Shirley Hull moved to the Chicago area. Larger offices had been rented at 608 South Dearborn in Suite 848, and Dr. Hull went to work to put RBP "on the map."

Dr. Ketcham continued as editor of the *Baptist Bulletin,* but it became obvious that the national representative's work was too demanding to do and still edit the *Bulletin.* When the Council of Fourteen met in May of 1955, they appointed Dr. Hull acting editor of the *Baptist Bulletin,* and Dr. Ketcham became the associate editor.

Upon his retirement in 1987 at the annual conference in Ames, Iowa, the Council of Eighteen presented the following resolution in honor of Dr. Hull:

Whereas our fellow servant, Merle Robert Hull, is approaching a well-deserved retirement as executive editor of Regular Baptist Press and is, therefore, laying aside the mantle of his many responsibilities, including treasurer of our Fellowship and editor of the *Baptist Bulletin;* and

Whereas he has faithfully served our Fellowship for some thirty-three years, beginning in Dayton, Ohio, and then in small downtown Chicago offices with five employees to the present ministry, facilities and staff at the Schaumburg location, serving an ever-expanding constituency of more than 6,300 churches; and

Whereas Shirley Hull has served as his faithful and devoted wife in the ministry of their home as well as the mutual work at Regular Baptist Press;

Be it therefore resolved that we, the messengers of the churches in fellowship with the General Association of Regular Baptist Churches, meeting for our 56th Annual Conference in Ames, Iowa, June 22–26, 1987, do express our deep gratitude to Dr. and Mrs. Hull for their ministry to our Fellowship, and express to God our thanksgiving for His effective use of His servants; and

Be it further resolved that we do honor God as we recognize the far-reaching effect of Dr. Hull's ministry through administration, preaching, writing and godly example; and we join his fellow workers at Schaumburg in rejoicing with great respect for his high standard of ministry and the deep relationship of love between us that will encourage us until we gather in Glory.

The resolution was passed unanimously, and Dr. and Mrs. Hull received a long standing ovation by the large crowd of messengers.

The October 1987 issue of the *Baptist Bulletin* was a tribute to the Hulls. Among many tributes from many friends and fellow laborers national representative Paul Tassell said the following:

Merle Robert Hull served the GARBC with sterling faithfulness for thirty-three years. I worked with him closely during eleven of those years. Dr. Hull was an executive editor of stellar character and superb competence. His warm heart, balanced judgment and editorial expertise made all the ministries of Regular Baptist Press Christ-honoring and Bible-centered. He was a trusted confidant, a triumphant champion of GARBC principles and a transcendent commentator on the religious scene in America through his perceptive editorials. Dr. and Mrs. Hull worked admirably as a team to bless the lives of thousands.

With appreciation for, and apologies to, the writer of the last 22 verses of Proverbs 31, this is my tribute to Merle R. Hull:

Who can find a discerning editor? His type is worthy of headlines. The heart of the Fellowship doth safely trust in him so that there is no fear of embarrassment. He will do good and not evil all the days of his life. He seeketh articles and news and worketh willingly with his hands on the typewriter. He is like the merchants' ships; he bringeth advertising revenue from afar. He riseth while it is yet night and readeth books and then writeth book reviews. He considereth an article and accepteth it. With literary expertise he doth edit it. He perceiveth that his magazine is good; his candle goeth not out by night. He layeth his hands to the paper and his hand guides the pen. He stretcheth out his heart to the reader; yea, he reacheth forth his hands to the subscriber. He is not afraid of letters to the editor, for he believeth in individual soul liberty. He surrounds himself with able staff members and up-to-date equipment. His wife is known in the Fellowship when she teaches in Regular Baptist Press Sunday School conferences. He produces fine literature and selleth it; he delights in sending Sunday School quarterlies to more than six thousand churches. Strength and honor are his clothing, and he shall rejoice in time to come. He openeth his mouth with wisdom, and his tongue is the law of kindness. He looketh well to the ways of Regular Baptist Press and eateth not the bread of idleness. The readers of the *Baptist Bulletin* rise up and call him blessed; the staff also, and they praise him. Many editors have done valiantly, but thou excellest them all. Popularity is deceitful and deadlines are relentless, but an editor that serveth the Lord is neither deceived nor discouraged. Give Merle Robert Hull the fruit of his hands and let his own works praise him.[4]

On Monday morning, November 12, 1990, Dr. Merle Robert Hull suddenly went to be with the Lord after suffering a massive heart attack.

A memorial service was held at Grace Baptist Church in Lombard, Illinois, on November 15. Pastor David Gower led in the invocation, Scripture reading and graveside service. Tributes to Dr. Hull were given by Dr. Gary Anderson, president of Baptist Mid-Missions; Dr. James Misirian, president of Shepherds Baptist Ministries; Dr. Paul Tassell, national representative of the General Association of Regular Baptist Churches; and Dr. Milo Thompson, president of Baptist Bible College and Seminary of Clarks Summit, Pennsylvania. The Rev. Wilbur Ellsworth, pastor of the First Baptist Church of Wheaton, Illinois, provided the special music. He was accompanied at the organ by Mrs. Jean Ellsworth. The Rev. Gary Moosey, pastor of West Hill Baptist Church of Akron, Ohio, delivered the funeral message. The victorious service was climaxed by the congregation's singing "When We All Get to Heaven."

Dr. Hull was survived by his wife, Shirley; a son, Tom Hull; a daughter, Jeanne Arnett; and a grandson, John Arnett.

I wrote in the January 1991 issue of the *Bulletin,*

Surely the words of Revelation 14:13 now include Merle Robert Hull: "And I heard a voice from heaven saying unto me, Write, Blessed are the dead which die in the Lord from henceforth: Yea, saith the Spirit, that they may rest from their labours; and their works do follow them."[5]

In 1981 Dr. Hull wrote:

The ministry of the Press has not been limited to the printed page alone. As editorial responsibilities have permitted, office staff members have also been active in conference work. Add to this the full-time service of traveling consultants, and the total of local church workshops would reach into the thousands in the almost thirty-year existence of the Press. In particular, the large regional conferences, dating back to 1962 at First Baptist Church of Mishawaka, Indiana, should be mentioned. Through the years they have made an immeasurable impact. As an example, the pastor of one of the Association's largest and most active churches stated that it was an RBP regional conference that gave him the vision and motivation for his ministry.

In addition to the present staff members, several other men and women have made vital, lasting contributions to Press work. They include Marjorie Raidt, Edgar R. Koons, F. Donald Drake, Vernon D. Miller and Darrell R. Bice.

Well, that's the Regular Baptist Press story . . . surely a major aspect of GARBC history.

As we leave it, consider one fact.

Every movement, good or bad, has succeeded in proportion to its output of printed matter . . . and the degree to which its followers have read that material!

Something to think about, isn't it?[6]

But we must go back to 1950 for now. The Regular Baptist Press idea was not the only accomplishment of 1950 for the GARBC. In February Dr. Ketcham headlined the second page of the *Baptist Bulletin:* "The Baptist Builders' Club." In a feature article he shared the burden of his heart about struggling young churches and sacrificing young (and sometimes older) preachers endeavoring to build church buildings in communities that desperately needed a gospel witness. Dr. Ketcham told how the Council of Fourteen had wrestled with the matter at their December 1949 meeting in Philadelphia and had agreed at that time to present to the GARBC constituency the Baptist Builders' Club.

The heart of Ketcham's burden is expressed in his own words as follows:

> How we wish that our people in lovely churches and comfortable circumstances could see this army of trained young preachers as they sacrificially, without thought of future place in the ministry, tackle the problem before them, and stay with it until a Gospel witness is established. Surely, beloved, we must help them, and help these local mission agencies that are trying to help them.
>
> With this overwhelming picture of the need all across this nation before it, the Council decided to take definite measures to do something about

meeting it, at least in part. It was decided to form a Baptist Builders' Club. The idea itself is not at all new—several Christian organizations are using the idea with marked blessing and success. The group is to be composed of individuals throughout our Fellowship who will sign a membership card, and promise to pay during the course of a calendar year not more than $10, payments to be made $2 at a time upon call of the committee in charge.[7]

The idea caught on, and through the years hundreds of churches have been helped. Several years ago the amount per call was raised to five dollars with a total of $25 per year. The grants are outright gifts. A few years ago an arrangement was made that provides qualifying churches a combination grant/loan. The combination provides for a revolving fund on the loan aspect of the Baptist Builders' Club grant. Grants are usually made in the $2,000 to $8,000 range with combination grant/loans going as high as $10,000.

The 1990 annual report of the Baptist Builders' Club revealed that during the past 40 years of the Club's existence 528 churches have been helped. Total grants to churches since the Club began total $1,491,800. Presently 1,395 people are active members in the Club. The Board of Administrators of the Club are as follows: Dale Murphy, chairman; Eugene Apple; Edward Fuller; Vernon D. Miller; Gerald P. Safstrom; Donald Tyler and W. Wilbert Welch.

Concluded Dr. Ketcham in the 1950 article on the Baptist Builders' Club:

> Surely such a procedure ought to make it possible for the G.A.R.B., itself, without becoming a mission agency, to put itself in a position where it can help somebody as well as being helped. The Council is confident that a thousand or two thousand dollars, or even a few hundred in some instances, given to a struggling church such as is described above, would be just the thing to put them over the hill and lift the burden, and allow them to go on to victory. Certainly we can do it as Baptists working together at the Baptist task, without being a Convention. Let us try it, at least, in His dear name.[8]

Try it we did! And work it did!!

End Notes

1. Kenneth Good, "Fifty-nine New Churches Received at the 19th Annual Conference," *Baptist Bulletin* (July 1950), p. 4.
2. R. T. Ketcham, "This Month with the Editor," *Baptist Bulletin* (July 1950), pp. 2, 25.
3. Merle R. Hull, *What A Fellowship!* (Schaumburg, IL: Regular Baptist Press, 1981), pp. 55, 56.
4. Paul N. Tassell, "A Tribute to Merle and Shirley Hull," *Baptist Bulletin* (October 1987), p. 12.
5. Paul N. Tassell, "Merle R. Hull in Heaven," *Baptist Bulletin* (January 1991), p. 29.
6. Hull, pp. 57, 58.
7. R. T. Ketcham, "The Baptist Builders' Club," *Baptist Bulletin* (February 1950), p. 3.
8. Ibid., p. 3.

21

Robert T. Ketcham was one of the original separatists. But he was not an isolationist. Neither did he think only Regular Baptists would go to Heaven. Neither did he limit his public ministry to Regular Baptist churches and Regular Baptist conferences. His title was "national representative," and he rightly assumed that he was to represent the GARBC to others. He was to win friends, if you please, for the GARBC. He was to inform other groups, as opportunities arose, about the message, position and goals of the GARBC. Consequently, he spoke in a variety of places to a variety of groups that held a variety of theological positions within the parameters of Biblical Christianity or fundamentalism. More than once he spoke at the Bible Presbyterian Church in Collingswood, New Jersey, pastored by Dr. Carl McIntire. Dr. Ketcham felt more at home with a Bible-believing Presbyterian like McIntire than he did with a Baptist infidel like Fosdick.

Dr. David Nettleton, former president of Faith Baptist Bible College, a past chairman of the Council of Eighteen and present pastor of Fellowship Baptist Church in Lakeland, Florida, tells about the time he heard Dr. Ketcham introduce Dr. McIntire to a large crowd at an ACCC rally. Ketcham ended his introduction by saying, "When I get to Heaven, I'm going to ask the Lord to allow me to immerse 10,000 Presbyterians in the pure river of water of life."

McIntire walked to the pulpit and declared, "I'm grateful to hear Dr. Ketcham admit there will be at least 10,000 Presbyterians in Heaven!" Such was the Scripturally magnanimous spirit of R. T. Ketcham. He spoke at Bob Jones University Bible conferences; New York's National Bible Institute Bible conferences; Moody Founder's Week Bible conferences; the Pinebrook Bible Conference, headed by Percy Crawford; the Gull Lake Bible Conference, directed by D. J.

DePree; the Sandy Cove Bible Conference, led by George Palmer; the Hawthorne Bible Church in Hawthorne, New Jersey; the Emmanuel Bible Church in Colorado Springs, Colorado; and the Moody Memorial Church in Chicago, pastored by his good friend H. A. Ironside. Many other non-GARBC conferences, churches and schools were on his schedule as year after year he represented nationally his beloved GARBC.

Dr. Ketcham did not accept the idea that because you shared the platform with a preacher of differing theological interpretations you took on all of that differing preacher's positions. It is almost amusing to hear some 1990s fundamentalists talk about "separation" being the primary characteristic of a true fundamentalist while in the same breath lauding W. B. Riley as a great fundamentalist. I agree that Riley was a great fundamentalist, but he certainly was not a separatist like Ketcham. Riley did not leave the Northern Baptist Convention until he was practically on his deathbed in 1947 at the age of 86. Ketcham had left the Convention in 1932, but he often ministered with Riley and always spoke well of Riley. He surely disagreed with Riley's staying in the Convention, but he admired Riley for fighting the liberals in the Convention. It is strange, therefore, when some 1990s fundamentalists criticize other fundamentalists for appearing on the same platform with men like Charles Stanley or Adrian Rogers who are battling liberalism in the Southern Baptist Convention. Dr. Ketcham often appeared in Bible conferences with Southern Baptist Robert G. Lee even when Ketcham disagreed wholeheartedly with Lee's remaining in a convention that tolerated liberalism in some of its seminaries.

Ketcham's attitude is exemplified in an editorial he wrote in the March 1951 issue of the *Baptist Bulletin:*

> Elsewhere in this issue will be found a letter of resignation from the trustees board of the Northern Baptist Seminary, written by Dr. Richard Clearwaters of Minneapolis. This is a forthright declaration and Dr. Clearwaters is to be highly congratulated for both his conviction and his courage in the whole matter. We have known for a long time that there is internal disturbance in Northern Baptist Seminary of Chicago, and we have known that not only some of the professors, but some of the Board members, have been registering a persistent protest over the direction that the Seminary is taking in reference to its subservience to the American Baptist Convention. It has been a source of real encouragement to those of us in the G.A.R.B. group as we have observed the position of some of the men like Dr.

> Clearwaters. Some may have felt that these men should have walked out of the situation long ago, but we are personally of the opinion that they were under obligation to stay with the Seminary until the last possible hope was gone of holding it to the line that it started out on many years ago. The Seminary was originally set up as a protest to the Northern Baptist Convention and its inclusive policy. Today the Seminary is one hundred percent sold out to the support of the Convention and its inclusive policy. Dr. Clearwaters remained with the school in an endeavor to avert this tragedy, and we congratulate him now upon his courage to withdraw when he sees that the men in the driver's seat are determined to follow the highway of the Convention.[1]

Many similarities exist between the Northern Baptist Convention of the 1920s and 1930s and the Southern Baptist Convention of the 1970s and 1980s; but there are also some distinctive dissimilarities. One major difference has been the ability of the Bible-believing leaders to capture the presidency of the Southern Baptist Convention for the past dozen or so years. Just suppose that in 1928 Dr. William B. Riley had been elected president of the Northern Baptist Convention and in 1929 reelected. Suppose H. O. Van Gilder had been elected president of the NBC in 1930 and 1931. Suppose Robert T. Ketcham had been elected NBC president in 1932. Don't you, dear readers, think the formation of the GARBC would have been postponed, perhaps indefinitely? If Riley and Van Gilder and Ketcham and Griffith had been winning some battles in the Convention and had been winning elections to the top position, don't you think they would have stayed in and fought a while longer?

That is somewhat the scenario in the Southern Baptist Convention of the past two decades. Bible-believing men like W. A. Criswell, Adrian Rogers and Charles Stanley have won some victories. They are convinced they ought to fight on. I may disagree with their staying in and not coming out *now,* but they believe they must "fight the good fight of faith" within the Convention right now. Ketcham would have, I believe, had patience with such men. He would have been very slow about criticizing a Jack Wyrtzen or a Warren Wiersbe or a Jerry Falwell for encouraging such men. After all, long-suffering is the fruit of the Spirit, and Ketcham surely was long-suffering to men like Riley and Clearwaters who really wanted to do the right thing.

People have said often that an institution or organization is just the lengthened shadow of a man. Surely down through the years the

GARBC has taken on the character of its early and best-known leader, R. T. Ketcham. We have stood firmly for separation from apostasy. And we have stood firmly for separation from those, like Billy Graham, who give aid and comfort to apostates. But as an Association we do not "shoot from the hip" at other Bible believers who may not quite see separation as we see it, yet. We were right out in front for separation from apostasy (in 1932). And we were the first ones to warn against Billy Graham's compromise and ecumenical evangelism. Dr. Ketcham was writing and preaching about Graham's "playing footsies" with liberals in the early 1950s while Bob Jones, John R. Rice and other fundamentalists were still encouraging and promoting Graham. Ketcham was not harsh with those who did not yet see the issue, but he certainly rejoiced when Wyrtzen, Jones and Rice took their stands against ecumenical evangelism and the 1957 New York crusade. (More on that in a later chapter!)

Labels can be libels. The practice by some fundamentalists to call other fundamentalists "neo-fundamentalists" or "pseudo-fundamentalists" or "new-image fundamentalists" is unhealthy. We Regular Baptists believe in autonomy and individual soul liberty. We do not believe one fundamentalist has to dot every *i* and cross every *t* like another fundamentalist. Making Bible versions or hemlines, harmonies and haircuts tests of fellowship may indicate a "hyper-fundamentalism" not really found in the Word of God. Recently one group of fundamentalists in a Baptist group began publishing a magazine that they promoted with the following arrogant words: "It is the only magazine from fundamentalists for fundamentalists." What unmitigated audacity! I wonder what M. H. Reynolds, publisher of another fundamentalist publication named *Foundation, A Magazine of Biblical Fundamentalism,* published in California, thinks of such a claim. And the *Baptist Bulletin*, for example, has been faithfully published by the GARBC since 1933, also truly a magazine from fundamentalists for fundamentalists.

Regular Baptist Press has also published an excellent book titled *Biblical Separation* in which Dr. Ernest Pickering said:

> Some people are by nature scrappers. They are not afraid to confront a situation immediately and take a strong and open stand. Some are by nature pugnacious and rather enjoy a good fight. Others, who may possess separatist convictions, are more reticent by nature to become involved in open

controversy. They will follow separatist convictions when driven to a decision, but they will tend to avoid a confrontation if possible. Many of these differences are reflections of varying personalities. Separatists are people too! There are different kinds of them. In fairness we must recognize and accept that and be careful lest we, too, carelessly mark as a compromiser someone who may not approach a problem in the same manner as we do. . . .

Some separatists see a new evangelical under every bush and a compromiser in every other pulpit. They are constantly "uncovering the dirt" about other brethren. They have just heard this, or they have just heard that. They see sinister meaning in perfectly innocent actions. It is this characteristic, probably more than any other, that is sometimes referred to by nonseparatists as part of the "separatist mentality." We would not hesitate to confess that this could be said of *some* separatists. On the other hand, we believe that it is not of the essence of separatism, and it would be most heartily repudiated by most separatist leaders.

Certainly separatists should immerse themselves in 1 Corinthians 13. Paul makes an interesting statement: "Love . . . believeth all things" (1 Cor. 13:7). Does this mean we should gullibly accept whatever we are told? Does this support the idea that we should accept everyone's Christian profession with no questions asked? No. We believe Lenski has a helpful observation when he says that love "refuses to yield to suspicions of doubt. The flesh is ready to believe all things about a brother and a fellow man in an evil sense. Love does the opposite . . ." (R. C. H. Lenski, *The Interpretation of St. Paul's First and Second Epistles to the Corinthians* [Minneapolis: Augsburg Publishing House, 1961], p. 560).[2]

The GARBC has not been built on the personality traits or personal whims of any one group of fundamentalists. We have built on the solid rock of Biblical doctrine and Scriptural position. We hold to God-given mandates and are not driven by personal or cultural preferences. We believe, as did R. T. Ketcham, that a fundamentalist can be militant without being mean or malicious. The following command is still part of the inspired, inerrant, infallible, authoritative Word of God: "Let your moderation be known unto all men" (Phil. 4:5a).

In 1950, Albert Williams was ordained by the Hedstrom Memorial Baptist Church, Buffalo, New York; Thurman Fuller by the Calvary Baptist Church, Anderson, Indiana; Jesse C. Howell by the Nottingham Baptist Church, Cleveland, Ohio; W. Denton Reilly by the Bible Baptist Church, Morrison, Illinois; Mark E. Jackson by the Grace Baptist Church, Binghamton, New York; Johnnie M. Kain by the First Baptist Church, Monroe, Iowa; Carson Fremont by the Emmanuel Baptist

Church, Dayton, Ohio; Albert Brower by the First Baptist Church, Wilmington, California; Lloyd R. Markley by Calvary Baptist Church, Susanville, California; John Bajema by the Calvary Baptist Church, Grand Rapids, Michigan; Austin D. Plew by the First Baptist Church, Maine, New York; George Carapelle by the Baptist Church, Danbury, Connecticut; George Myers by the First Baptist Church, Dresden, Ohio; W. Thomas Younger by the Glen Park Baptist Church, Gary, Indiana; Robert Johnson by the Capitol Baptist Church, Washington, D. C.; Elmer Ubbink by the Wealthy Street Baptist Church, Grand Rapids; Robert P. West by the Riverside Baptist Church, Decatur, Illinois; Donald B. Woodby by the Calvary Baptist Church, Mannington, West Virginia; and Stanley Holman by the Emmanuel Baptist Church, Toledo, Ohio.

In 1951 George Toensfeldt was ordained by the Calvary Baptist Tabernacle, Los Angeles; Everett G. Christensen by the Grace Baptist Church, Omaha, Nebraska; Warren W. Wiersbe by the Central Baptist Church, East Chicago, Indiana; Darris Hauser by the Independent Baptist Tabernacle, Jersey Shore, Pennsylvania; Don Bunge by the First Baptist Church, Austin, Minnesota; Curt Wetzel by the First Baptist Church, Lock Haven, Pennsylvania; Preble Cobb by the Liverpool Independent Baptist Church, Liverpool, New York; Jay Dyksterhouse by the Wealthy Street Baptist Church, Grand Rapids; Ralph O. Burns by the Worthington (Pennsylvania) Baptist Church; Elvin K. Mattison by the First Baptist Church, Vassar, Michigan; Quentin Kenoyer by the 31st Street Fundamental Baptist Church, Indianapolis; Clifford Roach by the First Baptist Church, Romeo, Michigan; Everett Wolfe by the First Baptist Church, Creston, Iowa; Everett Hawbaker by the First Baptist Church, Perry, Iowa; Albert Platt by the First Baptist Church, Atlantic City, New Jersey; Cecil C. Akam by the First Baptist Church, Dunkirk, New York; William Broughton and Orrin Christian by the Grace Baptist Church, Binghamton, New York; Charles Moore by the Hough Avenue Baptist Church, Cleveland, Ohio; Edward Wilson Wahl by the First Baptist Church, Kennedy, New York; and Don Reed Loomis by the First Baptist Church, Gallipolis, Ohio.

End Notes

1. R. T. Ketcham, "This Month with the Editor," *Baptist Bulletin* (March 1951), p. 2.

2. Ernest Pickering, *Biblical Separation* (Schaumburg, IL: Regular Baptist Press, 1979), pp. 226, 231.

22

Perhaps the most popular preacher of the twentieth century is Billy Graham. His ministry began in a relatively small church in Western Springs, Illinois, a suburb of Chicago. He actually became an evangelical celebrity when he began to travel for Youth for Christ in the 1940s. At the age of 29, in 1947, he became president of Northwestern Schools in Minneapolis, Minnesota. However, he spent most of his time in evangelistic crusades and in 1951 resigned his position to go into evangelism full time. Such a decision was a foregone conclusion since he had captured national headlines with his famous 1949 Los Angeles crusade. He subsequently had great meetings in Boston, Massachusetts; Columbia, South Carolina; and Pittsburgh, Pennsylvania. By the summer of 1952 he was the most attractive and famous preacher in America. Thousands were flocking to his meetings, and hundreds were responding to his invitations to receive Christ.

Unfortunately, he was courting the favor and official sponsorship of liberal preachers and liberal councils of churches. He was sending converts back to "the church of your choice." But in the glare of publicity and in the excitement of the huge campaigns, Graham's compromises went largely ignored. People were so hungry for something real in religion, and true believers wanted so much to see a real revival that Graham's errors of judgment were attributed to his youth and inexperience with the press and religious leaders. He was indeed popular. Who would dare to call attention to his compromises, his nurturing of what we now call ecumenical evangelism?

Enter Robert Thomas Ketcham! Yes, Dr. Ketcham was one fundamentalist who was willing to say in a national publication that all was not well with the popular, youthful, winsome evangelist. It took great courage and Bible-based convictions to do it, but Ketcham did not lack in either. On page 8 of the December 1952 *Baptist Bulletin* appeared an article by Ketcham titled "The Billy Graham Controversy." Wrote Ketcham:

> Dr. Graham recently closed a city-wide campaign in Pittsburgh, Pennsylvania. At the opening of his campaign he was interviewed by Mr. William McElwain, a reporter for the *Pittsburgh Sun-Telegraph*. In the issue of Saturday, September 6, 1952, Mr. McElwain writes his story concerning that interview. To quote three paragraphs from that article:
>
> "Graham stressed that his crusade in Pittsburgh would be interdenominational. He said that he hopes to hear Fulton J. Sheen at one of the masses at St. Paul's Cathedral tomorrow. He added:
>
> "Many of the people who have reached a decision for Christ at our meetings have joined the Catholic Church and we have received commendations from Catholic Publications for the revived interest in their church following one of our campaigns.
>
> "This happened both in Boston and Washington. After all, one of our prime purposes is to help the churches in a community. If after we move on, the local churches do not feel the effects of these meetings in increased membership and attendance, then our crusade would have to be considered a failure."[1]

When Graham responded that he had been misquoted, Mr. McElwain said the only real error was in his statement that Graham wanted to hear Bishop Sheen "at a mass," but that Graham would still like to hear him. When Dr. Ketcham wrote personally to Graham, Ketcham listed sixteen matters to which he asked Graham to reply. Ketcham's letter covered six typewritten, single-spaced pages. It was kindly and earnestly written on March 8, 1951. On March 24, 1951, Graham wrote a brief letter. The first paragraph said:

> Dear Dr. Ketcham: Your letter has just reached me here in Fort Worth and I make haste to answer. I shall never forget the first time I ever heard you preach. It was at the Moody Church during a Founder's Week Conference. You preached the greatest sermon on the Incarnation I ever heard. As you preached I was having my second date with the young lady who is now my wife. Certainly it was a memorable occasion. Ever since that time I have held you in the highest esteem and considered you one of the great preachers of our generation. I love you, believe in you and admire you tremendously.[2]

He then proceeded to dismiss all of Ketcham's questions about the Graham quotations with the following words: "Some of the quotes that you have picked up here and there were completely false; others were garbled and were texts out of context; a few were true."[3] Graham made no effort whatsoever to say which were false, which were garbled and which were true. Ketcham ended his article as follows: "We come back to our original thesis, that it is strange that Mr. Graham is so often 'misquoted.' Either the reporters across this country are generally a bad lot who are totally incapable of reporting anything accurately, or Mr. Graham is 'irresponsible' in what he says to them. Personally I am forced to believe the latter."[4]

In the June 1957 issue of the *Baptist Bulletin* another article by Dr. Ketcham appeared. It was titled "Billy Graham Finally Admits His Position." In the heart of the article Ketcham said:

> Dr. Graham says he will go anywhere, sponsored by anybody. I am wondering if that statement can be supported. Some six or seven years ago when the New York campaign was first discussed, a fundamental doctrinal statement was drawn up by the Evangelicals of New York City which was to be signed by all members of the Central Committee. The modernists refused to sign it and resigned. Dr. Graham thereupon refused to come to New York City because the Committee was not sufficiently ecumenical in representation. Later the evangelical fundamentalists of the whole metropolitan area approached Dr. Graham as to whether he would accept an invitation to conduct a New York crusade, sponsored wholly and only by the evangelicals of New York City. This he refused to do. He refused to come to New York unless the whole Council of Churches of New York City was included. So it cannot be said that Billy will "go anywhere, sponsored by anybody." At least, he would not go to New York sponsored solely and only by evangelical and fundamental interests. The only conclusion one can draw, therefore, is that by "anybody" he means that it must be an inclusion of all shades of doctrinal positions.
>
> It seems very strange to us that Dr. Graham turns down an invitation to come to New York issued by the friends of Calvary, and only comes when the enemies of Calvary are included.
>
> In the announcement of this policy, Dr. Graham flies straight into the face of clear and easily understood Scripture. In 1 Timothy 6:3–5 it is specifically stated that if any one comes who does not consent to wholesome words, even the words of our Lord Jesus Christ, that the true believer is to withdraw himself from him. By no stretch of the imagination can the word "withdraw" be made to mean co-operate in a great campaign.[5]

The fundamentalists in the New York area were especially upset that Graham would have blatant liberals on his central committee like Dr. Henry Van Dusen, president of Union Seminary. The 1957 New York crusade was "the last straw" for many fundamentalists who had tried to be patient and hopeful with Graham. Jack Wyrtzen of Word of Life separated from Graham and the New York City crusade. Bob Jones, Sr., and Bob Jones, Jr., broke with Graham, as did Dr. John R. Rice. Dr. Paul R. Jackson, president of Baptist Bible Seminary in Johnson City, New York, took a clearcut stand against the ecumenical evangelism represented by the Billy Graham New York City crusade. Dr. Joseph M. Stowell, pastor of the large and influential First Baptist Church in Hackensack, New Jersey, and a well-known radio preacher in the New York City area, led his church to stand against the compromise of the Graham New York meeting. In fact, all of the GARBC churches in the area stood with Stowell and his people. It was an unpopular stand, and some members of Regular Baptist churches broke with their pastors and left their churches or caused great tensions in those churches over the Graham issue. Across the country GARBC pastors really "took the heat" from evangelicals who would not take the Scriptural position.

Another issue that concerned fundamentalists was the Graham practice of sending converts back to liberal churches where the Bible was not honored and the gospel not preached. According to Dr. Ketcham, Graham's answer to his fundamentalist critics on this matter was as follows: " 'Apparently these brethren who make these statements have no faith in the Holy Spirit. The work of regeneration is the work of the Holy Spirit—the work of follow-up is the work of the Holy Spirit. The same Holy Spirit that convicted them of sin and regenerated them is able to follow them.' "[6] Dr. Ketcham's answer to that bit of sidestepping is classic. Ketcham wrote:

> Dr. Graham says that the same Holy Spirit who convicted them will follow them. And since He follows them we do not need to be concerned about where they go, for no matter where they go the Holy Spirit will follow them and bring them through. Well, if that is a sound conclusion, then it ought to work in both directions. Why not leave the matter of *conviction* and *regeneration* wholly in the hands of the Spirit, and save all of the campaign expense of Billy's preaching mission? If the Holy Ghost will follow and take care of them, without any consideration of the human instruments involved, then it

must necessarily follow that the same Holy Spirit could bring about their conversion without any consideration of human instruments. Since the Holy Spirit uses human instruments to bring to pass, through the preaching of the Word, conviction and regeneration in the heart of the sinner, it also follows that He uses human instrumentalities to bring that new-born babe on through to a solid relationship with his Savior, and a thorough training and upbringing in the Word of God. Now if these babes in Christ go into churches where such human instruments are not to be found, then what? No, it will not do to say that the Holy Ghost will take care of them. If He can take care of them after they are saved without any human instrumentality involved then He can take care of saving them in the first place, without any human instrumentality. This is one of the strangest arguments we have yet heard coming from the lips of Dr. Graham, in an attempt to justify his campaigns with these modernists and modernistic churches among his sponsors.[7]

Ketcham's pen was not reserved for purely polemical purposes, however. He wrote *God's Provision for Normal Christian Living,* an excellent exposition of Ephesians 6:10–18. The book was published by Moody Press and went through several editions. It is now being published by Regular Baptist Press. One of his most-loved books, *I Shall Not Want,* is an insightful exposition of Psalm 23. Dr. Ketcham also wrote nine of the fifteen GARBC Literature Items. These pamphlets are distributed free by the home office. His other books and magazine articles were wonderfully used of God to instruct and inform thousands. He sought to exhort with all long-suffering and doctrine both from the pulpit and with the pen.

End Notes

1. R. T. Ketcham, "The Billy Graham Controversy," *Baptist Bulletin* (December 1952), p. 8.
2. Ibid., p. 24.
3. Ibid., pp. 24, 25.
4. Ibid., p. 25.
5. R. T. Ketcham, "Billy Graham Finally Admits His Position," *Baptist Bulletin* (June 1957), p. 11.
6. Ibid., p. 12.
7. Ibid., p. 12.

23

The GARBC constituency has always been education-conscious. The training of young people in a Christian atmosphere, undergirded by a Christian philosophy of education, is essential to a movement like the GARBC. As 1953 opened, five "approved schools" were in happy fellowship with the Association. The GARBC Constitution says: "It shall be the policy of the Association to abstain from the creation and/or control of educational, missionary and other benevolent agencies" (Article VII, Section 1). Therefore, the "approved schools" have no organic connection with the GARBC, but they are characterized by Baptist doctrine, financial soundness and separation from apostasy and new evangelicalism. The five approved schools at the start of 1953 were Baptist Bible Seminary of Johnson City, New York, which had come into being in 1932, the same year the Association began; the Baptist Bible Institute of Cleveland, Ohio; Grand Rapids Baptist Theological Seminary and Bible Institute in Michigan; Los Angeles Baptist Theological Seminary, which had started in 1927; and Western Baptist Bible College in Oakland, California. Only one of them, Grand Rapids, is still in the same city and state at this writing! Los Angeles is now Northwest Baptist Seminary in Tacoma, Washington. Western is now in Salem, Oregon. Baptist Bible Seminary is now Baptist Bible College and Seminary of Pennsylvania in Clarks Summit, Pennsylvania. Baptist Bible Institute is now Cedarville College in Cedarville, Ohio. To the five have been added Faith Baptist Bible College and Seminary of Ankeny, Iowa (formerly Omaha [Nebraska] Baptist Bible College), and Spurgeon Baptist Bible College of Mulberry, Florida.

We decided to talk about education in the era including 1953 because of what Larry Ward dubbed "Miracle at Cedarville" in the June

1953 issue of the *Baptist Bulletin*. Without desiring to "play favorites," the author still wants to relate a special "quest for faithfulness" in the history of what we now know as Cedarville College.

The Baptist Bible Institute of Cleveland came into being in 1942. Since its beginning it had occupied classrooms in the educational building of the Hough Avenue Baptist Church of Cleveland. A large home served as a girls' dormitory, while the young men had to find housing where they could afford it. As the student body grew, a committee was appointed by the board to seek for suitable property. After fruitless searching, James T. Jeremiah of Emmanuel Baptist Church in Dayton, Ohio, brought stunning news concerning a college in the town of Cedarville, not too far from Dayton.

The committee investigated and discovered nine buildings in good repair on fifteen acres of a beautiful campus. Cedarville College had been chartered as a liberal arts college in 1887. Originally affiliated with the Reformed Presbyterian Church, it passed into the hands of an independent board in 1928. As the churches supporting the school began to join other Presbyterian denominations, the support and enrollment had badly dwindled. Only two solutions seemed feasible to the beleaguered board members: Either sell the college property to liquidate the operating deficit for the year, or transfer ownership to a group that would pay the debt and continue to operate the college!

A news release from the Baptist Bible Institute of Cleveland, as quoted in the *Baptist Bulletin,* explained the matter:

> "It was the proposal of the Cedarville College Trustees that the interested church group or school selected by them should assume full responsibility for any deficit in the present school year (estimated at $25,000). In return, of their board of twenty-one members, all except a quorum of ten would resign. The remaining quorum would first elect eleven new members designated by the new group, then they, too, would resign. The eleven new Trustees would then elect the remainder of their own Board of Trustees. In this manner, *the ownership and control of Cedarville College would be transferred completely into the hands of the new Board of Trustees to be operated without any restrictions or conditions."* [1]

The article went on to say,

> The two boards of trustees met in Cedarville College on Saturday afternoon, April 4. In a meeting charged with spiritual blessings indicative of

the reality of the presence of God, the ownership and control of Cedarville College passed into the hands of the Baptist Bible Institute of Cleveland![2]

The new school year got off to a good start with a week of special meetings with Robert T. Ketcham as guest speaker. Dr. Ketcham was so excited by what he saw and heard and felt at Cedarville that he penned the following words in the November 1953 *Baptist Bulletin:*

> I am not a prophet, but I venture a prophecy. If the board of trustees of the Cedarville Baptist College walk carefully and wisely before God, as I know they will, there is no reason in the world why, if the Lord tarries, in ten years from now there should not be a student body of at least one thousand in Cedarville. Ten years from now, and even possibly in half that time, Cedarville management should have drawn around itself a faculty and an administrative program and policy which will make Cedarville second to none in the field of academic training. In the providence and grace of God there is ahead of us a day at Cedarville when our Regular Baptist young men and young women can go to their own school and come out with diplomas that are prized as highly as any offered by any other sound, evangelical college in this country. Indeed I am not so sure but what my prophecy of one thousand is an underestimate. If Cedarville, as I know it will, moves on and takes its place in the academic world, not only will our own young people flock to it, but here too, will be a college of such high standing and trustworthiness as shall attract Baptist youth from the Conservative Baptist ranks, as well as from the "independent" field.[3]

What a prophecy! In 1989 Cedarville enrolled almost 2,000 students on a campus worth more than $30 million dollars with a faculty numbering more than 100 of the finest Christian scholars in the country. Dr. James T. Jeremiah and Dr. Paul Dixon have led the school since 1953, Dr. Jeremiah for 24 years and Dr. Dixon for 12 years (and still counting!). Cedarville's graduates are serving all over the world with distinction and a zeal to reach people for Christ.

Other "miracles" have happened through the years on the campuses of our other "approved schools." Years ago Grand Rapids College and Seminary moved out of the facilities of the old Wealthy Street Baptist Church onto a spacious campus in northeast Grand Rapids. Dr. W. Wilbert Welch led the school in almost a quarter of a century of continual building. Dr. Charles U. Wagner served as the president through December of 1990.

Under the leadership of G. Arthur Woolsey, the Baptist Bible Seminary became Baptist Bible College of Pennsylvania when it bought a Roman Catholic campus in beautiful Clarks Summit, Pennsylvania. Led through the years by stalwart men named Earle G. Griffith, Paul R. Jackson, G. Arthur Woolsey, Ernest Pickering, Mark Jackson and now Milo Thompson, the school continues to train faithful and competent soldiers of the Cross.

For 18 years John L. Patten led the Omaha Baptist Bible College. In the middle 1960s Dr. David Nettleton led the college to relocate in Ankeny, Iowa. The name was changed to Faith Baptist Bible College, and by the time Nettleton had completed his 15-year presidency, the campus was dotted by attractive and functional buildings. Dr. Gordon Shipp succeeded Nettleton. When Dr. Shipp went Home to be with the Lord, Dr. Robert Domokos became president.

Los Angeles Baptist Theological Seminary was led to relocate in Tacoma, Washington, by Charles U. Wagner. A new location beside beautiful Puget Sound also brought a new name, Northwest Baptist Seminary. Dr. William Bellshaw, the present president, was preceded by Ernest Pickering and J. Don Jennings.

Spurgeon Baptist Bible College was founded by Dr. G. Arthur Woolsey in Mulberry, Florida. Dr. Woolsey was followed in the presidency by John Polson, J. O. Purcell and Elvin K. Mattison. The present president is Timothy W. Teall.

Dr. Van Gilder led Western Baptist College for 16 years and relocated the school in El Cerrito, California. Dr. Fred Brock followed him and moved the school to Salem, Oregon. Dr. W. Thomas Younger followed Dr. Brock's tenure, and Dr. John G. Balyo became WBC president when Dr. Younger went back into the pastorate.

All of "our" schools have unique and special ministries. Their combined total enrollment for the 1989–90 academic year was 4,338 students. Two hundred twenty eight full-time and 122 part-time faculty are involved in teaching and training our young people. The total value of the seven campuses is more than $73 million.

The closing words of Dr. Ketcham's report on Cedarville may be applied to all our schools.

> Some years ago I remember hearing a song that was then popular, the title of which I think was "Did You Ever See a Dream Walking?" As I remember it, the first line went, "Did you ever see a dream walking? Well, I did."

I would like permission to lift that phrase out of its cheap and secular connotations, and say that that is exactly what I saw at Cedarville. The dreams and the prayers of God's people in our Fellowship all of a sudden materialized right there before our very eyes!

But now what do we do? Where do we go from here? The God Who gave to our blessed Fellowship in general, and to the Cleveland school in particular, this magnificent gift is able to develop and complete the hopes and dreams and aspirations of our people in the years ahead. But, as always, God works through people; and in this case we Regular Baptists are the people. . . . I may not enhance my popularity (however much I may have) by what I am about to say, but I would like to add a gentle reminder that perhaps it is time for all of our churches to take a new look at the necessity of supporting our *own* institutions and agencies, instead of spending over a million and a half dollars each year on projects outside our Fellowship. Understand, I am not suggesting that these extra projects be abandoned, but certainly there must be room somewhere for some adjustments. *We have a liberal arts college of our own now.* It is a gift of God to us. Our people *must* support it.[4]

End Notes

1. Larry Ward, "Miracle at Cedarville," *Baptist Bulletin* (June 1953), p. 9.
2. Ibid., p. 9.
3. R. T. Ketcham, "The Miracle at Cedarville, Ohio," *Baptist Bulletin* (November 1953), p. 14.
4. Ibid., pp. 13, 14.

24

The presidential candidates of 1952 and 1956, Dwight David Eisenhower and Adlai E. Stevenson, logged more miles than any previous presidential candidates. Both Eisenhower and Stevenson discovered just how vast the United States of America really is. During the 1950s R. T. Ketcham also found out how big our country is. Being the "national" representative and trying to cover the entire nation became a bone-wearying, exhausting job. Although the entire number of GARBC churches numbered just 760 in 1956 (there are 1,574 as of 1990), the churches were scattered from coast to coast. Early in Dr. Ketcham's work at the home office, the Council of Fourteen began to think about securing eastern and western regional field representatives. The rationale behind a home office and a national representative had been the desire to provide encouragement, services and ministry to the local churches. The establishment of Regular Baptist Press with Sunday School consultants Merle and Shirley Hull implemented that desire further. It was also the desire of the national representative to promote the GARBC personally wherever he went.

In 1957 the Council of Fourteen extended a call to Rev. Alfred Colwell to become the eastern regional representative. The Council of Fourteen had watched with great concern the heavy schedule of activities and services carried on by 68-year-old Robert T. Ketcham, and they realized he must have assistance in covering the country. Colwell's major work would be that of encouraging and ministering to pastors while at the same time preaching to their congregations. He would also get on the campuses of the approved schools and, as he had time, visit other schools to represent the GARBC as the local church-oriented, missionary-minded Association it is.

Alfred Colwell was a successful pastor for many years. From 1952 to 1957 he served as the state missionary of the Indiana Fellowship of Regular Baptist Churches. His productivity in that work was truly outstanding. New churches were started, older churches were brought into the Fellowship, a beautiful youth camp was purchased and developed, and pastors were enriched and encouraged by the fruitful, congenial counsel and ministry of Alfred Colwell.

He began his ministry with the GARBC in October of 1957. The calling of Colwell coincided with the Association's celebration of its silver anniversary. From 22 churches to 760 and the establishment of a strong and productive home office plus the establishing of Regular Baptist Press all testified to a healthy, vigorous, purposeful young-adult Association. And taking on a new field representative was just more evidence of the blessing of God on the first 25 years of the GARBC.

In 1958 the annual conference was excited about the Council of Fourteen's decision to extend a call to Rev. C. Allen Taff to become the western representative of the GARBC. At the time, Taff pastored the First Baptist Church in Richland, Washington. He earlier had served as pastor of the First Baptist Church of Wilmington, California. During World War II he served as a chaplain in the army. He moved to (of all places!) Paradise, California, and his work took place chiefly in the area west of the Rocky Mountains. Taff was considered a western pioneer, and he was just the right man to work with and challenge other pioneering servants of the Lord in the West.

Colwell served the Association fruitfully from 1957 to 1966 when he went Home to be with the Lord. Taff served from 1958 to 1962, when he left to become pastor of the Pleasant Valley Baptist Church in Chico, California. Surely the effectiveness of these men in promoting the work of the Association was considerable. Moreover, they took a tremendous load off the shoulders of Dr. Ketcham.

After Colwell died in 1966, then national representative Paul R. Jackson and the Council of Fourteen agreed unanimously to call Rev. Reginald L. Matthews as GARBC field representative. Dr. Matthews had had a long and distinguished pastoral ministry at Calvary Baptist Church of Norwich, New York; Parr Memorial Baptist Church of Petoskey, Michigan; Emmanuel Baptist Church of Toledo, Ohio; and Calvary Baptist Church of Grand Rapids, Michigan. Dr. Matthews was awarded the doctor of divinity degree by Grand Rapids Baptist College in 1963. He retired at the age of 65 in 1975. He was my pastor in Toledo during my college years (1951–55) and has been a valued friend through the years. Even at 80 years of age (in 1990) he still preaches quite regularly. He loved to keep good records, and during his tenure as GARBC field representative he preached in 37 states and 5 Canadian provinces, speaking in 800 local churches. Dr. R. L. Matthews had a great love for missionaries and world evangelism. He spoke in scores of missionary conferences during his work for the Association.

In 1959 Regular Baptist Press called Rev. Fred M. Barlow as its first Sunday School consultant. Fred Barlow was one of the most dynamic, energetic, hard-working, consecrated-to-Christ men who ever walked among us. He was born in 1921 and was saved as the result of a relentless visitation program by an Akron (Ohio) church. That is one of the reasons he never tired of promoting visitation evangelism. He graduated from Baptist Bible College when it was in Johnson City, New York. He pastored churches in New York, Ohio and Michigan. In 1968 he received an honorary doctor of divinity degree from Western Baptist College in Salem, Oregon. Dr. Barlow organized, promoted and conducted huge regional Sunday School conferences all over America for more than 20 years. Those conferences awakened apathetic preachers and laymen, instructed eager teachers and inspired hundreds of Sunday School teachers and workers to faithful (as Fred would say it!), fruitful, fervent, fearless, forceful service for Christ. No one who ever heard or saw Fred Barlow preach could forget his intensity. Some called him "machine-gun Barlow" because of his rapid-fire delivery, and how he loved to preach!

One of my greatest experiences in the ministry was a 12-day "barnstorming" trip around the state of Florida March 1–12, 1982. Dr. Barlow had helped to organize Sunday School attendance contests in several regions of the state. At each evening rally he would give out awards, promote the Sunday School and Regular Baptist Press, and then I would preach what he called "a bell-ringing" sermon. We drove from city to city in his old, big 1972 Cadillac. Dr. Barlow said to me, "Brother Paul, just change the oil in these old cars every two thousand miles, and they'll never quit!" Well, for 12 days we rode, promoted and preached. We started at Heritage Baptist Church in Lakeland on March 1, then to Calvary Baptist Church in Gulfport, then to Temple Baptist Church in Lakeland, on to Sun Coast Baptist Church in New Port Richey, to Calvary Baptist Church of Silver Springs Shores in Ocala, then to Gateway Baptist Church in Kissimmee, to Maranatha

Baptist Church in Orlando, to First Baptist Church in North Port and finally ended up at Broadview Baptist Church in Pompano Beach on March 12. What a whirlwind two weeks!

Little could I have guessed that Fred Barlow would be dead in less than a year. He contracted a fast-growing cancer and went Home to be with the Lord on February 22, 1983, at the age of 61. His funeral service was held at Heritage Baptist Church in Lakeland. Pastor J. O. Purcell spoke to a packed church auditorium. I had the privilege of reading a "Tribute to Daddy" written by his four children. Heaven's gain was surely the GARBC's loss. Regular Baptist Press had lost a great Sunday School champion.

Others who have served through the years as Sunday School consultants are Melvin Jones, Carl Elgena and James Dersham.

For many years now the Association has not had regional representatives. Why? Because the state associations began to engage men as "state representatives." As Regular Baptists know, no organic relationship exists between the GARBC and any state or regional fellowship. Each state fellowship is a separate, autonomous entity and is in no way obligated to, or controlled by, the national fellowship (GARBC). Our state fellowships are allies, however, and we enjoy cordial fellowship. Rather than centralize the work of the field representatives in the GARBC home office, wisdom dictated that each state fellowship have its own representative if and when it could afford it.

As of 1990, 13 such men serve across the country: Donald Radecki of California, Reese Johnson of Illinois-Missouri, Randall W. Patten of Indiana, Robert Humrickhouse of Iowa, M. O. Burman of Kansas (Mid-Continent Association), Maynard Belt of Michigan, Paul Lobb of Minnesota, Laurence R. Hilliker of New England, John McCullough of New Jersey, R. Craig Golden of New York, Lawrence Fetzer of Ohio, Leland Hufhand of Pennsylvania and James Maxwell of Wisconsin. These men meet with the GARBC national representative in the GARBC home office at Schaumburg, Illinois, every April for two or three days of seminars, workshops and sharing of ideas. Each state fellowship is responsible for paying the expenses of its representative. This system seems to work the best for all concerned.

Colwell, Taff and Matthews faithfully promoted the GARBC annual conference. So did the Regular Baptist Press consultants. And so do the state representatives. Through the years the annual conference has become a great family Bible conference with tremendous preaching, stirring music and warm fellowship. The Council carefully and prayerfully prepares the program. The home office conference coordinator works with a local committee from the conference area, and great meetings result. For many years Herman Scott worked as conference coordinator. For the past few years Milton Tyrrell has had that responsibility.

Perhaps one of the most difficult challenges in planning a conference is choosing the speakers. With 1,600 pastors, hundreds of missionaries, many evangelists and scores of college professors, the GARBC has many from which to choose. But there are only about 15 slots a year to fill! The program committee does its best to put together a slate of speakers that will stir interest, meet needs and really "ring the bell."

In 1954 the Walnut Street Baptist Church of Waterloo, Iowa, inaugurated the Ketcham Travel Trophy for the church having the most "messenger miles." The competition is friendly, of course, and churches do try hard to send as many messengers as possible when rivalries are developed. The Maranatha Baptist Church in Sebring, Florida, has won the trophy more times than any other church.

From time to time through the years the Council has invited special speakers from outside the Fellowship to minister to our messengers. The 1954 conference was held at historic Moody Memorial Church in Chicago. Dr. Richard Clearwaters of Minneapolis was the invited guest that year. At the 1955 conference in Kansas City, Missouri, the guest speaker was Dr. Sam Morris of Houston, Texas. In 1957 the Silver Anniversary Conference was held in Grand Rapids at the Civic Auditorium, and the evening speakers were Hall Dautel, R. T. Ketcham, Kenneth Masteller and Kenneth R. Kinney. Dr. Chester Tulga was guest speaker. Columbus, Ohio, was the site of the 1958 conference. Dr. M. R. DeHaan and Dr. Sam Morris were the guest speakers. Dr. DeHaan brought four messages during the week, and Dr. Morris brought the closing message on Friday evening. In 1959 the conference was held in Rochester, Minnesota, and the guest speaker, Dr. John Walvoord, brought two prophetic messages. Again and again during the 1950s the conference song leader was Harold Scholes, the conference organist was Hall Dautel and the conference pianist was Charles Bergerson.

But the major work of the churches was done at the local level as the conference enthusiasm was carried back home to the "grass roots" and the week by week, day by day work of the ministry was accomplished. As every experienced servant of the Lord knows, however, sometimes setbacks and discouragements occur in the work of the Lord. For example, in 1953 a roaring fire totally gutted the Hough Avenue Baptist Church of Cleveland, Ohio, pastored by John G. Balyo. The congregation and pastor were able to secure temporary quarters, and the new facilities that came later were bigger and better. It seems true to experience that hardships and even tragedies bring God's people together and cause them to pray more earnestly and work more fervently.

In January of 1954 the Campus Baptist Church of Ames, Iowa, pastored by Willard J. Martz, was led in a special week of meetings by Dr. J. Oscar Wells. In an effort to counteract some of the emptiness of modernistic ecumenicity offered at nearby Iowa State University, the evangelistic meetings were held during the same week the University sponsored meetings involving different religions.

The 1954 annual missionary conference at Riverside Baptist Church in Decatur, Illinois, pastored by George Bates, featured the Jay Dyksterhouses, bound for Chile; the Russell Ebersoles, bound for the Philippines; the Arthur Christmanns, headed for Brazil; and Rev. Robert Burns, ABWE deputation director. As an unusual feature of the conference the three couples gave their testimonies while dressed in clothing depicting their respective walks of life at the time of conversion: Mr. Dyksterhouse as a sailor, Mrs. Dyksterhouse as a chorister, Mr. Ebersole as a college baseball player, Mrs. Ebersole as the daughter of a missionary couple in the Philippines, Mr. Christmann as a horticulturist and Mrs. Christmann as an American teenager.

In the late summer of 1954, the First Baptist Church of Medina, Ohio, pastored by Kenneth Smelser, pitched a tent at the Medina County Fairgrounds. A high point of the fair ministry was the distribution of almost eight thousand gospel tracts. The church invited Rev. and Mrs. Ray Brubaker into the tent for four days with their Cathedral Caravan, and they ministered the gospel through music, gospel films, gospel magic and pointed preaching.

Christmas of 1954 was quite special for Rev. and Mrs. Fred Brock. The couple was given the keys to a brand-new 1955 Pontiac sedan by the First Baptist Church of Petaluma, California, in appreciation of Pastor Brock's ten years in the pastorate there.

In an effort to bring more people under the sound of the gospel, the Immanuel Baptist Church of Arcanum, Ohio, engaged in a new venture for the four Sundays of August 1955. Under the leadership of Pastor Tom Younger, the church held Sunday evening drive-in services on the church grounds. Average attendance was 275. Each family in attendance received an attractive packet of gospel literature.

Rev. Harry Ketcham, brother of R. T. Ketcham and pastor of the Hagerman Baptist Church in Waterloo, Iowa, and whose wife went to be with the Lord in the fall of 1955, wrote the following words for the January 1956 *Baptist Bulletin:*

> I have preached the unsearchable riches of Christ for 25 years. I have stood beside many sorrowing hearts and told them of the Christ that heals and satisfies broken hearts. I did it because I believed it with all my heart. But the time came when my own heart needed mending and satisfying. I want to assure you that He has done the same for me as I have always said He could and would for others. Heaven and the things of eternity are more real than ever. He is a wonderful Savior; I recommend Him to all of you. There is a Balm in Gilead that heals the sin-sick soul.[1]

The Calvary Baptist Church of Everett, Washington, made two people extremely happy. On behalf of the church, Pastor Mark Jackson presented a new outboard motor to Mr. and Mrs. John Schlener, missionaries to Brazil under ABWE. Not too far from Everett, the Tabernacle Baptist Church of Seattle reported that every time Paul and John Schlener started down an uncharted tributary of the Amazon in evangelizing, they could remember that the nearly 100 dollars (that's 1956 dollars!) of the purchase price of their boat was a memoriam to Willard Segerstom. Willard had recently gone Home. Before he went, he and his wife, Marie, had agreed that in the event of either of their deaths, the remaining spouse would urge people not to waste money on flowers, but rather if they wished to express their sympathy in a material way, they should put the money into a fund for a memorial in a missionary investment. This the friends of Willard Segerstom did, and the memorial fund amounted to about $93.

In a different form of outreach, the Fishermen's Chorus, a men's chorus of twenty-five, of the First Baptist Church of Mishawaka, Indiana, was active in extension work at the Hope Rescue Mission in South Bend and at the county jail and county infirmary, where the church held monthly services. The chorus, which included teenagers as well as men in their 70s, sang once a month in a Sunday evening service at the church.

Thus our churches continued to be one in doctrine but varied in outreach.

End Notes

1. "With the Churches [Waterloo, Iowa]," *Baptist Bulletin* (January 1956), p. 13.

25

We need to definitely settle this matter once and for all—now!" So exclaimed Dr. David Nettleton on Thursday afternoon, June 25, 1959, in Rochester, Minnesota, at a business session of the GARBC. He was talking about the pretribulational, premillennial rapture of the Church. The GARBC was from its beginning in 1932 an association of churches that taught and preached Bible prophecy. The Association was always strong on the "imminent return of the Eminent One," but a pretribulational statement had never been written into the GARBC doctrinal statement. At the time of Nettleton's declaration, the eschatological article, Article XVII, was headed: "Of the Resurrection, Personal, Visible, Pre-Millennial Return of Christ, and Related Events."

There were throughout premillennialism three positions on the rapture of the Church. For those who are unfamiliar with Bible prophecy, by "rapture of the Church" we mean the translation of the Church from earth to Heaven when Jesus appears suddenly in the air. This means dead believers will be resurrected and living believers will meet them in the air to join the Lord Jesus Christ forever. According to the apostle Paul, this could happen at any moment; and when it does, it will all take place in the "twinkling of an eye" (see 1 Cor. 15:51–57; 1 Thess. 4:13–18). The three premillennial positions include the pretribulational—Christ will come for His Bride, the Church, *before* the tribulation period; the midtribulational—Christ will come for His Church in the middle of the tribulation; and the posttribulational—Christ will come for His Church after the seven years of the tribulation period have passed.

The GARBC had taught the pretribulational position. The pastors of the local churches were strongly dispensational and pretribulational in their prophetic orientation. They had been greatly influenced by men like I. M. Haldeman, A. C. Gabelein, William Pettingill, H. A. Ironside and M. R. DeHaan. Franklin Logsdon, who had been a Regular Baptist pastor before succeeding H. A. Ironside as pastor of Moody Memorial Church in Chicago, was one of the greatest pretribulational preachers of the twentieth century. He once said to me, "Paul, in one of my study notebooks I have listed 150 reasons why the Church cannot go into or through the tribulation period." Such strong convictions on the part of Regular Baptist pastors and congregations put the GARBC solidly in the pretribulational camp.

At the 1959 conference the messengers were anticipating the opportunity of voting on a resolution that would precisely position the Association as pretribulational. The messengers were not all agreed on passing a resolution. Some thought the matter ought to become part of the Articles of Faith; nevertheless, the Council was convinced the matter could be settled by the passing of a resolution.

In the August 1959 issue of the *Baptist Bulletin,* Dr. Merle R. Hull editorialized about the 1959 conference. Said he:

> The business hours of this year's meeting were a particular joy to behold. The primary question, of course, related to the "rapture resolution." It was evident that all the messengers did not hold the same views on this resolution. Yet when the subject was presented, the speakers conducted themselves with perfect decorum. One did not sense the slightest evidence of bitterness or ill will. Again we must give some measure of credit, under God, to a leader—the reference being to Dr. Joseph Stowell's magnificent performance of his duties as conference chairman. . . . Voting was delayed until Thursday of the conference week, giving sufficient time for thought and discussion. It should be added that the Council spent an entire morning, in their pre-conference meeting, thoroughly and prayerfully considering the matter. The new resolution is a directive from the Association to the Council, instructing them "that in the future they present for fellowship in the General Association of Regular Baptist Churches, only those churches which believe that Christ's return for His church may occur at any moment. Further, that the Council approve only those agencies that hold this view of our Lord's return." The resolution was approved with only fourteen dissenting votes, and it should be added that some of these were negative only because of the feeling that the measure does not go far enough; that instead of a resolution, this should be made a part of the confession of faith. Thus the Association plainly declared itself with relation to this question, which is one of the most pressing issues of the day.[1]

In his report on that Thursday business session, Dr. Herbert C. Webber, pastor of Swissvale Baptist Church in Pittsburgh, Pennsylvania, said:

> The Associational business hour of the day was introduced by Chairman Stowell with a statement on Christian courtesy, Baptist democracy and friendly unanimity, all under the direction of the Holy Spirit. The Chair then called upon the secretary of the Council of Fourteen, Rev. Wilbur C. Rooke, who read to the Association a recommended resolution from the Council of Fourteen. . . . Upon motion and second, placing the resolution before the body, the Chair declared the matter open for discussion. In commendable orderliness and gracious spirit, a number of brethren took the floor to state their convictions, pro and con, regarding the resolution. When finally the vote was called for, and the Chair so responded, the body by a large majority approved the resolution.[2]

The GARBC has steadfastly remained true to that resolution. And, as we shall see in a later chapter, the statement of faith was finally amended to include a clear, strong pretribulational position.

The Rochester conference was quite significant for another reason—Robert T. Ketcham was not there! Earlier, on May 5, 1959, Ketcham had been in Detroit checking on possibilities for the 1961 conference. Prior to that he had visited his son, Donn, in medical internship in Decatur, Illinois. While he was in Decatur, Ketcham yielded to his son's urging to have an electrocardiogram made. Dr. Robert T. Ketcham was almost 70 years of age at the time, and his son had told him he probably would leave this old earth some day by way of a coronary. Donn had then described the classic symptoms of a heart attack. In Detroit, the elder Ketcham realized he was experiencing the exact symptoms his son had explained to him just weeks earlier. He finished his work in Detroit and took a train to Chicago. Murdoch continued the story:

> By the time he reached the Windy City, he realized that his symptoms were growing more severe. But instead of entering a hospital in Chicago, Ketcham went to a phone booth and called Donn. He offered no warning of his fears, knowing full well that his son would order him to a hospital in Chicago. Instead, he simply told Donn, "I'm coming down to see you; meet me at the train." Donn could not help but inquire as to why his father was paying this unscheduled visit. The reply was simply, "Well, I'm not feeling

very good, so I just thought I'd come down and see you. . . ." When Donn met the train, he knew in an instant that his father's situation was serious. Describing that moment, Donn said: "Dad got off the train looking like death warmed over. . . ." From May 5 to 12, Ketcham showed steady improvement. But on May 13 he suffered a severe relapse and almost died. For two days he lingered at death's door. Then he began to rally. In the weeks ahead he began to improve. After spending almost three months in the hospital, Ketcham was released.[3]

During his hospital stay Ketcham received almost 3,000 expressions of love in the forms of cards, letters and telegrams. After leaving the hospital he and Mrs. Ketcham took an extended vacation in the mountains of Pennsylvania, but the doctors told him he could not possibly go back to work before November. On pages 9, 10 and 11 of the November 1959 *Baptist Bulletin* appeared the bold headline: "An Open Letter from Dr. Ketcham." Excerpts from this unique letter will help us to understand something of the deep and abiding love relationship between R. T. Ketcham and the GARBC constituency. He wrote:

> I have been perplexed as to how I could contact the multitude of friends all over the world who stood so loyally by during my illness. I should like very much to write each one individually; but when I tell you that during my eighty-one days in the hospital I received 2,961 cards, letters and telegrams, you can see that that is impossible. To answer each one would put me back in the hospital again! The only way I can conceive of getting a word to most of this host of friends is through the pages of the *Baptist Bulletin*. . . .
>
> Well, the miracle is that there never was, and there is not now, a single moment of restlessness or irritation as I am laid aside and helpless. It is an amazement to myself. But God in His dear grace just taught me that I was not indispensable. He taught me that there were others who could do just as good a job as I thought I could. Even though I knew that the Rochester conference was to face a very serious matter, God took every thought of anxious concern away, and filled my heart with a peculiar peace hitherto unknown by me. And then how He wrought at Rochester!
>
> I must include in this personal chat with you a word of thanksgiving on the part of Mrs. Ketcham and myself for the precious ministry and care which was ours on the part of Pastor and Mrs. George Bates. Mr. Bates is pastor of our GARBC church in Decatur. Almost daily Brother Bates stopped in for just two or three minutes, leaving some precious nugget from the Book. I could tell that in many instances he had spent long moments in his study to get the truth he wanted me to have for that day into a nutshell. . . .

I am especially glad for the prospect of the month in the mountains, not only because I love them, but more so, because Mrs. Ketcham will have a chance to stay awhile among the mountains which were so dear to her in her girlhood. If you have never seen a Pennsylvania mountain in October, you have the sight of your life still before you. These have been real days of testing for Mrs. Ketcham. It has been a blessed experience for her, however, as she has seen the Lord give her peace and courage for the future when for awhile it looked as though she would travel the road alone. What a pillar of strength and comfort she has been!

Upon my return to the office, I shall probably give much time to writing. Hundreds have pled with me to put some of my sermons in print. This we will try to do. Eventually I will be able to take on a very *limited* schedule of speaking engagements, but nothing like it was before.

Well, I guess this will be all for now as I am a bit tired—and maybe you are too!

With a heart overflowing with love to you all, I am, with every good wish,

Yours and His.[4]

Ketcham did indeed recover but was never able to go at the pace he had for the first ten years of his tenure as national representative. And what a pace it was!

Dr. Hull wrote,

"Meanwhile, back at the Association, business was going on about as usual. After all, "Doc" himself had insisted years before that the GARBC was not a "one-man affair." It is also a testimony to a man's work when the organization he heads keeps functioning even when he isn't around. The Chicago office continued to operate smoothly. And the Association enjoyed a great annual conference, even handling the tricky pretribulation rapture issue. The conference really didn't seem quite the same without Dr. Ketcham, however. It was the first time in GARBC history he wasn't present.[5]

And the work of the Holy Spirit continued in the hearts of men, calling them into the ministry. One of the things that thrilled the heart of Dr. Ketcham during the 1950s was the tremendous number of young men from GARBC churches who were ordained to the gospel ministry in the span of one decade. A familiar phrase in a well-known gospel song goes: "Like a mighty army moves the church of God." Well, in the 1950s that "mighty army" was greatly strengthened by a host of young men who had enlisted for the blessed work of the pastorate. I have taken the space to list those ordained men of the

1950s. Many of them are still pastoring our strongest churches. Some have gone Home to be with the Commander-in-Chief. I know the list is long (and we won't do it with another decade), but you might be surprised at what memories or blessings will be recalled in your heart if you take the time to look over the next few pages. And notice how often the names of some churches keep showing up. What fruitful ministries!!

In November of 1951 William R. Weber was ordained by the Calvary Baptist Church of Ottawa, Kansas. Brother Weber was later awarded an honorary doctorate from Bob Jones University and went on to pastor the Ottawa church for the next 40 years. Albert Stover and Philip Babcock were ordained by the Trinity Baptist Church of Imlay, Michigan, on January 3, 1952.

Also in 1952 Morris Shirk was ordained by the First Baptist Church of Kent City, Michigan; Gerald Winters by the Berean Baptist Church of Grand Rapids; William Lancaster by First Baptist Church of Ferndale, Washington; Anthony Bourdess by Faith Baptist Church of Kansas City, Kansas; Robert Golike and Delbert Golike by Berean Baptist Church in Bunker Hill, Illinois; Paul Hubble and Edwin Henry by the Berean Missionary Baptist Church in Indianapolis; Clinton Housley by Garfield Avenue Baptist Church in Milwaukee; David E. Smith by First Baptist Church of Oakfield, Michigan; Gordon R. Lewis by First Baptist Church, Johnson City, New York.

Other men ordained in 1952 included Harold Carpenter by Struthers Baptist Tabernacle of Ohio; Hugh Rogers by Independent Baptist Church of Towanda, Pennsylvania; Charles Benedict by Nepperhan Avenue Baptist Church in Yonkers, New York; Paul King by East Leonard Baptist Church of Grand Rapids; Clarence Jeffers by First Baptist Church of Walnut Creek, California; Ward Harris by First Baptist Church of Shell Rock, Iowa; Raymond Dunn by the Fundamental Baptist Tabernacle of Medina, New York; Alfred Gerhardt and Charles Reif by Haddon Heights (New Jersey) Baptist Church; Eldon Brock and Dewey O'Dell by the Riverside Baptist Church in Decatur, Illinois; Edward Helmick and Devere Mayo by First Baptist Church of LaGrange, Ohio; Charles Livingwood by First Baptist Church of Hackensack, New Jersey; Richard Ahlgrim by Glen Park Baptist Church of Gary, Indiana; Leon Ditzell by Calvary Baptist Church of Trumansburg, New York; Kenneth F. Houser by Calvary Baptist Church in Sandusky, Ohio; Glen Gustafson by First Baptist

Church of Big Rapids, Michigan; Benjamin Garlich, Jr., by Berean Baptist Church in Youngstown, Ohio; Paul Gelatt, Jr., by Park Avenue Baptist Church of Binghamton, New York; Clifford Birdsall and Floyd Kester by Shickshinny (Pennsylvania) Protestant Church, Independent Baptist Testimony (aren't you glad that you read far enough to discover that name?!); Roscoe Smith by First Baptist Church in Mount Upton, New York; John Strong by First Baptist Church, Johnson City, New York; Calvin Rumley by Grandview Park Baptist Church in Des Moines, Iowa; Philip Peterson by Bible Baptist Church in Greenport, New York; Vernon Chandler by West Endicott (New York) Baptist Church; Paul A. Bustrum by College Baptist Church of Oakland, California; Truman Jingst by the Calvary Baptist Church of Quincy, Illinois; Vernon Weber by First Baptist Church of Mishawaka, Indiana; and Earl Dannenberg by First Baptist Church of Holland, Michigan.

In 1953 Allan Davis was ordained by First Baptist Church of Caldwell, New Jersey; Richard Turley by First Baptist Church of Hempstead, New York; Maurice L. Wilcox by Eighth Avenue Baptist Church of Sacramento, California; Virgil Bopp by Walnut Street Baptist Church in Waterloo, Iowa; Donald Waite by Berea Baptist Church of Berea, Ohio; Robert Cooley by Berean Baptist Church of Grand Rapids; Robert Chest by Ames Baptist Church of Ames, New York; Herbert Miller by Bible Baptist Church in Mount Vision, New York; Russell Shedd by Hydewood Park Baptist Church in Plainfield, New Jersey; Roland P. Globig by South Baptist Church of Flint, Michigan; Ronald Bantle by First Baptist Church of Hamburg, New York; Glen Schwenk by Galena Baptist Church of LaPorte, Indiana; Keith L. Gilmore by Bible Mission Baptist Church of Dresden, Ohio; Milton Barkley by Berean Baptist Church of Grand Rapids; Willard Reimer by First Baptist Church of Williamstown, Michigan; Clarke Spalding, Jr., by Northside Baptist Church of Lorain, Ohio.

Other men ordained in 1953 were John Wesley Depue by the Bridgewater Baptist Church of Montrose, Pennsylvania; Delbert Harrell by Lewis Avenue Baptist Church of Toledo, Ohio; Walter Buck by First Baptist Church of Onaway, Michigan; Guy Godfrey by Bethany Baptist Church of Los Angeles; Stuart Hussey and Thomas H. Price by the Trinity Baptist Church in Pasadena, California; Ralph R. Canfield by the First Baptist Church of Oak Park, Michigan; J. Allen Aardsma by Bible Baptist Church of Massapequa, New York; Merritt Dayton by the Venice Baptist Church of Venice Center, New York; Dr. Ralph

Montanus and Randall Speirs by First Baptist Church of Flushing, New York; Charles Cuthbertson by Evansville Baptist Church of Niles, Ohio; J. Woodrow Wright by Brown Street Baptist Church of Akron, Ohio; Jay DeBoer by the Calvary Baptist Church of Battle Creek, Michigan; James O. Taylor by Calvary Baptist Church of Mannington, West Virginia; Joseph Balbach by Englishville Baptist Church in Sparta, Michigan; Donald H. Opfer by the Grove Avenue Baptist Church of Racine, Wisconsin; Edwin S. Eloe and Robert E. Meyer by Grace Baptist Church in Omaha, Nebraska; David Wuth by Hayfork (California) Baptist Church; Willis Virtue by First Baptist Church of Johnson City, New York; Virgil Bunjer by Fundamental Baptist Church of Belmond, Iowa; Donald Worch by Immanuel Baptist Church of Arcanum, Ohio; Thomas Bunyan by Grace Baptist Church of Springfield, Massachusetts; Floyd A. Davis by Independent Baptist Church of North Jackson, Ohio; Gene Barnes by California Heights Baptist Church of Long Beach; Lynn Rogers and Richard Durham by Berea Baptist Church of Berea, Ohio; Jerome Casner by Immanuel Baptist Church of Columbus, Ohio; and Jack Dorris by First Baptist Church of Troy, Illinois.

In 1954 Charles Hawkins was ordained by First Baptist Church, Russell, Iowa; William Wood by Missionary Baptist Church, Michigan City, Indiana; Clifford Phillips by Cedar Avenue Baptist Church in Fresno, California; William Shellhammer by First Baptist Church of Newark Valley, New York; Robert Bearss by the North Chester Baptist Church of Conklin, Michigan; Charles R. Jones by the First Baptist Church of Fremont, Michigan.

Other men ordained in 1954 included Cletis Leverett by the Berean Baptist Church in Bunker Hill, Illinois; Martin E. Holmes by the First Baptist Church of Wauseon, Ohio; Carl Holwerda by Wealthy Street Baptist Church in Grand Rapids; Edwin H. Colson and Elwin W. Colson by Walnut Street Baptist Church in Waterloo, Iowa; Robert Evans by Eastside Baptist Church in Lorain, Ohio; Philip S. Lacy by Calvary Baptist Church of Onaga, Kansas; Ralph J. Poulson by First Baptist Church of Ferndale, Washington; Harold Cobb by First Baptist Church of Hallstead, Pennsylvania; Donald Geary by Grace Baptist Church of Smith Center, Kansas; Scott Janikula by Galilee Baptist Church, Seattle, Washington; William Compton by Memorial Baptist Church of Columbus, Ohio; Ed Woltzen by Temple Baptist Church in Omaha, Nebraska; Keith McIver by First Baptist Church, Lowell,

Michigan; and Daniel E. Gelatt by West Smyrna (New York) Baptist Church.

In 1955 Dr. David Seymour was ordained by the Grace Baptist Church of Binghamton, New York; Willis D. Booth by Faith Baptist Church of Strathmore, California; Gordon Wimer by First Baptist Church of Butler, Pennsylvania; Albert Crawford by Parr Memorial Baptist Church of Petoskey, Michigan; Frank Odor by First Baptist Church of LaGrange, Ohio; Merle Wood by First Baptist Church of Clarkston, Washington; Ralph G. Colas by Elimsport (Pennsylvania) Baptist Church; Stanley Brittain by Woodward Avenue Baptist Church of Grand Rapids; Dr. Jon Rouch by First Baptist Church of Mentone, Indiana; William Russell by Brookside Baptist Church of Cleveland; Frank McQuade and James Smith by the First Baptist Church of Hackensack, New Jersey; William B. Patterson, Jr., by Calvary Baptist Church of Cleveland; Louis Miller by Botna (Iowa) Baptist Church; Bruce Lemmen by Wealthy Street Baptist Church of Grand Rapids; and Willis Stitt by Seward Avenue Baptist Church of Topeka, Kansas.

In 1956 Alfred E. Nelson was ordained by First Baptist Church of Rochester, Michigan; Harold Willmington by Calvary Baptist Church in Quincy, Illinois; Gerald Russell by Calvary Baptist Church of Bellflower, California; George Slaughenhaupt by First Baptist Church of Hamburg, New York; Robert V. Dyer by Lynnwood Baptist Church of Lynnwood, Washington; Harold Green and Willis W. Hull by West Endicott Baptist Church of Endicott, New York; H. David Matson by First Baptist Church of Plymouth, Indiana.

Also ordained in 1956 were W. Robert Mattox by First Baptist Church of Johnson City, New York; George Bailey by North Baptist Church of Rochester, New York; Charles T. Butrin by Clintonville Baptist Church in Columbus, Ohio; Harold Proper by Birchwood Baptist Tabernacle of Elmira Heights, New York; Stanley Manus by Calvary Baptist Church, Concord, California; Donald Messenger by Union Baptist Church of Spencer, New York; Gerald Thurber and John Thurber by Silvis Heights (Illinois) Baptist Church; Alan Ames by Community Baptist Church of Stockton, New York; Gerald Montgomery by Tabernacle Baptist Church of Hazel Park, Michigan; Earle C. Harriman by Camden Baptist Church, Kipton, Ohio; and Robert Rogers by Berea (Ohio) Baptist Church.

In 1957 Ernest Francis, Russell Carnagey and Frank Hartwig were ordained by Calvary Baptist Church of Highland, Indiana; Donald

Drake by First Baptist Church of Hackensack, New Jersey; Paul Mayo by Berlin Heights (Ohio) Baptist Church; David Moore by Walnut Street Baptist Church of Waterloo, Iowa; Ira L. Howden by the First Baptist Church of Harvey, Illinois; Lee Webb by Cedar Avenue Baptist Church of Fresno, California; Vern L. Prugh and Virgil W. Moneysmith by the Burton Avenue Baptist Church of Waterloo, Iowa.

The year 1957 also saw the ordination of Jake Schopf by the Clover Creek Baptist Church, Tacoma, Washington; Richard Harding by Grace Baptist Church, Attleboro, Massachusetts; Gordon Shipp by First Baptist Church of Farmington, Iowa; Knute Orton by Temple Baptist Church, Omaha, Nebraska; George Ahlgrim by Glen Park Baptist Church of Gary, Indiana; Robert Barrett by the First Baptist Church of Buffalo, New York; Donald A. Parvin by First Baptist Church of Ogden, Pennsylvania; Richard Tice by First Baptist Church of Wilmington, California; Norman Walters by Coronado Baptist Church, Tucson, Arizona; Wallace A. Alcorn by the Garfield Avenue Baptist Church, Milwaukee; Robert Cowley, Roger Williams and Donn Ketcham by Belden Avenue Baptist Church of Chicago; Leonard A. Swanson by Prairie Dell Baptist Church of Iroquois, Illinois; Paul A. Heiniger by First Baptist Church of Grundy Center, Iowa; Howard Bolthouse by North Chester Baptist Church, Conklin, Michigan; William J. McClain by Lake City Baptist Church, Seattle, Washington; George Huffman and Charles Johnson by Glen Park Baptist Church, Gary, Indiana; and Myron Williams by East Side Baptist Church, Lorain, Ohio.

In 1958 Ralph Kemmerer was ordained by First Baptist Church, Galion, Ohio; Clifford Lones by the Blessed Hope Baptist Church of Springfield, Ohio; John L. Schroder by First Baptist Church, Austin, Minnesota; Harold Albert by Bible Baptist Church, Huntington Park, California; Elmer Davis by First Baptist Church, Plainfield, Illinois; David Henrikson by the Community Baptist Church, Silver Lake, Wisconsin; Donald Matheny by Rochester (Ohio) Baptist Church; Roy Watkins by Fundamental Baptist Tabernacle, Medina, New York; Jay Walsh by Lakeview (Michigan) Baptist Church; Kenneth Jobson by the First Baptist Church, Santa Susana, California; John Trautman by First Baptist Church, Angelica, New York

Others ordained in 1958 were George C. Berglund by the Grace Baptist Church, Austin, Minnesota; Russell Farrell by Grandview Park Baptist Church, Des Moines, Iowa; Robert Shackelford by Yeddo

(Indiana) Baptist Church; Richard McIntosh by Calvary Baptist Church, Norwalk, Ohio; Desmond J. Bell by Garfield Avenue Baptist Church, Milwaukee; Charles A. Nichols by First Baptist Church, Spearfish, South Dakota; Daniel Zimmerman by First Baptist Church, Grundy Center, Iowa; Leslie G. Newell by Federal Way (Washington) Baptist Church; William Buhrow by Cedar Hill Baptist Church, Cleveland, Ohio; Arthur Walton by Calvary Baptist Church, Meadville, Pennsylvania; and Paul Tassell by Emmanuel Baptist Church, Toledo, Ohio.

In 1959 Carlo Feriante was ordained by the Tabernacle Baptist Church, Seattle, Washington; Raymond Hill by the Temple Baptist Church, Tacoma, Washington; Paul Mathis by Bible Baptist Church, Huron, South Dakota; Francis Grubbs by First Baptist Church, Morristown, Minnesota; James F. Carmichael and Carl D. Ferguson by the South Baptist Church, Bay City, Michigan; Darrell R. Bice by the Litchfield (Ohio) Baptist Church; Lawrence Armstrong by First Baptist Church, Johnson City, New York; Wilbur E. Herzog by First Baptist Church, Pinole, California; William Burchett by First Baptist Church, Dunkirk, New York; Wayne K. Anderson by Newhall Baptist Church, Grand Rapids; Robert Obenchain by Temple Baptist Church, Boise, Idaho.

Other men ordained in 1959 included Robert Whatley by Community Baptist Church, Red Bluff, California; Herwin Scheltema by Wealthy Street Baptist Church, Grand Rapids; Ernest Thompson by Riverdale Baptist Church, Flint, Michigan; Norman Sanders by First Baptist Church, Bay City, Michigan; Willard Benedict by Nepperhan Avenue Baptist Church, Yonkers, New York; Raymond Guenther, Jr., by Burholme Baptist Church, Philadelphia; Roy L. Swanson by Tabernacle Baptist Church, Ithaca, New York; Richard R. Nelson by Maine (New York) Baptist Church; Walter Kronemeyer by Calvary Baptist Church, Grand Rapids; William Brown by the Calvary Baptist Tabernacle, Los Angeles; Edwin Metzler and Donald Hamman by the First Baptist Church, Mishawaka, Indiana; L. Duane Brown by First Baptist Church, Canton, Pennsylvania; Louis C. Tulga by the First Regular Baptist Church, Wellington, Ohio; W. C. Reynolds, Jr., by the Windsor Village Baptist Church, Indianapolis, Indiana; Leigh Adams by Oswego (New York) Baptist Tabernacle; and Jesse Eaton by Calvary Baptist Church, Lockport, New York.

End Notes

1. Merle R. Hull, "Editorials," *Baptist Bulletin* (August 1959), p. 7.

2. Ibid., p. 14.

3. Murray Murdoch, *Portrait of Obedience* (Schaumburg, IL: Regular Baptist Press, 1979), pp. 258, 259.

4. R. T. Ketcham, "An Open Letter from Dr. Ketcham," *Baptist Bulletin* (November 1959), pp. 10, 11.

5. Merle R. Hull, *What A Fellowship!* (Schaumburg, IL: Regular Baptist Press, 1981), p. 35.

26

The long months of the 1959–60 Chicago winter and the balmy 1960 spring days were not easy days or months for Robert T. Ketcham. His strength had been drained by the heart attack, and he knew he would be unable to carry on the demanding schedule he once had. He finally decided, after prayerful evaluation of his health and the needs of the Association, that his resignation as national representative was in order. He traveled to Long Beach, California, site of the June 1960 conference, with a settled heart.

This book is the record of the GARBC, and it surely would be incomplete without the full text of Ketcham's resignation and the full response of the Council of Fourteen and the conference messengers.

Beloved:

It has been my high joy and great honor to serve you as your National Representative for nearly twelve years.

As I walk through the halls of memory, I find its walls hung with some of the richest pictures of my forty-eight years in the Gospel ministry.

These have been perilous years. We have together come through crisis after crisis, as we have moved in one solid phalanx against the enemies of God, His Son, and His Word. We have had the constant joy of standing together in a great and growing Fellowship, as we have raised and maintained a witness to the glory of Christ, our Savior. The high and holy privilege of being one of your leaders in these glorious years has been accepted by me as a blessed commission by God Himself. The ministry of these years together will linger always as a sweet perfume of memory sanctified by the touch of His hand of blessing.

Since the founding of the GARBC in 1932, we have seen it grow from 22 churches to 932. We have seen the missionary giving of the churches reach the peak of almost four million dollars per year. We have seen many hundreds of new churches established and multiplied millions of dollars spent in the erection of new church buildings and the enlargement of old ones. And best of all, instead of a tapering off in all of these blessed accomplishments for our Lord, there is an increasing tempo of sacrifice, giving, and service in every area of our field of witness. For what small share God has given me during these twelve years in helping to bring this to pass, I am indeed grateful to Him and to you.

As an Association, however, we have not yet even come close to the possibilities of accomplishment which lie all around us. We must gird ourselves with ever greater determination to arise and possess the land than has characterized us in the past. Because of the increasing responsibility which rests upon all of us, I am convinced that I am no longer able to carry the terrific load of leadership which must rest upon your National Representative. As you know, one year ago a heart attack nearly took me Home. God, in His grace and in answer to your prayers, saw fit to restore me to practically a normal state of health. Severe damage was done to the heart, however, so while I feel well, I know I am not well. If I preserve my strength for less strenuous duties, I can have several years of active service in less responsible fields.

In view of my own somewhat limited capacity for the arduous tasks of the past, and realizing that someone else should be selected for this post, I hereby tender my resignation as your National Representative, at once. This does not mean that my love, prayers and service on behalf of this blessed Fellowship will cease. If I can be of service in any way whatsoever, I am yours to command.

Since you, as a Council, must now address yourselves to the task of selecting and recommending a new National Representative, and as an Association, you must prayerfully seek to know God's will, you shall have a constant and large place in my prayer ministry, that God's man for this hour will be made apparent to you and to him.

With every good wish, I am
Yours and His,
R. T. Ketcham
National Representative[1]

As Dr. Ketcham addressed the Council of Fourteen on that Thursday evening, June 16, 1960, in Long Beach, each Council member responded sympathetically and with some measure of sadness to his words. All were deeply grateful for what God had done through the dozen years of Dr. Ketcham's leadership.

On the following Monday night Dr. Ketcham read his resignation to the crowd of messengers gathered in the Long Beach Municipal Auditorium. Dr. Robert L. Powell then read a statement of appreciation and commendation (which is printed in full below) with the expressed desire that Ketcham remain in the home office as National Consultant as his strength permitted. After a long and moving standing ovation, the resignation was officially accepted. What a service it was! It opened with the congregation gloriously singing "Revive Us Again" and "Blessed Assurance" led by Pastor Harold Scholes and ended with a tremendous message by Dr. Carl Elgena from Titus 2:11. Dr. Elgena focused on the grace of God, which has made the sinner *redeemable,* our salvation *reliable* and the saint *responsible.*

Following is "A Statement Regarding Dr. Robert T. Ketcham":

In the course of normal human events, it must needs be that some of us serve our God for His appointed years. Then, by reason of failing strength, we find it inevitable that high and holy responsibilities must be passed on, as a sacred heritage, to the hands of others. Such experiences often cause great shock and sorrow to those who have loved, served and rejoiced together in the blessed ministries of God-ordained leaders in holy causes. Such a time has come to pass in the affairs of the General Association of Regular Baptist Churches in the resignation of our beloved and long-cherished leader, Dr. Robert Thomas Ketcham.

Having received the resignation of Dr. Ketcham as our National Representative, and being forced by circumstances beyond our control to act upon same, it seems most fitting that we should try to express to him, and to the entire brotherhood, our deep sentiment in regard to such a step.

We record herewith our abiding love of, and deep respect for, this man of God. Under Divine providence he has led the forces of independent Baptists for well over a quarter of a century. This leadership has eventuated in a New Testament fellowship of true believers, known as the General Association of Regular Baptist Churches.

We count it a joy that in the mercy of God, this man came "to the kingdom" for such a day as we have been passing through. He has shown great spiritual discernment through these years as he has rendered glorious service to God and his brethren. All of us are better Christians, better servants of our Lord and better warriors in the holy crusade for Truth because of God's rich bestowments upon and through him.

Our acceptance of Dr. Ketcham's resignation is with the deepest sense of loss. Yet it is tempered with the joy that God has spared him to us by bringing him back from the brink of the grave. This has been in answer to the fervent prayers of thousands of faithful servants of our glorious Savior.

We are happy to announce that he has consented to remain in a position of blessed service with us. He will be assuming at our request a place of employment more in keeping with his limited strength—that of National Consultant. We thank God for His gracious providence in allowing us to have our dearly beloved brother in our hearts and Fellowship a while longer.

It is altogether fitting on this occasion that we, the Council of Fourteen, bring to the entire Fellowship the sentiments which we all feel for our brother, Dr. Ketcham. Words are inadequate vehicles through which to convey deep emotions; but as best we can, we do, on behalf of this Baptist body, express to him our abiding love.

As a group of Regular Baptists we also extend our expressions of continued love and appreciation to Mrs. Ketcham. We trust that the future days of ministry for both of these dear servants may be rich and fruitful under God.[2]

This statement of action was unanimously adopted at the GARBC conference in Long Beach, California, June 20–24, 1960.

The above action of the Association messengers was formally presented to Dr. Ketcham in scroll form, with a typewritten copy for his files.

One man who worked closely with Dr. Ketcham for a number of years, Dr. Merle R. Hull, paid this tribute to Ketcham:

Those who knew Dr. Ketcham only through his preaching or writing could have concluded he was a firm, resolute—almost fearsome person to work with. He was firm; and he was resolute. But he was also a man of consideration and compassion. He was generous in his praise of office personnel. And fun! Visualize him waving a glass of Metrecal (a weight-reducing product, if you've forgotten) in one hand and a sweet roll in the other. They balanced each other off, he said! Hear him shouting into the radio to encourage his beloved White Sox. At office parties he was always ready for charades or any other kind of game. Start him telling stories about his Pennsylvania boyhood—getting his tongue stuck on a frozen ax head . . . marching straight ahead while the rest of the band had turned a corner—and you were in for some wholesome, hearty laughter. Working with him was fortunate, not fearsome.[3]

Dr. Ketcham's life and ministry did not end with his resignation in 1960; he served as the National Consultant for six years and lived beyond 1960 by 18 years! We will meet him again in a later chapter. The next chapter is a sermon by Dr. Ketcham.

End Notes

1. "Text of Dr. Ketcham's Resignation as National Representative," *Baptist Bulletin* (August 1960), p. 20.

2. "A Statement Regarding Dr. Robert T. Ketcham," *Baptist Bulletin* (August 1960), p. 21.

3. Merle R. Hull, *What A Fellowship!* (Schaumburg, IL: Regular Baptist Press, 1981), p. 32.

27

CALEB—THE MAN OF GOD

Robert T. Ketcham

It was crisis time in Israel. They were now ordered to move on into the possession of Canaan. They had sent some spies, you will recall, to find whether God had told the truth about His land. Back in Egypt God had described the land; but now that they were about ready to enter it, somebody suggested it would be a good thing to go and see what kind of a land it was! This, in itself, was a bad beginning. If you have a word from God, you don't need to spy on Him to know whether He is telling the truth. But twelve of them went.

Now the reports were in, and ten described the land as they had seen it. There is one interesting thing in the majority report that I think we ought to look at. They said, "And there we saw the giants; then we saw ourselves and we were grasshoppers in our sight; and so were we in theirs."

I have always thought that was somewhat of an accusation on the part of these ten against the giants of the land. I can just hear them saying to one another as they went back to camp: "That was a terrible thing that those giants should think of us as grasshoppers! They should have had more respect for us than that!"

Well, now, who started this grasshopper business anyhow? No giant said, "You're a grasshopper," until they said it themselves! They said they were grasshoppers, so why get so hurt and offended when the giants agreed with them! Apparently they said, "Now look, Mr. Giant, we *are* grasshoppers, and if you won't step on us we'll hop right back home and we'll never hop over here anymore." That was the majority report of the ten.

The minority report said it was a good land, and if God was pleased with them, they were well able to possess it. They wanted to go and take it over, but the crowd rose up to stone them.

I say it was crisis time in Israel. But God had a man. In fact, He had two men; but I can take time to deal with only one of them—the one who plays the prominent part in the immediate picture. God had a man in the hour of crisis. God always has men in the hour of crisis. A thousand cowards may be refusing to take their stand; but in every crisis that has ever confronted God's people, thank God one or two have been around who were God's men in the hour of crisis. Caleb was God's man for this crisis hour. Because he stood true, regardless of what others did, he found the reward they missed.

Today it is crisis time again for the people of God. It isn't Hittites, Jebusites, Perizzites or any other "ite" that has confronted the Church of Jesus Christ in this century. It is another crowd bearing different names and appellations. *Modernism.* Old-fashioned modernism. Bold, blatant modernism. A modernism that speaks of Jesus Christ as the Son of a German soldier without a blush of the cheek or a bat of the eyelash. A modernism that denies the very existence of God and says that any Messiah, "even though his name be Jesus," is "a dangerous man."

We move from that camp of the enemy into the camp of *neo-orthodoxy.* We can only mention these citadels in which the enemies of God's Church are entrenched. Neoorthodoxy came along with its protestations against the bold, blatant modernism of the old-fashioned school and said that they were going to come a little nearer orthodoxy. But when we study carefully what they have to say, we discover they say the same thing as the old-fashioned modernists, only in more subtle language.

Then along came *neoliberalism.* It professed to move a little closer to the orthodox and a little farther away from the heterodox and the neoorthodox. But when we analyze the position of the neoliberals, we discover they are no better and no nearer truth than the neoorthodox.

In my opinion, the most dangerous of all the enemies that have joined in creating the crisis hour for the Church of Jesus Christ is *neoevangelicalism.* That is the most dangerous of all. I can enter the pulpit anywhere; I can take my editorial pen and write as I please in the most blistering fashion in the denunciation of a Fosdick, a Nels Ferre or a Duncan Littlefair. And everybody in fundamentalist schools and churches will applaud me. But when I have to expose schools that have announced themselves as thoroughly evangelical and fundamental; when I have to combat men whose names have for years been household bywords of fundamentalists; when I have to cross bats and engage in arguments with men like Charlie Fuller, Harold Ockenga, Carl Henry and John Carnell; when I have to warn God's people against the compromise of such as these—instead of receiving applause, I am condemned.

You may as well get ready for the same treatment if you are going to be a modern Caleb. The hour is an hour of crisis, and it is heightened and brought to this point of danger—not by modernists, not by the neoorthodox, not by neoliberals. The crisis hour that confronts the Church of Jesus Christ in this particular day is the crisis that has been brought into existence by neoevangelicalism. This is where you will have to take your stand if you are going to be true to the Word of God.

Another element that adds to the crisis hour of the Church of Jesus Christ today is *ecumenicalism.* We are confronted with the idea everywhere that we should all get together in a great world church. We are told that all the fundamentalists should get together, regardless of how many entangling alliances some of the fundamentalists may have. Just because a man says he believes in the deity of Christ and all the rest of the things which we believe, we should cooperate with him in anything he wants to do. That seems to be the pattern of the day. But you may as well know now—and not have to find it out with bitter heartache later on—that you cannot cooperate with the fundamentalist who, on one hand, wants you to cooperate with him while, on the other hand, he cooperates with the modernists.

Another element that adds to the crisis hour of the Church of Jesus Christ is *worldliness.* We have had a lot to say about separation from apostasy. We need to speak out just as much, just as earnestly and just as pointedly about separation from the world. This is one of the things that startled me as I read Carnell's book, *The Case for Orthodox Christianity.* He calls the fundamentalists a "cult" and says the only reason we fundamentalists do not go to the movies is because we are afraid that if some other fundamentalist sees us going we will lose our standing in "the cult." He takes us all to task for being so radical against the dance. He says the Bible teaches the dance as a means to culture. It is a cultural thing. This is from a professor in what many people consider to be the outstanding fundamentalist school in this country. These are crisis hours! And somebody is going to have to stand up and face it and be counted.

Added to all of these is a spirit of *cowardice.* And underlying all of these is *shallow thinking.* Men do not think anymore. Radio, television and what-have-you have robbed us of the art of thinking. It seems pathetic and tragic to me that people cannot even put two and two together in a theological formula and come up with four as the answer.

I recall speaking with a group of men who were defending a certain section of the professed world of Christianity, arguing that this denomination did not deny the deity and the Virgin Birth of Jesus Christ. These men had read an article by Dr. Barnhouse, who said that this particular group was evangelical and ought to be admitted to the fraternity of evangelical denominations. Someone was arguing with me that this should be done. I said, "Well, I don't quite know how we can admit to the fraternity of evangelical denominations a denomination that denies the Virgin Birth of Jesus Christ."

"Oh," they said, "Dr. Ketcham, they don't deny it! Dr. Barnhouse says they don't."

So I quoted this sentence from page 62 of *The Desire of Ages:* "The people of Jesus' day came to him with their sorrows and their problems rather than to his brothers. This caused his brothers to be jealous because, being older than Jesus, they considered that they should have been the ones who received the attention."

After I quoted this statement to the group I was conversing with, every one of them sound fundamentalists (in fact, two of them fundamentalist preachers), I said, "Do you see anything wrong with that?"

Not one in the group of 11 people could think deeply enough to put two and two together and come up with the answer. They were so startled when I pointed out to them that if Jesus had older brothers, then He could not be *virgin-born.* They said, "Why, that is so!"

What I would like to know is why they had to wait for someone to come along and tell them so. Shallow thinking! Think! Think! Think! Get your Bible out and think it through; go to the bottom of its propositions and any proposition that is given you. Don't just ride along on the surface. Think your way through things like this, and you will come up with the answer.

Modernism, neoorthodoxy, neoliberalism, neoevangelicalism, ecumenicalism, compromise, worldliness, cowardice and shallow thinking all add up to just one thing in our day, namely, *crisis!*

Well, for hours like this we need some modern Calebs. These are days of hurricanes, tornadoes and earthquakes in old, established lines. The political world is being torn apart in an upheaval. It is utterly astounding to say nothing of frightening to see how men in high political realms seem to be unable to grasp the whole political situation that confronts the world today. Why in the wide world we just don't withdraw our ambassadors from Russia and close the door, only Heaven knows. Our own politicians are at each other's throats over issues, and nobody seems to have the answer. We are in an upheaval not only in the political world but in the educational world, the social world, the moral world and, God knows, the religious world. All these things are shaken and are being torn to pieces around us. If anyone had told me just a few years ago that we would be in the crisis that we are confronted with now in these various realms, especially in the realm that we call neoevangelicalism, I would have said he was a radical fundamentalist, too radical for even me. But these few short years have shown us that spiritual giants, theological giants are falling all around us. Political giants are falling all around us. Educational giants are falling all around us. The walls are breaking down everywhere!

Now I would like to make two or three observations concerning this man Caleb so that we might do our best to emulate him.

You will notice one thing said about him: He followed the Lord fully. He followed the Lord *fully.* He followed the Lord. He did not run ahead of Him in a wild fanaticism and a careless enthusiasm. He did not lag behind Him in a cowardly lethargy. He *followed* the Lord.

Two serious afflictions may lay hold upon the human body. One of them is paralysis. I remember going to the bedside of a dear old saint of God whose left side had been paralyzed for years. I said to her, "I'm sure you won't mind if I ask you to do something for me so that I may use it as an illustration."

She said, "If it's anything that's going to help you preach the gospel, Pastor, go ahead."

I said, "Would you mind moving that left hand of yours up to your cheek?"

She looked at me and smiled with a wry smile—one side of her face was all that could smile—and said, "Pastor, you know I can't do that."

I said, "Well, you just go ahead now and tell that hand to come up there. Order it to do it."

I shall never forget the look of determination that came upon that poor face as with all the energy and the power of her mind she ordered that left hand of hers to come up and touch her cheek. It remained quiet at her side. Her body would not obey her will.

We are the Body of Jesus Christ. And that's true of individuals, too, for He dwells within us. Did it ever occur to you to ask yourself the question, "Why did God purchase our bodies?" We are told in the Corinthian epistle that our bodies were purchased by the same awful price that was paid for the souls in them.

Christianity is not a set of principles or doctrines, although our principles and our doctrines must be correct. Christianity is a *Person*—the Person of Christ Himself living *His life* out through our bodies. Galatians 2:20 sets this forth with crystal clearness: *"Christ* liveth in me"; that is, in my *body.*

What could one do without a body? Absolutely nothing! The singer needs a body through which to display his talents. He couldn't sing without a throat. The pianist must have a body, or no one would ever hear him play. The housewife needs a body so she can cook her meals and keep her house. The carpenter must have a body, or he cannot saw a board or build a house. No matter how brilliant or talented one may be, he is absolutely helpless without a body.

Is it too much to suggest that this same truth applies to Christ? Christ must have a *body* through which He can display His manifold graces and powers. Beloved, that is exactly why He purchased our *bodies* with His precious blood. He is limited in this age to what He can do through these bodies of ours. He has no hands down here now but ours. He has no vocal organs down here now but ours. He has no feet but ours. That is why He bought this equipment (1 Cor. 6:19, 20). He is as helpless in this age without a body as we would be.

We are by no means belittling the power of Christ. Of course He can do anything He wants to, *but in this age He has voluntarily limited Himself to what He can do through yielded believers.* True it is that God is sovereign. But if God cannot limit His own sovereignty then He is not sovereign. For purposes best known to Himself, he has chosen to do His work in and through the yielded bodies of believers—bodies which He purchased for that express purpose. Oh, that God's own would lay hold upon this amazing truth. Our bodies are not simply the encasement of a saved soul. They are the dwelling place of the Lord. They are His to use as He will in the display of Himself.

Does He ask too much when He asks for the full possession of what He bought? Certainly not. This is *Christianity:* Christ living *His life* through a purchased body. When the Lord within us orders us to do thus and so, and we do not do it, we are a paralytic member. And just in proportion to the paralysis that we engage in or allow to take place in our individual lives, just in that proportion we slow up the output of the whole Church of Jesus Christ. If my left hand should become paralyzed tonight, you would see me tomorrow going around with my shoes untied. That's why the world sees the Church of Jesus Christ limping down the path when she ought to be marching as a great conquering host. There are too many spiritual paralytics. They are not obeying Him.

Then, of course, another difficulty is known as Saint Vitus's dance, which is an excessive activity. This is comparable to the fanaticism and the wildfireism of radicals. The Lord God needs men and women who will follow Him, not run ahead of Him in a fanatical separation, in a fanatical statement about situations, and not lag behind in a cowardly lethargy.

There is another way in which Caleb followed the Lord fully. He did not say, "I will do this but I will not do that." To follow the Lord fully is to do anything He commands. Our Lord said, "Ye are my friends, if ye do whatsoever I command you." Calebs do not pick and choose, they just *obey.* Caleb was just as ready to fight the giants as he was to carry the grapes. So many people are ready to do the sweet, the easy and the lovely friend-making duties; but when the defense of the name of Jesus Christ causes them to lose their friends or even a church, they draw back from following the Lord fully. Oh, it is so lovely to run around with a bunch of the grapes of Eshcol on your shoulder and to give everybody a grape. But to go over and take a giant in a public debate and in a position of separation and loyalty to the cause and Word of Jesus Christ, when your own friends will not understand you—that takes a Caleb!

I think Elijah had something of this in his experience. You remember he told Ahab off, then Jezebel told him off, and then he ran. Perhaps it was a good thing—when a woman like Jezebel gets after you, maybe you had better run. But I am reminded that after he ran (somebody said he ran nearly 100 miles), he sat down under that juniper tree and said, "Now, Lord, I only am left; let me die."

Now, of course, Elijah didn't want to die; he just thought he did.

If he really had wanted to die, there was a woman 100 miles back there just waiting to accommodate him; he would not have taken that marathon. He could have had it all over by this time if he had just waited around for Jezebel.

But it is what the Lord said to Elijah that interests me. He said, "Elijah, I have seven thousand who have not bowed the knee to Baal."

Well, I am not Elijah, but had I been I think I know what I would have said. "Lord, did you say there are seven thousand who have not bowed the knee to Baal?"

"Yes, Elijah."

I think I would have said, "Lord, will you trot some of them out here so I can see them?" This is a lonely business, you know. The best the Lord could say about them was "have not." Seven thousand "have-notters" and only one who had really done something about it. Where were they?

To follow the Lord fully means *cheerfully;* that is, without complaint. Obedience that is not cheerful is not obedience. Obedience that is not cheerfully given is essentially disobedience.

Some years ago I had a missionary in my church in Elyria, Ohio. He told us of being in a home on the West Coast where a little fellow got a little out of hand and wouldn't behave. His mother had taken him and set him down with considerable force into a chair. She said, "Now you sit there!" As she walked across the floor, he said, "Mama, I'm standing up inside!"

Did you obey God the last time you obeyed Him because you *had to* or because you *wanted to?* I remember on one particular occasion I went to my church board meeting where I had prayed about a thing for 18 months. The board looked at it for five minutes and threw it out the window. I smiled and said, "Okay." On the way home the Lord said, "Son, did you smile at that board tonight because you wanted to or because you had to?" Yes, we must obey God cheerfully.

To follow fully means to follow *constantly.* Without vacation! The Christian life is a moving picture of a walk. It is not a still picture of a pose. The Christian life isn't a pose of us standing. It is the life that is lived. It is the *constant walk* before the lens of the moving picture camera. No time out; no vacations.

Caleb was a *favored man.* He was spared in the hour of judgment. When the other ten fell by the plague, it was only two men, Joshua and Caleb, who lived in that awful day. So don't worry about the outcome.

Through the ages God's men have been at times the butt of jokes and jeers and gibes. Time has vindicated every one of them, and it will vindicate you. Noah was the butt of jokes and jeers for 120 years. One day he was vindicated. Daniel was at the wrong end of the whole proposition for a long time, but one day God vindicated him. The three Hebrew children were cast into the fiery furnace, but God vindicated them, and so He will you. He may not vindicate you by putting out the fire in the furnace, but He will glorify Himself in you, whether it be by life or by death.

There is a statement in Daniel 3:17 and 18 that I like. Nebuchadnezzar said to three young fellows. "Bow or burn!" Remember what they said? "Our God whom we serve is able to deliver us. . . . But if not, be it known . . . that we will not . . . worship the golden image." I like that. That's the kind of spirit we must have these days. "Our God is able to deliver us and to vindicate us. But if not. . . ." If for some strange mysterious reason He can get greater glory to Himself and produce a greater cumulative testimony and witness by our death, then let it be by death. But in any case it will be vindication.

Caleb was *an honored man.* Years afterward mothers would hold their little children up and say, "See Caleb and Joshua there, the only two men above twenty years of age whom God let live until now."

He would be an honored man at the council table in years to come when the younger men would sit around and say, "What shall we do now?" It was the old gray-haired Caleb who would say, "Well, let's review the history. In the face of all that has taken place in the present situation and in view of all that the Word of God has to say about the future, this is the wise thing to do."

Do you wait for that day when men will come to you, after you have served many years, and say, "Well, there is a person whose judgment is sound and whose leadership we can trust. Let's bring him into our councils." Do you long for a position in the Church of Jesus Christ like that?

Some of us are going toward the sunset. We can no longer sit at your council tables and say, "Young men, this is the way, walk ye in it." You are going to be the honored and the favored men and women in the days ahead. Caleb was a man of a different spirit, an "other spirit." God make you men and women like that.

In colonial days, Governor Endicott ordered that there be no more public prayer of any kind or description. Our Baptist forefather

Obadiah Holmes and others met together in a home to pray. Obadiah Holmes prayed and was cast into prison. People offered to pay his ransom; he refused any easement at all. He was taken to the whipping post, and the record declares that he was so soundly flogged and his body so torn and lacerated that for days he could lie only on the tips of his elbows and on his kneecaps. When the last lash fell, he looked up into the faces of his tormentors and said, "Gentlemen, you have whipped me with roses."

May God make us Calebs like that!

Paul R. Jackson

THE ERA OF PAUL R. JACKSON

1960–1969

28

The United States presidential election of 1960 was one of the most bitterly fought campaigns in our history. John Fitzgerald Kennedy defeated Richard Milhous Nixon 34,227,096 to 34,108,546, a margin of only 118,550 votes out of more than 68 million ballots cast. The biggest issue in the campaign was religion. John Kennedy was a Roman Catholic, and some newsmen and politicians and preachers were concerned over whether a Catholic President could resist pressures from the Pope. Most political observers believe that the turning point in the campaign was on the evening of September 12, when Kennedy spoke to a large crowd of "Protestant" preachers in a hotel ballroom in Houston, Texas.

Kennedy's speech before the Houston ministers was eloquent. He said he would not take orders from the Vatican; and that he would resign as President rather than do so. He said that there were far more critical issues in the campaign and that they should be discussed. . . . In New York, Baltimore, Chicago, and other Northern cities where there were large Catholic populations, expensive television time was purchased by the Democrats to broadcast and rebroadcast the selected portions of the speech made by Kennedy before the Houston ministers.[1]

Kennedy's campaign surged after the Houston confrontation.

In the end, the massive swing of Catholic votes to Kennedy . . . was the biggest factor in Kennedy's election. As Louis Bean put it, the statistics showed that "Catholic pride" was a stronger factor than "anti-Catholic prejudice" in bringing about Kennedy's victory.

With some 78 percent of the Catholics and 70 percent of the Negroes and 80 percent or more of the Jews voting for him, Kennedy took lop-sided majorities in the big cities, and thus in the big electoral-vote states they controlled. Looking at the Catholic vote as a whole, according to figures provided by Dr. George Gallup, the Democrats got 56 percent of the total in 1952, and 51 percent in 1956, but the figure went up by 27 percentage points to 78 percent in 1960. No other religious group showed a switch of that proportion.[2]

At their 1960 annual conference, the GARBC passed the following resolution:

Resolution: Re: Roman Catholicism and the High Political Offices of Presidency and Vice Presidency

Whereas: The historic position of the Roman Catholic Church has been opposed to full religious liberty and the separation of the church and state, as evidenced by Pope Gregory XVI's encyclical *Mirari Vos* in 1832 in which he condemned liberty of conscience, freedom of speech, freedom of the press, and separation of the church and state; and by Pope Pius IX's *Syllabus of Errors* in 1864 in which he insisted on the supremacy of the church's authority and denied the right of every man to the liberty of his own form of worship, and

Whereas: The Roman Catholic Church's *ex cathedra* decrees of Popes are regarded as eternally infallible, and

Whereas: The late Rt. Rev. John A. Ryan of the Catholic University of America and the Rev. Dr. Francis J. Boland of the University of Notre Dame, in their book, *Catholic Principles of Politics,* issued under Cardinal Spellman's *imprimatur,* insist: "Error has not the same rights as truth. Since the profession and practice of error are contrary to human welfare, how can error have rights? How can the toleration of error be justified? If there is only one true religion, and if its possession is the most important good in life for states as well as individuals, then the public profession, protection, and promotion of this religion and the legal prohibition of all direct assaults upon it must become one of the most obvious and fundamental duties of the state, for it is the business of the state to safeguard and promote human welfare in all departments of life." And

Whereas: Another American Catholic theologian, the Rev. Francis J. Connell, has written: "I believe that the state has the right of repression and limitation (although often it is not expedient to use it) when error is doing harm to the spiritual interest of the Catholic citizens. . . . However much we may praise the American system, as far as our land is concerned, it is not *per se* preferable to the system in which the one true church would be acknowledged and specially favored." And

Whereas: In those countries where Catholicism is the predominant religion and enjoys a great measure of state support, as in Spain and Ecuador,

Protestants are harrassed, restricted, and sometimes also persecuted, and

Whereas: A Catholic President in America would be subjected to certain pressures from his church,

Be it resolved: That the General Association of Regular Baptist Churches strongly recommend to both the Republican and Democratic political parties that they do not nominate a Roman Catholic for the high offices of the presidency and/or vice presidency of the United States.[3]

And so 1960 was a tumultuous year for American politics as leadership transfered from one political party to another and from one president to another. Such tumult was not present among Regular Baptists in Long Beach in June of 1960. The Council of Fourteen, after receiving Dr. Ketcham's resignation, had prayerfully settled unanimously on his successor. The man was Paul Rainey Jackson, who had just resigned the presidency of Baptist Bible Seminary in Johnson City, New York, after leading that strategic school from 1946 to 1960. Dr. Jackson was at the time chairman of the Council of Fourteen. The other 13 men who had come to trust and admire his leadership were vice chairman Robert L. Powell, secretary Wilbur C. Rooke, Joseph H. Bower, Carl Brown, Hall Dautel, Raymond F. Hamilton, William E. Kuhnle, Kenneth A. Muck, Harold L. Scholes, Joseph M. Stowell, Carl Sweazy, W. Wilbert Welch and G. Arthur Woolsey. The assembled messengers gathered for the annual conference were just as enthusiastic about Dr. Jackson as was the Council of Fourteen.

Paul R. Jackson was born in Flandreau, South Dakota, on May 16, 1903. When he was just a small boy, his family moved to Wibaux, Montana. Jackson met his future wife, Stella Chappell, on their first day of school in the first grade! When Jackson finished high school, he enrolled at Montana State College to become an electrical engineer. During his freshman year, the Holy Spirit moved upon his heart concerning full-time Christian ministry. The next year found him at Wheaton College, west of Chicago. After his graduation in 1926, he and Stella were married and pastored rural churches in North Dakota from 1926 until 1929.

The First Baptist Church of Strathmore, California, extended a call to Jackson in 1929, and he gladly accepted the invitation. During his five years there he became active in the newly formed California Association of Regular Baptist Churches. He was called to the First Baptist Church of Ceres, California, in 1934. He attended his first GARBC annual conference in Waterloo, Iowa, in 1938. From then on he was increasingly active in the GARBC. The Jackson family moved to Grand Rapids, Michigan, in 1945 in order to serve as interim pastor at Wealthy Street Baptist Church while Pastor David Otis Fuller was serving as a chaplain in the armed forces. He was honored by the Bible Institute of Los Angeles (Biola) with the doctor of divinity degree before he left Ceres.

Dr. Jackson was called to the presidency of Baptist Bible Seminary in Johnson City, New York, in 1946. The school grew under his leadership, and he influenced the lives of hundreds of future leaders for Christ and His Word. After 14 years of fruitful and productive academic life, he resigned just before the 1960 GARBC conference. The Jacksons were parents of Lois, married to Pastor William Russell; Mark and Donn, both longtime preachers.

Dr. Jackson had come to the fore in the 1958 annual conference when he brought the Monday-night keynote address titled "The Position, Attitudes, and Objectives of Biblical Separation," which later became GARBC Literature Item 12. In that message Dr. Jackson demonstrated the same Biblical balance that had characterized his two predecessors, Ketcham and Van Gilder. Regular Baptists had left the Convention in order to be free from denominational dictatorship and doctrinal deviation. That freedom was not for the purpose of simply "bragging" about our separation, but in order to use that freedom to do the real work of the ministry without the crushing weights of apostasy and denominationalism to encumber us. Separation must lead to service. Declared Jackson:

> Separation, as I have so often explained, is to the whole ministry of the Word of God and the service of Jesus Christ what sanitation and sterilization are to surgery. When you go into surgery you are not at all prejudiced against the practice of surgeons, and others who enter that room, to scrub and scrub and scrub! You want every germ destroyed. If there is any possible chance of an infection, you may be the victim of it, and you are well satisfied for sanitation at its ultimate and absolute to mark those who minister to you. But, as a matter of fact, no matter how long the surgeon scrubs, it will do no good until he finally takes hold of the scalpel and the other instruments to perform the surgery. Unless he ministers to you in the other spheres of medical attention, the sanitation is valueless to you. Cleanliness is only the necessary *condition* and *atmosphere* in which the real ministry of the surgeon takes place. It is not an end in itself, but it is an essential condition to the rightful end.[4]

In his tenure as national representative, Dr. Jackson would make that emphasis again and again. In the November 1961 issue of the *Baptist Bulletin* Dr. Jackson gave his "platform" for the GARBC. He listed three great objectives for the Association:

First, we provide fellowship and help for churches, whether they are large or small, old or young. Churches, as well as individuals, *need* fellowship. In isolation we are in danger of one of two evils: *pride* in the presumption that our church alone stands for the truth, or *despair* over the delusion that there are none who stand with us! These snares may be avoided by fellowship with a host of other faithful churches in the GARBC without the danger of being enmeshed in a great ecclesiastical machine. . . . A *second* major objective of the GARBC is to maintain the purity of the churches in doctrine and life. This involves the faithful teaching of the whole counsel of God and the fearless exposure of false doctrine and un-Biblical movements and men. This is not a popular responsibility, but it is a Biblical one! Paul *warns* every man as well as *teaches* every man in all wisdom (Colossians 1:28). . . . A third major objective of the GARBC is the establishment of new churches both at home and abroad. Many of our thousand churches have been founded through recent years. Many hundreds of these New Testament churches have also been established in other lands throughout the world. . . . The GARBC seeks to follow the entire Apostolic program, both as to the message and the methods. These principles have been conveyed to us in the Word of God, and are the marching orders for the churches of our day. Men's needs have not changed, and God's remedies have not changed. We seek therefore to be obedient to this Divine Commission as we encourage and fellowship with one another, exposing the evil that would destroy the souls of men, and go forth into all the world to preach Christ whereby men are saved, baptized, and gathered into New Testament churches. They in turn take up the same torch of truth and continue these God-given tasks until our Lord comes.[5]

As early as 1959 suggestions were made to Doctors Ketcham and Jackson that all agency men be excluded from the Council of Fourteen. In a memo to the Council from Dr. Ketcham, dated May 30, 1959, Dr. Ketcham wrote:

I am a little disturbed about these communications which, in fact, amount to the presentation of an amendment barring all salaried school and mission agency men from the Council. You will recall, brethren, that at Columbus, I suggested that we meet this situation by ourselves offering an amendment stating that not more than two salaried servants of schools or mission boards could be on the Council at the same time. You brethren rejected it on the grounds that it was dictating to the churches who they could and could not nominate for the Council. It was then by the suggestion of one of the school men, as I recall it, that the Council voted a ruled procedure governing their own affairs to the effect that when matters affecting our schools were under discussion, the school men on the Council should leave the Council room. The same was to be true of the mission agency men. I do not think that this restriction which was placed upon the Council by itself, in full agreement with the school men, was sufficiently publicized, which is probably my fault. At any rate, you will have an amendment to be read at Rochester, which will have to be acted upon a year later. During that year maybe we can educate our people to the point where they will not insist on the total elimination of all of our fine school and mission men.[6]

As it turned out, no amendment about Council makeup was presented at Rochester in 1959. The Council chairman, instead, appointed a committee to study the matter. The committee was made up of Joseph M. Stowell, chairman; G. Arthur Woolsey and James T. Jeremiah. At the 1961 conference at Winona Lake, Indiana, the first reading of the amendment was given: "At any one time there must be serving on the Council of Fourteen not less than ten men other than salaried servants of the approved agencies of the Association." These words were to be inserted at the end of the first paragraph of Article VI, Section 1 of the GARBC Constitution. The following year (1962) at Springfield, Massachusetts, the motion to amend was made by David Otis Fuller, seconded by Earl Leiby and carried.

While he was Council chairman, in December of 1959, Dr. Jackson appointed a search committee to find a man who would work as director of public relations for the GARBC and RBP. The committee members were William E. Kuhnle, chairman; and John G. Balyo. At the June 1960 council meeting, Merle R. Hull reported the work of the search committee had been successful and Edgar R. Koons had joined the office staff in April. When Koons saw the GARBC general fund figures in the red, he got an idea! Why not inaugurate a "penny campaign"? Just five pennies from each member in GARBC local churches, and the deficit would be eliminated. So the innovative Mr. Koons went to work and sent to the churches an attractive letter of appeal. A number of churches responded, all sending checks or money orders. Then one morning Pastor Homer Kirchner of the South Side Baptist Church in Chicago appeared in the doorway of Mr. Koons's office. In his hands was a parcel that he deposited on the desk of the surprised Mr. Koons. The contents? Two thousand nine hundred sixteen pennies! Later another parcel of pennies arrived from the Tabernacle Baptist Church of Seattle, Washington, where Pastor Forrest E. Johnson had collected 2,961 pennies! Actually, the best way to keep the general fund in the black is to put the GARBC on your church budget!

By now (1962) 17 people were working in the Transportation Building in Chicago. Their resources were taxed to the limit in preparing for the first Regular Baptist Press Regional Sunday School Workers' Conference at the First Baptist Church of Mishawaka, Indiana, April 5 and 6, 1962. Fred Barlow reported: "The warm hospitality of the local area churches, the fervent ministry of Dr. Louis Paul Lehman, the inspiration and information of the nearly 50 workshops, the consecration and cooperation of all office personnel, the premiere showing of the first RBP film, *The Sleeping Giant in Your Church,* all combined to make this a never-to-be-forgotten revival time to the 1,029 paid registrants and the hundreds of visitors from eleven states." I can say a hearty Amen to Brother Barlow, for I was there! And that regional conference was just the first of many under the splendid, fervent leadership of Fred Barlow.

The second one was held at First Baptist Church, Johnson City, New York, and it outdid the first one! On November 15 and 16, 1962, 1,214 Sunday School workers registered. Almost 400 seminary students attended many sessions, thus hiking the attendance to more than 1,600. Twelve states were represented. Dr. Lee Roberson was the guest speaker. Two hundred forty-five homes were opened in the Johnson City, Endicott and Binghamton area to provide 307 free beds for guests.

At the December 1962 Council meeting, Dr. Ketcham pointed out that the lease for the GARBC in the Transportation Building would expire in March of 1963. Dr. Merle Hull told of the great need for additional space not only for office personnel but also for storage and future expansion. R. L. Matthews moved that Dr. Jackson renew the present lease for two years, if possible, and secure additional rental space as needed. William E. Kuhnle seconded the motion and it carried. The wonderful blessing of God upon Regular Baptist Press and the like blessing of God upon the GARBC made growth inevitable. It would be only a matter of time when the Transportation Building would have to be vacated. There was also growing conviction that the GARBC ought to buy its own office facilities instead of continuing to rent.

Even though space was limited, Dr. Hull felt impelled to keep the momentum going. In the June 1963 Council meeting at Omaha, Nebraska, Dr. Hull announced the securing of Rev. Vernon D. Miller, pastor of Immanuel Baptist Church of Arcanum, Ohio, as editor of Sunday School papers. The expansion of Regular Baptist Press was indeed something to behold.

The Omaha conference was a record-breaking meeting. Seventy-eight churches were welcomed into the Association, an all-time high, a record that still stands. Only twice before had more than 70 churches come into the Association in one year: 72 in Johnson City, New York, in 1943; and 73 in Winona Lake, Indiana, in 1961. The number of churches in the Fellowship after the Omaha conference stood at an even 1,100. Commenting on the Omaha record, Dr. Jackson said:

> A fine group of churches is coming into the GARBC this year. Some are older churches that have severed ties with the American Baptist Convention because of its liberalism. Others are new churches the very existence of which indicates the missionary outreach of our people. The Lord enable us to found many more new churches this coming year![7]

Raymond Hamilton, one of the "founding fathers" of the GARBC, commemorated his twelfth anniversary as pastor of Belden Avenue Baptist Church of Chicago in 1963. He resigned in order to become American Secretary of the International Council of Christian Churches. Dr. Hamilton had gone to Belden from the Burholme Baptist Church of Philadelphia where he had pastored for four years. Previous pastorates included six years as R. T. Ketcham's assistant at Central Baptist Church of Gary, Indiana; four years at First Baptist Church of Pana, Illinois; and two years in Quincy, Illinois, where he established the Calvary Baptist Church. He became secretary-treasurer of the GARBC in 1934 and became a member of the Council of Fourteen when it was first formed. In 1948 he went to Amsterdam to represent the GARBC in the formation of the International Council of Christian Churches. Dr. Hamilton was president of the American Council from 1960 to 1963.

This chapter began with the election of John F. Kennedy to the presidency. It ends by recalling his assassination. It has been said that everyone remembers where he or she was on November 22, 1963, when Kennedy was shot to death by Lee Harvey Oswald. I was in my study at Bethany Baptist Church in Galesburg, Illinois. Dr. Paul Jackson was in Tacoma, Washington, for an Associational rally. Rev. Al Colwell was at the Calvary Baptist Church in Brazil, Indiana. Dr. Fred Barlow was at the Northampton Baptist Church, Cuyahoga Falls, Ohio. Dr. Robert T. Ketcham and Dr. Merle R. Hull were in their offices on the twelfth floor of the Transportation Building at 608 South Dearborn in Chicago. And God was on His throne, still sovereign, still making the wrath of man to praise Him and restraining the remainder of man's wrath (Ps. 76:12).

End Notes

1. Victor Lasky, *JFK, The Man and the Myth* (New Rochelle, NY: Arlington House, 1963), pp. 490, 491.

2. Ibid., p. 492.

3. "Minutes of GARBC Annual Business Meeting," June 1960, Long Beach, California. (Typewritten.)

4. Paul R. Jackson, "The Position, Attitudes, and Objectives of Biblical Separation," GARBC Literature Item 12 (Schaumburg, IL: General Association of Regular Baptist Churches, n.d.), pp. 3, 4.

5. Paul R. Jackson, "What Are the Objectives of the GARBC?" *Baptist Bulletin* (November 1961), pp. 8, 9, 12.

6. R. T. Ketcham, "Council of Fourteen Minutes," Rochester, Minnesota, June 1959. (Typewritten.)

7. GARBC Annual Report (Schaumburg, IL: Regular Baptist Press, 1963), p. 1.

29

Talents For Christ! For Regular Baptists those three words have come to stand for excellence. Teenage excellence. Dedicated excellence. Christ-honoring, Christ-serving excellence.

Talents For Christ is a national GARBC-sponsored program for teenagers. The program had its birth in 1963 when a Minnesota teenager, Pam Worden, wrote to Dr. Paul R. Jackson about her idea for a nationwide competition for high school young people coupled with scholarships to GARBC-approved schools. Pam had been involved in a small-scale state contest in Minnesota. She was motivated to make such competition a reality for Regular Baptist youth.

Dr. Jackson shared Pam's idea with Ed Koons. At the annual conference in Omaha in 1963, Mr. Koons shared Pam's idea with the Council of Fourteen. The Council gave him the green light to develop a Talents For Christ program for the GARBC. It was a big job with a multitude of details, but Koons and his able secretary, Mary Groe, were equal to the challenge. They wrote contest rules and regulations, obtained suitable music lists and outlined qualifications for writing, public speaking and Bible knowledge. They settled on the following categories for competition: piano, organ, male voice, female voice, brass, strings, woodwinds, journalism, female public speaking, male public speaking and Bible knowledge (a type of quiz or examination over a specified part of the Bible).

State or regional contests would be held first, with the winners going on to the national competition to be held at the site of the GARBC annual conference. One of the most challenging tasks was finding judges. Three judges for each of the eleven categories totaled thirty-three. That was no easy group to find! Mr. Koons had to develop publicity and find people on the state level who would promote and properly organize and choose judges. He also had to "sell" the program to all of the approved schools, for they would be the ones responsible to provide the scholarships: one year of free tuition for first-place winners and one-half year for second-place winners. Winners also received attractive trophies. The schools were happy to cooperate.

The first national competition was held in 1964 at Winona Lake, Indiana, and Pam Worden, the young lady who had hatched the whole idea, won first place in piano! She went on to Grand Rapids Baptist College for her training. After graduation and teaching applied music for a year, Pam took further training at Saint Mary's Hospital and became a registered nurse. She practiced nursing until her marriage to Stephen Green (not the recording artist). They have three beautiful daughters and reside in Mishawaka, Indiana.

Other winners at Winona Lake were Danny Smith, Linda Riggs, Carol Martin, Gale Guthrie, Linda Frye, Pamela Perryman, James Wolfe, Betty Meyers, Dawn Meyers, Nate DeLisi, Kay Porter, Joel Glessner, R. James Brawn, Carol Cass, Cynthia Schwan, Nancy Vines, Joseph Fleming and Bruce Hays. The winners had the additional honor of being pictured on the front cover of the August 1964 issue of the *Baptist Bulletin.*

Many people have invested a great deal of energy in Talents For Christ through the years. When Koons went back into the pastorate, I was asked to run the Talents For Christ program from my Iowa pastoral office. Mary Groe took care of the details and made it all possible. When I became national representative, David Cortner of Des Moines ran the program, assisted by Gretchen Tyrrell of the home office. In 1990 the Talents For Christ baton passed to David Uibel, minister of music at Emmanuel Baptist Church in Toledo, Ohio.

Thousands of young people have been challenged to use their talents for Christ through this program of competition. At the annual conference in 1989 at Columbus, Ohio, past winners from all over the country enjoyed a Talents For Christ 25th anniversary banquet. What a thrill to see those talented young people and to hear them testify as to how the Lord has since used their consecrated talents! And all because Dr. Paul Jackson read a letter from a Minnesota teenager and did something about it!

Other teenagers do not sing or play instruments or write essays or win Bible knowledge contests. But they are not forgotten by Regular Baptists. These handicapped teens are usually referred to as "retarded," and the first social agency or service ministry to receive approval status was Shepherds Home and School, whose official name is now Shepherds Baptist Ministries.

Shepherds grew out of a project undertaken in 1957 by an adult Sunday School class at Garfield Avenue Baptist Church in Milwaukee, where Dr. William E. Kuhnle was pastor. The teacher of the class was Dr. Viggo B. Olsen, now Daktar, the famous missionary physician to Bangladesh under ABWE. One of the couples in that class had a retarded son, Larry Cayton. Other couples in the class decided it would be a worthwhile investment of their time to study retardation. The project was taken to the pastor and deacons of the church, who gladly endorsed the idea. In December of 1957 the officers of the class met with the GARBC Council of Fourteen and outlined their dream for a home for the mentally retarded. In 1960 a constitution was written and officers were elected. In 1961 Andrew H. Wood became the executive director. Property was purchased in 1963 at Union Grove, Wisconsin. Construction was begun, and in June of 1964 the home and school opened with 36 boys and girls.

More than 500 people attended the dedication services for the first unit. Mr. and Mrs. Lawrence Cayton assisted Andrew H. Wood in cutting the ribbon to the entrance. Dr. Wood served Shepherds for the next 25 years with great blessing and the confidence of the GARBC constituency.

Dr. James H. Misirian succeeded Dr. Wood in 1986, and the ministry of Shepherds continues to expand. In 1990 Misirian coordinated the acquisition of 70 acres of land next to the existing facilities and has directed Shepherds' recently completed $1.2 million "A Greater Love Campaign," including breaking ground for a new chapel and gym and expansion of the kitchen facilities. One hundred sixty residents are now cared for by a full-time staff of 68 workers.

The GARBC has proved the liberals wrong when they say fundamentalists have no "social consciousness." Including Shepherds, five service ministries are approved by the Association. The Baptist Children's Home and Family Ministries, Inc., is headquartered in Valparaiso, Indiana, with branches in Ohio, Michigan and Iowa. It began in 1956 and last year (1990) had 55 residents. Altogether the Home served 292 people in such varied areas as child care, foster care, counseling, maternity, adoption and family life conferences. The ministries are directed by President Donald E. Worch.

In 1973 the Michigan Christian Home Association was organized in Grand Rapids, Michigan. This Baptist home for Senior Citizens provides independent apartment living and is also a licensed skilled nursing home. It presently serves 119 residents. Mr. Byron G. Wild is the administrator.

The Baptist Family Agency of Seattle, Washington, was led for many years by Rev. Robert Van Alstine, who recently retired. He was succeeded by Rev. Harold Hayes, a former military chaplain and pastor. The agency is responsible for 29 foster care children and has served about 50 families during the past year.

Baptists for Life is the newest GARBC-approved service ministry and is a Baptist pro-life organization engaging in educational and direct action ministries and providing seminars and training for crisis pregnancy center programs. It also offers medical ethics briefings and analyses of legislation dealing with pro-life issues. Baptists for Life is located in Grand Rapids, Michigan. Rev. Mark B. Blocher is executive director. Last year this ministry reached more than 30,000 people with its message and ministry.

Dr. Merle Hull pointed up the incalculable value of our service ministries with the following true story.

It arises from a background all too common in recent decades. A young girl in a tragic home circumstance; mistreated by her father. The situation became intolerable. And in her desperation, the girl came to one of the social agencies approved by the Fellowship. She came with a heart full of confusion and bitterness, feeling lost, lonely and unloved. Hearing the rules and regulations as given by the housefather, she felt trapped. For almost 12 years she had run her own life. Never had she listened to any instruction like that. Her instinctive impulse was to run; to get away from there.

But gradually, God worked in her life. Through the houseparents she began to feel loved. At church she learned that God also loved her—loved her as she was, full of hatred and sin. Then one day the Holy Spirit moved powerfully in her heart. She found herself at the front of the church pouring out her soul to God, asking Him to forgive her and trusting Christ as her Savior. She cried all the way back to the Home, but the tears were those of peace and joy.

Through the example of godly houseparents and the environment of spiritual devotion, she grew in Christ. She remained at the Home for more than five years. Looking back later, she stated: "I learned so many things. The main thing I realized was that I was a person, and with God my life could be something. I didn't think I was worth anything until I found Christ."

A happy ending, with additional happiness in the fact that this young woman now has a fine Christian husband and two lovely children.

Again, this account is but typical of many. In a time of broken homes, child abuse and neglect, drugs, promiscuity and endless evils, the work of the social agencies becomes increasingly vital.[1]

Another ministry that has blessed the lives of hundreds of thousands of young people is camp. Bible camping ministries have been used of the Lord to change people's eternal destiny and to direct still other people into lives of fruitful service. I have personally been involved in Regular Baptist camps since 1948, as a camper, a counselor and a speaker. I have seen literally hundreds of teenagers get right with God in camp meetings. At least one of our camps is on the top of a mountain—Pilot Lake Regular Baptist Camp outside La Porte, California. Two camps are located on islands—New Life Island Regular Baptist Camp at Frenchtown, New Jersey, and Camp Patmos on Kellys Island, Ohio. Two of them are known as "ranches"—Victory Ranch at Moreno, California, and Skyview Baptist Ranch at Millersburg, Ohio. Our GARBC Church Directory lists 27 camps that are approved by the state associations. The GARBC itself operates no camps. I have personally preached in 20 of these camps. My ministries have centered in youth camps, family camps, senior citizen retreats, men's retreats and pastors and wives' retreats. Meetings in camps are always special. They provide an atmosphere conducive to thinking, listening and meditating.

Why are youth camps successful? Many men and women who are candidates for the mission fields tell me they surrendered to the Lord for missionary service at a camp service. Many, many of my preacher friends tell me they dedicated their lives to the Lord at a summer camp or winter retreat. I well remember preaching one summer week at the Iowa Regular Baptist Camp. On Wednesday night I gave the invitation, and 92 young people came forward. And they were not coming casually or because a friend was coming. They were serious. Some were weeping quietly. Others were sobbing aloud. They had deep conviction and confession of sin and a determination to go home and burn dirty magazines and worldly records and cassettes. They made holy vows to follow the Lord in baptism or to attend Bible school. The decisions were truly life-changing. I meet these people, now grown, all over the country. They point to the camp meeting as the turning point in their lives.

One reason camping is so successful is the simple matter of getting the camper into an environment where he or she can get a concentrated dose of Biblical preaching and teaching. Old evangelists like Bob Jones, Sr., used to tell me how in the old days they would preach for weeks without giving an invitation. They would "pour it on" until people would practically beg the evangelist to give an invitation. *But* that happened because people then went to the meetings night after night after night, and the conviction of the Holy Spirit deepened and strengthened and broke the stubborn will of the listener. This is what happens at camp. When a teen is at camp, he does not go to a Sunday morning service and then go back into the world until next Sunday morning. He is at camp for a succession of days, and the Word of God and the Spirit of God have time to do something in the heart and mind of that youth. I have discovered that the break usually starts on Wednesday night, and decisions are made at each service thereafter until the end of the camp.

Another reason that camp is so successful is that campers are separated from the worldly influences brought upon them by radio, tapes, television and ungodly companions. They must listen to God's Word. They must listen to God's music. They must listen to godly companions and counselors. They begin to hear the truth about themselves, about sin, about salvation, about surrender and about service. And suddenly, it makes sense!

A different blessing from camping is that which comes to those who work at camp. Young people many times learn discipline and cooperation for the first time. They learn to obey, to set priorities and to think of others ahead of themselves. They realize that serving the Lord can be very practical.

Surely GARBC churches would not be as strong as they are today were it not for our camping programs. Certainly our approved schools would not have as many students as they do had it not been for the camps. And it is certain that our mission agencies have profited greatly from the ministries of our camps.

I have found that it is easier to impact men at men's retreats than just about any other type of meeting. Men seem more relaxed, more open, more willing to listen when they are in the atmosphere of a camp. And, oh, do they sing! Nothing compares with the singing at men's retreats. And the testimonies! And the prayer times and fellowship times. I really believe pastors are wise to encourage attendance at men's retreats because their men will come back home edified, enthused and enlightened. I am sure the same could be said for ladies' retreats.

Paul Jackson enjoyed camp ministries. He worked as many camps into his itinerary as his work load would permit. Through his years as national representative he showed the same loving interest in young people as he had as a college president for 14 years. He preached at the Baptist youth camp at Lake Ann, Michigan; conferences at Cape May, New Jersey; senior high camps at the Illinois-Missouri Regular Baptist Camp, Beechwood Lake Baptist Camp in Indiana, Glendawn Baptist Camp in Seattle, Washington, the Iowa Regular Baptist Camp, and the Regular Baptist Camp of Northfield, Massachusetts. Dr. Jackson knew the value of investing time and energy in camp meetings.

One of the finest camp directors in the United States for many years was the executive administrator of Lake Ann Baptist Camp in Michigan, Dr. Eldon Brock. He wrote:

Christian camping has been a major factor in recruiting Christian leaders—from faithful church members to the full-time Christian workers. Missionaries and pastors testify that they were saved or called to serve Christ at camp. Some will show you the place they were sitting in chapel. Others talk about the conversation they had with their counselor or the closing campfire they attended in identifying the time and place God met them.

A few people question the value of camping in comparison to the effort and cost, but a recent study of 3,905 randomly selected church leaders revealed camping provides the most prominent learning experiences that shape the Christian life. Various surveys show that 50 to 80 percent of these Christian workers made major spiritual decisions in a camp.

I have records for the past 14 years showing that at least 85 percent of the unsaved kids coming to camp made salvation decisions before going home. The testimonies at the close of camp also prove most of the Christian campers make spiritual growth decisions that give Biblical value to their relationship with God, family, church and others. . . . Camp is for the camper, not necessarily for the fun, ease or convenience of the staff. Camping involves planning and careful control of the program to make sure the camper's feelings and needs are cared for. The role of the camp staff is to give personal attention to each camper. This way the needs and interests of each one can be discovered. Then through loving direction they can be helped to see that Christ can meet their needs.[2]

The 1964 conference not only was the beginning of Talents For Christ, but it also was the start of a larger youth program at the annual conference. June 23 was designated "Youth Emphasis Day." In the morning 16 workshops were presented by the professors and presidents of the approved schools. In the afternoon the Talents For Christ contests were held. In the early evening two youth banquets were held featuring the musical groups from the schools and messages by John Reed and Wendell Kempton titled "Faith Spans the Ages." The day climaxed in the evening service, which featured a great youth choir and orchestra and a message from Dr. W. Wilbert Welch titled "By Faith We Understand."

End Notes

1. Merle R. Hull, *What A Fellowship!* (Schaumburg, IL: Regular Baptist Press, 1981), pp. 49, 50.
2. Eldon Brock, "Good Camps Produce Great Results," *Baptist Bulletin* (May 1986), p. 17.

Home office in Des Plaines

30

Our younger readers may not really appreciate all of the "blood, sweat and tears" that have gone into making the GARBC and RBP facilities what they are today. Neither may they appreciate the near ecstasy with which news was received by the staff that the Council had voted to proceed with an all-out effort to find new property. Thus the full story must be told in this chapter.

At the June 1964 Council of Fourteen meeting at Winona Lake, Indiana, Dr. Jackson reported that the need for additional space and room for expansion had become critical. He reported that Vernon D. Miller had done a great deal of field work and had reported that land in the Chicago area varied in price from $35,000 to $54,000 an acre. Miller indicated that the Association and Press would need at least two acres. Dr. Jackson said that the home office people had to have facilities that could provide for areas of expansion. Dr. Hull then outlined them as follows: editor for books, plus a secretary; editor of youth materials, plus a secretary; assistant editor of Sunday School papers; a full-time *Baptist Bulletin* editor; someone to oversee the Sunday School literature; storage space. Dr. Hull said all the curriculum personnel just listed would necessitate additional workers in the Business and Shipping departments so that RBP would conceivably take on ten to twelve more employees in the next six or seven years.

The Council and staff then listed reasons for remaining in the Chicago area: need for repairs on machines; excellent travel facilities for those on the road; mailing and shipping facilities readily available. It was moved by David Otis Fuller and seconded by David Nettleton that the men in the Chicago office investigate the matter further and bring one or two recommendations to the December meeting. The motion carried, and Vernon Miller went home after the conference and went right to work.

In November of '64 Miller reported to the Council that area surveys had been made in the cities of Chicago, Grand Rapids and Cleveland to determine available sites and facilities for office location.

Let Miller go on with the exciting story.

About August 15, the property in Des Plaines, Illinois, was brought to our attention. It was available from the General Telephone Directory Company. I notified Dr. Ketcham in a letter on August 21, and Dr. Jackson upon his arrival in the office, of the availability of this property. We then had a meeting with the Seay and Thomas Realty Company, with General Telephone Directory Company personnel, and with Gerald Lurie and Company's representative, who was to handle our interests in the purchase of the building, and who notified us of its availability. Following this meeting, we called a meeting of the Publications Committee and the chairman of the Council of Fourteen, requesting their advice.

On September 15, the meeting of the Council of Fourteen was held in the Des Plaines building. At this time it was determined that brochures stating the needs of the Chicago office should be made available to our Association.

On September 23, a letter was sent to the Council stating the availability of a free option which was to conclude in sixty days. Actually, this option is dated to December 8, at our request. In view of the availability of the option and the general opinion among the office staff of the advisability of considering this building, a telephone conference was called for by the chairman of the Council for September 26.

The Council responded in this conference with a vote for a referendum and authorized Dr. Jackson to proceed with the negotiations for the property.[1]

Dr. Jackson then wrote the following letter to all the GARBC churches:

Dear Regular Baptists:

This is probably the most important letter I have written to our pastors and churches. Please read it carefully. Pastor, your church is in the GARBC and this letter is official business of the Association. It is vitally important that each church vote on the recommendation from the Council of Fourteen to purchase the 1800 Oakton property.

The Regular Baptist Press is growing. Many new areas of publishing should be entered quickly. To do this we must have more room. We have explored many possibilities of renting, building or buying. We have prayed and planned. The staff and the Council have worked together on this problem. We believe that finally we have the answer from the Lord. The building described in the enclosed brochure is available. It meets all the qualifications which we had outlined in our study of our needs. Many prayers have been answered already, indicating His approval.

We have a 60 day option on this property, which did not cost us anything and which does not obligate us legally in any way.

The Regular Baptist Press is in a position to assume major responsibility for the cost of the property, although obviously many of our churches and people will share that obligation joyfully, if the churches vote to purchase.

Immediate action is necessary if we are to secure this building. *We need to hear from you not later than November 15.* We are enclosing a card to simplify the report on the vote of the church.

The plan is to make a down payment of $125,000 from RBP funds. We have official assurance of a 20-year mortgage at 5 1/2% from Equitable Life Assurance Society. The agreement provides for prepayment without penalty, which would enable us to pay the entire amount within ten years, thus saving a great deal of interest.

Careful research and planning has been done, and we are assured of the soundness of the building, and of the financial commitments that would be involved in the purchase.

Please read the unanimous recommendation of the Council: "The Council of Fourteen, after days of deliberation and prayer, wholeheartedly recommends to our churches the purchase of the property at 1800 Oakton Boulevard, Des Plaines, Illinois, for the sum of not more than $385,000."

Each church should vote "yes" or "no" on this recommendation. A "yes" vote does not involve the church in a financial commitment, beyond its own voluntary desire to help in this great work. Every church should vote, even though not giving financially to the GARBC. This property is needed because of the growth of the Regular Baptist Press. Every church using RBP material has a basic interest in seeing this wonderful property put to use for the Lord. Much more sound literature must be produced!

This purchase does not involve any centralization of authorities or activities. There are no plans to increase the personnel and program of the GARBC. The need is to provide area for more editors and secretaries for the Regular Baptist Press and space for adequate storage of materials. Increased volume of business also increases the demand for more room for shipping literature. There is no plan to install our own presses, for this would involve the expenditure of vast sums of money.

To assist in presenting this property, we are mailing a package of brochures like the one enclosed. You may wish to put some on your bulletin boards and use others as inserts. These brochures are designed to present the necessary information and to answer questions in the minds of the people.

Please bring this recommendation to the church for a vote in time to send the card to us not later than November 15. It would be a great help to us if you could vote on this in time to get the card back to us immediately after November 1. Would it be possible to distribute the brochures on Sunday, October 25, and vote that day, or Wednesday, the 28th, or Sunday, November 1? We would be most grateful if you would mail the card immediately.

Please pray with us that the will of the Lord shall be accomplished.
Yours in His wonderful name,
Paul R. Jackson, National Representative.[2]

Now let Vernon Miller continue his report to the Council on November 25:

Following this conference (telephone conference), brochures accompanied by letters and comments from the Council were mailed to our entire constituency. The response has been gratifying in that as of today, November 25, there are 804 favorable votes and 4 opposed; 579 yes votes were required in the referendum. On October 6, the option was received which had been signed by General Telephone Directory Company who leased the property, accompanied by a letter from Lincoln National Life Insurance Society in Fort Wayne, the owner of the building, guaranteeing the amount of $385,000 as the purchase price.

Application for the $260,000 loan from the Equitable Life Assurance Society of the United States was received on October 6, and signed at a later date. This application is now in New York for final processing.

The following items are included in the financial program as outlined in the loan application: The length of time will be twenty years with interest at 5 1/2% per annum. It will be repaid in equal, quarterly installments of $5,400 including interest. We are to have the right after one year to prepay up to $20,000 in any one year, non-cumulative, without charge, and to prepay additional amounts after five years with a charge of 5 percent during the sixth year declining one quarter percent per annum each year thereafter to not less than one percent.

A cash deposit of $2,600 was made to Equitable as a good-faith deposit. We have every assurance that this will be completed in time for our closing date, about December 8, or soon thereafter. We also secured the services of Mr. Edwin L. Brown, attorney for our Association, who had given us advice concerning the referendum, the required number of votes, and the procedure to be followed. He is checking all the documents and we are handling contracts which are now being written through his office.

Material necessary for the insurance company, the Equitable loan, and for other legal procedures was secured, including the original cost of the land

and improvements which was $412,000, complete building plans and specifications, complete certified survey of the property, and a complete breakdown of operating expenses including heating, cleaning and taxes, etc. In addition to this, an insurance schedule with types, amount, rates and co-insurance was secured in order to secure coverage on the building upon our taking possession of the property.

It is anticipated that the moving date will be January 18, 1965. Appreciation is expressed to members of the staff who furnished figures and facts, to the Council of Fourteen for its wholehearted approval, and to the churches of our GARBC for their wonderful response to the challenge.[3]

I do not know whether or not the Council sang the Doxology after Mr. Miller's report, but I'm sure they felt like doing it! What a story of the provision of God for His people! We agree with Council member W. Wilbert Welch, who said:

The move to Des Plaines by the Chicago office is the climactic evidence of Association maturity. First, there was the ready recognition of the need for the type of facilities which would enable the office to operate with far greater efficiency. Second, there was nationwide confidence that such a move did not stem from a growing hierarchical authority which would violate local church autonomy. Separating themselves as many churches have from a strong denominationally controlled background, only years of careful respect for the independence of the local church could have gained such confidence. Third, the amazing record of 820 congregations voting for the move with only four dissenting votes—a total proxy vote of 824 out of a possible 1156—is in itself one of the most unusual displays of unity and confidence probably ever recorded in Baptist history. Certainly the move to Des Plaines was a capstone event and prophetic of good things to come.

For every advance the praise belongs to the Lord. There is reason to believe that other Baptist bodies will look long at what God has done for the GARBC.[4]

Hall Dautel was equally enthusiastic. He said: "In appearance, facilities (transportation and otherwise), and price, without question this is the finest building that has been brought to our attention over the years. I feel that God has kept this for us at this time."[5] Said Joseph Bower: "The proposed building located at 1800 Oakton, Des Plaines, Illinois, is well constructed, compact in arrangement, adequate in facilities, central in its location, providential in its provision."[6]

James T. Jeremiah wrote: "The blessing of God is upon our

GARBC fellowship. Its witness for Christ and the Bible is ever expanding. It is obvious that adequate facilities must be provided for the Regular Baptist Press and our staff if the services to our churches are to be as desired and expected. I believe we need the Des Plaines, Illinois, property."[7] David Otis Fuller declared: "At first I wondered a bit about the advisability of spending such a large sum. But after seeing the building and realizing how suitable it was for our needs, and how much we pay out every month in rent, I feel we should make this purchase. The hour is late! The need is great! What we do we must do quickly! 'Where there is no vision the people perish.' May it not be said of us that our spiritual eyesight had developed myopia or astigmatism."[8]

R. L. Matthews said: "I heartily favor the purchase of the proposed new office building in Des Plaines. It is modern and will adequately care for present and anticipated needs."[9] Wrote William E. Kuhnle: "Having seen the property at 1800 Oakton Avenue in Des Plaines, Illinois, it is my personal judgment that God is in this matter. It is an excellent building for the needs now and future for the Regular Baptist Press and for the home office."[10]

Another Council of Fourteen member, Kenneth Muck, wrote: "Much prayer has been offered that a proper and suitable building might be either built or purchased. It seems very evident that the hand of the Lord has made possible the obtaining of such a building as the one in Des Plaines. From every viewpoint it meets the conditions which have been laid down."[11] Robert L. Powell said:

> Because we have all felt that we need a building for all of our offices, the national representative and staff, the Regular Baptist Press and all the staff members and all other workers of our Fellowship, we have been exploring this field for several years. Now there has come an opportunity to purchase a building well suited to our needs, under conditions and terms which we feel are reasonable and possible for us to meet. I am therefore casting my vote as one member of the Council of Fourteen to proceed with the purchase of same at the earliest date consistent with our methods of authorizing such a business transaction.[12]

David Nettleton expressed his conviction about the building: "I am convinced that the building in Des Plaines is very suitable for our home office and the work of RBP. The combination of advantages it offers are difficult to match. It is large enough, well constructed, across the street from a post office, has room around it for parking, and is immediately available. Let's move right in and be ready for more expansion."[13]

Wilbur Chapman Rooke wrote:

For two or three years I served on the Council of Fourteen on the committee appointed by the chairman to help seek a proper headquarters building. We looked in Cleveland as well as in Chicago but to no avail. When looking, however, several things seemed to stand out as the absolute essentials for a building for the GARBC: it must be adequate for a growing concern, it must be in a location that our girls would not be in danger as they go to and from work, it must be near the airport, it must be near the post office, and it must have parking space. When I saw the lovely new building which I feel the Lord has made available for the GARBC, I was thrilled beyond words to see that it more than fulfilled all of these needs.[14]

Robert L. Sumner said: "I have seen the proposed building to house our GARBC offices and those of the Regular Baptist Press and am very enthused about it. It is just what we need."[15]

Wrote W. Thomas Younger: "Having seen the Des Plaines property with its many features favorable to our growing needs, I feel we should purchase it for a permanent base of operation."[16] Last, but most assuredly not least, Joseph M. Stowell declared:

In my judgment, the proposed action regarding the Des Plaines property is one of the most important advances ever contemplated by our forward-moving Association, on a par with past decisions to put a full-time national representative on the field and the inauguration of our own Sunday School materials. I not only wholeheartedly and enthusiastically endorse the idea of purchasing property to house our offices eliminating this "down the drain" waste of high rent money—but I approve of this particular property which meets every requirement of our present needs and of all foreseeable needs for several years to come.[17]

What testimonies! No Council of Fourteen was ever more united and excited about a matter than the fourteen men who voted to buy the Des Plaines property. Little did Dr. Jackson and Dr. Hull realize when they called Vernon Miller to be Sunday School papers editor they would also get a man with business savvy and a good knowledge of buildings and property. But we serve a God Who is "able to do exceeding abundantly above all that we ask or think" (Eph. 3:20).

One man who was as happy as anyone else over the building purchase was Merle Robert Hull. For ten years he had labored under increasingly difficult conditions in that downtown Chicago Transportation Building. Then . . . well, let him tell you how he felt:

You've thought about something for a long while . . . discussed it as a possibility . . . enjoyed it as a pleasant dream.

Then one day it becomes a reality—and you can hardly believe it is happening!

That's the way the home office staff feels about the move to the new building in Des Plaines. The purchase has been authorized by the churches. (Latest vote count is 819–4.) The legal negotiations are under way. But after all these years in a Loop office building, to be going to our own now still seems a little unreal.

More and more, however, we're being brought back to earth. And it is a pretty busy, detailed earth, at that. Remember that last time *you* moved? How *can* so many things accumulate? You wonder whether you'll ever be able to remember all the items that must be checked off.

Of course, we don't have pots and pans, wardrobes, dining room tables, or trunks full of old love letters! But we do have books, *books,* BOOKS, file cabinets, desks, stencil cabinets, storage shelves, displays, stationery, typewriters—just to begin naming some things. . . . Once we get settled in our new quarters, and learn to find our *own* way around in all the extra space, we plan to have an open house so that everyone from near and far can come to see firsthand what the Lord has provided. In addition, any of you who chance to be traveling through the Chicago area are cordially invited to come in. Your map will quickly show you Des Plaines—just a little north and east of O'Hare Field. You don't even need to let us know you are coming—we're not set up to bake cakes, anyway!

Excuse me now, please—I have to go do some packing.[18]

Another man was smiling broadly about the new building. He was 75 years old, and on November 30, 1964, he wrote a letter to the Council of Fourteen. Robert T. Ketcham wrote:

Little did I dream 32 1/2 years ago that an action taken in this very building [the Loop's office building] would develop into the proportions of blessing and usefulness which our Association enjoys today. There were just a few of us here, but we were convinced that obedience dictated our action, and a God-given faith enabled us to obey. The years which have followed have been marked by Paul's oft-repeated phrase in his epistle, 'But God.' . . . As we come now to this latest expression of God's goodness to us in the securing of adequate facilities to carry on our ever-expanding ministry, I would like to give some definite, tangible evidence of my thanksgiving for whatever share He has allowed me to have in the accomplishments of our blessed Fellowship. Mrs. Ketcham and I would like, therefore, to make a gift of $1,000 toward the purchase of the Des Plaines property.[19]

That open house was held on May 22, 1965, and more than 400 showed up to go through the building God had so wonderfully provided.

End Notes

1. "Council of Fourteen Minutes," Chicago, Illinois, December 1964. (Typewritten.)
2. "Council of Fourteen Minutes—Des Plaines Property," Chicago, Illinois, December 1964. (Typewritten.)
3. "Council of Fourteen Minutes," Chicago, Illinois, December 1964. (Typewritten.)
4. Wilbert W. Welch, "Editorials," *Baptist Bulletin* (June 1965), p. 14.
5. "Approvals of the Council of Fourteen in the Report on the Des Plaines Property," Chicago, Illinois, December 1964. (Typewritten.)
6. Ibid.
7. Ibid.
8. Ibid.
9. Ibid.
10. Ibid.
11. Ibid.
12. Ibid.
13. Ibid.
14. Ibid.
15. Ibid.
16. Ibid.
17. Ibid.
18. Merle R. Hull, "It's Our Move," *Baptist Bulletin* (January 1965), p. 11.
19. Letter on File in Council Minutes, November 1964.

31

Nineteen sixty-six was a significant year in the United States. Medicare, the government program to pay part of the medical expenses of senior citizens over 65, began on July 1, 1966. President Lyndon B. Johnson in June ordered the bombing of the area around Hanoi, North Vietnam. By the end of the year more than 400,000 American troops were in South Vietnam. Here in the United States the protests against the war became more and more vocal and violent. President Johnson's popularity was shrinking. Republican Edward Brooke of Massachusetts was elected as the first black United States Senator since 1880.

While American boys were giving their lives in Vietnam, one great GARBC "soldier of the cross," Rev. Alfred F. Colwell, died suddenly. He surely was at the "front lines" at the time of his Home-going. He had served with distinction as the GARBC eastern representative from 1957 right on up to his death in 1966. His widow, Gladys, had also served with him. As "Al," as he was affectionately known, encouraged pastors, Gladys encouraged the wives of pastors. Gladys has remained active to this day (1990), and until recent years, she went to the annual conferences at her own expense and voluntarily worked at the registration desk. A new generation of preachers has arisen in the GARBC who "know not" Al Colwell, but, believe me, those of us who knew him and loved him have never forgotten him and his great contributions to the work of the GARBC.

Nineteen sixty-six was also the year of Robert T. Ketcham's "second" retirement. At the 1965 Des Moines conference Dr. Ketcham had indicated he would resign as National Consultant at the 1966 Grand Rapids conference. As J. Murray Murdoch said:

> The years gradually had sapped his strength. His dim eyesight necessitated that someone guide him as he walked. Even the process of walking

had become a chore at the age of seventy-six, and he seldom moved without the aid of his cane. If he did not recognize friends by voice, he could not identify them. But the years had not dimmed his sense of humor. He announced his retirement by saying: "This next year I'll be seventy-seven and I'll become a Regular Baptist with the right to vote at the 35th Annual Bible Conference." In recording that statement in the *Baptist Bulletin,* Edgar Koons said: "Great men have a sublime way of announcing events of major significance. . . . What better expression could have been spoken to announce that he was stepping down from his position of national consultant to assume his position and place as a loyal Regular Baptist."[1]

For our uninitiated readers' information, salaried servants who work in the GARBC home office have no voting privileges at annual conferences. Dr. Ketcham, therefore, had had no voting privileges for 18 years and was looking forward to the 1966 conference where he would.

The Council of Fourteen at their 1965 winter meeting made plans for a fitting "farewell" to Dr. Ketcham. On February 4, 1966, Dr. Robert Powell sent a letter to all pastors in GARBC churches. He spoke of Dr. Ketcham's upcoming retirement and said:

> The entire Association will surely want to take proper notice of this significant event. We all feel a sense of gratitude to God for giving us such a master workman as our National Consultant, and because of the sense of gratitude, many of us feel some worthy recognition should be given this warrior of faith. The occasion of his retirement is that he will have reached the age of seventy-seven, and in the course of human events that begins to tell on one's strength. And while he retires officially from his present position, yet he will never retire in the sense of quitting the work of the Lord as long as he is able to serve.[2]

Powell went on to explain how the Council believed that a well-planned love offering ought to be presented to Dr. and Mrs. Ketcham at the Grand Rapids conference. He suggested that a Sunday be set aside in May and expressed the hope of the Council that the churches of the Association would be generous. He finished his letter with typical Powell gracefulness:

> And, of course, the whole matter is strictly on a basis of a voluntary principle, as is always the case among us "independent Baptists." But we

believe that such an opportunity will be gladly and enthusiastically accepted by all of the fine people called "Regular Baptists," because to Dr. Ketcham more than any other man alive is the credit for keeping the cause of the GARBC alive and going at a good rate of growth. Hundreds of pastors and missionaries have felt that he is really their "father" in the scriptural sense of the word. All of us owe him a debt of gratitude for the work God has done through his surrendered life.[3]

The Council of Fourteen also directed Dr. Hull to devote an entire issue of the *Baptist Bulletin* to Dr. Ketcham. Dr. Hull announced the significance of the special issue in his lead editorial in the March 1966 edition:

For the first time in the *Bulletin's* thirty-three year history, the major portion of an issue is being dedicated to one person—Dr. R. T. Ketcham. Should anyone harbor even the momentary thought that in this we are exalting a man instead of the Lord, he has only to read the material presented this month to be set straight. It will be evident that what we are doing is *honoring* a man who has *exalted* the Lord. For such an act, there is clear scriptural precedent.[4]

The cover of the March 1966 issue carried an expression of Regular Baptist appreciation. It was headed simply "In Appreciation" and said:

Occasionally God thrusts upon some man more than ordinary responsibilities and then demonstrates to and through that man His sufficiency for every task.

Members of the Council of Fourteen have had the opportunity of colaboring with such a man in the person of Robert T. Ketcham. In the close contacts afforded in such a relationship the Council members have gained a new insight of his devotion to the Person of the Lord Jesus Christ, of his dedication to the Word of God, and of his courage to dare to stand for what he believes is right in the sight of God. Through more than fifty years of a rich public ministry these very qualities have enabled him to leave a vital spiritual impact on his generation. Without question the cause of evangelical Christianity has been enhanced because God chose and enabled this man to stand in the gap.

In view of Dr. Ketcham's announced retirement in June from active leadership in the General Association of Regular Baptist Churches, the members of the Council of Fourteen, in behalf of our national constituency, wish to express their appreciation for his dedicated life and energies, his courageous stand for truth, and his thirty-four years of leadership in our GARBC.[5]

Included in that special March issue was a tribute by Dr. Ketcham to his wife:

Without overstatement I can say that when I am in need of special help from God, I would rather have the prayers of my wife undergirding me than those of any other person on earth. One reason for this is that I know she *lives* where she *prays.*[6]

In response to Dr. Powell's letter, gifts poured into the home office designated for Dr. Ketcham's love offering. At the 1966 conference in Grand Rapids, Wednesday night was set aside for Ketcham's appreciation service. He was asked to preach, and after his moving message, Dr. and Mrs. Ketcham were presented a check for $13,643.42. I was there and I must say it was one of the most moving services ever to take place in a GARBC conference. Dr. and Mrs. Ketcham wept openly as did most of us in that crowd of 4,500 people. By the time all the monies had been received, the total love offering amounted to $14,110.

The highest honor that night, however, was not in the form of money but in the form of a citation that was read to the messengers as a resolution would be. It was passed by a unanimous vote and a standing ovation. It read as follows:

Citation
of the ministry of
Dr. Robert Thomas Ketcham
in relationship to the
General Association of Regular Baptist Churches

Dr. Robert T. Ketcham has given much of his ministerial life to the General Association of Regular Baptist Churches. In the providence of God he aided immeasurably in bringing the Association into existence and contributed largely to shaping its organizational structure and formulating its policies. As National Representative of the General Association of Regular Baptist Churches for twelve years his dedicated administrative gifts were used of God to implement the objectives of the Association and to expand its ministry and influence. With great devotion to Christ and to the Association he gave of himself unreservedly that the name of Christ might be honored and the witness of the Fellowship of Churches made effective and powerful.

There is no possibility of calculating Dr. Ketcham's influence upon the lives of thousands of people who have profited from his preaching ministry, his published writings of articles, pamphlets, and books, and his wise counsel. We wish, however, to give expression to our own sense of indebtedness and gratitude, and to assure Dr. Ketcham that he holds in our hearts a unique place of great love and affection.

Be it resolved, therefore, that the General Association of Regular Baptist Churches in session of the city of Grand Rapids, Michigan, at its thirty-fifth annual conference this twenty-second day of June, 1966, commend Dr. Robert T. Ketcham for his courageous and compassionate leadership in official capacity during the past eighteen years, and that we convey to him by this resolution the deep devotion of our grateful hearts.[7]

The 1966 conference also involved some weighty and crucial business. For several years Dr. Paul Jackson had been keeping the Council of Fourteen and the Association informed about what was going on in the Science Department of Jackson's alma mater, Wheaton College. The teaching of theistic evolution had been clearly documented. The matter saddened many GARBC pastors and missionaries who were graduates of Wheaton. Jackson was a 1926 graduate. Wheaton had awarded honorary doctor of divinity degrees to William E. Kuhnle in 1953 and Joseph M. Stowell in 1956. Dr. David Otis Fuller was a longtime member of the Wheaton Board of Trustees. He passionately fought against the teaching of "theistic evolution" by some professors, but to no avail.

With a deep desire to keep our approved schools from such decline, a strong resolution was passed in 1966 at Grand Rapids. Some wanted to make the 24-hour-day interpretation a test of fellowship, but the majority felt there should be room for differences of viewpoint with reference to "days." All were strongly opposed to evolution of any kind. The resolution passed by a majority vote and is still today adhered to as a guideline in school approval. It reads as follows.

A Re-Affirmation of Biblical Conviction Regarding Creation

Whereas: There are strong religious currents today moving contrary to historic Christian orthodoxy including subtle attacks against the verbal inspiration of the Word of God, the diminishing of its authority, the rejection of the miraculous in the Gospels, the propagation of the theory of the death of God, and even the proposal of Christian atheism; and

Whereas: Barthian neo-orthodoxy and scientism have made inroads in many ecclesiastical bodies, schools and mission boards; and

Whereas: A focal point of subtle attack on the Word of God is the creative account of Genesis 1 and 2, questioning the direct, immediate creative acts of God and implying that the account is allegorical, or mythical, and not to be regarded as a literal, historical record; and

Whereas: We have a thirty-four year history of separation from religious apostasy and a firm adherence to historic Christian orthodoxy and wish to do all possible to protect our Fellowship from the inroads of Barthianism, current neoevangelicalism, philosophical relativism and modern scientism, as well as to protest the vitiating effects of liberal theology upon both church and society; and

Whereas: The Grand Rapids Association of Regular Baptist Churches in annual meeting in September, 1960, overwhelmingly passed a resolution relative to creative days which states in part, "There are many who hold to six literal days of twenty-four hours each while there are other true, born again, earnest Christians who hold to an age-day interpretation, and such we would not for one moment wish to exclude from fellowship;" and

Whereas: Historically the six creative days have been, and are, interpreted by most of our Associational churches as twenty-four hour days, yet since such an interpretation has not been regarded as a doctrinal requirement for membership in the local churches, we would not therefore wish to exclude from Associational fellowship those holding other views (providing such views are within the framework of our doctrinal statement and historic Christian orthodoxy):

Therefore, be it resolved: That we, the messengers of the General Association of Regular Baptist Churches, in session in the city of Grand Rapids, Michigan, at our 35th annual conference this 21st day of June, 1966, reaffirm our belief in the full verbal inspiration of the Word of God without any admixture of error for its matter, including our acceptance of the opening chapters of Genesis as being neither allegory nor myth, but a literal, historical account of the direct, immediate creative acts of God; that man was created by a direct work of God and not from previously existing forms of life; and that all men are descended from the historical Adam and Eve, first parents of the entire human race; and

Be it further resolved: That we recommend to our fellowshipping churches a scriptural watchfulness on matters of doctrine clearly delineated in our Confession, lest there be a slow departure from the faith, while at the same time granting the exercise of our historic individual soul liberty in matters beyond the framework of our Confession and the plainly revealed Word of God; and

Be it further resolved: That we recommend to our autonomous but approved agencies, especially our schools as the fountainhead of our trained Christian servants, and our missions as a comparable fountainhead of worldwide evangelism and church building, that each hold fast our historic doctrinal convictions and guard itself against the inroads of Barthianism, neo-orthodoxy, scientism and academic idolatry, rejecting theological modernism and neo-evangelicalism, rejecting and refuting both naturalistic and theistic evolution, and accepting the clear statements of Scripture as having precedence over any pronouncements of science whenever such may appear to be in conflict,

Be it further resolved: That we instruct the Council of Fourteen to approve only such schools, missions and other agencies as refute both naturalistic and theistic evolution, and

Be it further resolved: That we instruct the Council of Fourteen to maintain a careful scrutiny of the approved schools, missions and other agencies of our Association in relation to their adherence to the stated doctrinal position of the General Association of Regular Baptist Churches.[8]

The developments at Wheaton were part of the growing influence of new evangelicalism that by 1966 had become a full-blown movement. It had its own college, Wheaton College. It had its own seminary, Fuller Theological Seminary. It had its own spokesman, Billy Graham. It had its own periodical, *Christianity Today.* It had its own organization, the National Association of Evangelicals. Dr. Jackson had tried a number of times to get Billy Graham to sit down with him to talk about the issues that affected so many Bible-believing local churches, but Graham refused to make or take time for such a meeting. Dr. Jackson had been Cliff Barrows's pastor at First Baptist Church in Ceres, California, but even that friendship was not enough for Graham to give Jackson some time. The GARBC would, however, maintain its Biblical position against a new evangelicalism that made concessions to unbelieving liberals, especially on matters that had to do with the first three chapters of Genesis.

End Notes

1. J. Murray Murdoch, *Portrait of Obedience* (Schaumburg, IL: Regular Baptist Press, 1979), p. 277.
2. Ibid., p. 278.
3. Ibid., p. 278.

4. Merle R. Hull, "Editorials," *Baptist Bulletin* (March 1966), p. 6.

5. *Baptist Bulletin* (March 1966), p. 1.

6. R. T. Ketcham, "My Partner in His Service," *Baptist Bulletin* (March 1966), p. 15.

7. "Council of Fourteen Minutes," Grand Rapids, Michigan, June 1966. (Typewritten.)

8. Ibid.

32

The words were ominous. They cast an eerie shadow. They were sobering. They were written by Merle R. Hull as part of the editorial page in the February 1965 issue of the *Baptist Bulletin:*

> Sometimes the greatest impact is created by coming directly to the point. With this thought in mind, omitting any buildup, we go immediately to the subject of this editorial.
>
> In the Christmas letter sent out by National Representative Paul R. Jackson and Mrs. Jackson, there appears this paragraph: "We would appreciate a special place in your prayers. Paul's doctor has just done a biopsy and reports that he has a mild malignancy in his lymph system. He is now taking medication. This condition is not sufficiently advanced to retard his ministry. We know that our Lord is able to direct the outcome to His own glory, and we have committed this to Him. We rejoice in the peace that He has given."
>
> No additional explanation needs to be attempted, and, we believe, no urging people to pray is necessary. The hosts of people across the country to whom Dr. Jackson has deservedly endeared himself will surely take it upon themselves to pray earnestly that this condition might be completely eliminated, to the glory of God. May he be sustained in the full force of his leadership abilities for many, many years, the Lord willing. Let us offer the prayers of faith to that end.[1]

Dr. Jackson was held up by the prayers of God's people, and for some time the dread disease remained in a state of remission. At the December 1964 Council meeting, Dr. Jackson had asked the Council to allow him to spend half of his time in the home office. He felt that so much traveling was sapping his energies physically, emotionally and spiritually. He needed time for administrative work, sermon preparation, prayer and writing. The Council gladly concurred with his request.

In 1967 that decision seemed even wiser. Dr. Jackson had keenly felt the resignation of western representative C. Allen Taff in 1962 and the death of Alfred F. Colwell in 1966. How happy he was when Dr. Reginald L. Matthews agreed to join the home office staff as field representative in 1967. The indefatigable Matthews would relieve Jackson of a great deal of road work.

In 1967 Dr. Jackson decided to put his pen to paper and write something that would be a lasting contribution to Bible-practicing Baptists everywhere. The result was *The Doctrine and Administration of the Church,* a presentation numbering 192 pages that covers all phases of the local Baptist church: its organization, government, ministry, doctrine, distinctives, outreach and discipline. The book was published in 1968.

In the foreword of the 1980 reprint, his son Mark wrote:

> How well I remember reading page after page of the handwritten copy of this book as it came from Dad's pen a number of years ago. He always loved the church, and his churches loved him. Later, as President of Baptist Bible Seminary and National Representative of the General Association of Regular Baptist Churches, he was one of the most respected and loved men in the ranks of fundamentalism. I was proud of him.
>
> He often said that a local church was the hardest thing in the world to kill. You can maim it, wound it, bleed it, and do it injustice—but it's hard to kill it because it is a divine institution and Christ is its Head!
>
> Dad's clear thinking about spiritual things, about the operation of the church, about the doctrine of the church, brought this book into being. Now it is accepted in many places as a standard work on local church administration.[2]

The book was a fitting climax to an exceptionally fruitful ministry.

But disease worked relentlessly in Paul Jackson's body. Lymphosarcoma was the name of the evil malady, and on May 15, 1969, the disease conquered Jackson's body, and he went Home to be with the Lord one day before his sixty-sixth birthday. His memorial service was held at the historic Belden Avenue Baptist Church in Chicago. The pastor, Dr. Gordon L. Shipp, in his tribute, said:

> On the rare occasions when a busy schedule allowed it, he [Dr. Jackson] attended services as a part of the crowd. If he was in the city, he was in the services of his local church. Seated by his wife, about one-third of the

way back in the center section, he soaked in the Word of God. He negated the nervousness that came to the pastor, who instinctively remembered his position in our Fellowship, with warm words coming right from the hearth of his heart: "Preacher, that message blessed my soul." You were certain he meant it!

Paul the apostle wrote: "Those things, which ye have . . . seen in me, do. . . ." Every member of every local church in our Fellowship could well follow Paul Jackson's example as a gracious, sensitive, and loyal church member. He knew when to be a part of the crowd. He recognized the need to "come up from the crowd." Our Fellowship will miss the leadership of this servant of God. This pastor and every individual in the local assembly will miss a member who rode in the gospel chariot with such grace that the entire congregation can only be far better because of it.[3]

Dr. R. T. Ketcham said:

Among the many compensations of the gospel ministry, there is one which stands high on the list. It is the friends God gives one along the way. All of us are thankful for many friends, but there is always an occasional individual who stands out above the others. Such a friend to me was Paul R. Jackson.

There was something about this brother which instantly challenged one's admiration *for* him and complete confidence *in* him. He was one who touched and molded the lives of those who worked closely with him. He was a lovable and gracious man. He was always available. He was never too busy to be approached by anyone in need of his help and counsel.

The work in the GARBC office revolves around deadlines. Certain things *must* be done and ready for printing or mailing at a given time. There can be no failure on the part of any staff member or department to have his work done promptly. No matter how close the deadline, and no matter how high the pile of work on his desk, Paul Jackson was *always* available. He was this to everyone—to a staff member with a personal problem or a pastor with a heartache and an overload of problems.

I have seen him on many occasions when someone in his office was consuming his time while he knew some department was hung up, and waiting for him to turn over his finished work. The person visiting him would never suspect from any indication from him that there was a deadline making its loud demands upon him.

My close business associations with Dr. Jackson extend over a period from 1944 to the time of my retirement in 1966. When one works as closely as Dr. Jackson and I did over a period of twenty-two years, there would have been plenty of opportunity to discover weakness in character, judgment and integrity. I can say that not once did I ever note any such weakness. He was dependable. Whenever there was an issue demanding forthright loyalty to Christ and the Scriptures, you could bank with certainty that Paul Jackson would be on the right side.

Let me cite an occasion which reveals how gracious he was and how people loved him for it.

His hospital bed was in Room 310 on the third floor of the Swedish Covenant Hospital. In this room he had suffered and languished for several weeks. On Thursday morning, May 15, at 9:50 he slipped away from it all to be with his Lord. Within ten minutes there were at least a dozen nurses in his room, many of them in tears. They said, "He was like a father to us—so kind and patient."

Yes, *that* was Paul Jackson. Lovable, gracious, dependable, loyal and completely sold out to his Lord.

That was Paul Jackson—my beloved friend, brother and co-worker for twenty-two wonderful, blessed and happy years in fellowship and service.[4]

One who worked closely with Dr. Jackson was Miss Ruth Ryburn, who said:

Probably I shall never understand this side of eternity why I was privileged to work for eight and one-half years for such a man as Dr. Paul R. Jackson. I'm thankful to the Lord for this rich experience, for the many things I learned from him, and for his patience with me. It was a very happy relationship. He worked conscientiously and hard, and he expected his co-workers to do the same; but he was always generous with praise for work well done. His consistent Christian life was a blessing and a challenge to me. . . . Someone has said, "A man is not known for his duration, but for his donation." Dr. Jackson actually had three outstanding ministries for Christ during his lifetime. He was a successful pastor, the president of a fine school and the leader of a great Fellowship. We know his works will follow him. . . . Again I say, "Thank you, Lord, for the privilege of serving as secretary to this man of God."[5]

The man who followed Dr. Jackson as president of Baptist Bible Seminary, G. Arthur Woolsey, said:

Writing to the Philippians, another Paul said, "I thank my God upon every remembrance of you." It is a reassured, albeit, most difficult privilege to speak in the memory of our beloved friend, and to speak in behalf of the many hundreds of men and women whose lives have been touched through the ministry of Baptist Bible Seminary and Dr. Paul R. Jackson.

Paul Jackson stood head and shoulders above the crowd. However, he was completely unaware of this. He never sought honor for himself. He didn't build a personal empire of any kind. He strove mightily for Another, his blessed Lord and Savior. His thought was for others. There has not been another person in my acquaintance quite as thoughtful of others, quite as gracious as Paul Jackson. He has left a deep and a lasting impression upon those lives with which he came in contact. His interests were many and varied. He was active in different areas of Christian service. Yet I believe that in a unique sense Baptist Bible Seminary stands as a living testimony to what he was and to what he believed. Someone has said that an institution is the lengthened shadow of a man. Certainly this is true of the institution Baptist Bible Seminary and the man Paul R. Jackson. For many years he and the Seminary were almost indistinguishable. Both he and his family built their lives into this institution.

He came to Baptist Bible Seminary in the year 1946. It was a small and struggling school operating on the Bible Institute level. The annual budget that year was something like $18,000. Fourteen years later he left a highly respected institution of higher education with degree-granting privileges. He left an institution that was thoroughly organized and financially stable, with a budget of over $400,000. In a very real sense, however, these statistics are not the meaningful ones, because Dr. Jackson left with the school a commitment. The school came to be what he was, and came to believe what he believed. Among his ideals were absolute loyalty to the Word of God, a vital missionary interest, an unbiased, Baptist stance, a Biblical emphasis on the local church and a devotion to balance as well as a highly effective academic program. The word "balance" was among his favorite terms. It summarized his entire philosophy. He was a broad man who saw all sides; he was a committed man who held very firmly to clearly stated convictions. At Seminary he influenced hundreds of young people. They now serve Christ around the globe. They carry with them the imprint of their association with a man of God. In their behalf, I say, "Thank You, Father, for sending your servant to touch our lives."[6]

The chairman of the Council of Fourteen at the time of Dr. Jackson's death was Joseph M. Stowell. He paid tribute to Paul Jackson in these words:

I know if Paul were yet here, he would be saying to us, "Stop talking about me, for I am nothing. Christ is all." But we cannot help thanking God for him. I think one of the greatest joys that was his, down in his heart, was his family. And what a tribute to him that his sons and daughter want to be in the same work that he was in. Like the Apostle John he could say, "I have no greater joy than to hear that my children walk in truth," and beyond that, out in the whitened harvest fields for Christ. One of his more recent joys was to know that his oldest grandchild, a granddaughter, is registered for this fall at Baptist Bible Seminary. This gave him great joy. . . . Beyond this, he was a faithful minister. He declared the whole counsel of God. He was not ashamed of the Bible. He stood for the old faith even when it cost him friendships, and sometimes popularity. A man of his native ability might have had even greater influence from a worldly standpoint in popularity had he been willing to compromise, but he stood for the truth. He was a faithful minister of Christ, and we honor him for this. In days when we see some whom he knew as schoolmates and friends departing into the arena of new evangelicalism and ecumenism, compromising here and there, we always knew where Paul Jackson stood. There was never a question about where he would stand—solidly for the old faith.[7]

In paying tribute to his father, Mark Jackson told how much he and his dad had wanted to go to the Holy Land together. Their plans did not materialize. Mark went on:

We did take a recent trip together, however, and I'll never forget it. We spent a month in Europe—Paris, Berlin, Frankfort, Geneva—and what a wonderful time we had. The fourth floor walk-up, no w/c hotel rooms ("so sorry, elevator broken"), price haggling, climbing around the Alps, menu reading ("I think you have it upside down"), praying together, preaching, what memories! . . . You will miss his wise leadership, his practical, balanced common sense, his inflexible stand, his spiritual counsel, his ability to put his finger on the issue and keep it there, his availability, his patience, his love.

I will miss these and more: the affection he reserved for his family, the phone call in the middle of the night ("It's the only time I know I can reach you"), the great times we had together as a family—all seventeen of us—the small talk, the "shop" talk, the bear hug and kiss that marked every greeting!

Driving home the day after the funeral, reflecting on what had been said and the honor and tribute paid to him on that triumphant occasion, I was humming the strains of the "Hallelujah Chorus" which had been played at the service. A smile crossed my lips and I realized something that made me happy. Dad loved music—when someone else made it! He never could carry a tune. Standing beside him in a song service would break you up. It was a family joke. He made the proverbial "joyful noise," but beyond that he rarely ever crossed the melody! But humming that grand "Chorus," it seemed I could hear that now silenced voice lifted in tumultuous triumph, joined with the saints and angels—singing baritone—in perfect harmony: "King of Kings and Lord of Lords . . . and He shall reign forever and ever!"

And as I write these words, I hear him say to me across the vast reach of space, ". . . My son, be strong in the grace that is in Christ Jesus. And the things that thou hast heard of me among many witnesses, the same commit thou to faithful men, who shall be able to teach others also. Thou therefore endure hardness, as a good soldier of Jesus Christ."[8]

Mark's brother, Donn, would concur with everything Mark said, but Donn had some of his own words of tribute. They are as follows:

Reflecting on Dad's picture by my illustration file, I realize that it illumines portions of the Word of God far more brilliantly than a hundred select anecdotes. The quality of his life reflects and manifests the truth he so gladly proclaimed.

Two passages have thrust themselves upon me as being particularly relevant to the life of Paul R. Jackson. I did not seek these; I have not been able to escape the parallel at any reading. I do not choose them just now, but have pondered and tested these specific truths against an individual life for a number of years.

Now I would share with you two separate verses which have burned in my heart and eyes many times—not because of a word study, the historical background or a touching story, but because on the road ahead of me I saw them demonstrated in real life.

An earthly servant. His life focused Matthew 20:28 in my mind because he was a servant. "Even as the Son of man came not to be ministered unto, but to minister, and to give his life a ransom for many." Even as failing strength made hospitalization and increasing care necessary, he never murmured, complained or made a demand. His only expression was that he hated to bother anyone. It was not his habit "to be ministered unto."

The set of his life was toward the advantage of others. I believe his devotion to the work of the church is apparent to all who knew him. Perhaps it is only necessary to attest that the attitudes displayed in public were never contradicted in private. His was tiresome, thankless labor, never festered with regret or resentment. Service was a privilege, under pressure or at ease. I knew Dr. Paul R. Jackson and I knew Dad. They were the same person. . . .

A heavenly wisdom. Some folk have been accused of being so heavenly minded that they are no earthly good. On the contrary, I am convinced that Dad was a good servant upon earth by reason of heavenly mindedness.

I believe on the basis of the definition in James 3:17 that I have observed a life practicing heavenly wisdom. "But the wisdom that is from above is first pure, then peaceable, gentle, and easy to be intreated, full of mercy and good fruits, without partiality, and without hypocrisy." Quite a checklist! Yet how instructive to both heart and head to observe the function of a wisdom which had the sweet dew of Heaven upon it. He was ever pursuing truth and purity. His honesty extended to every last literal penny. His relationship to God thus established, he was able with great success to walk in peace with men. . . . These two verses, Matthew 20:28 and James 3:17, have given me a better knowledge of my father. My father has given me a better knowledge of these verses. I would that they should stand as heartfelt tribute and loving remembrance to Dr. Paul R. Jackson, a servant of the Lord endued with wisdom from above and a wonderful father.[9]

Let the words of Merle R. Hull close this chapter:

One of the best testimonies to Dr. Jackson is the fact that those who worked closely with him in the Des Plaines office loved and respected him the most. Always considerate, always encouraging, always ready to help, he was a benediction and bulwark to the entire staff.[10]

The next chapter is a sermon by Dr. Paul R. Jackson.[11]

End Notes

1. Merle R. Hull, "Editorials," *Baptist Bulletin* (February 1965), p. 14.
2. Paul R. Jackson, *The Doctrine and Administration of the Church* (Schaumburg, IL: Regular Baptist Press, 1980), p. 9.
3. Gordon L. Shipp, "A Loyal Church Member," *Baptist Bulletin* (July 1969), pp. 10, 11.
4. R. T. Ketcham, "My Tribute to a Friend," *Baptist Bulletin* (July 1969), p. 12.
5. Ruth Ryburn, "A Rich Experience," *Baptist Bulletin* (July 1969), pp. 11, 12.
6. G. Arthur Woolsey, "The Lengthened Shadow," *Baptist Bulletin* (July 1969), p. 13.
7. Joseph M. Stowell, "Brother, Minister, Fellow Servant," *Baptist Bulletin* (July 1969), p. 11.
8. Mark Jackson, "Paul R. Jackson: My Dad," *Baptist Bulletin* (July 1969), p. 9.
9. Donn Jackson, "A Wonderful Father," *Baptist Bulletin* (July 1969), pp. 9, 10.

10. Merle R. Hull, "Editorial," *Baptist Bulletin* (July 1969), p. 2.

11. Paul R. Jackson, "Baptists and the Word of God," *Baptist Bulletin* (July 1969), pp. 5–7.

33

BAPTISTS AND THE WORD OF GOD

Paul R. Jackson, D.D.

This is a subject dear to my heart, for I became a Baptist because of the Word of God. I never lived in an area where there was a Baptist church until I pastored one! In elementary school days, I was a member of a Congregational church with a modernist pastor. He took me into the church membership unsaved. Later, after a change of pastors, we had a man who preached the gospel and I was saved. The church left the Congregational denomination because the members rejected liberalism and accepted the Bible. I was taught the Word of God. But with the interdenominational emphasis, I had no idea concerning the differences of teaching on church doctrine. On the basis of the Word I came to believe the things which Baptists believe and found myself unhappy in groups which did not adhere to the Bible on these distinctive issues. Finally, by the Lord's grace, I was led to a Baptist church where I found people who believed the whole Bible. There I found fellowship and unity. I came to realize that I was a Baptist simply because I had believed the plain teaching of the Word of God.

The Bible is the Word of God! It is God-breathed. It is infallible because it was given by inspiration of God—verbal, plenary inspiration. This has been the position of God's people throughout the centuries. With some, this has been only a doctrine of the faith to which they subscribed. There was too often a lack of practical application of this truth in daily life. It was not the infallible rule of faith and practice to all who confessed the doctrine. Let me illustrate:

> The principle of the sole authority of the Bible for faith and life was not an exclusive Anabaptist possession, but rather a foundation principle of all

Protestantism beginning with Luther himself, and was established against the Roman Catholic principle that the Bible and the tradition of the church together constitute the authoritative norm. The reformers, however, although emphatically proclaiming the principle, were not uniformly consistent in applying it, being led at times by theological and practical considerations to depart from the strict teaching of the Scripture. The Anabaptists, being Biblicists and usually unsophisticated readers of the Bible, not trained theologians or scholars, and having made a more complete break with tradition than the reformers, were more radical and consistent in their application of the principle of sole scriptural authority.

It was because of this principle of *sola scriptura* that Luther defied the pope, abolished the mass, taught the principle of justification by faith, did away with clerical celibacy, restored the office of preaching to a central place, discarded compulsory fasts and other human regulations, and taught salvation by grace through faith. But he was, in the eyes of the Anabaptists, not consistent with his own principles when he wrote: "It is true that there is not sufficient evidence from Scripture that you might be justified to begin infant baptism at the time of the early Christians after the apostolic period. But so much is evident in our time no one may venture with a good conscience to reject or abandon infant baptism which has so long been practiced." (*The Recovery of the Anabaptist Vision,* edited by Guy F. Hershberger, p. 171.)

In our own day many divide arbitrarily between fundamental and peripheral truths, and freely ignore plain commandments of God's Word in the interest of convenience, compatability or self-will. The great interdenominational movement of this generation has grown out of this compromising practice; at the same time their leaders have vocally defended the authority of the Bible.

Historically, Baptists have not only subscribed to the doctrine of Biblical authority, but they have sought to implement this truth in a practical manner.

To meet their opponents . . . Baptists have but to stand by their cardinal principle that the authority of the Lord Jesus Christ, as expressed to us through the Scriptures, is paramount with a true follower of Christ. When he says, Do this, whatever it may be, his loyal follower has no choice but to obey. And he cannot long persuade himself or persuade the world that it is obedience to do something quite different, under the plea that "it will do just as well." Nothing will do as well as unquestioning, exact, glad obedience to Christ's lightest word. *(A Short History of Baptists,* by Henry C. Vedder, p. 414.)

We have a great heritage! Through the past centuries our Baptist forefathers have preached and lived the truth with great boldness and conviction. They have faced many persecutions. In loyalty to our Savior, multitudes of these stalwarts have died as martyrs. Their boldness was not based upon human and organizational loyalties. They believed the Word of God! They could not alter nor deny that holy Book. They dared to defy customs and traditions, kings and councils, when they were contrary to God's Word. Revealed truth, not expediency, governed their lives. History reveals that the great central conviction of our Baptist forefathers was loyalty to the Word of God. It is Truth.

The current spiritual conflict is not new. It centers in the relationship of man to the Bible. Does this Book have divine authority over man? Does this Book sit in judgment upon man? Does this Book still speak with unqualified authority in this modern age? The liberals say "no" to all these questions. But Bible-believing Baptists say "yes." (Thank God for loyal believers outside the Baptists who also believe the Word of God!) This is the central religious conflict of today. But it is not new! Satan initiated his assault on the human race with an attack upon the Word of God. First he cast doubt: "Hath God said?" Then he openly denied the Word of God: "Thou shalt not surely die."

We believe with all of our hearts that the Bible is God's infallible revelation. Not all men who call themselves Baptists now subscribe to this truth! We cannot work and worship with them. God forbids us to do so. There can be no basis for unity and fellowship between those who are guided by faith in the Bible and those who are not.

The major battle between divergent forces within the "Baptist" family has its real basis in conflicting convictions concerning the Bible. Those who no longer accept the Bible as infallible do not always admit this basic difference in doctrinal position. By clouding the real issue they try to avoid offending multitudes who would resist an open denial of the Book. So we must understand that strategy is complex and confusing to the majority of people. May I identify several methods currently used by those who oppose the historic position of Baptists concerning the Scriptures:

1. The attitude of careless indifference toward parts of the Word. Such people proclaim faith in verbal inspiration—but not subject to the portions that oppose their philosophy! This careless attitude toward the authority of all of the Bible has given birth to interdenomination-

alism. It declares as unimportant such precious truths as baptism, eternal security, the sovereignty of the local church, etc. This attitude is dangerous and destructive. It has produced an ecumenical movement within the framework of redemptive truth. It minimizes much truth, and exalts expediency and human opinion. True Baptists are opposed to all of this! We always have been opposed. God grant that we always will be opposed, whatever the cost. These convictions are unpopular in the world. Those who seek to have the praise of the multitudes cannot afford to hold them! But if we genuinely believe that the Bible is indeed the Word of God, we can hold nothing less! God help us to believe the truth and to practice it in all consistency.

2. Another subtle method currently used to oppose the historic position of Baptists on the Scriptures is an appeal to interpret the Word in the light of science. While such men normally affirm faith in verbal inspiration, they are prone to declare the "troublesome" portions to be symbolic or mythological. This may as effectually destroy the message of the Bible as if its inspiration were denied. Actually, it is more subtle and dangerous than open unbelief.

This method is frequently employed in handling the Book of Genesis. It fosters the ego, exalts the authority of men and science, and will inevitably lead to more open infidelity. Baptists must not succumb to this modern trend.

The greatest danger from this assault is through our schools. Schools have historically provided the entrée for liberalism. This generation is no exception. We must guard with devotion our educational centers. We need not be ignorant to be spiritual! The Word is perfect, and we need have no fear about exhaustive study! But we must be loyal to the Scriptures at any cost, including the derisive criticism of those who actually oppose the authority of the Bible. This assault is characteristic of the neo-evangelical movement. These leaders repudiate fundamentalists and declare that our position sponsors obscurantism. They are unmindful that it was from men of our convictions on the Scriptures that have come the great revivals, the worldwide missionary movements and the establishment of universities and hospitals throughout the past centuries!

3. A third method of attack upon the Word comes from the neo-orthodox movement. Basically, this is the repudiation of the "outer Word" in contrast with the "inner Word." This philosophy is highly subjective and robs the Bible of its position of an objective revelation

from God. Such men deny that the Bible is given by verbal, plenary inspiration. They declare that the "Word of God" is what the Bible says to you. Such a position would leave us without a "court of appeal," without positive knowledge on eternal truth. There is no support in the Word for such teaching.

We are to "search the Scriptures"—not our minds. "Holy men of God spake as they were moved by the Holy Ghost." They spoke with *words,* and these words were controlled by the Spirit. Thank God that we have a Bible that is trustworthy to which we may go for wisdom and truth!

4. The fourth method of opposition is the open repudiation of the Book. This is illustrated by such men as Dr. Nels Ferre when he says in his book, *The Sun and the Umbrella:* "The use of the Bible as final authority for Christian truth is idolatry" (p. 39). What other authority is there? Thank God we are not dependent upon the authority of this man (or others like him) when he states that "Jesus never was or became God . . . such is the nature of the grand myth which at its heart is idolatry" (p. 83).

Surveys of thought in American seminaries indicate that a substantial number of tomorrow's leaders deny many of the basic truths. The inspiration, infallibility and authority of the Word of God are truths held by a small minority. This fact is prophetic of dark days ahead! We must use every opportunity to warn men of these false teachings and those that advance them. We must declare to all the world the truth as our Lord has committed it to us in the Word.

As we analyze the current conflicts within the Baptist movement, we are made aware of the need we have to stand together. While each believer and each church is responsible directly to the Lord, we do need the fellowship, counsel and prayers of our brethren. Our united proclamation of Biblical truth sustains a lighthouse in this dark world. Our united protest against the forces of infidelity sounds a needed alarm to men everywhere.

I wish that at this point I could be more optimistic. However, we all know that "evil men and seducers shall wax worse and worse." We shall not destroy the opposition to the Word of God. Apostasy shall increase in the end of this age. Nonetheless, we are commanded: "But *continue* thou in the things which thou hast learned and hast been assured of, knowing of whom thou hast learned them; And that from a child thou hast known the holy scriptures, which are able to make thee wise unto salvation through faith which is in Christ Jesus. All scripture is given by inspiration of God, and is profitable . . ." (2 Tim. 3:14–16). Finally, the truth shall triumph! He shall come and reign in righteousness! Let us, therefore, be "stedfast, unmoveable, always abounding in the work of the Lord . . ." (1 Cor. 15:58).

In the immediate future the consequences of believing the Book may include very strong persecution over all the earth. Many of our brethren suffer terribly in these days in Spain, Colombia, China and Russia. But even in America, where liberty has been unlimited, forces are now concentrating against Bible believers and the positions which we hold because of His Word.

Leading periodicals brand our position as "the extreme right" and highly dangerous. We are decried as bigots. The acceptance of this image of Bible believers is now very common. We cannot subscribe to the unbiblical philosophy of ecumenicalism, with "one world" and "one church"! Our refusal of this popular position exposes us to the contempt and persecution of those who are determined to establish their great dream.

Actually, we have not turned to "the right" in an extreme and dangerous position. We are continuing down the highway of truth where we and our spiritual forefathers have always walked. The only reason that we appear to be on the extreme right is because the liberal has swung so far to the left that we are now on his extreme right. Nonetheless, the general acceptance of the position of the liberal now gives us the reputation of extremists. We are accused of obstructing the unity and the peace of the church. And, they say, the peace is more important than the purity of the church! Therefore, our determined stand for the truth antagonizes the ecumenicists and those who accept their philosophy. The wider that acceptance grows, the greater will be the potential for persecution for those who cannot, for conscience sake, support that program.

We are left with a choice of one of two paths. We could yield to their pressure, ignore the Word of God and escape their wrath. Or, we could resist their pressure, stand for the Word of God and suffer the consequences. Brethren, there is no real choice! We must obey God's Word! Whatever the cost, we cannot become part of this compromising, rebellious movement! But make no mistake. It will cost dearly! Our Lord has warned: "Marvel not, my brethren, if the world hate you" (1 John 3:13). Also in John 15:18–20: "If the world hate you, ye know that it hated me before it hated you. If ye were of the world, the world would love his own: but because ye are not of the world, but I have chosen you out of the world, therefore the world hateth you. Remember the word that I said unto you, The servant is not greater than his lord. If they have persecuted me, they will also persecute you; if they have kept my saying, they will keep yours also."

There is rough water ahead! Unless our Lord comes for us quickly, we may soon pass through much persecution. May God give us a holy boldness, as He did to the apostles of old who prayed for this boldness (Acts 4:29). May we be able to say with the Apostle Paul: "We glory in tribulations also: knowing that tribulation worketh patience . . . experience . . . hope" (Rom. 5:3, 4).

The fact that apostasy will increase and persecutions will come must not cause us discouragement, fear, cowardice or surrender! God has placed us here to be witnesses. We are to hold forth the Word of life. The darker the night, the more evident is the need for the light of His Word. Brethren, as Bible-believing Baptists, we must be loyal to our Lord. We must adhere to His Word. We *must* at any cost, even of life itself!

There are radical elements and leaders in the mental health program in the United States and the United Nations. There are very disturbing evidences of a campaign to develop this movement into a means of liquidating the conservative opposition to both the political and religious liberalism. This is the most probable source of physical persecution that is now on the horizon. It is true that our Lord can overrule the unholy purposes of wicked men. He can protect us from these crises, or He can protect us through them, if He leads us by that path! I remind you of the courageous stand of the three Hebrew men so long ago when they were threatened by death in the fiery furnace. "Shadrach, Meshach, and Abednego, answered and said to the king, O Nebuchadnezzer, we are not careful to answer thee in this matter. If it be so, our God whom we serve is able to deliver us from the burning fiery furnace, and he will deliver us out of thine hand, O king. But if not, be it known unto thee, O king, that we will not serve thy gods, nor worship the golden image which thou hast set up" (Dan. 3:16–18). Praise God for such boldness, courage and faith! Our Baptist forefathers were marked by such faith and loyalty to the Lord! There may soon be opportunity for us to prove our devotion to Him.

The future for Bible-believing Baptists may also be marked by the proclamation of the Word of God. We must not allow ourselves to become preoccupied with the adversary and neglect our holy calling. Like Israel in the days of Nehemiah, we must build with the trowel while we defend with the sword. Controversy is not our objective. We are to preach the Word. However, controversy for the truth is a necessary part of our ministry by virtue of the adversaries and the commands of the Word.

I challenge all of our churches to fight the good fight of faith and to hold forth the Word of life to men everywhere. The time is short! The harvest is great! The laborers are few! Surely the Lord has put us here for such a time as this. The Word of God is the only light in the darkness, the only true testimony amid the babel of men's voices. The Lord help us to be faithful in this crisis hour.

The impending consequences for Bible-believing Baptists not only include the persecution from men and the responsibility of the proclamation of the Word, but also glorification by God. My brethren, remember that if we suffer with Him we shall be glorified together, and "that the sufferings of this present time are not worthy to be compared with the glory which shall be revealed in us" (Rom. 8:18). We serve a living Lord Who shall strengthen His servants in the crises and reward them in their faithfulness!

Joseph M. Stowell

THE ERA OF JOSEPH M. STOWELL

1969–1979

34

The year 1969 was a memorable one for a number of reasons. In January Richard M. Nixon gave his first presidential inaugural address. He had defeated Hubert H. Humphrey in November of 1968 with 31,785,480 votes to Humphrey's 31,275,166 votes. The electoral college results were Nixon, 301 votes; Humphrey, 191 votes; and George C. Wallace, 46 votes. As Nixon took office early in 1969, American troops in Vietnam had swelled to more than 540,000. In July Nixon began the slow, agonizing process of withdrawing those troops.

Also in July Senator Edward M. Kennedy drove his automobile off a bridge at Chappaquiddick Island, Martha's Vineyard, Massachusetts, in the late night hours of July 18. The body of Mary Jo Kopechne, a 28-year-old secretary, was found drowned in the car from which Kennedy had escaped.

On July 20, Neil A. Armstrong, a 38-year-old United States astronaut, became the first man to set foot on the moon. His partner on the Apollo II mission was Air Force Colonel Edwin E. Aldrin, Jr. Their feat electrified the world and put the United States solidly in first place in the race into outer space.

The year 1969 was also a memorable year for the GARBC. In reporting the 1969 annual conference at Fort Wayne, Indiana, Merle R. Hull wrote:

> Perhaps it was the temperature, which had Regular Baptists all warmed up and ready for action.
>
> Perhaps it was an indication—contrary to what some detractors have implied—that fundamental Baptists are a part of this fast-moving age as well as everyone else.
>
> Or perhaps the messengers caught a bit of the forward-looking spirit for which churches of the Fort Wayne area have become noted.

At any rate, it is probable that at no annual conference in GARBC history were as many significant and far-reaching decisions made as at the 38th Association meeting.

Note the major actions:

(1) A call to Dr. Joseph M. Stowell to become the new National Representative.

(2) Formation of a radio commission with instructions to proceed with plans for a worldwide Regular Baptist program.

(3) An invitation from the Council of Fourteen to Dr. William Kuhnle to be assistant to the National Representative.

(4) Dissociation of the GARBC from the International Council of Christian Churches.

(5) Plans for the formation of an International Baptist Fellowship.

(6) A proposed constitutional change to allow churches in Canada and U.S. possessions to fellowship in the GARBC.

President Truman, unable to move his program through the Senate and House in Washington, once labeled the legislators as a "do nothing Congress." Regular Baptists at Fort Wayne were apparently quite the opposite.

The call to Dr. Stowell was unanimous in the fullest sense. Not only was the vote itself without opposition, but no other person was seriously mentioned, even in informal conversations outside the conference sessions.[1]

Who were the members of the Council of Fourteen in 1969 that gave such dynamic leadership to the conference messengers? They are as follows: Joseph M. Stowell, chairman; Carl E. Elgena, vice chairman; W. Thomas Younger, secretary; John G. Balyo; Kenneth K. Elgena; Hugh Hall; James T. Jeremiah; David Nettleton; Kenneth Ohrstrom; Ernest Pickering; Harold Scholes; Paul Tassell; W. Wilbert Welch and G. Arthur Woolsey.

An interesting sidelight to the 1969 conference was the weather—it was hot, HOT, HOT! And the air conditioning for the auditorium malfunctioned! And Dr. Carl Sweazy preached for more than an hour one evening in that heat! No one who was there that night has ever forgotten it!

Joseph Mishael Stowell was born on January 28, 1911, at Colon, Michigan, into a farmer's family. Joseph accepted Christ as his personal Savior when he was just nine years old. He was baptized into the membership of the First Baptist Church of Colon and received excellent teaching and training from Bible-centered pastors in that struggling rural church. It was a fruitful church, however, and three

Stowells and Joseph H. Bower all went into the GARBC ministry from its ranks.

After Stowell graduated from Wheaton College in 1933, he became pastor of the Bethany Baptist Church of Dollar Bay, Michigan, way up in the Upper Peninsula, where 20 feet of snow in the wintertime is not uncommon. After his brief stint at Dollar Bay, he organized and pastored the Calvary Baptist Church in Hancock, Michigan, until 1935. During those years in the Upper Peninsula, Stowell served as president of the Lake Superior Bible Conference, which sponsored summer Bible camps for young people and their parents. In 1935 he organized and pastored the Brunswick Baptist Church in Gary, Indiana. During the four years he pastored in Gary, he drove to Michigan City, Indiana, to teach a weekly Bible class that ultimately became the Evergreen Baptist Church.

In June of 1938 Stowell married Corabelle Pease. She had grown up in a Baptist parsonage in Stanton, Michigan. She majored in Bible and music at the Moody Bible Institute. The Stowells were blessed with two daughters and one son. The firstborn, Margaret, is married to R. William Wheeler, pastor of the Emmanuel Baptist Church of Xenia, Ohio. The second, Joseph M. Stowell III, is president of the Moody Bible Institute in Chicago. The third, Hannah, is married to Clifford Jensen, missionary aviator in Brazil. The three Stowell children are graduates of Cedarville College.

In 1939 Stowell was called to the Tabernacle Baptist Church in Ithaca, New York, home of Cornell University. During his six years at Ithaca, Stowell ministered to students at the University. He returned to Michigan in 1945 to pastor the First Baptist Church of Bay City. In 1949 Stowell was called to the First Baptist Church of Hackensack, New Jersey. He succeeded Dr. Harry Leach, who had pastored the Hackensack church for 33 years. Dr. Stowell pastored there for 20 years. During all of those years Stowell was dean of the Monday Night Bible Institute in Hackensack.

Dr. Stowell earned a master's degree from the Winona Lake School of Theology in 1947. In 1960, that seminary chose him for the distinguished alumnus award. In 1952 he and Reginald L. Matthews made an around-the-world missionary preaching tour. He visited Brazil in 1956 and Jamaica in 1965. In 1948 he was asked to serve on the Baptist Mid-Missions Council. He has also served on the board of ABWE since 1950 and as ABWE vice president for many years. He has served on the board of trustees of Baptist Bible College of Pennsylvania since 1943, sometimes as chairman.

Dr. Stowell, like his predecessors to the office of National Representative, brought to the office wide and deep experience as a successful pastor, an expository preaching ministry and a love for worldwide missionary outreach. His love for the GARBC had been demonstrated many times over by his helpful and productive service on the Council of Fourteen.

Dr. Stowell's letter of resignation to the First Baptist Church of Hackensack surely reveals his pastor's heart. It is dated July 27, 1969, and says:

My dear People:

The servant of Christ must ever keep his mind and heart open to the leading of the Lord as to his place of service. He dare not allow himself to get so deeply rooted in one place that our Sovereign God cannot transplant him to another field.

After twenty happy and blessed years of that precious tie and privilege of being your pastor, the Lord of the harvest has made it clear that He has for Mrs. Stowell and me another work—that of serving as the National Representative and preacher on a proposed worldwide radio ministry of our General Association of Regular Baptist Churches.

It is a Biblical plan that churches of like faith and order are to work together. Several times in 2 Corinthians 8, churches are spoken of as acting in unison. [Verse 19] speaks of a certain one who was "chosen of the churches" to special ministry. At the 38th Annual Conference of our churches meeting at Fort Wayne, Indiana, June 23–27 of this year, the Lord moved in a marvelous manifestation of enthusiastic, Spirit-prompted unity as the churches extended a call to your pastor to become their leader. We now believe this to be of the Lord—and we cannot say "no" to Him, though our hearts long to continue with you in the work here. What a joy it has been to co-labor with you fellow believers led by our noble officers and workers. The ties of love, mutual esteem and confidence are stronger than you can know. Making this decision has been very difficult.

We are constrained of the Lord, however, to ask you to release us to take up our new ministry as of November 1st of this year.

We sense more and more the need for churches and Associations of churches like ours to courageously and "earnestly contend for the faith, which was once delivered unto the saints" (Jude 3) and against the growing apostasy of our times. Though deeply sensing personal insufficiency for the task of leading a large portion of God's "faithful remnant" in these last days, yet our dependence is upon Him to whom all power is given. There is "a cause" that involves the preservation of Bible Christianity in the world (1 Sam. 17:29). The time is short—the coming of the Lord draweth nigh. We sense a Divine urgency in this call.

After having given twenty of the prime years of our lives to the work here, we are trusting our blessed Lord for some good years yet for this great ministry of wide influence and leadership that is before us as an open door from Him. He has promised in Ezekiel 36:11 that "He will do better unto you than at your beginnings."[2]

And so Dr. Stowell, at the age of 58, embarked upon an adventure that would carry him through an entire decade. After having lived in parsonages all her life, Mrs. Stowell would move to Chicago with her husband to set up housekeeping in an apartment.

The Council asked Dr. William E. Kuhnle to become assistant to the national representative. His major responsibilities would deal with the fledgling radio ministry tobe instituted by Dr. Stowell, who had had continuous radio ministries spanning 30 years. Promoting the broadcast, preparing radio booklets and answering the mail generated by the broadcast would be Dr. Kuhnle's responsibilities. If Dr. Stowell was to carry on all of the normal work of the office of National Representative, someone would surely have to relieve him of the day-to-day details of producing a half-hour weekly radio broadcast.

Dr. Kuhnle was born in Detroit, Michigan, in 1910. He graduated from Moody Bible Institute in 1935. While working at the Moody radio station, WMBI, he met beautiful Edna Stephenson, an accomplished vocal soloist. They were married in 1937. From 1937 to 1941 Dr. Kuhnle served as assistant to two great pastors of the Walnut Street Baptist Church in Waterloo, Iowa, P. B. Chenault (killed by a drunken driver in 1939) and Robert T. Ketcham. In 1941 Dr. Kuhnle was called to the pastorate of the Garfield Avenue Baptist Church in Milwaukee, Wisconsin, where he served for 28 years, until his call to the home office in 1969. He served on the executive committees of ABWE, Grand Rapids Baptist College and Seminary and Shepherds, Inc. His busy life included serving as president of the Alumni Association of Moody Bible Institute. He served on the Council of Fourteen for 18 years and as the beloved chairman of the Chaplain's Commission for many years.

Both Dr. Stowell and Dr. Kuhnle had been vigorously involved in radio ministries. Dr. Stowell had maintained broadcasts over WHCU in Ithaca, New York; WBCM in Bay City, Michigan; and for many years over WJRZ in Hackensack, New Jersey. Dr. Kuhnle had begun a radio ministry in 1941 in Milwaukee known as *The Gospel Hour*. By 1969 the broadcast was aired over nine stations, including two stations in the Philippines.

Dr. Stowell was convinced that the GARBC national representative ought really to represent the Association nationally. He felt that Regular Baptists were "talking to themselves" most of the time. True, the outreach of Regular Baptist Press had helped to correct that shortcoming somewhat. But there was much yet to do. By their very nature as separatists, Regular Baptists often felt uncomfortable about their national representative speaking in churches, conferences or campuses that were not really Regular Baptist by affiliation. Dr. Stowell strongly believed that such an attitude was unhealthy. If the Association were to make an impact on other groups and "make friends" for its viewpoints and positions, we would need to be willing to go to them and deliver our message.

This Dr. Stowell had done as a young pastor in Michigan. He became friends with Rev. John Rader, founder and director of the Gitche Gumee Bible Camp in Eagle River, Michigan, just a few miles from Copper Harbor, in the farthermost point of the Upper Peninsula. Dr. Stowell became president of the camp board. In 1937 he asked a young man by the name of Charles Hart to lead the singing for the summer camps. When Hart arrived on the campgrounds, he fell in love with the place *and* with the director's daughter, Joyce Rader! Hart stayed for the summer, eventually married Joyce and, when John Rader died in 1957, succeeded his father-in-law as camp director. He held that post until his retirement in 1981. He still is active as a camp board member and helps his successor, Mel Jones, in any way he can.

Dr. Stowell continued to serve as camp board president even after moving to Gary, Indiana, in 1935. All through the years since, even after Dr. Stowell moved to Ithaca, New York, and had to sever his official relationship with the camp in 1939, Gitche Gumee Bible Camp has been a friend and ally of the GARBC. A good share of the speakers at Gitche Gumee every summer are Regular Baptists. In the summer of 1990, for example, Regular Baptists speaking at Gitche Gumee were John Blodgett, Paul Beals, Clair Saliers, Paul Tassell, Manfred Kober, W. Paul Jackson, Charles Davis and David Warren. And the speaker for the October 1990 Senior Saints' Retreat was none other than 79-

year-old Joseph M. Stowell! Dr. Stowell has spent a lifetime making friends for the GARBC and making people aware of what the GARBC is. That was his primary, basic reason for a national radio broadcast.

Just as importantly, Dr. Stowell wanted a broadcast that would clearly present the gospel. His missionary heart had always been concerned for souls. He longed to see people evangelized, and he knew by experience that the radio was an excellent medium of getting out the message of salvation. His conviction had been that every local church in the GARBC ought to be busy in outreach to the lost, busy in making people understand Regular Baptist principles and busy proclaiming the whole counsel of God. He felt that the national representative ought to set the pace.

As 1970 neared, Dr. Stowell and Dr. Kuhnle had to secure a program producer and radio agent. He came in the person of James Draper, who had worked with Radio Bible Class. Mr. Draper contacted radio stations, negotiated contracts for air time and generally was the "troubleshooter" as agent. As producer he aided Kuhnle and Stowell in putting together a broadcast format, secured proper music and did the "nuts and bolts" work of putting it all together with the recording studio personnel.

A name! What would be the name for the broadcast? Taking a cue from *The Lutheran Hour* and *The Reformed Hour*, some strongly suggested *The Regular Baptist Hour*. But after much prayerful brainstorming, the name *Living Reality* was chosen. The theme songs—"In Times Like These You Need a Savior" and Paul R. Jackson's favorite gospel song, "The Solid Rock"—introduced and closed the broadcast. At first the special music was provided by the Music Departments of the approved schools, but that proved to be impractical and cumbersome for the most part; so Draper put together a fine men's chorus from the Chicago area and called them "The Living Reality Singers." Through the years they produced two long-play albums.

Dr. Kuhnle was the program "host" or announcer, and Dr. Stowell was the *Living Reality* preacher.

A nationwide broadcast generated a huge volume of mail and other office work. Dr. Stowell prevailed upon Margie Williams to take on the awesome task. Miss Williams had worked with Dr. Stowell at First Baptist Church in Hackensack; so she knew his personality and work ethic and was happy to follow him to the Des Plaines office. A great deal of the work involved answering questions from listeners.

This Dr. Kuhnle did. With his great background as a pastor and Bible scholar, he was a "natural" for that responsibility. Both Margie and Ruth Ryburn worked as secretaries for Dr. Kuhnle's "letter ministry," but Margie's main work had to do with opening the mail, processing the checks and sending out the radio booklets. Radio booklets? Yes, each month's radio messages (four or five) were printed in an attractive booklet the size of the *Our Daily Bread* devotional booklets put out by Radio Bible Class of Grand Rapids.

As stations were added and the mail increased, more help was needed. Dr. Matthew's wife, Grace, had worked for Radio Bible Class when she and Dr. Matthews resided in Grand Rapids. She joined Margie in the office, and the two of them worked smoothly to make *Living Reality's* ministry and outreach efficient and effective. Dr. Stowell's primary responsibility, of course, was the preparation and delivery of the radio messages. The recording studios were about 20 miles from Des Plaines, in the Wheaton area. Dr. Stowell and Dr. Kuhnle would go to the studios and spend an afternoon at a time, usually recording a month of messages and announcements. The studio personnel and Draper would then put the program together, package it and mail it to the many stations scattered across the country. Draper would also handle the details of receiving the bills from the stations and making sure they were paid.

Money! That was a problem. Stowell, Kuhnle, Draper and the Council of Fourteen had agreed that the broadcast would be top-quality with no gimmicks and no "begging for money." The prayerful hope was that the churches would support the broadcast in the main, and that individual listeners would pick up the rest of the tab. But it was a constant struggle. The log of stations ultimately numbered close to one hundred, including the prestigious Moody network and some foreign stations. There were times, however, when Regular Baptist Press had to come to the rescue and pay some of the bills. This dismayed Dr. Stowell, and he worked valiantly throughout his tenure as national representative to make the broadcast a "pay-as-you-go" operation.

Looking back over the 1970s one can see how *Living Reality* blessed many lives. Hundreds and hundreds of letters attest to that. Thousands of radio booklets went around the world. Dr. Stowell's ministry was, without a doubt, greatly multiplied as a result of *Living Reality.* It would be up to Dr. Stowell's successor to decide whether or not the broadcast would continue into the next decade. But that is another story for another chapter.

During the December 1969 Council of Fourteen meeting in Des Plaines, Dr. Stowell and Dr. Merle Hull approached me, Paul Tassell, with an invitation to join the home office staff as national youth representative. At that time I was pastoring the Campus Baptist Church of Ames, Iowa, and had a productive ministry to the students of Iowa State University. I had also been writing, at the request of Dr. Hull, the RBP youth materials called *Active Christian Teens (ACT)* for a couple of years at my desk in Ames. I accepted their invitation and moved to the Des Plaines office on April 5, 1970. It was an exciting time. New personnel. A new radio broadcast. A relatively new office building. And the opportunity to travel among the churches in behalf of our teenagers.

My responsibilities included writing the materials, overseeing the work of Talents For Christ (Edgar Koons was back in the pastorate) and setting up the program for Youth Days at the annual conference. In addition to those challenges, I preached a couple hundred times a year in camps, youth rallies, junior high and senior high school assemblies, and even public school assemblies! We changed the name of the youth materials to *Wise Active Youth (WAY)*, expanded the annual youth program at the conference from one day to two days and generally promoted our young people wherever and whenever possible.

After three years, however, it soon became obvious that my position, "National Youth Representative," and the *WAY* materials were unnecessary in the youth economy as it was developing among our churches. The state fellowships were waking up to the necessity for youth emphasis, and they were doing a great job. All over the country state fellowships sponsored "Funtastics," "Sports Jambo-ees," "Leadership Conferences" and, of course, great summer youth camps. As far as written materials were concerned, some were "coming into their own." Many churches used Word of Life, still others used *Positive Action for Christ (Pro-Teens)* and others used Awana. Just as the hard decision was made by RBP to discontinue *My Devotion* in face of the unquestioned popularity of *Our Daily Bread,* so I concluded that our youth ministries are best carried on at the state and local levels with each church using the written materials best suited to its youth group. I resigned as national youth representative and on February 18, 1973, returned to Iowa, to the pastorate of the Grandview Park Baptist

Church in Des Moines. I continued to write the *WAY* materials until RBP phased them out. Another development in our churches in the early 1970s that has increased through the years is the calling of full-time youth pastors to our church staffs. This, too, has been healthy and points up again that centralization of programs in a home office is not always the answer for Regular Baptists.

As the GARBC moved into its fifth decade, the 1970s, it was sound doctrinally, sound financially and sound organizationally. The Council of Fourteen, the invention of R. T. Ketcham in 1938, continued to serve the Association well. The Council had undergone some refinements a couple of times, but it was sound and practical. In 1948 at the annual conference in Grand Rapids, the Association had voted that "any Councilman completing two consecutive terms of two years shall be ineligible for election for at least one year." In Springfield, Massachusetts, in 1962, the messengers had voted that no more than four men who are "salaried servants" of approved agencies may be on the Council at any given time. Dr. Merle R. Hull wrote:

> With the growth of the Fellowship, an enlargement of the number seemed in order, and in 1973 the Council of Fourteen became the Council of Eighteen. Nine are now elected each year.
>
> From the beginning, of course, the GARBC constitution specified that no employee of the Association itself could vote. None of them, therefore, may be on the Council.
>
> The Council regularly meets twice each year—immediately prior to the annual conference in June and again the first part of December.
>
> For several years, representatives of state and area fellowships as well as representatives of all approved agencies have been invited to attend and observe the June Council meeting (except for executive sessions). These men, while permitted to offer comments or ask questions, are nonetheless only observers. They exercise no influence on Council policy or decisions.
>
> The matter of regional representation on the Council has been considered from time to time. In fact, as far back as 1953 a plan for dividing the Association into districts, each district to be represented on the Council, was presented on the floor of the Association in a business session. It failed to pass, and at no other time to date has the proposal gained widespread sympathy. Actually, the value of regional representation would seem to be only psychological. The Council is not like a legislative body in Washington or a state capital. It has nothing to dispense for the special benefit of any area. It acts in the interests of Association churches as a whole.

With the modifications just explained, Dr. Ketcham's plan for organization continues to function.[3]

End Notes

1. Merle R. Hull, "Editorials," *Baptist Bulletin* (August 1969), p. 21.

2. "Council of Fourteen Minutes," Des Plaines, Illinois, December 1969. (Typewritten.)

3. Merle R. Hull, *What A Fellowship!* (Schaumburg, IL: Regular Baptist Press, 1981), p. 26.

35

The world is reading! People are reading magazines. More than 19 million copies of *Modern Maturity* are sold every month. *Reader's Digest* has a circulation of 16 million per month. *National Geographic* sells more than 10 million per month. Both *Newsweek* and *Sports Illustrated* have circulations of more than 3 million per month. *Popular Science, Seventeen* and *Golf Digest* sell more than 1 million copies each per month. The average daily circulation of the *Wall Street Journal* is 1,931,410. *USA Today* has an average daily circulation of 1,341,811; the *Los Angeles Times,* 1,119,840; the *Washington Post,* 812,419; and the *Chicago Tribune,* 740,154.

As far as books are concerned, all-time best-sellers are Benjamin Spock's *Baby and Child Care,* 39,200,000; the *Merriam-Webster Dictionary,* 19,700,000; *New American Roget's Thesaurus,* 17,600,000; Dale Carnegie's *How to Win Friends and Influence People,* 17,400,000; J. R. R. Tolkien's *The Hobbit,* 14,500,000; and George Orwell's *1984,* 12,800,000. And those statistics have mainly to do with the United States of America and English-speaking-reading people.

But people all over the world are reading! They are reading newspapers, magazines, pamphlets, paperback books, hardcover books, fiction, nonfiction, prose, poetry, how-to books, religious books and political manuals. People are definitely, continuously, eagerly reading. Politicians know this. Cultists know this. Specifically, New Age proponents know this. The world has its proverbial nose stuck in a book!

At the 1973 annual conference in Kansas City, Dr. Stowell introduced the Council to Rev. Virgil Riley. For many years Mr. Riley had worked with an interdenominational organization that specialized in the distribution of literature to missionaries around the world. As funds were made available, the organization would give literature free of charge to the missionaries. Riley was, however, a Regular Baptist, and he longed to see a literature ministry that was unashamedly baptistic and separatist for our Regular Baptist missionaries. Dr. Stowell and the Council listened sympathetically and enthusiastically to Riley's "dream," and before the annual conference was over, Gospel Literature Services had been born as the Missionary Literature Department of Regular Baptist Press. And "Mike" (as the big, tall, handsome Irishman was affectionately called) Riley had been appointed its first director.

Mike and his wife, Jayne, moved into the Des Plaines office to begin a ministry that would span 15 years for them (until their retirement). The Rileys were tireless workers. They traveled among the churches telling of the great need of the Regular Baptist missionaries for tracts, discipling materials and Sunday School quarterlies. Mike would preach and promote, preach and promote, then come back to the office to correspond with missionaries about proposed literature projects. He and Jayne, with minimal help, would then go to work sorting, counting and packing box after box after box of materials.

The great burden of the Rileys was to make our churches see the need to put Gospel Literature Services on their missionary budgets. The going was tough at first, but gradually the churches began to respond. In addition to churches, individuals caught the vision and became regular contributors. Slowly, year by year, the number of projects increased—and so did the number of dollars. One of the more popular luncheons at the annual conference each summer was the Gospel Literature Services luncheon hosted by the Rileys. Mike would "report" and mission executives present would tell of the great value GLS had been to their missionaries over the past 12 months. The Rileys faithfully and fervently laid a solid foundation for a ministry that is growing faster than ever as the GARBC and RBP go through the 1990s.

In 1971 the chairman of the Council appointed a committee to clarify the Articles of Faith. Since 1932 there had been developments in the so-called evangelical world that tended to cloud and confuse certain areas of theological declarations. The charismatic confusion, the differences on creative days and the varying viewpoints on eschatology were some of the areas that called for precise statements. The GARBC was not interested in "changing" the articles of faith, only in "clarifying" them. The men appointed were Dr. David Nettleton, chairman; Dr. Ernest Pickering and Dr. Donald J. Sewell. Their work culminated in the June 1975 and June 1976 annual conferences, where the messengers voted to accept the clarified Articles of Faith.

However, the "culmination" did not occur before a rather vigorous "storm" of debate had taken place over the doctrine of election. The Clarifications Committee had been encouraged to include in the statement of faith an expression of belief in the doctrine of Biblical election. The Council heard the statement on election and agreed to have it presented and recommended to the Association. The constitutional procedure called for two readings before the voting messengers at successive annual conferences. It was given its first reading at the conference in Ocean Grove, New Jersey, in June 1974. However, when the Council met for their December meeting in 1974, Dr. Stowell advised the Council to drop the matter because it would be too divisive. The Council accepted the advice and instructed the Council chairman, Dr. Carl E. Elgena, to inform the churches of their decision. The letter written to the churches by Dr. Elgena in February of 1975 is as follows:

Dear Pastor,

I have been instructed by the Council of Eighteen to pen an epistle to you as the chairman of the Council regarding the Article on Election which was read to our Association at the Ocean Grove Conference.

The Council of Eighteen is concerned that the good spirit of warmth and unity continue in our great Fellowship; therefore, many hours were given over to a full discussion of this Article at our December meeting, with the following conclusions:

#1 The purpose and responsibility of the revision of the Confession of Faith Committee was to clarify, enlarge and strengthen our Articles of Faith. It was never intended that there would be any change or alteration of the essence of our doctrinal statement.

#2 Our Fellowship has always been identified as Calvinistic in its theology, but has never officially adopted the limited atonement view which may be held by some godly men in our Fellowship.

#3 We repudiate Arminianism and we believe that this is clearly set forth in our present Articles of Faith.

#4 We want to give leadership to the many young men in our Fellowship who may be moving to extremism in their methodology almost to the extent of excluding the Sovereignty of God in the affairs of men, and on the other hand very definitely making clear that, as an Association, we do not hold the view of limited atonement.

#5 We are Biblicists and we are Baptists!

We believe you will note that our present Articles of Faith make it very clear where we stand on the doctrine of Election, and to add such an article at this time would literally change and alter the Constitution which we have lived with for nearly 42 years. The Council, therefore, does not plan to recommend to the Association any changes or additions at this time.

Dear Pastor, will you note *Article VIII* on the atonement. "We believe that the salvation of sinners is *wholly of grace. . . .*" Note *Article IX:* ". . . the new creation is brought about in a manner above our comprehension, *solely* by the power of the Holy Spirit in connection with divine truth, so as to secure our voluntary obedience to the gospel." Note *Article Xb:* ". . . that it is bestowed not in consideration of any works of righteousness which we have done; but solely through faith in the Redeemer's blood, His righteousness is imputed to us." Note *Article XIV* on the security of the saints.

I believe, as Chairman, I would like to make this statement concerning the Article on Election which was read at Ocean Grove. The entire Council believes this was a very clear and concise statement which rather accurately gave expression to where our Fellowship has always stood on this great Bible doctrine. I shall make one more statement. *The entire Council indicated that this statement expressed in a very admirable fashion their own personal views on Election.* We must not allow extremism in any direction to mar what God has so wonderfully blessed down through these 42 years. I hope my letter, which I will stuff in the envelope with other mail from the Home Office, in order to save postage, will clarify our stand and define our course of action.

God bless you and keep you true to Him in these difficult but challenging days.

May God's best be yours in the brand new year . . .

Sincerely for souls,
Carl E. Elgena, Chairman
Council of Eighteen, GARBC[1]

The proposed article that was read at Ocean Grove in 1974 read as follows:

We believe that all men are totally depraved, without ability to come to God, and are hopelessly lost, but that God, in sovereign grace and apart from any consideration of foreseen human merit or response, and in perfect consistency with human responsibility, chose some before the foundation of the world to be recipients of His grace in Christ.

As the Gospel is preached to all the nations, these elect ones are caused to hear it and their hearts are opened by the Holy Spirit, so that they freely and gladly receive Christ as their Saviour, thus becoming children of God (John 6:44, 65; Acts 13:48; Rom. 8:29, 30; Eph. 1:4–6).[2]

After the reading of the above statement at the 1974 conference, the debate began around the country. Some tried to bring R. T. Ketcham's name into the matter. He responded in the following words:

For 43 years we have believed what the Bible has said to us about Election and we have all been happy. Now why this sudden confusion? Dr. Good quotes on what I say in my books about Election and then he winds up his paragraph by saying, "Therefore, Dr. Ketcham is a Calvinist." I made these statements not because I am a Calvinist, but because I am a Biblicist. I believed what I taught years before I ever heard of John Calvin. I emphatically deny that I have built my theology around what Calvin or any other man has said or taught. I have built it around the Book. Now, why must I be labeled as a Calvinist? I am a Biblicist. I have thought all my brethren were, too. Let us not run off now and follow a man who insisted that the State have a part in controlling the church. Why should we insist upon being called by the name of a man who engineered the burning at the stake of a man named Servetus? I have always given invitations to the unsaved to confess Christ. Not to do so would be like slamming the door in the face of one who was ready to come.[3]

When the annual conference convened at Winona Lake in 1975 and the business session was called to order, Dr. David Nettleton was given permission to read a statement about the proposed article. His statement contained three major points about the article: (1) the reason for the article; (2) the history of the article; (3) the nature of the article. Under the first point Dr. Nettleton said: "It was never meant to divide us, but rather to give expression to that which was commonly believed among us. The reason for it is that simple and that pure."[4]

Under point two, the history of the article, Dr. Nettleton explained that in June of 1972 he had asked Dr. Ernest Pickering to write an article on election. Pickering replied: "Frankly, I do not think I can produce a definition that will satisfy everyone in our Association. . . . However, I will send you this with the understanding that it may be thought unwise to introduce it because of potential division. I will understand perfectly if this is the case."[5]

Still under point two, Nettleton said:

The article which was submitted was broadened a bit and was later submitted to the Council for review. By June of 1973, the entire work of the committee was printed for Council review, and with it was the first draft of the election article. With some alteration the election article was again submitted to the Council in June, 1974, in its present form, and was so read to the Association.

Because of the nature of the article, it was agreed that inasmuch as the Council had advance notice of it, the entire Association should also be given much time to consider it. It was originally scheduled to be read first and officially in June, 1975, but was read in 1974, unofficially (i.e., not as a first official reading, but it was done with Council agreement) in order to see if there would be any reaction. (There was.)

When the Council met in December, 1974, it was decided that it would be unwise to put this on the schedule of an official first and second reading and vote. In order to sound forth a clear note, the entire Council expressed agreement with the article, but in order to preserve unity, yet with some diversity, it was agreed that the article should not be officially introduced.[6]

Since Nettleton reported that "the entire Council expressed agreement with the article," that entire Council should be identified. They were as follows: Fred R. Brock, Jr., L. Duane Brown, Russell Camp, Ralph G. Colas, Floyd A. Davis, Carl E. Elgena, Daniel Gelatt, Mark Jackson, J. Don Jennings, Wendell Kempton, David L. Moore, David Nettleton, Ernest Pickering, Wilbur Chapman Rooke, Donald Sewell, Paul N. Tassell, Donald Tyler and G. Arthur Woolsey.

Under his third point, the nature of the article, Nettleton had four things to say.

a. We believe it is scriptural. The fact that certain famous theologians of the past have embraced it and included it in their theological package, or the fact that famous men have opposed it—these facts have neither guided nor deterred us. The Bible presents a sovereign God who acts as He pleases, One who is the first cause, One who causes, wills and determines as He chooses. We, as a committee, did not choose to please self or others when we expressed ourselves.

b. Secondly, it is a sound statement. It is not extreme or "hyper." It can be carried too far, but many good truths can be carried to dangerous extremes. That does not negate or exclude the truth.

The article gives God the glory and makes the clay subject to the potter. It is not a humanistic philosophy leading to wrong practices, but a truth which recognizes the leadership and sovereignty of God and causes us to cooperate with Him.

The article is in agreement with many great confessions of faith and is in agreement with many outstanding theological textbooks used in sound schools today.

We have not crossed wires with our great Association leaders of the past, and the present Council has endorsed this expression of truth.

c. It is a balanced statement. In an attempt to avoid questions and controversy, we clearly stated that God's election was "in perfect consistency with human responsibility," so the two great truths were wedded in one balanced statement.

As an Association, we believe in a great outreach of evangelism and missionary effort and we so expressed ourselves by these words, "as the gospel is preached to all the nations these elect ones are caused to hear it. . . ."

Let there be no question as to the beliefs of the committee and Council along these lines. We believe that human responsibility should be taught, preached and stressed, but we believe that the great majestic truth of the sovereignty of God in election should stand out as well.

We are neither apathetic or fatalistic in the matter of men's souls. We believe that the sovereign purposes of God are effected by the greatest outreach possible—even greater than we have ever known so far. We only desire to reach out as He guides and empowers.

d. The article is controversial. We sensed this somewhat and thus proceeded carefully, but we did not fully grasp the great interest and reaction.

However, it is to be noted that the controversy is not new. Before this matter was ever read to the Council, attacks against the truth it expresses were being made widely and noble men were being offended. We believe that the raising of the standard was a word in due season.[7]

Dr. Nettleton commented on the "emotional climate that makes it unwise for us to take action on the election article." He then said:

"Therefore, Mr. Chairman, I move that we as an Association support the Council in its decision to refrain from presenting this particular article for first reading."[8]

Nettleton immediately, however, told the messengers that a second motion would follow. Wrote Nettleton:

It was necessary to know what the second motion would be before voting on the first one. Therefore, I explained that the second motion would present the same statement on election, but that it would be presented as a "testimony" and not as a test of fellowship. No one would be excluded by refusal or reluctance to accept it, but it would clarify the position of the

Association on this particular doctrine. With the knowledge that a second motion was immediately forthcoming, the motion to refrain from making the statement a test of fellowship (the first motion) carried with a vote of 1,148 for the motion and 109 against.[9]

The second motion was read as follows: "I move that we, the messengers of the General Association of Regular Baptist Churches, gathered in annual session at Winona Lake, Indiana, June 1975, declare ourselves in agreement with the Council of Eighteen in its endorsement of the following statement on Election."[10]

The statement was then read and the motion was seconded and discussed. Suddenly, Rev. Louis A. Lowndes, pastor of the Urbandale Baptist Church, Battle Creek, Michigan, came to the podium and presented a substitute motion. His preface to his substitute motion and the motion are as follows:

I do not feel that the statement on Election speaks for the majority among us, because of one little phrase. Of course I realize that others may disagree and others may find other phrases that they would disagree with: but the phrase, "or response" in the Election statement does not speak for me. I'm not a "five-point" Calvinist; I respect the men who are; I look up to them and in the past have appreciated their fellowship, but if I adopt *this* statement I am saying that God's foreknowledge is to be interpreted in the light of hyper-Calvinism. That God chose some without any consideration of foreseen human merit I heartily agree—but I do *not* agree that He moved without any foreknowledge of human response. It would *seem* to me that the voting messengers have already indicated their support of the Council of Eighteen, and I among them. . . . It seems to me that in supporting the Council of Eighteen we should bring an end to the discussion of Election. Why do we need to adopt *any* statement on Election? I believe that our constitution and our doctrinal position tell us clearly where we stand, and we don't *need* a statement on Election. Therefore, if I'm not out of line with parliamentary procedure, I'd like to offer a substitute motion. . . . In support of the Council of Eighteen's statement, which I have just read, and in view of the vote of our voting messengers today, to support the Council's decision recommending that the statement on Election not be given a first reading status here at Winona Lake, and recognizing the Baptist position of soul liberty, and in the interest of ending further controversy over this issue, I move that the matter of Election be dropped.[11]

The substitute motion passed by a vote of 665 to 401. The "election matter," therefore, was officially "dropped."

Hopefully, the discussion sparked new interest throughout our churches in the study of Bible doctrine. The discussion and its outcome also demonstrated again the GARBC's resilience. We can differ on some debatable issues and remain friends and even continue working together. If some feel strongly that they cannot work with others who differ with them on matters like election, they are free to leave the Association. As Ketcham and other Regular Baptist leaders have said through the years, "It is much harder to get into the GARBC than it is to get out." Article V, section 1, of the GARBC Constitution reads:

> Any fellowshipping church may withdraw from the Association at any time and for any reason sufficient to itself. Christian ethics would suggest that reason for such withdrawal should be filed with the Association, but such action is not mandatory. In conformity with the historic Baptist position, the property rights of such a church can in nowise be legally prejudiced or endangered by such withdrawal.[12]

Over the next few years after the election controversy, several churches left the Association. Some gave as their reason that "the GARBC is too Calvinistic," and others said they withdrew because "the GARBC is too Arminian." But there was good evidence of unity in the voting on the rest of the recommendations of the Clarification Committee. Half of the Articles of Faith were passed with flying colors at Winona Lake in 1975 and the other half just as enthusiasti-cally at the Seattle Center Opera House in the beautiful state of Washington in 1976.

Back in Des Plaines, Illinois, the GARBC and RBP staff members were working in increasingly crowded conditions. Hard to believe? Well, maybe, but the blessing of God was so abundant upon Regular Baptist ministries that a seemingly spacious building in 1965 seemed to "shrink" in 1974. The continuing success of Regular Baptist Press under Dr. Hull's steady leadership, the growing work of Gospel Literature Services and the expanding outreach of *Living Reality* were making demands of new dimensions. There was always, of course, the need for storage space, and renting such space was expensive and inconvenient.

Dr. Stowell appointed a staff committee, headed by the Rev. F. Donald Drake, RBP book editor, to search for something bigger and better. The committee looked at buildings and sites in and around the Chicago suburban areas and even in other cities. I personally can remember visiting with other Council of Eighteen members and the office staff committee about a building located across the street from Belden Regular Baptist Church in Niles, east of Des Plaines. Belden Pastor Gordon L. Shipp was understandably excited about that piece of property, but it just didn't quite ring the bell. And then the committee found the United States Life Insurance Building at 1300 North Meacham Road in Schaumburg! Dr. Hull wrote:

> Schaumburg is one of the true "new frontiers" in the Chicago area; a fast-growing, developing community. And the office is located a mere block from Woodfield shopping center, possibly the largest, most elaborate in all of greater Chicago. The property has already appreciated in value, and should continue to do so.[13]

So 1976, the bicentennial year of the United States, saw the GARBC and RBP in beautiful new surroundings. Since the last move had been only eleven years earlier, many of the staff members were "veterans" at the moving business! And since Schaumburg was only about ten miles from Des Plaines, no one had to go to all the trouble of changing residences. The new property had plenty of parking area and room for a warehouse/shipping building that was added to the beautiful office building under the watchful eye of Vernon Miller, who supervised the project. The Des Plaines property sold quickly and easily, providing $500,000 toward the downpayment of the new building, which sold for $1,100,000.

End Notes

1. "Council of Eighteen Minutes," Des Plaines, Illinois, December 1974. (Typewritten.)
2. Ibid.
3. *Fundamental Baptist Fellowship Information Bulletin* (May–June 1975), p. 2.
4. David Nettleton, *Chosen to Salvation* (Schaumburg, IL: Regular Baptist Press, 1984), p. 150.
5. Ibid., p. 150.
6. Ibid., pp. 150, 151.
7. Ibid., pp. 151, 152.
8. Ibid., p. 153.

9. Ibid., p. 153.

10. Ibid., p. 153.

11. "Minutes of GARBC Annual Business Meeting," June 1975, Winona Lake, Indiana. (Typewritten.)

12. "Constitution and Articles of Faith," GARBC Literature Item 1 (Schaumburg, IL: General Association of Regular Baptist Churches, n.d.), p. 3.

13. Merle R. Hull, *What A Fellowship!* (Schaumburg, IL: Regular Baptist Press, 1981), p. 43.

Home office in Schaumburg

36

When Robert T. Ketcham had his severe heart attack just two months before his seventieth birthday in 1959, few people would have predicted he would live 19 more years. His retirement from service in the home office had taken place in 1966, but he continued to preach for the next several years. The inevitable march of time and the relentless aging of his body brought even Ketcham's preaching days to an end as he neared his eighty-fifth birthday. One of his last sermons was delivered from a stool in 1974 in Grand Rapids, Michigan, during the annual Bible conference of the Grand Rapids Baptist Seminary. On Friday, February 22, he preached from Galatians 5:1 a message titled "Declaring the Word of Truth." In defining Scriptural liberty, Ketcham declared: "Well, it means that something has been done to me which makes it possible for me to do something which I could not formerly do. Namely, obey Christ."[1] Obedience! That was the hallmark of Ketcham's life and ministry. That is why J. Murray Murdoch titled his biography of Ketcham, *Portrait of Obedience.*

Dr. Ketcham suffered a severe stroke on December 19, 1976. After struggling in the hospital for 35 days, he returned to his apartment. The stroke had affected his speech, and he had to walk with a quad cane or walker. He was confined to his Chicago apartment by the end of 1977. On June 30, 1978, he suffered another severe stroke, which extensively weakened his limbs and throat. He choked when he tried to swallow, and his great voice was ineffective. Dr. Ketcham's condition worsened as he passed his eighty-ninth birthday on July 22. After spending almost a month in Chicago's Swedish Covenant Hospital, he was admitted to an extended care facility.

Mary Ketcham stood at her husband's bedside although communication with him was virtually nonexistent. She knew there was little likelihood of his getting any better. Ruth Ryburn accompanied Mrs. Ketcham to the hospital on August 20, and his condition was unchanged. On Monday morning, August 21, Mrs. Ketcham was summoned to the hospital. Before she arrived, Dr. Robert Thomas Ketcham had been called into the presence of his Lord Jesus Christ.

Dr. Joseph M. Stowell immediately sent out from the National Representative's office a letter to all of the pastors of the Fellowship, informing them of the funeral service to be held at the Belden Regular Baptist Church in Niles, Illinois. On August 24, 1978, members of the Council of Eighteen and friends from all over the nation came to pay their respects to the great preacher and leader. Pastor Gerald P. Safstrom opened the service by saying:

> We are met here today in memory of Dr. Robert T. Ketcham who some sixty years ago bowed to his sovereign Lord and said: "Lord, I have absolutely nothing to give you except obedience. That I can and will give You. What You will do with this absolutely useless vessel, I do not know. All I can do is obey. The rest of it is in Your sovereign hand." History has recorded much of the favor of God upon his life. Eternity will reveal the complete story of God's sovereign grace in the outworking of obedience. The words "but God" as stated by the Apostle Paul in Ephesians chapter 2, verse 4, are the fitting epitaph to his life.
>
> If our beloved Dr. Ketcham were here today, he would no doubt pray thusly—and I quote from a message of his years ago: "Precious Savior, help these dear ones to find out something about Thyself which they could never have known apart from this experience." And we trust that this experience today will be a means to the end of knowing something more of the greatness and grace of our loving Lord.[2]

National representative Joseph M. Stowell said:

> I suppose that more than any other one man, Dr. Ketcham was responsible for the building of our Association. Now with more than fifteen hundred churches, it was his life and his heart, in the latter years of his life. He gave his very best for it. He guided its direction and established its structure and was used of God to maintain its position, which still continues to this very hour. . . .
>
> And I suppose that if there is any one outstanding characteristic of his ministry above others it was his great heart for Christian missions. How many missionaries, I wonder, are there out on the field today who are there because

they yielded their lives to Christ for service under the ministry of Bob Ketcham? I know! That great theme of missions in his life and ministry affected my own life and ministry and gave a pattern of great interest for Christian missions.

. . . I've come to pay tribute from our beloved Association; from our pastors whom he loved and counseled; from the people in the pew who felt that he was their friend; and from the missionaries scattered all around the world who look back to a day at camp or a missionary conference or in the churches where he served when life-determining decisions were made, and they turned their backs upon personal plans and their own will and yielded everything to the will of God to go out to the regions beyond where the name of Christ, in many instances, had not yet been given.[3]

Former pastor of Belden Regular Baptist Church, Dr. Gordon L. Shipp, said:

In the seven years that God allowed me to preach here, Dr. Ketcham was my "amen corner." And if you can't preach with Dr. Ketcham in your "amen corner," hang up your ordination certificate and get out of the business. I praise God. And I extend my sympathies to this dear family, but I know that they wouldn't want him back here. He's with his Savior.[4]

Dr. John G. Balyo was asked to bring the funeral message. Among other things he said:

Perhaps we ought to stand at the graves of some of God's great men. Maybe we ought to remember what they believed and what they fought for and how they suffered and how they triumphed.

Have you ever seen a great tree stand tall against the sky? But then age and weather finally felled it. You passed by, looked where the tree used to stand and there was only a great empty space against the sky.

I am told that the Japanese produce dwarf trees which are only a few feet high. You may see a pine tree or maple tree in a dish, and the tree is only about three feet in height. They stunt the trees by continually cutting the roots. I think we live in a world of mostly little men, midgets, dwarfs, because they are not deeply rooted in *great* principles, *great* loyalties, *great* truths and *great* faith.

Dr. Ketcham *was*. He was a great man, one of God's tall men. And today there is a great empty space against the sky. He was a man of integrity. He was a man of great compassion. I shall never forget the warmth of his messages when he spoke about tears gathered by God in a bottle. I shall not forget in Council meetings, hearing him sob sometimes when he prayed for pastors or missionaries. I shall not forget the tenderness of a genuine compassion. I shall not forget his great ability. . . .

Oh, how I loved him. He was a great man and a dear friend, and now he is with the Lord he loved so much. And I am looking forward to the time when I am going to say "Hello" to the Lord Jesus and greet Dr. Bob again. Amen and Hallelujah![5]

In the October 1978 issue of the *Baptist Bulletin* the following tribute appeared from the heart and pen of Council of Eighteen chairman Paul N. Tassell.

What Thomas Jefferson was to the United States of America, Dr. Robert T. Ketcham was to the General Association of Regular Baptist Churches. As Jefferson was the major force in the writing of the Declaration of Independence, so Ketcham was the major spokesman and writer for hosts of Baptists declaring their independence from the tyrannical infidelity of the Northern Baptist Convention fifty years ago. As Jefferson's thinking was prominent in the writing of the United States Constitution, so Ketcham's incisive and precise thinking is interwoven throughout the constitutional and organizational genius of the General Association of Regular Baptist Churches, which had its official beginning in 1932.

Dr. Ketcham was a many-faceted man. He was a warrior who knew that the pen is mightier than the sword. His opponents were often made to feel the sharpness of his inky sword as he defended the doctrinal positions of the GARBC. In correspondence, in editorials, in pamphlets, in booklets and in Associational literature items, Dr. Ketcham could parry and thrust with an expertise born of the Spirit of God and perfected by the constant use of the Sword of the Spirit, the Word of God.

His pen was not just an instrument of spiritual warfare, however; he often used that pen as a shepherd's rod or staff. His treatises on Ephesians 6 and Psalm 23 are just two examples of how edifying, how encouraging and how enlarging his expositions could be to our hearts.

But Dr. Ketcham was first and foremost a preacher. How he could preach the Word! How he could exalt Christ! How he could expose error! He had the God-blessed ability to make Old Testament characters live before his listeners. He could make New Testament incidents absolutely unforgettable. (Do you recall his exposure of the modernist's foolish attempt to explain away the miracle of the feeding of five thousand?) Dr. Ketcham believed in the inerrancy of God's Word, and he preached that Word confidently, courageously and compassionately. Like a farmer, he plowed a straight furrow. Harvests have many times followed his patient sowing. Heaven is already peopled with many of his ingathered sheaves and shall be even more so through the coming years.

The words spoken by Pastor A. G. Brown at the funeral service of Charles Haddon Spurgeon may be aptly applied to Robert Thomas Ketcham: "Champion of God, thy battle long and nobly fought is over! The sword, which clave to thy hand, has dropped at last; the palm branch takes its place. No longer does the helmet press thy brow, oft weary with its surging thoughts of battle; the victor's wreath from the Great Commander's hand has already proved thy full reward."

Dr. Ketcham was an evangelistic example and a pastoral pattern. Our Regular Baptist churches need to exercise that Scriptural zeal which so wonderfully characterized his missionary vision and vitality. We as pastors need to feed and guard our sheep with the same Scriptural faithfulness that demanded separation from doctrinal degradation and denominational deceit. By the grace of God, we will preach the same gospel and exalt the same Christ he preached and exalted until that day when we join him in the Glory.[6]

End Notes

1. J. Murray Murdoch, *Portrait of Obedience* (Schaumburg, IL: Regular Baptist Press, 1979), p. 289.

2. Ibid., p. 313.

3. Ibid., pp. 314–316.

4. Ibid., p. 318.

5. Ibid., pp. 321, 323.

6. Paul Tassell, "Champion of God," *Baptist Bulletin* (October 1978), p. 9.

37

Joseph M. Stowell's ten years as national representative were exciting and action-packed years. In 1970 Dr. Ernest Pickering was named president of Baptist Bible College of Pennsylvania, and Dr. Wendell Kempton was selected to be president of the Association of Baptists for World Evangelism.

In 1971 the Internal Revenue Service issued a group ruling that exempts all GARBC churches from federal income tax and determines officially that contributions to GARBC churches are legally deductible. The file number of the ruling is T:MS:EO:R:2. The Association also has a group ruling number: 2194.

In 1972 David Marshall was named general director of Evangelical Baptist Missions, and ABWE moved into its new headquarters in Cherry Hill, New Jersey. Beating Senator George McGovern, Richard Nixon won his second term to the presidency of the United States in one of the biggest landslides in American political history.

In 1973 Evangelical Baptist Missions moved to Kokomo, Indiana, and Dr. W. Thomas Younger became president of Western Baptist Bible College in Salem, Oregon.

In 1974 Northwest Baptist Seminary was established at Tacoma, Washington, with Dr. Charles U. Wagner as president, and Arthur B. Cunningham became president of Hiawatha Baptist Missions. The first Informissions Conference was held at Grand Rapids Baptist College. President Richard M. Nixon resigned from the presidency over the Watergate scandal.

In 1975 Dr. John Patten retired from Faith Baptist Bible College. Dr. Reginald L. Matthews retired as GARBC field representative after eight fruitful years, and Mrs. Matthews completed her work with *Living Reality*. They moved to Clarks Summit, Pennsylvania, where

Dr. Matthews became an instructor at Baptist Bible School of Theology.

In 1976 the home office moved to Schaumburg, and a Southern Baptist, Jimmy Carter, became president of the United States, defeating President Gerald Ford in a close election.

In 1977 Norman Bosworth became director of the Regular Baptist Children's Home in St. Louis, Michigan. Regular Baptist Press celebrated its twenty-fifth anniversary, and Hiawatha Baptist Missions moved to its new headquarters in Grand Rapids.

In 1978 Dr. William Kuhnle retired as assistant to the national representative. Dr. James T. Jeremiah became chancellor of Cedarville College after serving as its president for a quarter of a century. Dr. Paul Dixon succeeded Dr. Jeremiah as president.

In 1979 Dr. W. Wilbert Welch completed 20 years as president of Grand Rapids Baptist College and Seminary. Dr. Mark Jackson became president of Baptist Bible College of Pennsylvania. Dr. John Polson became president of Spurgeon Baptist Bible College in Mulberry, Florida, and Dr. William Fusco was named president of Denver Baptist Bible College.

As Dr. Merle R. Hull noted:

> The decade of the 70s also saw a number of faithful, dedicated Regular Baptist leaders finish their earthly course. Among these were George Milner, Robert L. Powell, Earle G. Griffith, Forrest E. Johnson, Joseph McCaba, Robert Reynhout, Gerard Knol, Lloyd Morris, Leon Wood, Marjorie Raidt, John Ruhlman, Sr., Ruth Herriman and A. D. Mohr.[1]

And 1979 was the year when Joseph M. Stowell resigned as national representative of the GARBC. But he was not finished working even though he was 68 years of age! He gladly accepted the invitation of Dr. Wendell Kempton to become the international representative for ABWE.

As Dr. Stowell prepared to leave the GARBC home office, he told the messengers at the 1979 Dayton (Ohio) annual conference that we in the GARBC must always be vigilant. We were reminded by our outgoing leader that dozens, perhaps scores, even hundreds of denominations, organizations, seminaries, charitable institutions and evangelistic enterprises that started in a strong, Scriptural position had eventually backslidden into a greater or lesser degree of apostasy.

Then Dr. Stowell declared with that dynamic, dignified voice of his: "We are set to defy history!" What a Biblical battlecry! And so the GARBC continues to defy the historical trend toward unfaithfulness and apostasy.

Like the national representatives before him Dr. Stowell, during his tenure as national representative, advised hundreds of pulpit committees, wrote thousands of letters, counseled hundreds of college and seminary students and preached in hundreds of places to multiplied thousands of people.

Dr. Joseph M. Stowell walked among us as a spiritual giant. His dignity and strength of conviction were always benedictions. He never wavered in his love for the Lord Jesus Christ. He never tarnished the testimony of the gospel by tawdry stories or cheap gimmicks or shady lifestyle. In an age when some radio and television personalities were disgracing the Christian ministry, Joseph Stowell moved among us as a Christian gentleman. He was never, like some self-proclaimed fundamentalist leaders, pompous and arrogant. He was never a rampaging bull in the evangelical china shop. Neither was he afflicted with the "Elijah syndrome," the attitude that "I, even I only, am left." He knew there were at least "seven thousand" others "who have not bowed the knee to Baal."

I first met Dr. Stowell on the platform of the Billy Sunday Tabernacle at Winona Lake, Indiana, in June of 1964. I was the speaker for the Friday morning 11:00 hour, and Dr. Stowell, being the chairman of the Council of Fourteen, was the conference moderator. During the offertory, Stowell leaned over to me and quietly asked me to tell him about the church I was pastoring. I was only 29 years of age and nervous. I told him I was pastoring the Bethany Baptist Church in Galesburg, Illinois, and that I had led the church into the GARBC just three years ago in 1961 when the church was just five years old. He assured me he would be praying for me as I preached. When it came time to present me to that big crowd in the Tabernacle, he introduced me with grace and sensitivity. Just six years later he asked me to serve on his team as national youth representative; and in 1978 I was, as Council of Eighteen chairman, working closely with him. I grew to know him well and love him in the Lord.

Dr. Stowell has proved that a man can be a gentleman while being a gladiator. A man can be saintly while being soldierly. A man can be holy without being haughty. A man can be obedient to the Bible without being obnoxious to his brethren. A man can indeed speak the truth in love. He can indeed be a true Baptist without believing that only Baptists are going to Heaven. He can be a true fundamentalist and a true separatist without demanding that every other fundamental separatist dot every *i* and cross every *t* exactly as he does. Dr. Stowell has been a role model for all of us preachers.

At the Tuesday evening session of the annual conference in Dayton, on June 26, 1979, the Stowells were presented with a farewell gift from the churches of more than $12,000. All their children and grandchildren were called to the platform to join in honor of their parents. Dr. John White read the following resolution, which was adopted unanimously.

Whereas, the beloved Apostle Paul said, "We beseech you, brethren, to know them which labour among you, and are over you in the Lord, and admonish you; and esteem them very highly in love for their work's sake" (1 Thess. 5:12, 13), and

Whereas, Dr. Joseph M. Stowell has faithfully served the General Association of Regular Baptist Churches as its National Representative for these ten years, and

Whereas, he has demonstrated care and concern for pastors and people throughout our Fellowship, and

Whereas, he has consistently, carefully and Biblically spoken as our national voice in a day of rapidly changing theological and social standards, and presented a clear stand on Biblical church separation and the fallacies of neoevangelicalism, and

Whereas, his personal and family life has been godly and above reproach, serving as a standard for pastors, missionaries and laymen, and

Whereas, our lives have been enriched, encouraged and educated by his personal and pulpit ministry which has brought "a word in season" during discouragement, despair and indecision, and

Whereas, his dear wife has served with him to the glory of God and the good of our Fellowship,

Be it therefore resolved that we, the messengers of the churches at the 48th annual conference of the General Association of Regular Baptist Churches, meeting in Dayton, Ohio, June 25–29, 1979, do express to Dr. and Mrs. Joseph M. Stowell our sincere and abundant thanksgiving along with deep appreciation for tireless service and sacrifice for the cause of Christ and the General Association of Regular Baptist Churches, for exemplary living, good preaching, faithful leadership, godliness and tenderhearted concern for a large, scattered family of churches, and

Be it further resolved that we commend them to the grace of God and His tender care as they move into yet another chapter of their lives. We further pledge our love, friendship and support at the throne of grace as the Word of God continues to be a lamp to their feet and a light upon their pathway.[2]

The following chapter is a sermon by Dr. Stowell.[3]

End Notes

1. Merle R. Hull, *What A Fellowship!* (Schaumburg, IL: Regular Baptist Press, 1981), p. 43.

2. "Dr. Joseph M. Stowell," *Baptist Bulletin* (July–August 1979), p. 26.

3. Joseph M. Stowell, "Retrospect and Prospect," *Baptist Bulletin* (July–August; September 1979), pp. 25–30; 13, 14.

38

RETROSPECT AND PROSPECT

Joseph M. Stowell, D.D., D.Hum.

I first was introduced to the GARBC in 1933. I had just finished college and was on a college gospel team as the speaker traveling through the Midwest and the Northeast. Our first assignment on that tour was at Central Baptist Church in Gary, Indiana, where Dr. Robert T. Ketcham was the pastor. Then we went up into Michigan, a stronghold of Regular Baptists at the state level long before the national Association was begun.

That summer I was introduced to some wonderful pastors and churches in the GARBC. By contrast, we were in a number of churches that weren't quite the same. God spoke to my heart as I was seeking direction for my future ministry, and it appealed to me that in the GARBC were my people. This was where I belonged. From the beginning of pastoral life and ministry, therefore, I cast my lot with the Regular Baptist movement. And I look back with no regret. You are my people. Mrs. Stowell and I love you dearly. When we come to meetings and put our hands in yours and see your faces, our hearts leap with joy. Our lives are made rich by the Christian friends we have, especially those within our own Fellowship. You mean a great deal to us.

Retrospect

My text is found in Psalm 78:1–7. Here is a recitation by the Spirit of God of Israel's history given with divine purpose and import to seek to save and direct the future generations in the way of God:

> Give ear, O my people, to my law: incline your ears to the words of my mouth. I will open my mouth in a parable: I will utter dark sayings of old:

Which we have heard and known, and our fathers have told us. We will not hide them from their children, shewing to the generation to come the praises of the LORD, and his strength, and his wonderful works that he hath done. For he established a testimony in Jacob, and appointed a law in Israel, which he commanded our fathers, that they should make them known to their children: That the generation to come might know them, even the children which should be born; who should arise and declare them to their children: That they might set their hope in God, and not forget the works of God, but keep his commandments.

God has a deep-seated concern for succeeding generations. We sometimes speak with concern about second- and third-generation Christians who have been reared in a Christian culture. Some become gospel-hardened, careless and indifferent to the great truths of the gospel and their import. They are often soft and weak.

The force of history demands that to maintain a movement as it began we have to constantly and prayerfully be instructing our children in the precepts that brought such a movement into being. This text tells us that God raised up a testimony in Jacob which future generations were not to forget.

In 1932, in America, God raised up a testimony in Christendom. It was for the Word of God and for the testimony of Jesus Christ. That testimony and witness have lived now almost half a century. We have in our midst second-, third-, perhaps even fourth-generation people who were not there in those beginning days. Somehow we must help them catch the spirit and convictions of the beginning so that we do not lose our moorings. We must maintain the same testimony with which we began. Our roots are important. They teach us needed lessons.

Baptist history, we believe, antedates the Reformation. We talk about our Anabaptist heritage that preceded the great Protestant Reformation. Many of those early Anabaptists bear a martyr's crown tonight. They were slain for the sake of Jesus Christ. In mockery they were taken to a lake or river and immersed under the water until they drowned and went to Heaven, bearing a martyr's crown. We have a great spiritual ancestry.

Let me quote from *The New Schaff Herzog Encyclopedia of Religious Knowledge.* Volume one defines Baptists in this way:

Baptists have always professed to base their doctrine and practice exclusively upon New Testament precept and example. If they have failed to realize their aim, it has been due to imperfect understanding of the New Testament Scriptures or to the imperfection inherent in human nature. Baptists find their spiritual ancestry in all individuals and parties that during the early Christian centuries, the Middle Ages and the Reformation time in the spirit of obedience and loyalty to Christ sought to stay the tide of incoming pagan and Judaizing error, or in times of general apostasy endeavored to restore Christianity to its primitive purity and simplicity (p. 456).

Catch the import of that. True Baptists have always sought to stay the ever-rising tides of pagan error. I suppose in all of Christendom the most guilty party to introducing paganism into Christian thought is the Roman Church. It has not changed in that regard, even though some Baptist leaders of our time say the hope of the world is that eventually Protestants and Baptists will reunite with Rome and join hands for Christ. That is incompatible in our thinking. We are against pagan error in Christendom.

We need also to stay Judaizing error, which means a religion of salvation by works. Almost all the major denominations of the world are guilty here. We must cry from the housetops that salvation is by grace through faith plus nothing. And we must ever keep that clarion call ringing across the lands until Jesus comes.

We are now in times of grave and specific apostasy. Baptists must with vigor oppose it. The Baptist movement—the true Baptist movement—has always sought to restore the churches to primitive purity in doctrine, in manner of life, in ministry and in simplicity. These were the characteristics of the GARBC nearly half a century ago and must continue to be because paganism runs throughout Christendom; Judaism is ever extant; the final great apostasy is upon us; and the churches have lost their purity and simplicity. This puts our beloved Association in the mainstream of Baptist history. Those groups which have departed from this four-fold thrust have deviated and hardly deserve the name Baptist.

It is my candid judgment that today the Southern Baptist Convention is further down the road in departure than the Northern Baptist Convention was when we left it years ago. Not only is liberalism entrenched deeply in their schools, leadership and literature, but the Convention is also infiltrated by the charismatic movement with all of its error. We are living in the last times. The need for our Fellowship has increased with the passing of the years. This cause brought our

Association into being and made us a separatist movement outside the camp with Christ.

The early Baptists in America were hated and persecuted. Recently I said to Georgi Vins, "Our Baptist forefathers in this country knew something of persecution also." I read a thought-provoking statement recently. The author said that next to the Jews in the world, Baptists have been persecuted more than any other religious group. And by the way, we have not persecuted others. We have been the recipients of persecution, not the givers of it.

The early Baptists in America—persecuted as they were—scattered, and soon caught the missionary spirit and fire that sent our spiritual forefathers throughout the colonies and across the mountains and prairies. They became deeply involved in home missions and later in foreign missions. Local associations sprang up, not only for fellowship but to organize for missionary effort and to reach out to the next towns and the regions beyond.

In those days there was no national convention of Baptists in the North. They did have every year in the month of May what were called the May meetings or anniversaries of the missionary societies. You remember the wonderful record of Adoniram Judson and his coworkers who pioneered in foreign missionary work. Our early spiritual forefathers were caught up in that world vision that would not let them rest until they had reached out beyond the sea and across the lands to those who had not heard the wonderful message of the gospel of Christ. The records indicate that those May anniversary meetings of mission societies, attended by great numbers of people from the churches, were highlights in their spiritual lives.

There were local associations and state associations or conventions. Eventually, in 1907, the Northern Baptist Convention was organized. Its annual meeting replaced the May meetings of the mission societies. It promoted missions in the tradition of the May anniversaries, and it was especially successful in home missions among the bilingual peoples whom they welcomed to our shores. But history tells us that from its very inception the Northern Baptist Convention was a mixed multitude of modernists or liberals and fundamental believers. Because of this it was doomed to fragmentation. It was unbelievable that it could continue with that duality of belief and purpose harboring within its ranks. Its inclusive policy really included two religions that were mutually exclusive. A break had to come, and we were the pioneers in that break—the Bible Christians who followed the commands of Christ to "come out from among them, and be ye separate, saith the Lord, and touch not the unclean thing."

There was about the same time in the North another group called the Freewill Baptists who, by their very name, indicated their theology. This was quite a large group. These two groups constituted the preponderance of the Baptists in the north at the beginning of the twentieth century.

William Warren Sweet, in his *Story of Religions in America,* says this about those early pioneer Baptists: "Frontier Baptists generally accepted a mild form of Calvinism and there was little doctrinal discord among them, though out-and-out Arminianism was strongly condemned" (pp. 314, 315). But concurrent with this was the rather large Freewill Baptist movement, which was Arminian in viewpoint.

Four years after the Northern Baptist Convention was formed, a union between these two rather large groups was consummated. The Northern Baptist Convention group and the Freewill Baptists merged and became one.

The basis of their union was several-fold. In part, the Freewill Baptists were asked to accept the doctrine of grace and the Convention Baptists were asked to accept the doctrine of freedom and responsibility of man. And as often happens when a union of two diverse groups holding different views is accomplished, each group relinquished some of its convictions and had a moderate attitude toward what formerly was held to be worthwhile and strongly adhered to. That meant the Northern Baptist Convention developed into an almost adoctrinal group of people. It is manifest by the fact that it consistently refused (even though the fundamentalists sought to get it to do so) to adopt a confession of faith. And to this day, it has never done that. Each group was weakened by this union.

In such a climate as this throughout the North, modernism grew until it captured much of the leadership and the control of the schools, the mission societies and the Convention machinery. By 1920, when the Convention met in Buffalo, New York, the battle was joined between the fundamentalists and those who denied the faith. True, it was a losing battle, but nevertheless the battle had to begin.

Three years later, the Baptist Bible Union was formed. Dr. Ketcham told me that it was born in the heart and mind of Dr. R. E. Neighbour, then pastor of the First Baptist Church in Elyria, Ohio—

one of our churches now. Among those joining with him on the original committee were such men as William L. Pettingill, a great prophetic teacher and one of the consulting editors of the Scofield Reference Bible.

The Baptist Bible Union encompassed the South and Canada as well as the North. Its first meeting was held in Kansas City under a big tent where more than three thousand people gathered. After that first meeting, the organizing committee lost its leadership and the big three in fundamentalism in Baptist circles emerged to take control: Dr. J. Frank Norris of Fort Worth, Texas, in the South; Dr. T. T. Shields of Jarvis Street Baptist church in Toronto, representing Canada; and Dr. W. B. Riley of First Baptist Church in Minneapolis, representing the North. Each of these leaders had his strong points. Each was a genius in his own right, but like many a genius had some faults and weaknesses.

This movement sensed that it was necessary to have an educational institution. It purchased with all liabilities and assets the Des Moines University, a Convention school. Sad mistakes were made. One was to keep many of the faculty members and students who did not really stand where the Baptist Bible Union stood. Eventually, the debacle of Des Moines took place. Riots followed led by the students and faculty. The school was closed down never to open again. With that shadow over the Baptist Bible Union, it never regained its impetus, though its message had been used of God for that time.

By 1932, in the midst of the Great Depression, the Baptist Bible Union held its last meeting at Belden Avenue Baptist Church in Chicago. Interestingly enough, not one of the big three was present. They had given up their leadership, and a little band of people decided it was time to have an association of *churches,* which the Union was not. The last meeting of the Baptist Bible Union became the first meeting of the General Association of Regular Baptist Churches.

A year or two later when Dr. J. Frank Norris saw what was happening, he tried to bring Temple Baptist Church of Detroit into the Fellowship and rise to a place of leadership so he could capture this ...association for himself. He was thwarted in that plan. Then he set out to organize the World Baptist Fellowship, from which the Baptist Bible Fellowship emerged when a group separated from him later on.

God has been with us through all these years of our history and has kept us true in a wonderful, separated testimony. It has cost to stand. Some of those early pastors had to lose their pension funds and face retirement with nothing saved. But they paid the price no matter what the cost.

Certain influences shaped our destiny, and you must know about them. At the beginning of the fundamentalist movement there was a series of books published on the fundamentals of the faith. These raised the issue of true Christianity versus modernism. A strong influence for good was the Bible conference movement which began before the turn of the century. All across the land Bible conferences sprang up where great crowds of people gathered to hear the Word of God proclaimed and taught. Many of these people were not hearing it in their churches. There developed from this movement an early confession of faith that set forth the great fundamentals of the faith. It became a standard for many struggling believers in that time.

Concurrent with this was the Bible institute movement. It had a great influence on our beginnings. In my judgment, we would not be what we are today had it not been for the influence of the Bible conference and Bible institute movements. Most of our early pastors were Bible institute graduates. They were trained in English Bible and taught to teach the Word of God. They were trained in personal evangelism and soul-winning, and were imbued with a great spirit of missionary zeal.

Dr. Harold J. Ockenga, visiting the mission fields in Africa some years ago, said to his surprise almost all the missionaries had what he called a Bible institute mentality. He seemed to decry this. On the other hand, he must have recognized that there was something about what he called the Bible institute mentality that drove people around the world for Christ and missions. In our schools, let's not lose that touch that will imbue young people with the need to obey the Great Commission and to lay down their lives simply and humbly for the sake of Christ out there in the regions beyond.

Another great influence at the beginning of our movement which still lingers, and I trust with strong vitality, was the influence of the Scofield Reference Bible and a little booklet written by Dr. Scofield called *Rightly Dividing the Word of Truth.* These brought into the very heart and structure of our movement a dispensational approach to the Word of God that made us premillennialists. In those days, pretribulation rapture and premillennialism were thought of in the same breath as a rule. We are dispensationalists. We are premillennialists. All of this established for us and developed in our midst a Biblically based world view which had in its structure the coming of Christ and drove us to be a missionary movement.

In the early history of the GARBC, a great concern that caused a lot of discussion of those early leaders (Dr. Ketcham, Dr. Van Osdel and men associated with them) was the matter of Christian missions. Will we have our own mission societies? Will we approve mission societies and recommend them to the churches? Among those involved in those discussions were leaders of missions, including Dr. Hawkins, president of Baptist Mid-Missions; Mrs. Peabody, president of ABWE, then called the Association of Baptists for Evangelism in the Orient; Mrs. Sweet from the China Mission. It was decided we would not own and operate our own missions but approve mission societies. We have seen those mission societies grow beyond our fondest dreams until they circle the globe, receiving millions upon millions of dollars. They now have nearly two thousand missionaries. The sun never sets upon them.

Let me remind you that our separatist Baptist position set us free to do the work of God in His way. That structure of separation gave us an unhindered and uninhibited range to carry out the work of God as we felt God wanted it to be done. And that is still important in this hour. Nobody dictates to our churches—the national representative, the home office or the Council of Eighteen do not nor do they desire to have any authority over any local church.

At the beginning there developed in our midst a threefold thrust. It is still extant today. Number one, our churches were great Bible-teaching centers and had Bible conferences. I remember [when I was] a high school lad Dr. William Pettingill [came] to our little village church for a great Bible conference on prophecy. Roy L. Brown, perhaps the finest chart Bible teacher that we have known, came on more than one occasion with his charts. Oh, what those meetings meant to me as a young man and how they instilled in my thinking a certain firm structure of theology and Christian service that I have never lost. Our pulpits were filled with doctrinal preaching. In my judgment that is what has kept us from being cursed by the charismatic movement. The charismatic movement thrives on a vacuum of Bible teaching, and our churches do not have that vacuum.

Along with this developed the faith principle of giving. In many of the old Convention churches people knew little about tithing or faith promises. They struggled to get enough to support the pastor, to say little about supporting missions. Almost every church had what it called a ladies' aid society. Its purpose was, by one means or another, to raise enough money to pay the preacher. Those who provide the money often run things. These were often sincere, earnest ladies. They had soup suppers and sales of various kinds—bake sales, rummage sales; sometimes a minstrel show. Someone wrote a little tract on the subject, "God Wants Heart Money and Not Stomach Money." A new day dawned in the church that accepted the faith principle of financing. And what blessing came.

Also, from our beginning, our churches and pastors believed in the inerrancy of the Bible. It's not a new thing among us.

The second thrust is this. Our churches were not only Bible-teaching centers but great centers of evangelism. Our pastors were taught and trained in personal evangelism. They had evangelistic meetings. I, for one, do not believe the day of evangelistic meetings is passé. God's Spirit is not limited. Oh, that revival would break out in our midst and create great spiritual resurgence among God's people and a spiritual awakening among the lost! These preachers had a burden for lost souls. They gave invitations, inviting people to come to Christ. They longed to keep the waters of the baptistry stirred. Their hearts would break if a Sunday went by without a soul or months without a baptism service. In the old Convention days, to save water bills or to save carrying the water to the baptistry, churches might have a baptismal service two or three times a year—if there were any converts. But our people learned that the more often you baptize people, the more you are going to have to baptize. It is better not to keep people waiting six months to be baptized after they are saved. Keep the waters stirred. Oh, may we never lose that evangelistic fervor—Bible preaching, evangelistic zeal and deep warm-hearted involvement in the enterprise of Christian missions at home and abroad. As Wesley said, "The world is our parish."

Prospects

In Haggai 2:19 there is a striking text, "Is the seed yet in the barn?" Let me lay before you this proposition: The granaries of God are not yet filled. The age is ebbing away. We may well be living in the eleventh hour. Is all the seed in the barn? No, there are multitudes who have not heard. Do we care? "Is it nothing to you, all ye that pass by?" Do we have the heart of Paul who said, "I must go to the regions beyond"?

It is written that we must take bread to those for whom nothing is prepared. There are hungry multitudes out there, and we have a message from God for them. They're dying one by one, going down to Christless graves. Many of them have not yet so much as heard the name of Jesus. In our churches in the beginning—and it must be true now or we die—the pastor looked upon himself as a recruiting officer for world conquest, and the church was thought of as a recruiting center for world conquest. At the youth rallies, young people were pled with to yield their lives to Christ for service. The schools were looked upon primarily, at the beginning, as Christian training centers. It is written in 1 Kings 8:43, "Hear thou in heaven thy dwelling place, and do according to all that the stranger calleth to thee for: that all people of the earth may know thy name, to fear thee."

Mrs. Stowell and I were in the Philippines with Don and Polly Taber, frontier missionaries there. They'd had a vacation Bible school that summer under a tent. Some young people from a leading family in the community were saved. The father was an attorney, the mother was one of the leading educators in that section. They came to the Wednesday night meeting to hear the visiting American preach. God laid on my heart to plead with those who were there to recognize that they were lost and at a given point in time to personally accept Christ as Savior.

This couple, members of a liberal church, said to me, "No one ever told us before that at a point in time we have to receive Christ as our Savior."

On Saturday the missionaries went to that home on some matter of business. They brought the subject up again and said, "No one ever told us before that at a point in time we had to receive Christ as our personal Savior by faith." That day they did just that and were brought into the kingdom of God. There are multitudes like them in our world.

Mrs. Stowell and I were in Jamaica. We went into a tax-free shop and were waited on by a well-dressed, lovely appearing Jamaican lady. I said to her (she apparently had heard the gospel), "Have you ever been born again?" She said, "No, but I would like to be." And that day, in a few moments, she received Christ and became the possessor of eternal life.

We can find people like that out there in the mundane, sensual, secular, wicked world with its paganism if we reach out to them with the compassion of Christ in our hearts.

I was preaching in our church at Union Grove, Wisconsin, a year or two ago on a Sunday morning, and God's Spirit broke through in a very unusual way. The first person to raise his hand for salvation was an old, old man. When we started singing the invitation song, this elderly man came tottering down the aisle, took my hand, and in sincerity of heart said to me, "Am I too old to come?" You know what I said to him? "No, there's room at the cross for you." He came. The barn is not filled; all the seed is not in; the granary bins are not running over and the multitudes die without Christ.

A year or two ago I was preaching in the great historic Jarvis Street Baptist Church in Toronto. When I closed the meeting I said, "Is there anybody here to whom God is speaking who is now ready to receive Christ as your Savior?" I scanned the audience for hands and suddenly a piercing cry rang out over the auditorium from a man who was hidden from me behind one of the plants at the end of the platform. He had lifted his hand, and I hadn't seen it. He cried out something like this, "Here I am, over here!" He didn't want to be left out. Oh, dear friends, out there across the mountains and the sea and across the street there are people who, down in their hearts, don't want to be left out. When you explain the way of the gospel to them and ask them if they're born again, they'll say, "No, but I would like to be." There is room for these at the cross.

This is the spirit of our movement. It has been from our inception, and we are bound of God and the Scriptures to maintain it in the framework of our separatist position.

We are not ugly, fighting fundamentalists. We are militant fundamentalists, terrible as an army with banners, remembering His banner over us is love. We are not passive fundamentalists. Let me remind you, it's only a short step from being a passive fundamentalist to becoming a neoevangelical. We must concentrate within our separatism to teach and preach the Word of God inerrant in every part, to do the work of an evangelist, and to reach out with broken hearts and loving arms to a lost world, for all the seed is not yet in the barn.

I say this humbly. Mrs. Stowell and I are singularly blessed, and we take no credit to ourselves. Our children grew up in a great church that loved the pastor and prayed for him and his family. We didn't thrust our children into God's work, but every one of them is now in the service of Christ. Oh, how our hearts are made glad. Our oldest daughter is married to one of our pastors; our son is one of our pastors;

and our youngest daughter and her husband are going to the mission field.

Oh, beloved in church life, let us not rest until the best of our youth forget money-making, creature comforts, the materialism that curses our age and lay their lives upon an altar of living sacrifice for Christ. Missionary fields are white unto harvest and our Lord has said, "The laborers are few." That statement is as applicable today as when He said it. There's a great labor bottleneck. "How can they hear without a preacher?" Oh, may God speak to some young heart, some older couple, and may they hear the call of Christ to give their lives for service. May they burn the bridges behind them and launch out into the deep no matter what the cost, for all the seed is not yet in the barn. The granaries of God are not yet filled.

Paul N. Tassell

THE ERA OF PAUL N. TASSELL

1979—

39

Paul Norman Tassell was born on July 20, 1934, in Toledo, Ohio. I was saved in a GARBC church in Toledo, Ohio, in 1941 under the ministry of Pastor James T. Jeremiah of Emmanuel Baptist Church. My mother led me to Christ after Dr. Jeremiah's Sunday evening message. In 1943 he baptized me into the membership of Emmanuel. On July 20 of 1948, my fourteenth birthday, I surrendered my life to Christ for the ministry at the Regular Baptist Camp at Lake O'Dell, Lakewood, Ohio. I was ordained at the Emmanuel Baptist Church on October 27, 1958, when Joseph H. Bower was my pastor. Dr. James T. Jeremiah preached my ordination sermon. I received my ministerial education at Bob Jones University in Greenville, South Carolina, culminating in the Ph.D. degree in the summer of 1958.

While at BJU I met Doris Jaeger from Trenton, New Jersey. She was reared in a godly Plymouth Brethren family. Doris graduated from BJU in June of 1956 with a degree in elementary education. Mr. and Mrs. Asher Jaeger consented to our marriage, and we were wed at the Woodside Gospel Chapel in Trenton on August 4, 1956. The Lord has blessed our union with three children: Jann Patricia, who is married to Bert Mayhak; Jill Priscilla, who is married to Rev. Nathan Osborne; and Joseph Paul Tassell, who married Deborah, the daughter of former ABWE missionaries, Rev. and Mrs. Arthur Christmann. Deborah was born in Brazil. Doris and I have six grandchildren.

My first pastorate was the Second Baptist Church in Elberton, Georgia, where I ministered from the beginning of my senior year at BJU in September of 1954 to the end of my doctoral work. I preached my last message there on August 31, 1958. My second ministry was the Bethany Baptist Church in Galesburg, Illinois, where Doris and I served from November of 1958 to February of 1965. The Lord then called us to the Campus Baptist Church in Ames, Iowa, adjacent to the Iowa State University. While in Illinois I edited the state fellowship's paper, the *IL-MO Trumpet,* for four years. In Iowa it was my privilege to serve as chairman of the Iowa Fellowship's Council of Ten. In both states we were very active in the camp programs. I pastored in Ames from February of 1965 to April of 1970, when I went to the home office in Des Plaines to serve as national youth representative. After three years I was called to the pastorate of the Grandview Park Baptist Church in Des Moines, Iowa, where Doris and I served from February of 1973 to August of 1979.

When Dr. Stowell announced at the 1978 conference that he would be retiring after the 1979 conference, the Council of Eighteen began to pray about his successor. That particular Council was made up of Paul N. Tassell, chairman; John G. Balyo, vice chairman; John Polson, secretary; Joseph H. Bower; Donald M. Brong; L. Duane Brown; Paul Dixon; Jack W. Jacobs; David Jeremiah; Richard G. Mohr; David Nettleton; Ernest Pickering; J. O. Purcell; Wilbur Chapman Rooke; Joseph M. Stowell III; Ben E. Strohbehn; Donald Tyler and John White, Jr.

At the Council of Eighteen meeting in December of 1978 at Schaumburg, much time was spent in prayer and discussion. I was asked to leave the room, and more than an hour later I returned and was told by vice chairman John G. Balyo that the Council had voted to recommend me to the messengers at the annual conference in Dayton, Ohio, in June of 1979 as the successor to Dr. Stowell. It was a humbling albeit happy moment, because I knew something of the burdens of the office. But I also knew my brethren on the Council trusted me. We all knew we were utterly dependent upon the Lord for wisdom and strength to fulfill our responsibilities.

Grandview Park Baptist Church is one of the greatest churches in the GARBC. When I went there in 1973 I thought I might stay until the Rapture or retirement! But God had other plans for me and my family, and we had to convey to the congregation what had taken place at the December Council meeting.

At the 1979 conference in Dayton, Ohio, the messengers voted to accept the recommendation of the Council of Eighteen. Since Doris and I had had more than six months to pray about our future ministry, I was prepared to accept the call of the Association to the office of National Representative. On Friday evening of the conference Dr.

John White read the following resolution, which was adopted by an enthusiastic and unanimous vote of the messengers.

Resolution #7
Dr. Paul N. Tassell

Whereas Dr. Paul N. Tassell has been chosen by the General Association of Regular Baptists to serve as its National Representative, and,

Whereas the task lying before Dr. Tassell is monumental in size, and national in scope, and,

Whereas the problems of compromise, lethargy, theological error, inefficiency, inaccuracy and self-gratification are ever present, and,

Whereas the challenges of evangelism, church planting, education, pastoring, training, publication, fellowship and great preaching are worldwide objectives of our fellowship of which Dr. Tassell is now National Representative, and,

Whereas the Word of God has admonished us to pray for our leaders and faithfully support them as they labor;

Therefore be it resolved that we, the messengers of the churches at the 48th Annual Conference of the General Association of Regular Baptist Churches, meeting in Dayton, Ohio, June 25–29, 1979, do commend him to the Grace of God, and shall pray fervently for him that he may have purity of life, power of leadership, clarity of purpose, compassion of heart, communication skills and convictions consistent with God's Word and the stated purposes of the GARBC, and,

Be it further resolved that we will encourage, support and assist him and his family as they assume these new responsibilities.[1]

My first responsibility after moving to Schaumburg was to prepare for the radio ministry. Dr. Stowell and I worked together for the last two months of the summer of 1979 in order to effect a smooth transition from one administration to another. I had conducted radio ministries in all four of my pastorates. In Elberton, Georgia, I had had a half-hour weekly broadcast on Sunday afternoons. In Galesburg, Illinois, in 1959 I had begun a weekly broadcast over WGIL called *Bethany Bible Thoughts* on Sunday mornings after the 8:00 news. The two pastors who succeeded me there have kept that broadcast going, and *Bethany Bible Thoughts* is now the longest continuous broadcast in WGIL history, spanning more than 31 years. In Ames, Iowa, I had a daily morning broadcast called *Coffee with the Parson.* At Grandview Park Baptist Church in Des Moines, we had a daily broadcast called

Gospel Views from Grandview over three stations that covered most of Iowa. We also broadcast our morning worship service. So I was familiar with radio broadcasting.

However, when I came to Schaumburg, *Living Reality* was still having financial problems. To complicate matters further, Dr. William Kuhnle had retired—and so had Mrs. Grace Matthews. I told the Council of Eighteen I would do my best at the broadcast for one year, and if we were not in a pay-as-you-go, in-the-black financial situation at the end of that year, I would recommend the broadcast be terminated. Our radio agent and producer, James Draper, and I worked very hard during the next 12 months; but when we came to the end of that year, we were still $7,000 in the red. Our churches were not adequately supporting the broadcast financially. The Council then voted to accept my recommendation to end the ministry known for 11 years as *Living Reality*.

Two things should be noted about the broadcast. First, Dr. Stowell had indeed been successful in making the GARBC known to many people in Christendom who previously had known nothing about us. However, my evaluation of our ministries had convinced me that our major ministry in reaching new people for our cause was not through radio but through Regular Baptist Press—its Sunday School materials, Vacation Bible School materials and books. The second thing we should note is that *Living Reality* had become just one of many gospel broadcasts. By that I mean our going off the air really did not deprive anybody of the gospel. All of our broadcasts were either preceded by, or followed by, other good programs like those of J. Vernon McGee, Richard DeHaan, David Jeremiah. My ministries as national representative would concentrate on the pulpit and the pen.

Most of this book has had to do with men. But we need to give honor to one lady who surely served the GARBC as faithfully and selflessly as any man ever did. Miss Ruth Ryburn came to the GARBC home office in 1944. She served every national representative, including Van Gilder, Ketcham, Jackson, Stowell and Tassell. She was "Miss Competence" and "Miss Efficiency." She probably knew more about the details of the GARBC than any other living person. She not only was an excellent executive secretary, but she also was responsible for the registration desk at the annual conferences. She knew hundreds of Regular Baptists by name. She knew preachers and missionaries and their wives and their children—and in some cases their grandchildren!

Her memory was phenomenal.

Miss Ryburn lived for many years with the Ketchams. Ruth not only worked regular hours at the office, but she would often do work for Dr. Ketcham during after-office hours. Dr. Ketcham had great problems with his vision, but Ruth would sometimes read for him and provide research materials for him that enabled him to do far more than he otherwise could have. When it came time for Ruth to retire in 1982, she had served as the national representative's secretary for 38 years! She was my secretary for just three of those years, but what a friend and fellow-laborer she was during that time! She was competent in her duties, circumspect in her decorum and compassionate in her desire to get out the gospel.

When Ruth had to retire in late 1982 due to failing health, we were all saddened to see her leave. For the last eight years she has been confined to a nursing home in Mason City, Iowa. I am sure that great rewards await her in heavenly places. She was always loyal to her Lord, to her church, Belden Regular Baptist Church in Niles, Illinois, and to her pastors. She loved to travel. It had been her hope that upon retirement she would be able to visit mission fields and do some work for missionary families, but that dream never came true for Ruth.

End Note

1. "Council of Eighteen Minutes—Resolution #7," Dayton, Ohio, June 1979. (Typewritten.)

40

Violence marked the year 1980. It really began on November 3, 1979, when 63 Americans plus 27 others were taken hostage at the American Embassy in Tehran, Iran. The hostage-takers were radical, militant student disciples of the Ayatollah Khomeini. They demanded the return to Iran for trial former Shah Mohammad Reza Pahlavi, who was receiving medical treatment in New York City. When President Jimmy Carter attempted to rescue the hostages, his plan was foiled, and eight Americans were killed and five wounded in the ill-fated rescue effort. As it later turned out, 52 of the hostages (eleven had been released earlier) were held a total of 444 days and were released just moments after Ronald Reagan was inaugurated on January 20, 1981. The Iranian hostage-taking triggered all kinds of security measures in airports and military installations around the world. Those of us who must do a great deal of flying in our ministries felt the tension almost immediately. Chicago's famed O'Hare Airport introduced severely tight security measures. It seemed that armed police officers were everywhere. The safety of ambassadors became a chief concern for nations around the globe. God's people were encouraged more earnestly than ever to pray for the ambassadors for Christ who were stationed on all seven continents.

Violence was also felt in the realm of nature. In the state of Washington, on May 18, 1980, Mount Saint Helens "blew its top" with a force estimated to be 500 times as powerful as the atomic bomb that leveled Hiroshima, Japan, on August 6, 1945. The awesome eruption, followed by others on May 25 and June 12, killed at least 60 people while causing a minimum of $3 billion in economic losses.

On December 8, former Beatle John Lennon, who boasted in the 1960s that the Beatles were "more popular than Jesus," was shot to death in front of his apartment building in New York City. The killer was a former mental patient named Mark David Chapman.

Elsewhere, Liberian President William R. Tolbert was assassinated in a military coup on April 12. On September 17 former Nicaraguan President Anastasio Somoza Debayle was assassinated in Paraguay. Violence seemed to be everywhere.

The really big news of 1980 was the November 4th election of Ronald Wilson Reagan to the presidency of the United States. Reagan polled 43,899,248 votes to incumbent Jimmy Carter's 35,481,435 votes. The electoral college margin was a thumping 489 to 49 for Reagan. The stunning landslide extended to the United States Congress where Republicans gained control of the Senate and took 33 House seats from the Democrats. It was an exciting victory for conservatives in both religion and politics. Christians throughout the United States rejoiced that the man in the White House was anti-abortion, pro-prayer and generally anti-liberal in his policies. It was quite a significant year to be the national representative of the General Association of Regular Baptist Churches.

While many changes took place throughout the world, some things remained the same in 1980. Jack Nicklaus won his fourth United States Open and his fourth PGA championship, while Tom Watson won his third British Open. And the GARBC stayed the same doctrinally, positionally and evangelistically—fundamentalist and Baptist in doctrine, separatist positionally and missionary-oriented evangelistically. We continued about our business of evangelizing, baptizing and catechizing.

Nineteen eighty was a busy year at the home office as we made preparations for our Fiftieth Conference in 1981, which was to be held at the Billy Sunday Tabernacle at Winona Lake, Indiana. Two major projects kept many people busy throughout 1980, and they were both well done. First, Merle R. Hull, Herman S. Scott and Timothy L. Clement collaborated in the production of a general overview of the Association's first 50 years. Dr. Hull was responsible for the text of the book, Scott for the design and Clement for the illustrative artwork. As Dr. Hull described the book: "The words are mine, but it is Herman Scott who chose the type and format, selected pictures and worked out all such details."[1] The book was titled *What A Fellowship!* It was only the third attempt at putting into print the general history of the GARBC. Dr. Joseph Stowell in 1949 published his *Background and*

History of the General Association of Regular Baptist Churches. In the 1970s Dr. Calvin Odell, an instructor at Western Baptist College, published *The General Association of Regular Baptist Churches and Its Attendant Movement.* Both of those booklets have been out of print for a number of years. Dr. Hull's 78-page work was published in 1981 by Regular Baptist Press in time to be available for the great conference at Winona Lake.

The second project was the preparation of a 48-minute multimedia presentation called *A Living Treasure.* I worked with Mr. Carl Brandon of ABWE and a committee of historians and communication experts on this project,but it was the artistic genius of Carl Brandon that made the project a success. Literally hundreds of photographs were taken out of which the final set were chosen. All aspects of the work at Schaumburg were photographed. All of the agencies were represented photographically. The story of fundamentalism generally—and the formation and growth of the GARBC specifically—were put on film. The narrator was a professional from New York City. The presentation had its premiere showing at the conference on Wednesday evening. The multimedia presentation was then made into a regular film production, and copies for rental are still available through the home office. Both projects, the book and the film, took a great deal of time and energy but were well worth the expenditures. They impacted literally thousands of lives.

The 1981 conference was the fifth time our Association had met at Winona Lake. Previous conferences were in 1961, 1964, 1971 and 1975. Winona Lake's fascinating history as a conference site goes all the way back to the 1890s. Prominent speakers such as William Jennings Bryan ("the Commoner"), Dr. Wilbur Chapman, Evangelist Gypsy Smith, Dr. G. Campbell Morgan and Billy Sunday graced its platform. The 1981 conference was the last for the GARBC at Winona Lake, since the Health Department has condemned the Billy Sunday Tabernacle. But the 1981 conference was memorable, and the crowds exceeded 5,000.

The theme for the fiftieth was "Our Heritage." I gave the Monday night address. The morning messages were preached by Rev. Ronald Graef, "Our Heritage of Prayer"; Dr. David Nettleton, "Our Heritage of Preaching"; Dr. John G. Balyo, "Our Heritage of Prophecy"; and Dr. Joseph M. Stowell, "Our Heritage of Perspective." The morning Bible Hour was the responsibility of Dr. Ernest Pickering each day. The evening messages were preached by Dr. Mark Jackson, "Devotion to Christ"; Dr. Carl E. Elgena, "Contending for the Faith"; Dr. Donn Ketcham, "Missions"; and Evangelist Eldon Weaver, "Evangelize!"

A special feature of that special conference was titled "Just Reminiscing," held on Tuesday and Thursday afternoons. Dr. W. Wilbert Welch was the moderator, and we heard from Ruth Ryburn, Merle R. Hull, Fred Brock, Donn Ketcham, Wilbur Chapman Rooke, James Thomas Jeremiah, Ray Hamilton and Charles Dear, Sr. They told of the early leaders, the early conferences, the early struggles and the early victories. There were tears and laughter and many choruses of "Amen" as we walked down memory lane with some of our "older" folks. That anniversary conference had as its moderator, John G. Balyo; its song leader, Don Krueger; its organist, Mrs. Roger Kilian; and its pianist, Robert Welch.

As we moved into the 1980s, a tendency to go off on tangents seemed to characterize some fundamentalists. There were some who wanted to introduce new "tests of fellowship" that were certainly not part of early fundamentalism. Nor were they Scriptural or baptistic. Dr. Hull rightly read the pulse of fundamentalism in general and the GARBC in particular when he wrote:

> The violent protests and demonstrations of the 60s faded from the scene in the 70s. But it was a difficult decade. For the first time in history a president resigned because of a scandal. Inflation became a foremost national concern. The international situation was tense. Gasoline shortages—and skyrocketing prices—beset the country. Moral standards continued to decline. Homosexuals sought acceptance, and succeeded in getting themselves identified as gays—a horrendous misnomer. Women's rights, symbolized by the bitterly controverted Equal Rights Amendment, became a major issue. A restlessness, an uneasiness permeated all areas of the country.
>
> A bit of this restlessness seemed to seep into the GARBC during the 70s, though not over the same issues. The Fellowship did continue to grow, receiving a total of 376 churches from 1969 to 1979. But at the same time a substantial number—183—were removed from the list in the same period. Some of these found it necessary to dissolve. Some merged with other churches. Some simply stated they wanted to be "independent"—a great error in terminology, for *every* GARBC church is fully independent. Some were led by pastors into the orbit of competing Baptist "empires" that developed during the decade. As a prime example of the restlessness, in the same year one church voted out of the GARBC because they felt the

Association was "too Calvinistic"; and another left because they thought the Association was "not Calvinistic enough![2]

By the time I came to the National Representative's office, the issue was the King James Version of the Bible. I spoke to this issue at Winona Lake in words that were later incorporated into my September 1981 *Information Bulletin:*

Make no mistake about it! *The battle* in Christendom today is over the inerrancy of the Word of God as originally given. New evangelicalism has lost that battle. Claiming to believe in Biblical infallibility, new evangelicals have conceded Biblical inerrancy. In his book, *The Battle for the Bible,* Dr. Harold Lindsell has documented the sad and sickening willingness of new evangelicals to give up belief in the inerrancy of God's Word. The GARBC stands unashamedly, unabashedly and unwaveringly for the inerrancy of the Word of God. We believe with all fundamentalists that verbal-plenary inspiration demands inerrancy.

The integrity of the Bible calls for its inerrancy. The infallibility of the Bible necessitates its inerrancy. Our GARBC statement of faith declares: "We believe in the authority and sufficiency of the Holy Bible, consisting of the sixty-six books of the Old and New Testaments, as originally written; that it was verbally and plenarily inspired and is the product of Spirit-controlled men, and therefore is infallible and inerrant in all matters of which it speaks."

There is a great need today for a Biblically balanced, Scripturally sage, spiritual statesmanship in fundamentalist circles. While we stand guard against new evangelicals who would desert and betray the doctrine of Biblical inerrancy, we must also resist *new fundamentalists* who would seek to create a new test of fellowship among true fundamentalists, a test that neither our fathers nor their fathers were called upon to meet. I speak of those who would insist upon the so-called *Textus Receptus* as the only satisfactory text-type and the King James Version as the only acceptable translation. In this day when we should be wholeheartedly standing for the grand standard of Biblical inerrancy, let us not allow ourselves as fundamentalists to be drawn away to a fuss over translations and/or a debate over Erasmus vs. Westcott and Hort. We would do well to heed the wise words of Dr. Kenneth I. Brown, Dean of the Detroit Baptist Theological Seminary: "The TR defenders hold strongly to the Textus Receptus as the best, in fact the only, text-type. Most of the leading fundamental writers and scholars through the years have not held this to be so. Nearly all of the fundamental men who have written materials dealing with the New Testament prefer the Alexandrian text-type. The reasons for this [preference] are sound textually. Those who accept the

Alexandrian text-type are not radical, apostate nor heretical. Actually, this position better represents the center of Biblical scholarship and orthodox Christianity. It certainly provides basic answers to some difficult doctrinal matters which otherwise face difficulty in proper exegesis and interpretation. *There seems to be no valid reason why the serious student of the New Testament should not use with profit several translations, each with value in its own strength. Defense of the Textus Receptus does not represent the center and heart of Christianity. Such a defense need not be pursued." (A Critical Evaluation of the Text of the King James Bible* by Kenneth I. Brown, pp. 28, 29, published by Detroit Baptist Theological Seminary). Fundamentalists, therefore, must resist both the new evangelicals and the new fundamentalists if we would clearly, courageously and consistently define and defend the cardinal doctrine of Biblical inerrancy.[3]

My reference to "new fundamentalists" created quite a stir among some of the brethren; so in January of 1982 I wrote the following epistle to all of the pastors in the GARBC:

Dear Pastors of GARBC Churches:

A number of you have written or called me during the past several weeks asking me to clarify my annual conference reference to "new fundamentalists." My September 1981 *Information Bulletin* also referred to "new fundamentalists." My clarification must first have to do with what I did NOT say. I did *not* say that anyone who prefers the King James Version of the Bible is a new fundamentalist. I myself prefer the KJV in my preaching ministry. *Neither* have I ever been guilty of "ridiculing the Dean Burgon Textus Receptus position."

I trust that the following clarification will indeed create "light" and not "heat." If you will refer to page 3 of my September 1981 *Information Bulletin,* you will discover what I *did* say: "We must also resist *new fundamentalists* who would seek to create a new test of fellowship among true fundamentalists. . . . I speak of those who would insist upon the so-called Textus Receptus as the only satisfactory text-type and the King James Version as the only acceptable translation." The new fundamentalists are, therefore, people who *insist* there is *only one* acceptable text-type and *only one* acceptable translation of the Bible.

Fundamentalists have *never* held such a position; therefore those who *now insist* on such a position are *new* fundamentalists; that is, they hold to a position that *old* fundamentalists did *not* hold. Dr. Robert L. Sumner proves my point conclusively in his fine booklet entitled *Bible Translations* in which he answers the question: What Is the Historic Fundamentalist Position? Dr. Sumner quotes the greatest fundamentalists of the century who *all* held that the 1901 American Standard Version was superior to the KJV. Those fundamentalists preferred the use of the KJV in public ministry but *never* made anyone's preference of a version or text-type a test of fellowship of true fundamentalism. He quotes John A. Broadus, B. H. Carroll, James M. Gray, J. Gresham Machen, Alan MacRae, Carl McIntire, G. Campbell Morgan, John R. Rice, William B. Riley, C. I. Scofield, Louis Talbot, R. A. Torrey, Benjamin Warfield and other great fundamentalists. You may order Dr. Sumner's booklet for 50¢ from Sword of the Lord, Murfreesboro, TN 37130.

Let me urge you to send for the best brief work on this whole issue I have yet seen. Written by Douglas S. Chinn and Robert C. Newman, *Demystifying the Controversy over the Textus Receptus and the King James Version of the Bible* may be ordered for $2 from the Interdisciplinary Biblical Research Institute, P.O. Box 145, Hatfield, PA 19440. Another very helpful book, *The Truth about the KJV Controversy* by Dr. Stewart Custer, may be ordered from the Bob Jones University Press, Greenville, SC 29614. Price: $1.95.

Brethren, many of you and your congregations prefer and use the New American Standard Bible. Many of you and your congregations prefer and use the New International Version. Many of you and your congregations prefer and use the King James Version. In accordance with the GARBC 1972 resolution many of you have given "great care" to "the study and use of any and all 'new translations.' " You have discovered that the NASB and NIV are excellent and trustworthy translations. As fundamentalists we have no right to demean or belittle you because of your preference. Whether you hold up a KJV or NIV or NASB, you can confidently declare, "Thus saith the Lord."

Brethren, there is much work to be done for your Savior in 1982. We Regular Baptists need to be busy preaching the Gospel, establishing churches and edifying our congregations. Let us not allow ourselves to be swept into a controversy that is both needless and divisive.

We agree with Dr. Sumner's summation: "We have no objection if some refuse to use or honor any translation but the King James Version. We wish them Godspeed and count them our friends. We, too, love it and seek to defend it from its critics. But we think any who make exclusive use of that translation a test of fellowship are wrong, especially when they infer a recommendation of another version—which has been translated by competent evangelical scholars—is a departure from the faith. This is not the historic fundamentalist position!"

Sincerely in Christ,
Paul N. Tassell, Ph. D.[4]

In September of 1981 Dr. William E. Kuhnle went Home to be

with the Lord. The following tribute was sent to Mrs. Kuhnle:

We, the Council of 18 of the GARBC, assembled in Indianapolis, Indiana, December 2 & 3, 1981, do hereby pay tribute to one of our brethren, a man of God, Dr. William Kuhnle, who has gone to be with the Lord during this past year.

Brother Kuhnle was a dedicated and devoted pastor. He served admirably as chairman of our Chaplains' Commission and performed in an outstanding manner over many years, during which he gained the deep and abiding respect of the chaplains and of the officials in our government.

As an assistant to a national representative of the GARBC, Brother Kuhnle served faithfully among us.

Dr. Kuhnle was a beloved brother who loved as a friend and labored well as a fellow-servant. He is greatly missed and will be long remembered.

We express our sympathies to Mrs. Kuhnle and pray that God will comfort her continually.[5]

Others who finished their earthly course between June of 1981 and June of 1982 were Evangelist Elton Crowell, Chaplain Lawrence Horton, Professor Calvin Odell, Rev. Dale Fleming, Dr. Leander Roblin, Rev. Milton R. Gelatt, Rev. Andrew Marsteller, Dr. John L. Patten, Dr. Irving Penberthy, Rev. Kenneth Sanders, Dr. Frank Waaser, Rev. W. Harvey Taylor, Dr. Kenneth Muck and Rev. Adam Galt. How much richer and more precious Heaven becomes as each blood-washed saint enters its portals!

Between June of 1982 and June of 1983 the following faithful Regular Baptists became absent from the body and present with the Lord: Rev. Harold L. Day, Rev. L. E. Mustain, Rev. Carl Anderson, Rev. Clair C. Lawson, Mr. Peter Schoon, Rev. Glenn H. Davis, Rev. J. Harold Jefferis, Rev. Roger Mills, Dr. Floyd Davis, Dr. Fred M. Barlow, Dr. Raymond F. Hamilton, Rev. Robert J. DeBoer, Rev. H. D. Halsey, Dr. Howard A. Keithley and Dr. George Lawlor.

The most publicized religious happening in the United States of 1983 was the Supreme Court's decision against Bob Jones University. At the 1983 annual conference the GARBC voting messengers passed the following resolution supporting BJU:

Whereas the Supreme Court of the United States of America on May 24, 1983, has shocked the nation's religious leaders with its decision to deny Bob Jones University tax exemption, and

Whereas the Constitution of the United States guarantees that Congress shall not prohibit the free exercise of religion, the justices of the Supreme Court (with one exception) decided to do just that; they stated: "On occasion this Court has found certain governmental interests so compelling as to allow even regulations prohibiting religiously based conduct;" thus on the basis of so-called "established public policy" and "the common community conscience" the Court has removed religious liberty, and while we do not necessarily agree with the position of Bob Jones University on its racial policy nor do we appreciate its unbecoming attitudes publicly expressed when the Supreme Court decision was handed down, we do express our concern that the Internal Revenue Service ruled that the University was *uncharitable,* thus denying it tax exemption; which policy the University insisted was its doctrinal belief, and

Whereas this unprecedented action now establishes that government bureaucracy can and does sit in judgment of what is acceptable as "public policy" and so religious freedom and its exercise no longer exists in unlimited form.

Be it therefore resolved that the messengers of the General Association of Regular Baptist Churches meeting in Niagara Falls on June 27—July 1, 1983, request prayer for these governmental leaders and alert our churches and agencies to this very real danger facing religious freedom.

Be it further resolved that we assure the leaders and students of Bob Jones University of our prayers and sincere concern.[6]

For me, the Niagara Falls, New York, conference of 1983 was one of the finest meetings the GARBC has ever held. The evening speakers and their topics were as follows: Charles U. Wagner, "The Bible: The Foundation and Authority of Our Belief"; Robert V. Dyer, Jr., "The Local Church: Principles for Growth"; David Nettleton, "Sanctification: The Position and Purity of Our Belief"; Allan E. Lewis, "Missions: The Extension of Our Belief"; and Ernest Pickering, "The Rapture: The Culmination of Our Belief." I had the privilege of bringing the Bible messages for the 10:00 sessions Tuesday through Friday. My subjects from the Gospel of John were "The Lamb of God," "The Temple of God," "The Water of Life" and "The Light of the World." The attendance at Niagara Falls was excellent, the scenery was beautiful, the weather was pleasant, the fellowship was refreshing and the ministries of music and preaching were superb. The God of the Word was exalted, and the Word of God was expounded. What a week!

Conference joy was mixed with sorrow, however, when two well-known Regular Baptists suddenly went to be with the Lord. Right at the end of the conference, Doris Marquardt, beloved wife of Rev. Elmer F. Marquardt, passed away. Just a few days later, Dr. Fred Brock slipped into the presence of the Lord from Seattle, Washington.

In November Rev. Arthur B. Cunningham, executive director of Continental Baptist Missions, died quite unexpectedly. He had ministered to the annual conference of the Arizona Association of Regular Baptist Churches, and had decided to stay over to preach on Wednesday night, November 9, 1983, at the Sahuaro Baptist Church, then pastored by Richard G. Mohr. It was Brother Cunningham's last message. Also in November, Dr. Mead C. Armstrong passed away. He was 76 years of age at his death and had touched many hundreds, yea thousands, for Christ. Dr. Armstrong had taught Bible and theology at Baptist Bible Seminary from 1943 to 1962. He also served as registrar and director of admissions. From 1962 to 1967 he was pastor of First Baptist Church of Hallstead, Pennsylvania. In 1967 he joined the Cedarville College faculty and taught there until his retirement. What a joy it is to be able to say with Paul: "For to me to live is Christ, and to die is gain" (Phil. 1:21).

End Notes

1. Merle R. Hull, *What a Fellowship!* (Schaumburg, IL: Regular Baptist Press, 1981), p. 8.
2. Ibid., p. 40.
3. Paul Tassell, "New Evangelicalism—Concession of Inerrancy," *Information Bulletin* (September 1981), p. 3.
4. Paul N. Tassell to Pastors of GARBC Churches, January 1982, General Association of Regular Baptist Churches, Schaumburg, Illinois.
5. "Council of Eighteen Minutes," Schaumburg, Illinois, December 1981. (Typewritten.)
6. Ibid.

41

One of the all-time best-selling books (it ranks number seven in sales, with more than 12.8 million copies sold) was simply titled *Nineteen Eighty-Four*. It was written by George Orwell, a pen name for a British writer whose real name was Eric Blair. Orwell was born in 1903 at Motihari, Bengal, India, the son of a customs officer. He had written several well-received books before penning *Nineteen Eighty-Four* just one year before his death on January 23, 1950, at the age of 47. Orwell's experiences included service with the Indian Imperial Police in Burma, combat in the Spanish Civil War and work with the British Broadcasting Company Far Eastern Service during the war years of 1941 to 1945. In *Nineteen Eighty-Four* Orwell warned the world of the impending consequences and catastrophes that would plague the world because of totalitarianism, whether capitalist, communist, fascist or socialist. When he died in London in 1950 his book was a sensation, and for 34 years people looked toward the year 1984 with misgivings and anxiety.

Nineteen eighty-four did arrive. And it was a mix of good and bad, but it did not turn out to be as cataclysmic as Orwell had predicted. Soviet President Yuri V. Andropov died in Moscow on February 9. On February 3 Navy Captain Bruce McCandless and Army Lieutenant Colonel Robert Stewart were launched into space by the space shuttle *Challenger,* and on February 7 they became the first men ever to fly free of a spacecraft. From April 26 to May 1 President Reagan visited China for the first time. On July 12, Democratic presidential nominee Walter Mondale chose a woman, United States Representative Geraldine Ferraro of New York, as his vice presidential running mate. On October 31, the Prime Minister of India, Indira Gandhi, was assassinated by two of her own bodyguards in New Delhi.

The big news in the United States was the election of Ronald Reagan to a second term as President. The election was the most one-sided in American political history. Reagan garnered 54,281,858 votes to only 37,457,215 for Mondale. The electoral college score was 525 to 13 in favor of Reagan, who at 73 years of age was the oldest man ever elected President. He was clearly one of the most popular presidents ever. He had survived an assassination attempt in 1981.

Nineteen eighty-four was a world in which Regular Baptists had to deal with blatant materialism, brazen immorality and barbaric popular music. A new curse called AIDS had been unleashed upon the world. To further perplex Bible-believing Christians, Islam, Buddhism and Hinduism were experiencing unprecedented revivals. Bible colleges were struggling to stay alive. Charismatic television evangelists were being exposed as money-grabbing charlatans, while many genuinely Biblical local churches were grappling with the problems brought about by shifting demographics.

In the midst of the struggles and challenges, God was still calling and equipping men for the ministry. Fred C. Hand was ordained by the Bethesda Baptist Church of Brownsburg, Indiana; Robert Anderson by Trinity Baptist Church in Indianapolis; Bob Bolton by Munising (Michigan) Baptist Church; Michael Windsor by Blaine Baptist Church, Minneapolis; Lee Kliewer by First Baptist Church, Hackensack, New Jersey; and Jon Paul Mitchell by Discovery Baptist Church, Gig Harbor, Washington.

The year also marked a milestone for Rev. and Mrs. C. Allen Taff, who celebrated their fiftieth wedding anniversary and 50 years in the ministry. Taff, who had served as GARBC western representative from 1958 to 1962, celebrated while pastoring the Chinook Baptist Church in Pasco, Washington. On the other end of the age spectrum, John R. Gowdy, who had been their youth pastor for three years, accepted the call of Temple Baptist Church in Portsmouth, Ohio, to its pastorate. Another youth pastor, Rev. James Vogel, after serving the youth since 1977, was installed as senior pastor of First Baptist Church in Johnson City, New York.

One of the highlights of 1984 for me was the visit to the home office of Rev. and Mrs. Georgi Vins and their interpreter, Mary Smalenberger. Brother Vins reported on the persecution and oppression being suffered by the fundamental Baptists of Russia. At that time, at least 180 pastors along with many other Christian workers were in prison. Many of them were suffering as a result of beatings and lack of medical attention. Our meeting was a mixture of tears, smiles and perplexity at how difficult it is to communicate through an interpreter! (And Mary is an excellent one!)

Another highlight of the year for Mrs. Tassell and me was the tenth anniversary of Maranatha Baptist Church in Sebring, Florida, one of the most unusual churches in the GARBC. The church is located right in the center of Maranatha Village, a retirement community for Regular Baptist-oriented retirees. What a happy, lively place! The tenth anniversary was celebrated by a Sunday through Friday Bible conference. I was privileged to speak every day. Pastor Roy Hamman hosted the conference as only he can host. Others participating in the conference were Charles Cuthbertson, Allan Lewis, J. O. Purcell and G. Arthur Woolsey.

In 1934 Harry Ketcham had led a group of 75 believers out of the Northern Baptist Convention church in Boonville, Indiana. Fifty years later former pastor Lee R. Russell and I celebrated the golden anniversary of Boonville's Calvary Baptist Church. Charles J. Ketcham presented a biographical chronology of his father, Harry, and a scrapbook to the church library.

A great soldier of the cross, Rev. Earl V. Willetts was honored at the age of 82 by Cedarville College when a new dormitory was named Earl Willetts Hall. In making the presentation, Dr. Paul Dixon characterized Mr. Willetts as singular in his contributions to the cause of Christ in Ohio and throughout the GARBC. Willetts had served as pastor of Calvary Baptist Church in Bellefontaine, Ohio, from 1934 to 1947 and at Berea (Ohio) Baptist Church from 1947 to 1973. He was a trustee at Cedarville for 37 years. His son, the late Jack Willetts, received the first teaching certificate granted by Cedarville College.

May of 1984 was Homegoing time for Rev. Ewing Walters at age 81. His pastorates included South Baptist Church of Flint, Michigan; White Lake Baptist Church of Montague, Michigan; and Faith Baptist Church of Mattoon, Illinois. He endeared himself to many across the country when he served as fields director of the Fellowship of Baptists for Home Missions.

At the annual conference in Seattle, Regular Baptists met an issue head on. The resolution read as follows:

Women's Role in Church and Home

Whereas the ordination of women to the Christian ministry is being advocated in both liberal and evangelical circles; and

Whereas women's subordination to male authority in the church and home has become a subject of controversy; and

Whereas there is outright rejection by a number of evangelicals of some of Paul's teaching in the New Testament regarding women, calling his instructions rabbinical and erroneous; and

Whereas some of the evangelical women's caucuses have both misinterpreted Scripture and also objected to the revealed names of God in the desire to eliminate gender-specific language;

Be it resolved that the messengers of the General Association of Regular Baptist Churches, meeting in Seattle, Washington, June 25–29, 1984, affirm their adherence to the New Testament teaching that women are not legitimate candidates for ordination and that God has committed to men the important responsibility of leadership and authority in the church and in the home (1 Cor. 11:3; Eph. 5:21–24; 1 Tim. 2:11–15; 3:1–7).

Be it further resolved that we recognize Christian women's spiritual equality with Christian men (Gal. 3:26–29), affirming that subordination is not equivalent to inferiority (was not Christ equal to and yet subordinate to the Father?), and that women's role in the church and home has its own unique function and dignity.[1]

Regular Baptist women are surely a talented and treasured company of believers. In June of 1984 Mrs. Tassell and I were given the high and holy privilege of speaking at the annual Empire State Ladies' Spiritual Advance at First Baptist Church in Johnson City, New York. Speaking to almost 1,000 ladies is an awesome experience for a man! But Chairwoman Esther D. Camp, the charming hostess for the conference, put us all at ease with her humor and grace. The music, testimonies and auditorium services all made for a great time of encouragement and edification for the ladies of New York State.

Two women who have been mightily used of the Lord among GARBC women during the 1980s are Mrs. Myrtle Thompson, director of the Women's Department of Baptist Mid-Missions, and the assistant director, Miss Sallie McElwain. Another woman who has blessed thousands of women (and men!) with the productions of her pen is Donna Poole, author of the popular *Baptist Bulletin* column, "The Christian Woman." Among other women who have impacted many women in our churches are three named Ruth: Ruth Kempton, Ruth Nettleton and Ruth Wagner. But we must also take note of 1,600 women who live in cities and villages all across our great country known as GARBC "pastors' wives." They are gifted, gracious, generous, gritty, game, glowing, godly girls who literally inspire the alliterative efforts of their homiletical husbands!

In the GARBC home office, Ruth Ryburn was succeeded by Marianne Baltensperger, who has served the national representative and the Association since 1982. In the Regular Baptist Press offices, Gladys Hawkins and Patricia Brannen Carapelle have each served for more than 30 years.

And we are indebted for all of eternity to the thousands upon thousands of women in our churches who remind us of the godly women noted by Paul in Romans 16: "I commend unto you Phebe our sister, which is a servant of the church which is at Cenchrea" (v. 1); "Greet Mary, who bestowed much labour on us" (v. 6); and "Salute Tryphena and Tryphosa, who labor in the Lord" (v. 12). Obviously, women do not have to become "ordained ministers" to serve in the work of Christ. Thank God for our Regular Baptist women who obey the Bible and do not seek what God has clearly reserved for men.

The 1980s were years marked by many transitions. Some local churches are involved in transition periods regularly when pastors resign or retire. This happens to approximately 100 of our 1,600 churches each year. About half of them (or 50) contact the home office for help in locating prospective pastoral candidates. This means I have dealt with about 600 pulpit committees during the past 12 years. If a church's pastor has had a ministry of 20 to 30 years, the chances are good that no one on the pulpit committee has had any experience whatsoever as a pulpit committee member! In order to aid our pulpit committees I wrote an *Information Bulletin* on the work of the pulpit committee. Dated November of 1981, the bulletin deals with the Constitution of the Pulpit Committee, the Consultations of the Pulpit Committee and the Candidates and the Pulpit Committee. This valuable bulletin is free in any quantity to any church from the GARBC home office.

The decade of the 1980s was also a decade of transition in the GARBC-approved agencies. Two-thirds (12) of them changed leadership during those ten years, some of them more than once.

After serving 24 years as president of Baptist Mid-Missions, Dr. Allan E. Lewis turned the reins of leadership over to Dr. C. Raymond Buck, who in turn passed the baton of leadership to Dr. Gary Anderson.

Continental Baptist Missions began the decade led by Rev. Arthur Cunningham, who died in office and was succeeded by Rev. Charles Vermilyea.

Dr. Mark Jackson was president of Baptist Bible College and Seminary of Pennsylvania at the beginning of the 1980s. Dr. Milo Thompson was president when the decade ended.

Dr. David Nettleton completed his 15-year presidency of Faith Baptist Bible College early in the decade. He was succeeded by Dr. Gordon L. Shipp, who died suddenly while in office. The decade ended with Dr. Robert Domokos at the FBBC helm.

Dr. W. Wilbert Welch closed out a quarter of a century as president of Grand Rapids College and Seminary and was succeeded by Dr. Charles U. Wagner, who resigned in 1991 to return to the pastorate.

The decade began for Northwest Baptist Seminary in Tacoma, Washington, with Dr. Charles U. Wagner, who was followed by Dr. J. Don Jennings and Dr. Ernest Pickering. Their tenures totaled only a little more than four years. They were followed by Dr. William Bellshaw, who has continued through the decade.

Spurgeon Baptist Bible College in Mulberry, Florida, was served in the 1980s by Dr. John Polson, Dr. G. Arthur Woolsey, Rev. J. O. Purcell and Dr. Elvin K. Mattison. Rev. Timothy W. Teal was installed as president in September of 1990.

Dr. W. Thomas Younger finished nine years as president of Western Baptist College in Salem, Oregon, in 1981. He was succeeded by Dr. John G. Balyo, who served out the decade.

Rev. Robert Van Alstine completed a long tenure as executive director of the Regular Baptist Child Placement Agency in Seattle, Washington, in 1990. He was succeeded by Rev. Harold Hayes.

After a quarter of a century as executive director of Shepherds, the Regular Baptist ministry to the mentally retarded, Dr. Andrew H. Wood retired and was succeeded by Dr. James H. Misirian II.

The decade was also rather turbulent in that the GARBC saw the loss of one mission agency and two schools during that ten-year period. The longtime home mission, Fellowship of Baptists for Home Missions (which had brought more churches into the GARBC than any other agency) merged with the Galilean Baptist Mission to form Baptist Mission of North America. However, in 1990 BMNA went out of business through a series of financial failures by Church Buildings

Committee, an arm of BMNA. At the time of the merger, Dr. Austin D. Plew was president of FBHM, and Rev. David E. Smith was director of the Galilean Baptist Mission. Dr. Plew was the first president of BMNA, and Dr. Harold Garland was the last.

In early 1985 the trustees of Los Angeles Baptist College voted to give the school to Dr. John MacArthur. In a May 1985 *Baptist Bulletin* editorial, Dr. Merle R. Hull wrote:

> The departure of Los Angeles Baptist College from separatist Baptist ranks—while the actual impact on the GARBC will be minimal—was an unexpected and disappointing development. . . . The LABC board of trustees voted to offer the presidency of the school, with its total asset value of approximately three and a half million dollars, to Dr. John MacArthur. (It should be noted that the vote was not unanimous; three board members opposed the action and two abstained from voting.) Dr. MacArthur accepted the offer; the school will be renamed "The Master's College," and will no longer be a part of Regular Baptist life. . . .
>
> Many people have asked incredulously how the board could take such a momentous action all by itself. But according to the structure of the school, the board was acting within its rights. Nor is there necessarily any reflection upon Dr. MacArthur. He, too, had a perfect right to accept. And the opportunity would have been almost irresistible. How often does a man have college property and facilities worth millions of dollars offered to him with no strings attached?
>
> But the fact is that Dr. MacArthur is purposely not a Baptist. Whether he is a thoroughgoing, consistent separatist is uncertain. He does hold a position of church polity different from that which Baptists have for centuries believed is Scriptural. Dr. MacArthur holds—and aggressively teaches—that churches are not run by the congregational membership, but by a self-perpetuating board of ruling elders. . . .
>
> One observation seems imperative in respect to this event. Our pastors and people must review and reestablish their belief in the Biblical teaching regarding local church government. If the "ruling elder" view begins to permeate the churches, the effect could be chaotic. Hosts of churches now smoothly and harmoniously carrying on the work of the Lord could be divided and destroyed.[2]

At the 1985 annual conference in Springfield, Illinois, the following resolution concerning Los Angeles Baptist College was passed by the messengers:

> Since the trustees of Los Angeles Baptist College voted to call to the presidency of that college Dr. John MacArthur; and

Inasmuch as Dr. MacArthur is not a Baptist and has taught and put in practice a type of local church government that is contrary to our historic position and our Biblical conviction of congregational government; and

Inasmuch as the school has been renamed "The Master's College" and its new president has declared in print "there will be widening of the base of the college from its Baptist nomenclature . . ."; and

Since Dr. MacArthur has already issued an appeal for students and financial help from Regular Baptist churches for the Master's College;

Be it resolved that we, the messengers of the General Association of Regular Baptist Churches in attendance at this annual conference, June 24–28, 1985, in Springfield, Illinois, go on record as approving the statement made and published by the Council of Eighteen which says:

We deeply regret the loss of a formerly GARBC-approved college for the following reasons:

1. The college is no longer a Baptist college.

2. The college has sacrificed its identification with the GARBC.

3. The college is in danger of sacrificing some Baptist distinctives which we hold as Biblical convictions. In particular we are concerned that the Baptist distinctive of congregational government of the local church will be sacrificed. Dr. John MacArthur by his own profession is not a Baptist; nor is he baptistic in church polity. We do believe he is consistent in the renaming of the college which reflects his position.

4. The college has deeply disappointed many churches and people who have over the years invested money as well as their very lives in LABC precisely because it was a Baptist college.

The Council of Eighteen recognizes the fiscal crises which in part precipitated the unanticipated action of the board of trustees. We therefore strongly encourage our churches to support more substantially our approved schools by contributions and by recommending our schools to the young people of our churches.[3]

Following closely on the heels of the loss of LABC was the loss of Denver Baptist Bible College and Seminary. The Denver schools had applied for approval status in 1977 when Dr. Bryce B. Augsburger was the president. At the 1977 conference in Des Moines, Iowa, a thorough report on the schools was brought to the Council by Dr. Donald M. Brong and Dr. Gordon L. Shipp, who had been appointed to investigate the schools for the Council. Paul Tassell moved that the Denver Baptist Bible College and Seminary be approved. The motion was seconded by Ralph Colas and carried unanimously.

Dr. Augsburger completed 13 years as president of the Denver schools in 1979 and was succeeded in the DBBC presidency by Dr. William R. Fusco. Dr. Fusco retired because of health reasons in the summer of 1984 and was succeeded by Dr. L. Duane Brown, who had resigned from the pastorate of the Southwest Calvary Baptist Church in Houston, Texas, to assume his duties at DBBC on August 1, 1984. The school had been plagued with financial problems for many years. Finally, in 1986, Dr. Gordon L. Shipp, president of Faith Baptist Bible College in Ankeny, Iowa, and DBBC president Dr. L. Duane Brown led their boards of trustees in working out a merger between the two schools. As a result, Shipp became president of Faith Baptist Bible College *and* Seminary. Dr. Brown accepted a call to the pastorate of the Parsippany (New Jersey) Baptist Church.

Understandably, many folks were upset at the loss of two schools in so short a time; but not quite so understandably, they aimed their frustration at the Council of Eighteen. The situation that developed at Los Angeles Baptist College was indeed especially frustrating, and some thought the Council was indirectly to blame. Of course, it was not. When the Council met for its winter meeting at Schaumburg in December of 1984, there was no hint of a deal between LABC trustees and John MacArthur. In fact, some Council of Eighteen members had been approached by LABC board members about the possibility of their being interested in the presidency of LABC. When, therefore, the deal was made with Dr. MacArthur two months later, the Council was just as surprised as anyone else.

Nevertheless, that restlessness and frustration mentioned by Dr. Merle Hull in *What A Fellowship!* (p. 40) continued to grow in the hearts and minds of some people. It finally erupted onto the floor of the 1987 annual conference in Ames, Iowa. A motion was made and seconded "that the Council of Eighteen use greater care in its review and approval of our schools." The motion asking messengers to vote that the Council Education Committee "use greater care" inferred the committee was not already using proper care. And such was not the case. The Council Education Committee was made up of three of the most conscientious men who have ever served on the committee: Chairman Lawrence Fetzer, Clay Nuttall and John Wood. The messengers were confused by such a motion, and the vote demonstrated the confusion. The vote was in favor of the motion 355 to 312.

In 1987 Western Baptist College in Salem, Oregon, came under fire when the WBC board of trustees was found to have one trustee who was a member of a church in the Conservative Baptist Association. One faculty member belonged to a CBA church. Western's critics strongly alleged that the college was somehow "compromising" or "building bridges to the CBA." However, Dr. Balyo, the WBC president, defended the action of the college saying the CBA churches involved were fundamental, separatist churches and WBC had no intentions of building bridges to the CBA or the National Association of Evangelicals. Actually, there is nothing in the GARBC Constitution that would forbid a member of a CBA church from serving in a GARBC-approved school. Although it would generally be thought unwise by many Regular Baptists, the actual decision would have to be made by the autonomous Western Baptist College board.

At the 1989 annual conference in Columbus, Ohio, a motion was made "that the Association instruct the Council of Eighteen to monitor and advise Western Baptist College to remove eventually all full-time faculty, administrative staff and board members who are members of churches in fellowship with the Conservative Baptist Association."[4] The motion seemed to be out of order in the thinking of many people because the GARBC Constitution makes the following statement: "It shall be the policy of the Association to abstain from the creation and/or control of educational, missionary and other benevolent agencies" (Article VII, Section 1). The motion to "monitor and advise" seemed to indicate "control." The motion was voted upon and passed 669 to 515.

At the same Columbus conference a proposed amendment was put on first reading by a voting messenger, not with the blessing of the Council, that all agency heads be barred from the Council of Eighteen. For many years the Association had allowed four agency men to serve on the Council. The proposed amendment generated a great deal of discussion because the restlessness, frustration and unhappiness of a segment of the Association continued to allege that agency men on the Council was really a basis for "our problems."

The Council of Eighteen's position and that of the national representative was mailed to all of the churches in November 1989. The *Information Bulletin* generated much debate throughout the Fellowship, and all viewpoints were thoroughly aired. Dr. Tassell's *Information Bulletin* read as follows:

Who Should Serve on the Council of Eighteen?

During the annual conference of the GARBC in Columbus, Ohio, in June of this year, a motion was made by one of the messengers to amend the

GARBC constitution. The wording of the proposed amendment is as follows: "No salaried servant of the approved agencies shall serve on the Council of Eighteen."

During its June meetings, the Council of Eighteen passed the following resolution in opposition to the proposed amendment.

"Whereas, The officers of the General Association of Regular Baptist Churches 'consist of a Council of Eighteen men (members of fellowshipping churches)'; and

"Whereas, These men as nominees 'subscribe in writing to the Constitution and Articles of Faith of the General Association of Regular Baptist Churches,' which include a clear statement concerning the absolute right of the local church to govern itself free from the interference of any hierarchy of individuals or organizations, these men being nominated by the local churches and elected by their messengers; and

"Whereas, The Constitution of the General Association of Regular Baptist Churches does not permit at any one time more than four salaried servants of the approved agencies of the Association on the Council of Eighteen; and

"Whereas, The above stated controlling principle guarantees that at any one time fourteen of the men on the Council of Eighteen will be pastors or laymen from the Association churches; and

"Whereas, The salaried servants of the approved agencies who have served on the Council of Eighteen through the years have done so with distinction, often because of their years of prior pastoral experience and exposure to the local church scene because of their many travels; and

"Whereas, These salaried servants have provided strong leadership to the Council of Eighteen without any threat to local church sovereignty;

"Be it therefore resolved, That we, the Council of Eighteen of the General Association of Regular Baptist Churches, meeting in session prior to the 58th annual conference in Columbus, Ohio, on June 26–30, 1989, reaffirm our belief in the present composition of the Council of Eighteen as outlined in our Constitution; and

"Be it further resolved, That we, the Council of Eighteen, given the history of our Association, throughout which the messengers have established existing constitutional policy and a satisfaction therewith, express our opposition to the proposed amendment to change the present constitutional composition of the Council of Eighteen."

I agree with the Council of Eighteen. I believe the proposed amendment is both unnecessary and unwise.

The Amendment Unnecessary

There is nothing in the present GARBC Constitution that requires any agency men to serve on the Council. The only reason agency men are nominated and elected is because that is what the churches want. Every year churches voluntarily nominate agency men, and every year voting messengers at the annual conference voluntarily elect agency men to the Council. It has been very obvious through the years that the vast majority of our churches and conference messengers are in favor of having agency men on the Council of Eighteen. If the majority do not want agency men on the Council, all they have to do is refrain from nominating them and electing them.

In reality, ALL Council members are also members of GARBC local churches. An individual is not really elected as a college president or missionary agency president but as a member of a fellowshipping church. Article VI, Section 1, of the GARBC Constitution declares: "A Council member who ceases to be a member of a fellowshipping church shall immediately cease to be a member of the Council of Eighteen."

There are those who constantly call the Council of Eighteen elections "popularity contests." Are not all elections "popularity contests"? Of course they are! In the first century when the Twelve were called upon to solve the problem of some of the widows being neglected, the Twelve said to "the multitude of the disciples," "Wherefore, brethren, look ye out among you seven men of honest REPORT, full of the Holy Spirit and wisdom, whom we may appoint over this business" (Acts 6:2, 3). Note that word REPORT. It has to do with REPUTATION.

It stands to reason that men will be nominated and elected to the Council who are well-known. There is nothing wrong with that. Through the years we in the GARBC have quietly and humbly chosen our Council members without politicking and hoopla. We have quietly allowed the Holy Spirit to guide us in our choices. We have believed the words in Psalm 75:6, 7: "For promotion cometh neither from the east, nor from the west, nor from the south. But God is the judge: he putteth down one, and setteth up another." We have heeded the wise advice of Jeremiah 45:5: "And seekest thou great things for thyself? seek them not."

I remember how surprised I was the first time I was nominated for the then Council of Fourteen and how very surprised I was when I was elected. Positions of responsibility and service and leadership should be accepted humbly, not sought after. And if our churches want to nominate and elect salaried servants of our agencies, they ought to be allowed that option.

Amendment Makes False Assumptions

The proposed amendment implies there is something wrong about agency leaders serving on the Council of Eighteen. For the past two or three years we have been told that agency men have "different agendas" from pastors. We have been told that agency men will vote on issues in a manner that will benefit their agencies, not necessarily in the best interests of the GARBC.

There is an awful lot of misunderstanding about the Council of Eighteen and its work. I would very much like to shed some light on the subject since enough heat has already been stirred up by insinuations that local churches are somehow being violated when agency men serve on the Council of Eighteen.

We need to understand that the Council of Eighteen agenda is quite simple and rather "cut and dried." The December meeting is primarily given over to the finalizing of the annual conference program and the matter of finances. The Council members are there to serve the Association. There are no hidden agendas. For over twenty years I have sat in Council meetings, and I have never heard an agency man try to push his "agenda." The June meeting is largely given to hearing annual reports from the national representative and the executive editor and the reports and recommendations of each of the committees. The Council seeks no control over any local church or agency. No Biblical principle is violated by allowing a mix of agency men and non-agency men to serve on the Council together.

Council Not a House of Representatives

Some people think the Council of Eighteen is similar to the United States House of Representatives. Therefore, they say, we ought to have "regional representation" on the Council. That idea has never caught on in the Association, and there are some sound reasons why. First, the Council members are not on the Council to push regional causes or programs. The Council prepares the annual conference program and oversees the work of the Home Office. Second, congressional representatives dole out financial benefits to their districts. The congressmen who make up our House of Representatives may want a new highway or a new dam or a new bridge for their districts and they politick for it. That is surely not the business of the Council of Eighteen! The Council's range of responsibility is a very limited one that serves the Association as a whole. Regional issues are not involved and neither are regional finances. The national representative does not serve regional issues and neither does the RBP executive editor.

Out of sixteen hundred local churches we elect only eighteen men to serve us, and it really does not matter what region or state they come from. They are on the Council to serve the Association, not to represent their district, state or region. The same is true of the agency men. They are not on the Council to serve their agency constituency but to handle the strictly defined responsibilities of Associational business.

The men who first structured our Association did a wonderful piece of work. They depoliticized as much as possible the work and relationships of our Association. Our pastors through the years have worked closely and harmoniously with our educational, missionary and service agencies. Let us not now polarize our churches and agencies by ostracizing our agency men from service on the Council.

Let us allow our churches the privilege each year to decide whether or not they want agency men nominated and elected. The present constitution gives that freedom. We do not need an amendment. If the churches do not want agency men on the Council, all they have to do is refrain from nominating them and electing them. Past experience indicates an overwhelming desire on the part of our churches to put agency leaders on the Council, never more than four at any time. That surely seems fair to me.

The Amendment Unwise

The proposed amendment to prohibit agency men from serving on the Council is unwise. Let me list the men from agencies who have served on the Council of Eighteen through the years. Some of them have also served on the Council before or after their agency days: Bryce B. Augsburger, John G. Balyo, William G. Bellshaw, Fred R. Brock, L. Duane Brown, Paul Dixon, John R. Dunkin, William Fusco, Earle G. Griffith, Mark Jackson, Paul R. Jackson, J. Don Jennings, James T. Jeremiah, Wendell Kempton, Kenneth Muck, David Nettleton, Ernest Pickering, John Polson, J. Irving Reese, Gordon L. Shipp, Milo Thompson, H. O. Van Gilder, Sr., Charles U. Wagner, W. Wilbert Welch, John White, G. Arthur Woolsey and W. Thomas Younger.

The above list of twenty-seven men reads like a GARBC "hall of fame." What a sad mistake it would have been to have missed the wisdom, spirituality and expertise of those men just because they were led to accept places of agency leadership! Twenty-four of those men served many years as pastors before becoming agency men. Does the proposed amendment imply that men of God called out of the pastorate to train young men and women for ministry somehow do not now qualify to serve our Association on its Council? Why should this be? Why not make such a prohibition for state representatives or for pastors who serve on school or mission or service agency boards? Why pick on agency leaders? Why penalize agency leaders for being chosen of God to direct ministries that are so vital to all of our churches? That does not seem wise to me, and I doubt if it seems wise to the vast majority of our churches.

I believe a ban on agency leaders serving on the Council is unwise because such a ban would rob us of great experience. It seems logical to me that if anyone would know the heartbeat of the GARBC, it would be the agency leaders who minister in fifty to one hundred churches a year. I know from personal experience that my travels among our churches for the past ten years have given me more insight and more depth of comprehension about our churches than twenty-five years of pastoring just four churches could teach me. How could it be unwise for just four agency leaders to counsel with fourteen non-agency men? Surely the present Council makeup is balanced, fair and wise.

Another reason a ban on agency men would be unwise is the very nature of the Council's work. The major part of the Council's work has to do with giving direction and help to Regular Baptist Press and the GARBC Home Office. The RBP and GARBC Home Office ministries parallel in many ways the work of our missionary, service and educational agencies. Our offices in Schaumburg employ between forty-five and fifty people. Regular Baptist Press alone is more than a $4 million per year operation. We have $2.5 million worth of property and buildings to tend. The financial and personnel management skills of our agency leaders have been of inestimable help to all of us at the Home Office through the years. I believe it would be unwise to take such expertise away from the Council.

In my ten years as national representative I have been blessed year after year as I have watched the Holy Spirit direct the annual conference voting messengers to choose just the right mix of pastors, state representatives and agency leaders. While some may be well-intentioned and sincere in their efforts to tamper with a God-blessed system of electing our leaders, I personally think such an amendment to be unwise.[5]

When the annual conference convened at Niagara Falls, New York, in June of 1990, the amendment issue had been talked about and written about more than any other item of business in recent Association meetings. When the vote was finally taken, the 1,908 voting messengers soundly defeated the proposed amendment: 1,172 voted no; 736 voted yes. Thus the Constitution stays the same, and it is still permissible to have up to four agency men on the Council if that is what the churches desire.

End Notes

1. "Council of Eighteen Minutes," Seattle, Washington, June 1984. (Typewritten.)

2. Merle R. Hull, "Editorially Speaking," *Baptist Bulletin* (May 1985), p. 17.

3. "Los Angeles Baptist College and The Master's College," *Baptist Bulletin* (July–August 1985), p. 30.

4. "Motion Made by L. Duane Brown," GARBC Annual Conference, Columbus, Ohio, June 1989. (Typewritten.)

5. Paul N. Tassell, "Who Should Serve on the Council of Eighteen?" *Information Bulletin* (November 1989), pp. 1–4.

42

My first seven years as national representative had given me the opportunity to travel widely among our churches. As 1986 unfolded, I became increasingly aware of a segment of fundamentalism that was increasingly majoring on minors and making personal preferences equal to Scriptural convictions. They were failing to heed Ernest Pickering's wise exhortation on page 234 of his book, *Biblical Separation:*

> We must avoid the danger of elevating our own personal tastes or opinions to the level of divine revelation. People with strong convictions (and most separatists are such) have difficulty distinguishing between their opinions and scriptural principles. In an effort to avoid appearing wishy-washy or uncertain in areas of doctrine, some separatists go to an extreme and take hard, irrevocable stands on every minor issue as though it were a major item of the faith.[1]

Some fundamentalists were making these the tests of fellowship: the King James Version or the use of hand microphones while singing or the wearing of pantsuits by women or the length of a man's sideburns. Some were going far beyond Biblical separation from apostasy and Biblical separation from new evangelicals who willingly encourage apostates to all kinds of so-called "degrees" of separation that are not found in the Bible. Such "hyper-separatists" do not represent the kind of Biblical position taken by the Van Gilders, Ketchams, Jacksons, Stowells and present GARBC leaders. Ostracizing a pastor or other leader who may invite a speaker to his platform that you wouldn't is a violation of that brother's autonomy and an overstepping of your rights as a fundamentalist. If a Robert T. Ketcham could work on the platform with Northern Baptist W. B. Riley, why do you think a modern-day Regular Baptist cannot encourage a fundamentalist today who may not yet be all the way out of some associations we would avoid?

So I went to our 1986 conference at Grand Rapids with my heart full. My burden was to steer our great Association away from an unbiblical hyper-separation that was surely dishonoring to God and hurtful to the cause of Christ. My annual report for the 1986 conference was later sent to the churches as a September 1986 *Information Bulletin.* The entire bulletin read as follows:

The following message was given as my National Representative's report on Tuesday morning, June 24, 1986, at the annual conference of the GARBC in Grand Rapids, Michigan. It is a plea, not a denominational edict. It is not a "papal decree," but one man's studied and prayerful evaluation. I am not angry with anyone nor do I seek to "muzzle" anyone. My plea is for independence and autonomy, for the right to disagree agreeably as brethren who are dedicated to the basic principles and practices of Regular Baptists. It is written in the spirit of Robert T. Ketcham, who said: "It is not at all inherent in the issue itself that to be a good Baptist, one must be a poor Christian in his attitude to all other evangelical denominational groups" (quoted from GARBC Literature Item 15, "Is It a Sin to Be a Baptist?" by R. T. Ketcham).

This is my seventh annual report to you messengers, and I have a heavy burden on my heart today which I would like to deliver to you. My report is going to consist of an answer, an exhortation and a challenge.

First of all, the answer. Around the country for the past couple of years, people who are *outside* the GARBC have said again and again, "The GARBC is going soft." And that talk has apparently permeated and pervaded the thinking of some of our own pastors who write to me and talk to me and say the GARBC is going soft. I'd like to ask a question and then try to answer it. *About whom are they talking?* What do they mean when they say the GARBC is going soft? Do they mean the home office staff in Schaumburg? Well, I know all of those men well. I can assure you that Dr. Merle Hull, our Executive Editor, has not gone soft. He stands right where he did when Dr. Robert T. Ketcham asked him to come to Chicago and serve in that office way back in the middle 1950s, some 32 years ago. They certainly can't mean Dr. Merle Hull.

Well, do they mean Herm Scott, our Marketing Director? He's been with us for 15 years, a loyal church member in his Regular Baptist church. He certainly hasn't gone soft.

What about our Business Manager, Milt Tyrrell? Not only is he a fundamentalist and a separatist, but our business manager in his office in

Schaumburg often wins people to Christ right across from his desk—salesmen who come in to talk to him about business. They surely can't mean Milt Tyrrell.

Well, do they mean our Southwestern representative for Regular Baptist Press, Mel Jones? No sir. Mel is a separatist of the first order.

What about Dr. Jim Dersham, our Managing Editor? Has he gone soft? Well, Denver Baptist Bible College in their last commencement didn't think so. They awarded him an honorary Doctor of Divinity degree. Part of the reason was his uncompromising stand for the Word of God.

What about our Vacation Bible School Editor, Donald Anderson, whom you saw (well, you didn't see him, you heard him) last night? Why, he's such a separatist he won't even eat Graham Crackers! They surely can't mean Don Anderson.

What about Dr. Mark Jackson, our new director of Gospel Literature Services, who has pastored in our churches through the years, who has recently been president of one of our great schools and who will now lead the Gospel Literature Services ministry? I tell you, Dr. Mark Jackson stands exactly where his father, Paul R. Jackson, stood.

Well, how about our dedicated ladies? Have they gone soft? Not on your life.

Well, that leaves me. These people who say the GARBC has gone soft, are they talking about the National Representative? My position as a separatist, fundamentalist and as a Regular Baptist is identical to what it was when I took my first pastorate in 1954, 32 years ago. There probably isn't anybody alive who gives more time to propagating the position of the General Association of Regular Baptist Churches than I do. I teach our position; I preach it; I write it; I sell hundreds of Dr. Pickering's book *Biblical Separation* every year. I distribute tens of thousands of our GARBC literature items, and I stand forthrightly for Biblical separation without apology. It can't be me.

Well, maybe they mean our approved agencies. Is that what they mean when they say the GARBC has gone soft? Well, I know all the leaders of our schools, all the leaders of our mission agencies and our social agencies. Each has its own individuality, and there is diversity among them, but they are solidly committed to our doctrinal position and our separation from the apostasy and New Evangelicalism. I have been on our campuses through the years, and certainly there is diversity. But there's room for diversity in the GARBC.

Well, do they mean our Council of Eighteen? Our churches nominate our councilmen, the messengers from our churches elect them, they sign their names to the statements of allegiance to our position before their names go on the ballot. Of course, there are diverse viewpoints on debatable things among those men. They may differ on people and places of ministry within the evangelical, fundamentalist arena, but I don't think that's any reason to call any of them soft. Just because one man may preach somewhere where you wouldn't preach doesn't mean that man is soft. And just because a councilman may be different from you doesn't mean he's soft—he's just different from you. That may be a good thing!

Well, what about our churches? Nobody ever said we're perfect, but the General Association of Regular Baptist Churches was founded to oppose doctrinal deviation, and our churches are bound together by true-to-the-Bible articles of faith. We were also founded to oppose any form of denominational dictatorship. We are not a convention, coercing our churches, nor are we a denomination exercising dictatorship over our people. Listen, folks, the GARBC is a fellowship. According to our Constitution, and I'm quoting now, "Upon the recommendation of the Council of Eighteen at the annual meeting of the GARBC, and the majority vote of the Association, a church shall be received into fellowship. (Note the word 'fellowship,' not 'membership.' A Baptist church cannot be a member of anything outside itself. It can declare itself in fellowship with any body of Baptists on earth, but cannot be a member.)" Now listen, a fellowship ought to be an enjoyable experience. Dr. Robert Ketcham used to speak often of "our happy fellowship." Having declared ourselves as agreed on our doctrinal and separatist distinctives, we surely ought to respect each other's autonomy and the right of all of us to exercise independence in our ministries without calling those who differ with us "soft" or "neo" or something worse. We must never allow the GARBC to be taken over by a paranoid syndrome that looks with suspicion on anyone who does not do or say exactly as I do or say. A fellowship should not be characterized by a gestapo-like mentality where every preacher is always checking up on every other preacher. We're in the GARBC because we want to be, and we're here as a fellowship of fundamental, separatist Regular Baptists. Sometimes some fundamentalists remind me of teenagers who are always trying to prove how macho they are by challenging others to be as daring and macho as they are. Or we've divided ourselves into camps like little boys who say my dad can beat your dad. Men, we can be strong fundamentalists without always having to beat our hairy chests while proclaiming our superior militancy. If a man really loves his wife, he doesn't have to always be telling everybody. I do not believe the GARBC has gone soft. Let me tell you what I do believe is happening in the GARBC as a movement.

Number 1—We're growing in grace. Now that's Scriptural. We're learning to be gentlemen as well as gladiators as a movement, and there's nothing wrong with that.

Number 2—We're learning to speak the truth in love, and that, too, is Scriptural. Our founders, like Robert T. Ketcham, left us that kind of an example. Many of us here today can remember Dr. Ketcham many times preaching with tears; warring with the enemy does not preclude weeping over the enemy. Debating with brethren on points which are legitimate questions doesn't mean demeaning the brethren. We have through 54 years in the General Association of Regular Baptist Churches had many differences. It is not true that differences are something new in this fellowship, but through the years the GARBC has had a great fellowship despite our differences. There is room for debate on the subject of plurality of elders. We do not believe in elder rule, but surely some of us who are strong men on pastors and deacons can live with some fellows who talk about plurality of elders. It is in a real sense a matter of semantics, and you may disagree with me on that. But there's room for that kind of disagreement. We have always had different degrees of Calvinists in this Association—some are 2-point, some are 4-point, some are 6-point! We even differ a little bit in Grand Rapids on the subject of versions. We may differ on whether or not we ought to be involved with the American Council of Christian Churches. We have some differences about where we ought to minister as it relates to non-GARBC fundamental and evangelical circles. And, thank God, we're learning to speak the truth in love with each other. That doesn't mean you're going soft.

Number 3—We are becoming more and more aware of what Dr. Paul R. Jackson wrote more than 20 years ago. We're finally catching up with Ketcham and Jackson on some of these things. Dr. Jackson wrote, "Separation is to our GARBC movement what sanitation is to surgery." Scrubbing is not an end in itself, and separation is not an end in itself. And we got out of the Northern Baptist Convention so that we could be free—free to preach the truth, free to evangelize, free to plant churches, free to do the work of the Great Commission. Separation is not an end in itself, it is a means to an end.

Number 4—The GARBC has traded denominational rigidity for associational latitude—not doctrinally, not as we relate to the apostasy, but our churches and pastors are surely at liberty to conduct themselves as they sincerely believe God is leading them. If we cease to believe and practice such autonomy, we cease to be an associational fellowship and become something less baptistic and even less Biblical.

Number 5—We are more clearly seeing our responsibility to contend for the faith. Contending for the faith is not sniping at your brother—your brother pastor. Contending for the faith is not writing letters, demeaning brethren who differ with you on some debatable point. We're to contend for *the faith.* Now let me say something as the National Representative of the GARBC. Let me say something as a rock-ribbed, died-in-the-wool separatist. Let me say something as one who has no use for blood-denying, Bible-rejecting, namby-pamby, wishy-washy, white-livered, yellow-backed, thumb-sucking, toe-kissing liberal preachers. Let me say, God *does* work through other people in this world besides Regular Baptists. Jack Wyrtzen is not a

Nels Ferre or a Harry Emerson Fosdick. John MacArthur is not a Bishop Oxnam or Karl Barth. Warren Wiersbe is not a Norman Vincent Peale . . . (I know all about Moody Bible Institute's bringing Billy Graham in for their 100th anniversary; I don't like that and I'm sure you didn't like that), but let me tell you something—with all of their failings and shortcomings and lack of separatist position, and they've always been interdenominationalists—we ought to know that—but with all that, Chicago would be a spiritual wasteland if it were not for Moody Bible Institute. Hey, listen, where would the spiritual need of Tennessee ever be met if it were up to the GARBC? Don't knock Don Jennings and the Tennessee Temple Schools. Where would Tennessee be without them? What have we done for South Carolina in the last 54 years? You may not agree with everything about Bob Jones University, but South Carolina would be a spiritual wasteland without it. What about North Carolina? Thank God for Piedmont Bible College. Let's stop training our guns on fellow soldiers and train them on some real enemies who are diametrically opposed to the faith.

When this Association started in 1932, there were 207 million Protestants in the world of all stripes—liberals, evangelicals, fundamentalists, neo-orthodox, everything—207 million. Today there are 324 million. That's an increase of 57%. In 1932 there were 151 million Buddhists in the world. Today there are 245 million. That's a 63% increase. Buddhism has increased 6% more in the last 54 years than has Protestant Christianity. In 1932 there were 331 million Roman Catholics in the world. Now there are 565 million. That's a 70% increase. In 1932 there were 230 million Hindus in the world. Today there are 500 million. That's a 117% increase, and this past weekend in Aurora, Illinois, which is 35 miles from our Schaumburg office, the largest Hindu Temple in North America was dedicated at a cost of $2.5 million. *That's our enemy!* In 1932 there were 202 million Moslems in the world. Today there are 1 billion. That's a 500% increase. Multi-million dollar mosques are right now being constructed in Boston, Chicago, Detroit, Houston, Los Angeles, Montreal, New York, Philadelphia, San Diego, San Francisco, Toronto and Washington, D.C. Ladies and gentlemen, let's contend for *the faith.* The Buddhists and the Hindus and the Moslems and the Modernists and the Mormons and the Mariolaters are taking it away from us. While we're squabbling with our fly-swatters swatting mosquitos, they're challenging giants.

What is the fallout of loose talk about the GARBC going soft? Let me share some comments from laymen who came to me as I traveled from border to border and coast to coast in the last year. These are laymen who came up to me and said, "I've heard some of our schools have gone liberal." Why, that's ridiculous. Of course, they haven't gone liberal. Those poor laymen didn't even know the meaning of the term liberal, but that's the fallout of this kind of loose talk. Another one said, "Is it true that some of the Council of Eighteen members no longer believe in Biblical separation?" Not on your life. Somebody else said to me, "Why does the GARBC allow some of its school professors to drink wine?" Now whoever spread that rumor is a liar. To quote a famous grammarian at Grand Rapids Baptist College, "That just ain't so!" Another one said, "How come the GARBC doesn't take a stand against liberals anymore?" You see, that's the kind of fallout from loose, unfounded talk. That's my answer.

Now, here's my exhortation. Brethren, my heart is burdened that we close ranks and refrain from the kind of petty bickering that has ruined the Bible Presbyterian denomination and the International Council of Christian Churches and other groups through the years who majored on fighting their comrades instead of their enemies. Listen, oh listen to me. Listen to the words of Paul in Galatians 5:15. "But if ye bite and devour one another, take heed that ye be not consumed one of another." I beseech you pastors and other messengers to work with me in Scripturally counteracting the soft talk. We are separatists, we are true fundamentalists, and we are concerned that we only be *Biblical* separatists and *Biblical* fundamentalists, not some stereotype caricature. Are you with me? Will you stand with me?

Now, here's my challenge. As an Association we need to get busy doing what Paul Beals was talking about this morning. The Council of Eighteen last Friday evening appointed a blue ribbon committee of men who will aid me in leading the GARBC in the next several years in church growth and church planting. They are Don Tyler, John White, Larry Fetzer, Norm Nicklas and Bob Wright. . . . They have directed me to restructure my schedule in order to have time in the home office to plan and promote multiple church conferences and seminars on church planting and to write materials which will help our pastors step-by-step in how-to fashion to mother a church. I'm going to have to cancel some meetings and revamp my schedule, but this must take top priority in our fellowship. Our goal, well Dr. Beals mentioned in his message that by 1991 he thought it very possible that 500 new churches could be started in our Fellowship. I would like to think that by the year 2000 every single one of our 1,600 churches would start another church. That means in 14 years we would number 3,200 churches instead of 1,600. I can't imagine a church not being able to start another church in 14 years. And we're not simply going to stand up here and say we ought to do it. By God's grace we're going to provide some materials to help you to do it; we're going to provide some conferences and seminars and literature to show you how-to. I believe that's the need of the hour. Sure, we're separatists. We're free from the apostasy. We're free from the compromise of conventionism. *And we're free to get busy for God.* May God help us to do it.

The following paragraphs are taken from a letter written by Dr. A. Donald

Moffat to Dr. Tassell on July 16, 1986. Dr. Moffat has served as a missionary to Brazil under Mid-Missions, [as] a representative for ABWE, as state representative for Ohio and now [as] an assistant to the Pastor at Maranatha Baptist Church in Sebring, Florida. He is a son-in-law of R. T. Ketcham. At age 76 he is still very active in our fellowship.

"This morning we heard your report to the Fellowship. It was excellent! You spoke with clarity and forcefulness. It brought back memories of Dad Ketcham. He would have spoken in exactly the same manner.

"I, personally, have been disturbed by those of our Fellowship who have gone into a position of isolation. They will not have Wiersbe, Strauss, Sugden and the like. What bothers me most is that they defend their position by saying it was Dr. Ketcham's position. Nothing could be farther from the truth than that! Dad ministered at Pine Brook, Keswick, Sandy Cove, Montrose, Schroon Lake, Moody and such places. He was at these places year following year. He counted as close friends Warren Wiersbe, Jack Wyrtzen, Percy Crawford, Bishop Culbertson, Lehman Strauss, Dr. Pettingill and others. They did not see eye to eye with our GARBC position; however, they were (and are) brothers in Christ. Dad fellowshipped with both these men and their ministries.

"Few people know that the last year that Dad Ketcham was alive, it was Warren Wiersbe who went to Mother and Dad's apartment in Chicago almost every week. He read the Scriptures to Dad, prayed with him and talked of things spiritual. Warren wanted Dad to have his funeral in the Moody Memorial Church because he was afraid that our Belden Regular Baptist Church would not be big enough.

"Let me say again—your message set things straight."[2]

End Notes

1. Ernest Pickering, *Biblical Separation* (Schaumburg, IL: Regular Baptist Press, 1979), p. 234.

2. Paul N. Tassell, "An Answer, an Exhortation and a Challenge," *Information Bulletin* (September 1986), pp. 1–4.

43

One of the most meaningful actions of the Council of Eighteen was taken in Grand Rapids, Michigan, in June of 1986. The Council and the national representative had talked about the need of a church-planting impetus in the Association for a couple of years. I wrote an *Information Bulletin* for March of 1984 titled "A Strategy for Establishing Churches in the U.S.A." (still available free from the home office). In that bulletin I spoke about The Underlying Problems, The Undeniable Priority, The Understanding Pastor, The Underlining Procedures, The Undaunted People, The Undergirding Power and The Undiluted Promises. That *Information Bulletin* stirred many hearts and generated a great deal of correspondence over the next two years. Finally, at the pre-conference meeting of the Council of Eighteen in 1986, we felt led of the Spirit to put actions with our words. The result? The Blue Ribbon Committee on Church Planting and Church Growth. The purpose of the committee would be to hold two conferences per year on the "how-to" of church planting and church growth. These conferences would utilize the best talent and experience we could find in our Association. The rationale was simple but sure: If the GARBC is to survive as a viable force for God into the twenty-first century, we must get busy building our present churches while at the same time establishing scores of independent, fundamental, separatist, soul-winning, Bible-teaching, Christ-honoring local Baptist churches.

Dr. Donald Tyler was appointed chairman of the Blue Ribbon Committee. He has pastored the Bethesda Baptist Church in Brownsburg, Indiana, since 1959. He has led that church in steady, solid growth for three decades. From a congregation of fewer than 100, he has seen it grow to a membership of more than 2,000. As leader of the Blue Ribbon Committee, he has taken the lead by challenging his church to start new churches in Indiana. The other committee members are as follows: Howard Bixby, Kenneth Davis, Vernon D. Miller, Rich McGhee, Norman Nicklas, Larry Smith, Paul N. Tassell, Charles Vermilyea, John White and Robert Wright.

So far excellent conferences have been held in Brownsburg, Indiana; Clarks Summit, Pennsylvania; Grand Rapids, Michigan; Ankeny, Iowa; Salem, Oregon; and Hemet, California. The first conferences were two-track: Church Planting and Church Growth. The conference at Grand Rapids April 30—May 2, 1990, included a third track on church leadership. All future conferences will include all three tracks. For April of 1991 plans were to hold the conference on the campus of Cedarville College in Ohio (April 29—May 1). The conference after that was scheduled for October 28–30, 1991, in the Kansas City area. For those two conferences three new seminars were to be presented: "Tools and Resources for Use in Church Growth" by Robert Wright; "Tools and Resources for Use in Church Planting" by Norman Nicklas and "Tools and Resources for Use in Church Leadership" by Howard Bixby.

These conferences are really producing! Already a number of churches have been planted as direct results of the information, instruction and inspiration given in these sessions. Church growth has also resulted from putting into practice some of the methods and motivations learned at the Blue Ribbon conferences. The new track on leadership has also proved productive. The spiritual and Scriptural benefits from obeying the Great Commission are eternal.

As the months of 1986 came and went, the strategic ministry of Gospel Literature Services experienced a change of leadership. Virgil Riley and his wife, Jayne, had served since 1973. "Mike" Riley, as director of GLS, had endeavored for 13 years to alert our churches and pastors to the great need of our missionaries for literature. Riley's work was one of pioneering and breaking new ground, for Regular Baptists had not hitherto known much about providing literature on a large scale free to our missionaries. We all had to learn to give. Although GLS is connected with Regular Baptist Press, it is not subsidized by the Press. GLS is totally dependent upon gifts from churches and individuals for its ongoing ministries. When the Rileys came to retirement time, they could justly be proud and grateful for what God had used them to do. They had laid a solid, Scriptural foundation upon which the next director could build with confidence and fruitfulness. But who would that next director of Gospel Literature Services be?

Dr. Mark Evan Jackson was born on October 28, 1928. He was born again in September of 1936 at the First Baptist Church of Ceres, California, and baptized there in 1938 by his pastor who was also his father, Paul R. Jackson. He graduated from Baptist Bible Seminary in Johnson City, New York, in 1950. He and his wife, Irene, have four children and seven grandchildren. His pastorates over a period of 30 years included First Baptist Church of Dedham, Massachusetts; Calvary Baptist Church, Everett, Washington; Bethel Baptist Church, Kalamazoo, Michigan; Calvary Baptist Church, Muskegon, Michigan; and Walnut Ridge Baptist Church, Waterloo, Iowa. From 1979 to 1986 he served as president of Baptist Bible College of Pennsylvania. One would be hard pressed to find a man more prepared and qualified for the GLS directorship than Mark Jackson, who received an honorary doctorate from Cedarville College in 1976. Between 1969 and 1985 he served as director and planner for 17 tours to Israel, Egypt, Jordan, Russia, England, Europe, Greece, Italy, Turkey and Hong Kong. He is the author of *Ready, Set, Grow!* which is in its fifth printing.

In the churches where he pastored, missionary budgets were greatly increased, and vital missionary interests were incorporated into church life. His insight into missionary needs is further enhanced by his serving on the board of Association of Baptists for World Evangelism. He travels extensively to mission fields ministering to missionaries, working on long-range literature plans with missionaries and representing the work of Gospel Literature Services and the spread of the gospel through the printed page.

The total income for GLS in the last GARBC fiscal year of May 1, 1989, to April 30, 1990, was $125,792.96. Dr. Jackson would like to see that sum grow to a million dollars annually as our churches catch the vision of getting gospel literature into the hands of the multiplied millions, yea, billions of people on this planet earth. The missionaries are more and more turning to GLS, for they know they have a real friend in Mark Jackson, who will do everything in his power to find the monies necessary to fund the crucial projects planned by the missionaries. Let Dr. Jackson share his burden with you through the following paragraphs from his 1990 report at the Niagara Falls conference:

> Gospel Literature Services is a ministry of our churches. Until we get to Heaven, we will not fully know the importance of the work we carry on for

missionaries through Gospel Literature Services.

The domino effect of the distribution of literature can be illustrated in the following account of a single two-cent gospel tract. One of our missionaries in the Philippines, along with five or six members of one of the churches, stood in a busy marketplace and passed out 14,000 tracts in 90 minutes! You have to stand in the middle of a clamoring crowd of pushing, pulling, yelling people to understand how quickly thousands of tracts can be given out.

One tract fell into the hands of a Roman Catholic college professor. The truth of the tract grasped his mind and heart. He shared it the next morning with all his jogging partners and later in the day with three of his university classes. Then he read it at a meeting of the entire faculty!

How can you calculate the effective worth of a two-cent tract!?

In months past we have been sending tracts to missionaries in "large" bunches of 5,000 and 10,000. Now the missionaries are bolder in their requests, and the churches are increasingly generous in their support, and the numbers have increased ten-fold. Requests are being met now for 50,000 and 100,000 tracts.

The above illustration of one small part of the GLS ministry will have to suffice for purposes of this report. The story of a quarter of a million dollars' worth of Sunday School and VBS material, Bibles, New Testaments, specially printed literature such as that produced for Project Utah, six tons of material sent to Romania, more than $50,000 worth of Bibles sent into Russia and a thousand other similar projects have made this year without doubt the most exciting year in the 17-year history of GLS and the most demanding of my 40 years in the ministry.

And I have enjoyed every minute of it!

Please pray for GLS, for missions, for missionaries, for literature outreach and even for individual pieces of literature that they will fall into the hands of just the right people and be effective in their salvation.

Right now as you read—during our annual conference in Niagara Falls—BMM missionaries and hundreds of short-term missionary helpers are walking the streets and sidewalks of small cities in Utah knocking on doors and giving Mormons literature that was produced by GLS and paid for by hundreds of our churches and supporting friends. . . .

Our outreach to the Eastern Europe countries and Russia will continue as long as the churches continue to send funds. The long-range work will be carried out through the work of our missionaries who will be making ministry journeys into those countries. Literature will be made available to them to take to these needy fields. It is our objective to gather a "war chest" of $100,000 to begin to meet their needs. Your continued help in this ministry as churches and friends will be tremendously appreciated by the people who have lived so long behind the terrible curtain.

Mrs. Jackson and I want to thank the hundreds of churches and thousands of friends who have been so gracious to us and to GLS over these years of our ministry at GLS. You have made the long, hard journeys much more pleasant by your hospitality, your support and your friendship.[1]

End Note

1. "Report on Gospel Literature Services," by Mark E. Jackson, Director, *1990 GARBC Annual Report* (Schaumburg, IL: Regular Baptist Press, 1990), p. 12.

Vernon D. Miller

44

How does a man say farewell to people he has known and loved for 33 years?"[1] Dr. Merle R. Hull posed that question in his final editorial in the September 1987 *Baptist Bulletin.* He went on to answer his question in the following words:

> Well, he does it inadequately—at least in my case. To fully transfer the feelings of my heart to paper is beyond me. . . .
>
> I am thankful for you, our *Bulletin* constituency through the years. You have been patient, understanding, responsive and a delight to serve. I even enjoyed the occasional letters that suggested my editorial judgment was missing in action. These helped me, and I have always stood for people's right to express their reactions.
>
> I am thankful for our great Association. Being made up of people not yet perfect, it has its weaknesses. To me, however, it is still the greatest Fellowship of believers this side of Heaven. I thank God for the rare privilege I have had of working with Dr. Ketcham, Dr. Paul Jackson, Dr. Joseph Stowell and Dr. Paul Tassell. And I am thankful for the various persons who have been my co-laborers in the Chicago–Des Plaines–Schaumburg offices. Some of us are in positions where our names are better known, but in the Day of Christ these who work so faithfully behind the scenes will receive their deserved recognition. I especially want to mention the support, encouragement and faithful work of my wife through all these years. . . .
>
> To my successor, Brother Vernon Miller, I wish the Lord's blessing and a double measure of love, knowledge and all judgment that he may approve things that are excellent in an increasingly confused world.[2]

Earlier in this book we paid tribute to Dr. Hull. His impact upon the GARBC was far-reaching and lasting. On his last day in office, his secretary somehow managed to get his car keys. Some of our men got a red carpet-runner and stretched it from the office steps to his car.

Then all of the employees lined up on both sides of the carpet and applauded Dr. Hull as he made his way from the office to his car for the last time as Regular Baptist Press executive editor and editor of the *Baptist Bulletin.* I considered it an honor to open the car door for him. Dr. Hull continued to be active in a preaching ministry until his death in November 1990.

How do you choose a successor to a man who has served you for 33 years? On June 25, 1986, Council of Eighteen Chairman John G. Balyo appointed a Search Committee with the mission of finding God's man to succeed Dr. Hull. The committee was comprised of Wendell Kempton, chairman; William Fusco and Richard G. Mohr. The committee met on September 5, 1986, and followed through with having personal interviews with Dr. Hull, Patricia Brannen and Dr. Tassell. The interviews centered around putting together a profile covering the man who would succeed Dr. Hull. The committee concluded carefully and prayerfully that the next man should be one who is theologically in agreement with the GARBC Articles of Faith, is holding separatist convictions (that would include both personal and ecclesiastical separation), is possessed with technical ability, is capable of administrative skills, is an acceptable public speaker and is a man who does not mind being in a number-two position. Furthermore, he should be one who has a compatible personality and an evangelistic spirit. As the committee refined and elaborated upon the profile, it decided the man should have a proven track record, including consistent convictions. He should be a man of strong moral character and a man whose past ministries have evidenced the obvious blessing of God.

During the next two weeks, the committee kept in touch with one another and finally narrowed their attention to one man—Vernon D. Miller, who had earlier worked alongside Dr. Ketcham, Dr. Hull, Dr. Jackson and Dr. Stowell. A meeting between the committee and Mr. Miller took place on October 20, 1986, in Chicago. The meeting lasted four hours as the committee engaged in an in-depth interview. After the interview was concluded, the committee met without Miller and decided they should follow through with two areas of responsibility: (1) A meeting that would include Mr. Vernon Miller, Dr. Paul Tassell and Rev. Richard Mohr should take place; (2) there should be written references submitted from those who have worked alongside Mr. Miller.

The meeting including Miller, Tassell and Mohr took place on

October 31, 1986. Pastor Mohr submitted in writing a synopsis of the meeting to William Fusco and Wendell Kempton. The consensus of that report was that Dr. Tassell was extremely satisfied with the interview, Vernon Miller was willing to move ahead and Richard Mohr felt that an additional important step had been completed. The references concerning Miller were positive and encouraging. Therefore, with the approval of Miller and Tassell, the committee came before the Council of Eighteen on the evening of December 1, 1986, and enthusiastically recommended Vernon D. Miller as the next executive editor. As Dr. Kempton completed his excellent and thorough report of the work done by the Search Committee, there was a tremendous sense of God's definite leading. Miller was invited into the Council room. There he spoke of his vision for the future of Regular Baptist Press, the GARBC and the *Baptist Bulletin*. After opening the meeting for questions, which were answered thoroughly by Miller, Dr. Balyo asked for a vote on the recommendation. The Council voted unanimously to extend the call to Mr. Miller. There was a loud chorus of amens, and Miller was called into the room to be told the good news. Spontaneously, we all sang the Doxology!

Vernon D. Miller was born on September 27, 1932, in a small town called McClure, Illinois. Miller's parents, Homer and Marie Miller, farmed several hundred acres in the Mississippi Valley. When he was old enough to do so, Vernon worked in the fields with horses and sometimes mules. In the late 1940s Miller's small church called a Regular Baptist man as pastor. He pointed the young people to the Regular Baptist camp at Lake Bloomington. There Miller heard Robert Ketcham for the first time. A year later he enrolled at the Moody Bible Institute. At Moody he met Alice Wright, who two years later became his wife. They were blessed with five children, all of whom graduated from Cedarville College and also married Cedarville College students. The Millers have ten grandchildren.

They began their pastoral labors in Carterville, Illinois, in 1954, followed by a pastorate at Faith Baptist Church in Mattoon, Illinois. In 1960 Vernon and his wife moved to Cedarville, Ohio, where he engaged in another year of study at the College. Shortly thereafter he accepted the pastorate of the Immanuel Baptist Church in Arcanum, Ohio. While he was in Arcanum, he was invited to join the Regular Baptist Press staff in Chicago as the first editor of the take-home papers. After seven years at that post, he left to work with Church

Building Consultants, with which he was connected until coming to Schaumburg in 1987.

Upon taking up his responsibilities at Schaumburg, Miller declared:

> We must sound a certain note in the midst of the barrage of material hammering at our minds today. This is an exciting communications hour and we have something to say to the world.
>
> Regular Baptist Press must continue to align its position with the Word of God and believe that the Word is capable of giving life. We must plant the Word in the very earliest days of our children's lives and be constantly aware of methods and ministries that will enhance the teaching of the truth. But the method must never hide the message.
>
> Regular Baptist Press is in a unique position to print what its staff and constituency believe, not simply find out what sells. Our concern is to be true to Biblical distinctives, loyal to our heritage and effective in our methodology.
>
> We must not be wooed away by the desire for a wider market if it means watering down the truth.
>
> We could drop several distinctives, dodge the issues, drop the name Baptist and be quite like any nondenominational publishing house. But then we would not be needed, even though we might be better accepted by some who do not place a priority on the content to be taught and learned.
>
> Regular Baptist Press has a Biblical reason to exist, a baptistic reason to serve fundamental Baptist churches and a better motivation to serve our constituency.
>
> We must equip the worker to produce the product—fully equipped lives who will also share the gospel.[3]

In his three-plus years as executive editor, Dr. Miller (an honorary doctorate from Cedarville College) has demonstrated skill in administration and motivation. He has a keen ability to recognize talent in a person and to fit that person to a specific job. The *Bulletin* is now a 48-page magazine, and every area of Regular Baptist Press is growing and glowing.

As we bring this account of a quest for faithfulness to a close, we must mention the unique work of a unique man, David Nettleton. When the old Belden Avenue Baptist Church in Chicago was made the victim of the wrecker's ball, Dr. Nettleton begged from Pastor Gordon Shipp the wood from a deacon's chair. With that beautiful wood, Dr. Nettleton went into his workshop, turned on his lathe, and made some beautiful gavels. He made one for me that I treasure highly. He, of course, has one. And he used it fairly and firmly during his years as chairman of the Council of Eighteen. As he relinquished his chairmanship at the June 1990 annual conference, he surprised the new chairman with a gift—the last gavel made from that Belden wood. John White, the new chairman, was ecstatic!

I like to think of those gavels as batons—batons that are passed in a relay race. The GARBC started at Belden in 1932, but something more valuable than wooden gavels has been passed down through the years into the 1990s. It is the message preached by Dr. Howard C. Fulton at that first meeting of the GARBC in Belden in 1932. In a great message titled "What Regular Old Fashioned Baptists Stand For," Fulton said:

> The subject is significant of the fact that Baptists stand for something. . . . Some Baptists stand for some things that other Baptists do not and will not stand for; and some so-called Baptists do not stand for much of anything. It is the purpose of our deliberations this morning to consider old-fashioned, blood-bought, born-again, deep-water, Christ-honoring, Bible-believing, historic Baptists. . . .
>
> The reason the Baptist faith has stood the test of time and persecution, fire and sword, and come off victorious is because it is the truth. Truth has nothing to fear from truth. Truth cannot contradict truth. If we hold the truth of God and the truth of God makes us what we are, then we cannot compromise with error in order to unite. When two people who differ, one right and the other wrong, compromise, then they are both wrong, for then one departs from the truth and the other does not come to the truth. To compromise the truth is to surrender the truth and stand in error. How can we cooperate with and support those who deny the great verities of the historic Baptist faith; those who say the Bible is not the inspired Word of God but a man-made book; those who say that Jesus Christ is not the virgin-born Son of God and God the Son but the illegitimate son of Joseph and Mary, born out of wedlock or the product of evolution; those who say that the death of Jesus Christ was exemplary and not expiatory; those who say that Jesus Christ did not rise bodily from the dead, and is not coming back personally into this world of men? . . . We are old-fashioned regular Baptists because the New Testament makes us such. . . .[4]

When it comes time for me to pass the baton of my responsibilities to my successor, I intend to give him "the Belden message" preached by Fulton and all other faithful Regular Baptists down through these six decades of quest for faithfulness.

End Notes

1. Merle R. Hull, "Editorials," *Baptist Bulletin* (September 1987), p. 20.
2. Ibid.
3. "Meet the New Editor," *Baptist Bulletin* (September 1987), pp. 21, 34.
4. Merle R. Hull, *What a Fellowship!* (Schaumburg, IL: Regular Baptist Press, 1981), pp. 16, 17.

45

BIBLICAL SEPARATION—FIVE QUESTIONS WITH ONE ANSWER

Paul N. Tassell

The Bible doctrine of sanctification is vital to New Testament Christianity. "For this is the will of God, even your sanctification" (1 Thess. 4:3). Bible teachers talk about positional, progressive and perfect sanctification. We are saved from the penalty of sin; we are being saved from the power of sin and some day we will be saved from the very presence of sin. We are set apart *from* sin and set apart *for* God! Sanctification is, therefore, both negative and positive. Biblical separation is the practical outworking of sanctification. Personal separa-tion from ungodliness and ecclesiastical separation from unbelief are clearly responsibilities of the obedient believer. The one passage of the Word of God that epitomizes the Biblical doctrine of separation is 2 Corinthians 6:14—17:1:

> Be ye not unequally yoked together with unbelievers; for what fellowship hath righteousness with unrighteousness? and what communion hath light with darkness? And what concord hath Christ with Belial? or what part hath he that believeth with an infidel? And what agreement hath the temple of God with idols? for ye are the temple of the living God; as God hath said, I will dwell in them . . . and walk in them; and I will be their God, and they shall be my people. Wherefore come out from among them, and be ye separate, saith the Lord, and touch not the unclean thing; and I will receive you, and will be a Father unto you, and ye shall be my sons and daughters, saith the Lord Almighty. Having therefore these promises, dearly beloved, let us cleanse ourselves from all filthiness of the flesh and spirit, perfecting holiness in the fear of God.

Commenting on the above passage, Robert Gromacki said:

> ... Separation is basically positive, toward God, but it can only take place after departing from sin and unholy alliances. . . . The concept behind "be separate" is to mark off boundaries beyond which you will not go. These fences of restriction must be based upon obedience to the revealed truth of Scripture.[1]

William L. Pettingill has written on the same passage:

> In the awful apostasy of these last days, there are churches, and many of them, alas! which have become hopelessly separated from God and the truth of God in all their testimony. Destructive critics occupy their pulpits, ungodly men, denying the Lord that bought them. They have turned away from the truth, and turned unto fables. They bring reproach upon the Lord Jesus by denying His Virgin Birth, and by denying the need and efficacy of His blood atonement. In such a case, I do not think a believer ought to hesitate a single moment. He certainly should come out from among them and be separate.[2]

On the same passage, Charles Caldwell Ryrie says: "This injunction applies to marriage, business, and to ecclesiastical and intimate personal relationships."[3] In this day of appalling apostasy and incredible infidelity, Paul's Corinthian message is needed more than ever.

The Prohibition

The Scriptural prohibition is clearly and forthrightly stated: *"Be ye not unequally yoked together with unbelievers."* The Biblical rationale for ecclesiastical separation from apostate religious bodies could not be plainer. Paul enforces the prohibition with five rhetorical questions. Each question expects an answer best expressed with the words *absolutely none.* Let us examine them closely.

The prohibition is first supported by *true logic:* "For what fellowship hath righteousness with unrighteousness?" *Absolutely none!* Paul's logic echoes the age-old reasoning of the prophet Amos: "Can two walk together, except they be agreed?" (Amos 3:3). *Absolutely not.* There is no logical or reasonable way a true believer in Scriptural righteousness can fellowship with the unrighteousness being tolerated and condoned in some of the mainline denominations affiliated with the National Council of Churches. For example, the United Methodist

Church has promoted a study guide titled *Other Perspectives: Christian Views of Homosexuality.* One United Methodist piece of promotion reads:

> This four session study explores various aspects of homosexuality in the light of Biblical research, theological thinking and medical and behavioral findings. The study does not advocate any one particular approach but encourages individuals and/or groups to examine a variety of attitudes and information as an aid to clarifying their own beliefs and decisions.[4]

Every righteousness-loving believer knows there is only ONE right view of homosexuality and that is summed up in Leviticus 18:22: "Thou shalt not lie with mankind, as with womankind: *it is abomination."* There is no way logically that a Bible-believing Christian can stay in an apostate denomination that tolerates an unrighteous view of vice and degradation.

Paul's second question supports the prohibition with *true learning:* "And what communion hath light with darkness?" *Absolutely none!* How consistent is John with Paul!

> And this is the condemnation, that light is come into the world, and men loved darkness rather than light, because their deeds were evil. For every one that doeth evil hateth the light, neither cometh to the light, lest his deeds should be reproved. But he that doeth truth cometh to the light, that his deeds may be made manifest, that they are wrought in God (John 3:19–21).

According to Psalm 119:105, a believer is taught by God's Word, which is "a lamp unto my feet, and a light unto my path." Isaiah declared, "To the law and to the testimony: if they speak not according to this word, it is because there is no light in them" (Isa. 8:20). Paul told the Ephesians, "And have no fellowship with the unfruitful works of darkness, but rather reprove them. For it is a shame even to speak of those things which are done of them in secret. But all things that are reproved are made manifest by the light: for whatsoever doth make manifest is light" (Eph. 5:11–13). Jude describes apostates with these words: "Raging waves of the sea, foaming out their own shame; wandering stars, to whom is reserved the blackness of darkness for ever" (Jude 13). There is no way a Spirit-taught believer enlightened by the Word of God can have any communion with the religious darkness of the apostasy.

The Pauline prohibition is also supported by *true loyalty:* "And what concord hath Christ with Belial?" *Absolutely none!* How can anyone be truly loyal to the Lord Jesus Christ and be in concord with His archenemy, Satan? How can one who professes to believe the Virgin Birth stay in a church or denomination that teaches Jesus was the product of an illicit sexual relationship between a whoremongering soldier and a promiscuous Jewish maid? How can any one who believes in the sinlessness of our Savior be in concord with a denomination that denies His deity, His sinlessness, His teachings and His triumphant, bodily resurrection? Loyalty to Christ demands separation from Belial. Loyalty to the Savior demands separation from Satan. Jesus exposed the Pharisees for the religious frauds they were when He told them in no uncertain terms:

> If God were your Father, ye would love me: for I proceeded forth and came from God; neither came I of myself, but he sent me. Why do ye not understand my speech? even because ye cannot hear my word. Ye are of your father the devil, and the lusts of your father ye will do. He was a murderer from the beginning, and abode not in the truth, because there is no truth in him. When he speaketh a lie, he speaketh of his own: for he is a liar, and the father of it. And because I tell you the truth, ye believe me not (John 8:42–45).

The issue is between the Savior and Satan! You cannot be loyal to both. Neutral you cannot be. The Lord Jesus Christ has been betrayed and scorned by so-called liberalism. To remain in apostate denominations is to join that betrayal.

The fourth apostolic question supports the prohibition with *true love:* "Or what part hath he that believeth with an infidel?" *Absolutely none!* First Corinthians 13 is the great love chapter of the Bible. In verse 6 of that passage we are told that love "rejoiceth not in iniquity, but rejoiceth in the truth." If that is so, and it is, how can a true believer be unequally yoked together with an infidel? How can anyone who *loves* truth, yea, who *rejoices* in truth, remain in a denomination or religious organization that scoffs at Biblical truth? The liberals like to talk about love, but Jesus said: "If ye love me, keep my commandments" (John 14:15). John wrote: "He that saith, I know him, and keepeth not his commandments, is a liar, and the truth is not in him. But whoso keepeth his word, in him verily is the love of God perfected: hereby know we that we are in him" (1 John 2:4, 5). *There is simply too much sloppy agape in Christianity today!* True love does not sell out the truth and betray the Bible and compromise the church. John also wrote: "By this we know that we love the children of God, when we love God, and keep his commandments. For this is the love of God, that we keep his commandments: and his commandments are not grievous" (1 John 5:2, 3). Our wishy-washy, namby-pamby, white-livered, yellow-backed religious world needs to hear the command of the psalmist: "Ye that love the LORD, hate evil" (Ps. 97:10). If a gardener truly loves flowers, he must and will hate weeds.

Paul's last question supports his prohibition with *true life:* "And what agreement hath the temple of God with idols?" *Absolutely none!* Idols are lifeless. The psalmist tells us: "The idols of the heathen are silver and gold, the work of men's hands. They have mouths, but they speak not; eyes have they, but they see not; they have ears, but they hear not; neither is there any breath in their mouths. They that make them are like unto them: so is everyone that trusteth in them" (Ps. 135:15–18). Apostates are idolaters. They have deified man and at the same time humanized God. "Professing themselves to be wise, they became fools, and changed the glory of the uncorruptible God into an image made like to corruptible man, and to birds, and fourfooted beasts, and creeping things" (Rom. 1:22, 23). Such idolatrous and shameful humanism seems to lead to the pits of homosexuality and lesbianism, for Paul goes on to say: "Wherefore God also gave them up to uncleanness through the lusts of their own hearts, to dishonour their own bodies between themselves: who changed the truth of God into a lie, and worshipped and served the creature more than the Creator, who is blessed for ever" (Rom. 1:24, 25). Paul calls believers "the temple of *the living God*" (2 Cor. 6:16). And believers alive unto God must not have any agreement with ungodly and satanic idolatry. Paul had made that point earlier in 1 Corinthians 10:19–21: "What say I then? that the idol is any thing, or that which is offered in sacrifice to idols is any thing? But I say, that the things which the Gentiles sacrifice, they sacrifice to devils, and not to God: and I would not that ye should have fellowship with devils. Ye cannot drink the cup of the Lord, and the cup of devils: ye cannot be partakers of the Lord's table, and of the table of devils." No wonder John said: "Little children, keep yourselves from idols" (1 John 5:21). The prohibition, therefore, "Be ye not unequally yoked together with unbelievers," is supported by true logic, true learning, true loyalty, true love and true life. All five Pauline questions reveal the utter inconsistency of fellowship with unbelievers.

The Procedures

In 2 Corinthians 6:17 Paul told us how to implement the prohibition against unequal yokes. First, *"Come out."* That is *my parting.* Regular Baptists are "come-outers." In every age it has been the will of God for His people to come out of the place of unbelief. Israel "came out" of Egypt. In Revelation 18:4 we read: "And I heard another voice from heaven, saying, Come out of her, my people, that ye be not partakers of her sins, and that ye receive not of her plagues." It may sound smart and even "spiritual" to talk about "infiltrating the major denominations" with a gospel witness or "staying in to fight the apostate denominational leadership," but all such action is plain disobedience to God's command to "Come out."

There are those who say the day of battle against the mainline denominations is over, but I heartily disagree. There are still thousands of people and pastors in mainline denominations who still believe the gospel and the Bible. They need to be encouraged to obey God and "come out." The National Council of Churches has for many years spearheaded the apostasy in our nation. The *Reader's Digest* has exposed the left-wing extremism of the NCC. In January of 1983 the CBS television program *60 Minutes* further unmasked the NCC. Surely God's people must come out of such unbelief.

The second procedure is found in the words, *"Be ye separate."* That is *my position.* Just who are those bodies that make up the National Council of Churches? One of the leaders is the American Baptist Churches in the U.S.A., once known as the Northern Baptist Convention. They have a new name but are characterized by the same old infidelity. The other groups making up the NCC are as follows: African Methodist Episcopal Church; Armenian Church of America; Christian Church (Disciples of Christ); Christian Methodist Episcopal Church; Church of the Brethren; Coptic Orthodox Church in North America; The Episcopal Church; Friends United Meeting; Greek Orthodox Archdiocese; Hungarian Reformed Church in America; Lutheran Church in America; Moravian Church in America; National Baptist Convention of America; National Baptist Convention, USA; National Council of Community Churches; Orthodox Church in America; Russian Orthodox Church in the USA; Philadelphia Yearly Meeting of the Religious Society of Friends; Polish National Catholic

Church of America; The Presbyterian Church (USA); Progressive National Baptist Convention; Reformed Church in America; Serbian Eastern Orthodox Church; Syrian Orthodox Church of Antioch; Ukrainian Orthodox Church in America; The United Church of Christ; and The United Methodist Church. From all these "Be ye separate."

The third procedure enjoined upon us is *"Touch not the unclean thing."* That is *my purity.* The less we have to do with apostates, the better. Some of my fundamentalist brethren think it necessary to listen to men like Cardinal Bernardin and Martin Marty of Chicago, but I would respectfully suggest that we do not need any advice from men who have never been friends of Biblical fundamentalists. In fact, listening to liberal church leaders is a violation of Psalm 1:1: "Blessed is the man that walketh not in the counsel of the ungodly, nor standeth in the way of sinners, nor sitteth in the seat of the scornful." God blesses obedient and holy servants. The GARBC may not be the biggest or the richest, but let us be sure we are as pure and as obedient to God as we can be.

The Promises

There are some wonderful promises given to believers who obey the prohibition and procedures of 2 Corinthians 6:14–17. The first one has to do with *reception:* "I will receive you." That has to do with *the favor of God.* Oh, to have the smile of God on one's ministry! If you want just crowds and outward success, you can join Disneyland. But *pleasing God is our major priority.* If we can get crowds and great success while being obedient, well and good. But let us never sacrifice obedience on the altar of bigness and super success.

The second promise has to do with *relationship:* "And will be a Father unto you, and ye shall be my sons and daughters, saith the Lord Almighty." That has to do with *the family of God.* Once again the matter of obedience is here highlighted, for obedience is a family matter. The unsaved are referred to by Paul as "the children of disobedience." Obedient children of God will be happy as they revel in their relationship with God the Father. Who cares what the world thinks as long as God is pleased? The conclusion has to do with *renewal:* "Having therefore these promises, dearly beloved, let us cleanse ourselves from all filthiness of the flesh and spirit, perfecting holiness in the fear of God" (2 Cor. 7:1). That has to do with *the fear of God.* In his great commentary on 2 Corinthians, Charles Hodge says:

> This verse [2 Cor. 7:1] properly belongs to the preceding chapter. It is the appropriate conclusion of the exposition there made. . . . Though the work of purification is so often referred to [as having God] as its author. . . . This does not preclude the agency of His people. They are to work out their own salvation, because it is God Who worketh in them both to will and to do. If God's agency in sanctification does not arouse and direct ours; if it does not create the desire for holiness, and strenuous efforts to attain it, we may be sure that we are not its subjects. He is leaving us undisturbed in our sins."[5]

Hodge goes on to say the *fear of God* "is the motive which is to determine our endeavours to purify ourselves. It is not regard to the good of others, nor our own happiness, but reverence for God. We are to be holy, because He is holy."[6]

May the prohibition, procedures and promises of this great Corinthian passage be always in the warp and woof of Regular Baptists. *Amen!*

End Notes

1. Robert G. Gromacki, *Stand Firm in the Faith* (Schaumburg, IL: Regular Baptist Press, 1978), pp. 108, 109.

2. William L. Pettingill and Richard P. Poleyn, *Bible Questions Answered* (Grand Rapids: Zondervan Publishing House, 1978), p. 193.

3. Charles Caldwell Ryrie, *The Ryrie Study Bible, King James Version* (Chicago: Moody Press, n.d.), p. 1653.

4. *The United Methodist Reporter* (November 9, 1984).

5. Charles Hodge, *Second Corinthians* (Grand Rapids: Wm. B. Eerdmans Publishing Company, 1953), p. 174. Used by permission of the William B. Eerdmans Publishing Company.

6. Ibid., pp. 174, 175.

APPENDIXES

APPENDIX A

The registered messengers for the first meeting of the GARBC, May 15–18, 1932, at Belden Avenue Baptist Church, Chicago, Illinois

Rev. H. C. Fulton, Chicago, Illinois
Charles E. Crawford, Chicago, Illinois
Fred Blumberg, Chicago, Illinois
Charles W. Boman, Chicago, Illinois
Ralph L. Erickson, Chicago, Illinois
Dr. J. E. Conant, Chicago, Illinois
A. O. Odegard, Chicago, Illinois
Charles F. Fields, Chicago, Illinois
G. B. L. Johnson, Chicago, Illinois
Walter E. Gillespie, Chicago, Illinois
David E. Gillespie, Western Springs, Illinois
A. E. Heiniger, Niles Center, Illinois
J. R. Humphries, Aurora, Illinois
James Williams, River Grove, Illinois
M. E. Hawkins, Mishawaka, Indiana
A. G. Annette, Grundy Center, Iowa
Carey R. Moser, Eldora, Iowa
Wesley K. Howland, Brownsdale, Minnesota
Rev. George W. Kehoe, Faribault, Minnesota
G. H. Dahlberg, Park Rapids, Minnesota
Leo Sandgren, Austin, Minnesota
A. E. Berglund, Morristown, Minnesota
Rev. D. J. Davies, Saint Paul, Minnesota
Rev. Earle G. Griffith, Toledo, Ohio
Rev. Charles F. Fredman, Toledo, Ohio
Dr. Oliver W. Van Osdel, Grand Rapids, Michigan
Rev. I. Van Westenbrugge, Grand Rapids, Michigan
Rev. Clyde E. Wood, Grand Rapids, Michigan
Rev. Theron W. Wood, El Monte, California
Rev. Gordon A. Whipple, San Dimas, California

APPENDIX B

CONSTITUTION OF THE GENERAL ASSOCIATION OF REGULAR BAPTIST CHURCHES

(As amended at the June 1980 annual meeting)

Article I. Name

General Association of Regular Baptist Churches.

Article II. Purpose

Section 1. To maintain an Association of sovereign, Bible-believing, Christ-honoring Baptist churches; to promote the spirit of evangelism; to spread the gospel; to advance Regular Baptist educational and missionary enterprises at home and abroad; to raise and maintain a testimony to the truth of the gospel and to the purity of the church; to raise a standard of Biblical separation from worldliness, modernism and apostasy; to emphasize the Biblical teaching that a breakdown of the divinely established lines between Bible believers and apostates is unscriptural and to be a voice repudiating cooperation with movements which attempt to unite true Bible believers and apostates in evangelistic and other cooperative spiritual efforts.

Section 2. The acquisition or disposition of any properties necessary to implement the provisions of Section 1 of this Article shall be authorized by (1) a majority vote of messengers present and voting at any annual meeting, or (2) by a mail referendum majority vote of the fellowshipping churches, when a decision relating to property cannot await an annual meeting of the Association.

Article III. Meetings

A meeting of the Association shall be held annually for the transaction of business, the election of officers and the conducting of a Bible and missionary conference at a date and place to be fixed by the Council.

Article IV. Fellowship and Voting Privileges

Section 1. Procedures for approval of churches desiring to fellowship with the GARBC. Any Baptist church on the North American continent, the United States and her territorial possessions which is not in fellowship or cooperation with any local, state or national convention, association or group which permits the presence of liberals, liberalism (modernism or apostates), and which church subscribes to the Constitution and Articles of Faith of the General Association of Regular Baptist Churches contained in the current Church Directory, and which desires to fellowship with the GARBC shall:

(a) Make application to the Home Office of the GARBC in writing. This request should be made by the church clerk and contain the date of the meeting of the church in which this action to seek fellowship took place.

(b) Shall have had a recognition council of Regular Baptist pastors and messengers for the purpose of examining the constitution and bylaws of the church to determine if it is a properly constituted and functioning Baptist church.

(3) Upon the recommendation of the Council of Eighteen at the annual meeting of the GARBC, and a majority vote of the Association, the church shall be received into fellowship. (Note the word "fellowship," not "membership." A Baptist church cannot be a member of anything outside itself. It can declare itself in fellowship with any body of Baptists on earth, but cannot be a member.)

Section 2. Each church shall be entitled to a maximum of six voting messengers from its membership to be sent to the annual meeting, two of whom shall be empowered to sit on the Elections Committee, but each church is urged to send as many non-voting messengers as possible. Each year every voting messenger shall subscribe to the Constitution and Articles of Faith of the Association prior to taking his seat in the annual meeting.

Section 3. No salaried servant of the Association shall be entitled to vote.

Article V. Cessation of Fellowship

Section 1. Any fellowshipping church may withdraw from the Association at any time and for any reason sufficient to itself. Christian ethics would suggest that reason for such withdrawal should be filed with the Association, but such action is not mandatory. In conformity with the historic Baptist position, the property rights of such a church can nowise be legally prejudiced or endangered by such withdrawal.

Section 2. Any fellowshipping church which is publicly known to be no longer in agreement with the Constitution and Articles of Faith of the Association and has not voluntarily withdrawn itself from the Association may, upon satisfactory evidence of disagreement being presented by the Council, and upon its recommendation, be removed from the rolls by majority vote of the Association.

Section 3. Any fellowshipping church which for a period of three years has failed to send an annual report or a messenger to the Association meeting or in no other way has evidenced continued interest in the Association may be dropped from the rolls at the discretion of the Association on recommendation of the Council.

Article VI. Officers and Their Election

Section 1. The officers of the Association shall consist of a Council of Eighteen men (members of fellowshipping churches). Nine men shall be elected annually for a period of two years.

All nominees for the Council of Eighteen shall subscribe in writing to the Constitution and Articles of Faith of the General Association of Regular Baptist Churches.

A Council member who ceases to be a member of a fellowshipping church shall immediately cease to be a member of the Council of Eighteen, his successor being the next highest nominee in the previous election.

At any one time there must be serving on the Council of Eighteen not less than fourteen men other than salaried servants of the approved agencies of the Association.

Also any Councilman completing two consecutive terms of two years shall be ineligible for election for at least one year.

Section 2. The Council shall meet at the annual conference immediately after its election and shall appoint individuals to care for the various matters relative to the work of the Association, such as a treasurer, a secretary, and such committees as missions, education, social agencies, publications and other committees appropriate to the ministry of the Association. The Council may appoint regional representatives.

Section 3. The Council shall appoint one of its members as Chairman of the Council, and he or someone appointed by him shall moderate the public meetings of the Association.

Section 4. The Council shall be elected in the following manner. Each church in fellowship with the Association shall meet in business session and nominate as many names for the Council as it may desire. These names shall be sent to the secretary of the Association at least six weeks in advance of the annual meeting. The secretary shall make proper tabulation of all lists, and the eighteen highest names shall be considered the nominees, except that not less than fourteen men other than salaried servants of approved agencies of the Association shall be nominees. Each church in fellowship with the Association shall designate any two of its messengers to serve on the committee of election. At an announced time during the annual conference, at the call of the secretary, the committee shall meet, at which time the list of eighteen nominees shall be presented to it and each member shall cast a ballot for not more than nine. The nine highest shall be elected to the Council for a two-year term, except that at any one time there must be serving on the Council of Eighteen not less than fourteen men other than salaried servants of the approved agencies of the Association.

Section 5. All new members of the Council shall be presented at the closing session of the annual conference and shall assume their Council duties as of that session.

Section 6. It shall be the duty of the Council to make recommendations to the Association for the furtherance of its work, and to implement and put into operation all actions and policies of the Association. The Council shall be authorized to secure the services of such administrative and office personnel as shall be required to carry on the work of the Association, except for the National Representative. He shall be recommended by the Council and approved by a two-thirds majority vote of the messengers present and voting at any annual meeting of the Association. All salaries shall be determined by the Council. Its authority is that which is committed to it by the Association, and any of the actions of the Council or of any salaried servant of the Association may be called up for review by the Association at any annual meeting.

Article VII. Approved Agencies

Section 1. It shall be the policy of the Association to abstain from the creation and/or control of educational, missionary and other benevolent agencies.

Section 2. Any agency (mission, social, education, etc.) desiring the approval of the Association shall make application in writing to the Council of Eighteen.

Section 3. In order to qualify for such approval, an agency must carry the name Baptist in its title or its subtitle and must be sound in doctrine, organization, business administration and ethical practices. It shall be the duty of the Council to: (a) Authorize an appropriate Council member, who shall select such assistance as necessary and pursue an in-depth study of the applying agency. (b) This committee shall prepare a complete report to the Council, including its recommendation. (c) The Council shall act on the report and, if favorable, recommend to the annual meeting of the GARBC the approval of said agency. Majority vote of the Association shall constitute approval. (d) All such agencies shall be reviewed and approved by the Council annually.

Section 4. The list compiled annually by the Council shall be published and advertised to our churches as approved agencies.

Article VIII. Amendments

This Constitution may be amended at any annual meeting of the Association by a two-thirds vote of the messengers present and voting, provided the proposed amendment shall have been presented in writing at the previous annual meeting of the Association.

ARTICLES OF FAITH

(As clarified at the June 1975 and 1976 annual meetings)

I. Of the Scriptures

We believe in the authority and sufficiency of the Holy Bible, consisting of the sixty-six books of the Old and New Testaments, as originally written; that it was verbally and plenarily inspired and is the product of Spirit-controlled men, and therefore is infallible and inerrant in all matters of which it speaks.

We believe the Bible to be the true center of Christian unity and the supreme standard by which all human conduct, creed and opinions shall be tried (2 Tim. 3:16, 17; 2 Pet. 1:19–21).

II. The True God

We believe there is one and only one living and true God, an infinite Spirit, the Maker and supreme Ruler of Heaven and earth; inexpressibly glorious in holiness, and worthy of all possible honor, confidence and love; that in the unity of the godhead there are three persons, the Father, the Son and the Holy Spirit, equal in every divine perfection and executing distinct but harmonious offices in the great work of redemption (Exod. 20:2, 3; 1 Cor. 8:6; Rev. 4:11).

III. The Holy Spirit

We believe that the Holy Spirit is a divine person, equal with God the Father and God the Son and of the same nature; that He was active in the creation; that in His relation to the unbelieving world He restrains the evil one until God's purpose is fulfilled; that He convicts of sin, of righteousness and of judgment; that He bears witness to the truth of the gospel in preaching and testimony; that He is the Agent in the new birth; that He seals, endues, guides, teaches, witnesses, sanctifies and helps the believer (John 14:16, 17; Matt. 28:19; Heb. 9:14; John 14:26; Luke 1:35; Gen. 1:1–3; John 16:8–11; Acts 5:30–32; John 3:5, 6; Eph. 1:13, 14; Mark 1:8; John 1:33; Acts 11:16; Luke 24:49; Rom. 8:14, 16, 26, 27).

IV. The Devil or Satan

We believe in the reality and personality of Satan, the Devil; and [we believe] that he was created by God as an angel but through pride and rebellion became the enemy of his Creator; that he became the unholy god of this age and the ruler of all the powers of darkness and is destined to the judgment of an eternal justice in the Lake of Fire (Matt. 4:1–11; 2 Cor. 4:4; Rev. 20:10).

V. Creation

We believe the Biblical account of the creation of the physical universe, angels and man; that this account is neither allegory nor myth, but a literal, historical account of the direct, immediate creative acts of God without any evolutionary process; that man was created by a direct work of God and not from previously existing forms of life; and that all men are descended from the historical Adam and Eve, first parents of the entire human race (Gen. 1; 2; Col. 1:16, 17; John 1:3).

VI. The Fall of Man

We believe that man was created in innocence (in the image and likeness of God) under the law of his Maker, but by voluntary transgression Adam fell from his sinless and happy state, and all men sinned in him, in consequence of which all men are totally depraved, are partakers of Adam's fallen nature, and are sinners by nature and by conduct, and therefore are under just condemnation without defense or excuse (Gen. 3:1–6; Rom. 3:10–19; 5:12, 19; 1:18, 32).

VII. The Virgin Birth

We believe that Jesus was begotten of the Holy Spirit in a miraculous manner, born of Mary, a virgin, as no other man was ever born or can be born of woman, and that He is both the Son of God and God the Son (Gen. 3:15; Isa. 7:14; Matt. 1:18–25; Luke 1:35; John 1:14).

VIII. Salvation

We believe that the salvation of sinners is divinely initiated and wholly of grace through the mediatorial offices of Jesus Christ, the Son of God, Who, by the appointment of the Father, voluntarily took upon Himself our nature, yet without sin, and honored the divine law by His personal obedience, thus qualifying Himself to be our Savior; that by the shedding of His blood in His death He fully satisfied the just demands of a holy and righteous God regarding sin; that His sacrifice consisted not in setting us an example by His death as a martyr, but was a voluntary substitution of Himself in the sinner's place, the Just dying for the unjust, Christ the Lord bearing our sins in His own body on the tree; that having risen from the dead He is now enthroned in Heaven, and uniting in His wonderful person the tenderest sympathies with divine perfection, He is in every way qualified to be a suitable, a compassionate and an all-sufficient Savior.

We believe that faith in the Lord Jesus Christ is the only condition of salvation. Repentance is a change of mind and purpose toward God prompted by the Holy Spirit and is an integral part of saving faith (Jonah 2:9; Eph. 2:8; Acts 15:11; Rom. 3:24, 25; John 3:16; Matt. 18:11; Phil. 2:7, 8; Heb. 2:14–17; Isa. 53:4–7; 1 John 4:10; 1 Cor. 15:3; 2 Cor. 5:21; 1 Pet. 2:24).

IX. Resurrection and Priesthood of Christ

We believe in the bodily resurrection of Christ and in His ascension into Heaven, where He now sits at the right hand of the Father as our High Priest interceding for us (Matt. 28:6, 7; Luke 24:39; John 20:27; 1 Cor. 15:4; Mark 16:6; Luke 24:2–6, 51; Acts 1:9–11; Rev. 3:21; Heb. 8:6; 12:2; 7:25; 1 Tim. 2:5; 1 John 2:1; Heb. 2:17; 5:9, 10).

X. Grace and the New Birth

We believe that in order to be saved, sinners must be born again; that the new birth is a new creation in Christ Jesus; that it is instantaneous and not a process; that in the new birth the one dead in trespasses and in sins is made a partaker of the divine nature and receives eternal life, the free gift of God; that the new creation is brought about by our sovereign God in a manner above our comprehension, solely by the power of the Holy Spirit in connection with divine truth, so as to secure our voluntary obedience to the gospel; that its proper evidence appears in the holy fruits of repentance, faith and newness of life (John 3:3; 2 Cor. 5:17; 1 John 5:1; Acts 16:20–33; 2 Pet. 1:4; Rom. 6:23; Eph. 2:1, 5; Col. 2:13; John 3:8).

XI. Justification

We believe that justification is that judicial act of God whereby He declares the believer righteous upon the basis of the imputed righteousness of Christ; that it is bestowed, not in consideration of any work of righteousness which we have done, but solely through faith in the Redeemer's shed blood (Rom. 3:24; 4:5; 5:1, 9; Gal. 2:16; Phil. 3:9).

XII. Sanctification

We believe that sanctification is the divine setting apart of the believer unto God accomplished in a threefold manner; first, an eternal act of God, based upon redemption in Christ, establishing the believer in a position of holiness at the moment he trusts the Savior; second, a continuing process in the saint as the Holy Spirit applies the Word of God to the life; third, the final accomplishment of this process at the Lord's return (Heb. 10:10–14; 3:1; John 17:17; 2 Cor. 3:18; 1 Cor. 1:30; Eph. 5:25–27; 1 Thess. 4:3, 4; 5:23, 24; 1 John 3:2; Jude 24, 25; Rev. 22:11).

XIII. The Security of the Saints

We believe that all who are truly born again are kept by God the Father for Jesus Christ (Phil. 1:6; John 10:28, 29; Rom. 8:35–39; Jude 1).

XIV. The Church

We believe that a local church is an organized congregation of immersed believers, associated by covenant of faith and fellowship of the gospel; observing the ordinances of Christ; governed by His laws; and exercising the gifts, rights and privileges invested in them by His Word; that its officers are pastors and deacons, whose qualifications, claims and duties are clearly defined in the Scriptures. We believe the true mission of the church is the faithful witnessing of Christ to all men as we have opportunity. We hold that the local church has the absolute right of self-government free from the interference of any hierarchy of individuals or organizations; and that the one and only Superintendent is Christ through the Holy Spirit; that it is Scriptural for true churches to cooperate with each other in contending for the faith and for the furtherance of the gospel; that each local church is the sole judge of the measure and method of its cooperation; that on all matters of membership, of polity, of government, of discipline, of benevolence, the will of the local church is final (1 Cor. 11:2; Acts 20:17–28; 1 Tim. 3:1–13; Acts 2:41, 42).

We believe in the unity of all New Testament believers in the Church which is the Body of Christ (1 Cor. 12:12, 13; Eph. 1:22, 23; 3:1–6; 4:11; 5:23; Col. 1:18; Acts 15:13–18).

XV. Baptism and the Lord's Supper

We believe that Christian baptism is the single immersion of a believer in water to show forth in a solemn and beautiful emblem our identification with the crucified, buried and risen Savior, through Whom we died to sin and rose to a new life; that baptism is to be performed under the authority of the local church; and that it is prerequisite to the privileges of church membership.

We believe that the Lord's Supper is the commemoration of His death until He come, and should be preceded always by solemn self-examination. We believe that the Biblical order of the ordinances is baptism first and then the Lord's Supper, and that participants in the

Lord's Supper should be immersed believers (Acts 8:36, 38, 39; John 3:23; Rom. 6:3–5; Matt. 3:16; Col. 2:12; 1 Cor. 11:23–28; Matt. 28:18–20; Acts 2:41, 42).

XVI. Separation

We believe in obedience to the Biblical commands to separate ourselves unto God from worldliness and from ecclesiastical apostasy (2 Cor. 6:14—7:1; 1 Thess. 1:9, 10; 1 Tim. 6:3–5; Rom. 16:17; 2 John 9–11).

XVII. Civil Government

We believe that civil government is of divine appointment for the interests and good order of human society; that magistrates are to be prayed for, conscientiously honored and obeyed; except in those things opposed to the will of our Lord Jesus Christ Who is the only Lord of the conscience and the coming King of Kings (Rom. 13:1–7; 2 Sam. 23:3; Exod. 18:21, 22; Acts 23:5; Matt. 22:21; Acts 5:29; 4:19, 20; Dan. 3:17, 18).

XVIII. Israel

We believe in the sovereign selection of Israel as God's eternal covenant people, that she is now dispersed because of her disobedience and rejection of Christ, and that she will be regathered in the Holy Land and, after the completion of the Church, will be saved as a nation at the second advent of Christ (Gen. 13:14–17; Rom. 11:1–32; Ezek. 37).

XIX. Rapture and Subsequent Events

We believe in the premillennial return of Christ, an event which can occur at any moment, and that at that moment the dead in Christ shall be raised in glorified bodies, and the living in Christ shall be given glorified bodies without tasting death, and all shall be caught up to meet the Lord in the air before the seven years of the Tribulation (1 Thess. 4:13–18; 1 Cor. 15:42–44; 51–54; Phil. 3:20, 21; Rev. 3:10).

We believe that the Tribulation, which follows the Rapture of the Church, will be culminated by the revelation of Christ in power and great glory to sit upon the throne of David and to establish the millennial kingdom (Dan. 9:25–27; Matt. 24:29–31; Luke 1:30–33; Isa. 9:6, 7; 11:1–9; Acts 2:29, 30; Rev. 20:1–4, 6).

XX. The Righteous and the Wicked

We believe that there is a radical and essential difference between the righteous and the wicked; that only those who are justified by faith in our Lord Jesus Christ and sanctified by the Spirit of our God are truly righteous in His esteem; while all such as continue in impenitence and unbelief are in His sight wicked and under the curse; and this distinction holds among men both in and after death, in the everlasting felicity of the saved and the everlasting conscious suffering of the lost in the Lake of Fire (Mal. 3:18; Gen. 18:23; Rom. 6:17, 18; 1 John 5:19; Rom. 7:6; 6:23; Prov. 14:32; Luke 16:25; Matt. 25:34–41; John 8:21; Rev. 20:14, 15).

APPENDIX C

GARBC COMPARED WITH OTHER CHURCH GROUPS AS OF 1990

Groups	Year Founded	Number of Churches Now
American Baptist Church	1907	5,817
Assemblies of God	1914	10,173
Baptist Bible Fellowship	1950	3,500
Baptist General Conference	1852	803
Christian Missionary Alliance	1897	1,436
Conservative Baptist Association	1947	1,126
Evangelical Covenant Church	1900	577
Evangelical Free Church	1884	850
Evangelical Methodist Church	1946	138
GARBC	1932	1,574
Grace Brethren Churches	1939	300
IFCA	1930	692
Southern Baptist Convention	1845	36,531

APPENDIX D

MEN WHO HAVE SERVED ON THE COUNCIL OF FOURTEEN OR EIGHTEEN

Charles Alber
A. G. Annette
Barney Antrobus
Bryce B. Augsburger
Bryce B. Augsburger II
John G. Balyo
George Bates
William G. Bellshaw
Charles Benedict
Joseph H. Bower
Fred R. Brock, Jr.
William Brock
Donald M. Brong
Carl Brown
L. Duane Brown
Russell Camp
James M. Carlson
P. B. Chenault
Richard Christen
Ralph G. Colas
Hall Dautel
Floyd A. Davis
Kenneth Dodson
Paul Dixon
John R. Dunkin
Carl E. Elgena
Kenneth K. Elgena
Richard Elvee
Lawrence G. Fetzer
D. O. Fuller
William Fusco
Daniel Gelatt
David Gillespie
R. Craig Golden
David Graham
John Greening
Earle G. Griffith
J. Edward Hakes
Hugh Hall
Raymond F. Hamilton
William Headley
Robert Houchin
Mark Jackson
Paul R. Jackson
W. Paul Jackson
Jack Jacobs
J. Don Jennings
David Jeremiah
James T. Jeremiah
Forrest Johnson
Clarence Keen
Howard Keithley
Wendell Kempton
Robert T. Ketcham
Kenneth Kinney
William E. Kuhnle
John Lineberry
S. Franklin Logsdon
Donald J. MacKay
Clarence Mason
R. L. Matthews
W. A. Matthews
Richard G. Mohr
David L. Moore
Kenneth Muck
Ralph Neighbour
David Nettleton
Clay Nuttall
Kenneth Ohrstrom
Ernest Pickering
John Polson
Ford Porter
Robert L. Powell
J. O. Purcell
J. Irving Reese
Wilbur C. Rooke
William Rudd
Robert Ryerse
Leo Sandgren
Harold Scholes
Donald Sewell
Gordon L. Shipp
E. C. Shute
Virgil Stoneking
Joseph M. Stowell
Joseph M. Stowell III
Ben Strohbehn
Robert L. Sumner
Carl Sweazy
C. Allen Taff
Paul N. Tassell
Milo Thompson
Donald Tyler
H. O. Van Gilder, Sr.
Charles Wagner
W. Wilbert Welch
John White, Jr.
Orlan Wilhite
Arthur F. Williams
John Wood
G. Arthur Woolsey
Leroy Wortman
W. Thomas Younger

APPENDIX E

GARBC AND RBP HOME OFFICE STAFF AS OF FEBRUARY 1991

Association
Marianne Baltensperger
Paul Tassell
Gretchen Tyrrell
Milton Tyrrell

Editorial Department
Joan Alexander
Donald Anderson
Jonita Barram
Patricia Carapelle
Cindy Carr
James Dyet
Annette Haskins
Mary Ann Kaspar
Vernon Miller
Norman Olson
Rosanne Pletcher
Heidi Ray
Janis Salzman
Sonya Shafer
Brian Weber
Valerie Wilson
Linda Zimmerman

Customer Service
Penny Fales
Gladys Hawkins
Isabelle Hollenbaugh
Linda Jones
Carol Lechner
Wendy Sorensen
Linda Wood

Receptionist
Karen Treu

Shipping/Maintenance
Elly Anderson
Gloria Dyet
David Fox
Diane Garmany
James Iverson
Irene Jackson
Keith Mauch
Greg Meyer
Paul Stump

Marketing
Melvin O. Jones
Anthony Woolford
Constance Woolford
Sharon Youngmark

Gospel Literature Services
Judy Emery
Mark Jackson

Graphic Arts/ Production
Brenda Bopp
Dan Garmany
Doug Jennings
Jim Johnson
Eleanor Kennedy
Carla Kuehl
Terry Powell
John Shafer

APPENDIX F

ANNUAL CONFERENCE SITES

1932	Chicago, Illinois
1933	Buffalo, New York
1934	Gary, Indiana
1935	Grand Rapids, Michigan
1936	Chicago, Illinois
1937	Johnson City, New York
1938	Waterloo, Iowa
1939	Paterson, New Jersey
1940	Erie, Pennsylvania
1941	Pontiac, Michigan
1942	Waterloo, Iowa
1943	Johnson City, New York
1944	Grand Rapids, Michigan
1945	(Canceled because of war restrictions on travel)
1946	Waterloo, Iowa
1947	Atlantic City, New Jersey
1948	Grand Rapids, Michigan
1949	Cleveland, Ohio
1950	Buffalo, New York
1951	Oakland, California
1952	Des Moines, Iowa
1953	Philadelphia, Pennsylvania
1954	Chicago, Illinois
1955	Kansas City, Missouri
1956	Seattle, Washington
1957	Grand Rapids, Michigan
1958	Columbus, Ohio
1959	Rochester, Minnesota
1960	Long Beach, California
1961	Winona Lake, Indiana
1962	Springfield, Massachusetts
1963	Omaha, Nebraska
1964	Winona Lake, Indiana
1965	Des Moines, Iowa
1966	Grand Rapids, Michigan
1967	Seattle, Washington
1968	Rochester, New York
1969	Fort Wayne, Indiana
1970	Denver, Colorado
1971	Winona Lake, Indiana
1972	San Diego, California
1973	Kansas City, Missouri
1974	Ocean Grove, New Jersey
1975	Winona Lake, Indiana
1976	Seattle, Washington
1977	Des Moines, Iowa
1978	Lakeland, Florida
1979	Dayton, Ohio
1980	San Diego, California
1981	Winona Lake, Indiana
1982	Denver, Colorado
1983	Niagara Falls, New York
1984	Seattle, Washington
1985	Springfield, Illinois
1986	Grand Rapids, Michigan
1987	Ames, Iowa
1988	Anaheim, California
1989	Columbus, Ohio
1990	Niagara Falls, New York
1991	Indianapolis, Indiana

Projected

1992	Milwaukee, Wisconsin
1993	Des Moines, Iowa

APPENDIX G

OUR PASTORS—WHO THEY ARE AND HOW THEY LIVE

Robert G. Parr and Rex M. Rogers

PART ONE

Clergymen, more affectionately known as pastors, play an important role on the stage of American social life. Faithful pastors visit us soon after birth, later guide our spiritual development, assist our families in interpreting political and social events, officiate at our weddings and those of our children, counsel us in old age and nearly always lay each of us to rest.

It is surprising, therefore, that preachers have rarely been the subject of serious scholarly study. Only in the past 20 years have researchers conducted important scientific inquiries, first with mainstream Protestant clergymen, later with evangelical (broadly defined) preachers and recently with fundamentalist preachers.

Pastors in the General Association of Regular Baptist Churches (GARBC) have never been the subject of a carefully implemented national survey. However, with an estimated membership of more than 250,000 (1987), the GARBC is one of the largest avowedly fundamentalist associations in the United States. Consequently, the GARBC represents an important fundamentalist body, one likely to attract more research in the future.

GARBC Survey

We developed and mailed a survey to all GARBC pastors, promising participants we would report our findings to *Baptist Bulletin* readers. We designed our research principally to examine the social and political attitudes of GARBC pastors. We also asked pastors to evaluate questions about various lifestyle standards or "separation issues," as well as questions detailing personal background characteristics.

Between March and May 1988, we mailed 1,805 questionnaires, and by July, 992 questionnaires had been returned. This response yields a return rate of 55 percent, with all areas of the country fairly well represented. Those [readers] familiar with survey research will recognize this result as an outstanding rate of return. In addition, according to recent GARBC annual directories, approximately 7 percent of GARBC churches do not have pastors at any given time. This condition would typically reduce the return rate, but our numbers nevertheless reflect a high level of pastoral interest.

With a survey as extensive as this one (130 items), this article could focus on a number of subjects, including abortion, views on work and poverty, attitudes toward marriage and divorce issues, social and political concerns or attitudes toward the role of women in society. We have chosen to emphasize two themes: pastors' personal background characteristics and lifestyle standards.

Pastor Characteristics

Pastors in the GARBC form a remarkably similar group of individuals. For example, of 992 respondents, only 16 (1.6 percent) are nonwhite (7 black, 5 Hispanic, 4 Asian or Native American Indian). Approximately 94 percent have an earned college degree or higher, with more than 36 percent having graduated from seminary.

Similarity in the identification of political party was also striking. More than 54 percent of GARBC pastors call themselves "Republicans"; if pastors who call themselves "Independent, closer to Republican" are added to the first group, the figure climbs to 96 percent. Amazingly, of 992 respondents, only 8 (less than 1 percent) call themselves "Independent, closer to Democrat" or "Not very strong Democrat." Not even one pastor identifies himself as "Strong Democrat."

More than 98 percent of GARBC pastors consider themselves conservative in ideology, of whom 68 percent are "Very conservative." Only 8 pastors (less than 1 percent) call themselves "Moderate," while only one labels himself "Somewhat liberal." Needless to say, one rarely finds such unanimity on the American social scene today.

Pastors' ages range from 22 to 76 for an average of 44 years of age. About 63 percent of GARBC pastors come from rural or small-town settings. Approximately one half minister in rural or small-town environments, while one half labor in suburbs or cities.

Sociologists would call the heritages of GARBC pastors middle class. Their fathers usually worked in labor/unskilled (43 percent) or clerical/service (23 percent) occupations, with 72 percent having earned a high school diploma or less. About 73 percent of pastors' mothers were housewives, with 75 percent holding a high school diploma or less.

The pastors who responded to this survey have given little thought to leaving the ministry. Twenty-nine (29) percent have never considered doing so, and an additional 41 percent seldom give it a thought. Only 4 percent indicate they often entertain the possibility.

One other pastoral characteristic was especially interesting. More than 71 percent of GARBC pastors call themselves a "Fundamentalist," while only 8 percent prefer the label "Evangelical." Another 6 percent checked "Fundamentalist" plus "Other," the additional identity, including such labels as Baptist, Bible Believer and Evangelical Fundamentalist. Five (5) percent of the men (limited almost exclusively to those in the Midwest) used the terms "Biblicist" or "Biblist."

Several pastors reveal uneasiness with using labels, refusing to accept any of the ones suggested. Some of the comments include: "Evangelical seems to point to one who will substitute love for doctrine; Fundamentalist has become a term that is stuck to anything radical." "I am a Fundamentalist in the historic sense, not as seen by the media." "It depends on the background of the person to whom I am talking. I am a Fundamentalist with ministers, a Bible-believing Christian with Christians and a Christian with the unsaved." "I am a Fundamentalist theologically and an Evangelical practically, only because Fundamentalist is interpreted by some to be social practices of dos and don'ts instead of being theologically defined."

When we examined Evangelicals separately, we discovered they are younger (average 38 years), rarely found in the East and the recipients of higher levels of education (62 percent seminary graduates). They more than likely come from homes where the father worked as a white-collar professional, and the education levels of both parents were higher (though the mother was less likely to be employed outside the home).

Lifestyle Standards

We asked the pastors to indicate their approval or disapproval of Christians participating in 12 selected activities. These 12 activities represent lifestyle standards that many people believe measure an individual's degree of "separation" from the world and its practices. Again, a remarkable similarity emerges in the patterns evident in our statistical analysis.

More than 96 percent registered disapproval of Christians participating in dancing; more than 98 percent disapprove of social drinking; more than 97 percent disapprove of Christians purchasing lottery tickets; more than 99 percent disapprove of Christians using tobacco; 98 percent disapprove of membership in secret societies; and 99 percent disapprove of gambling.

Other items indicated more debate: 85 percent disapprove of Christians attending movie theaters; 64 percent disapprove while 14 percent are uncertain and 23 percent approve of the use of playing cards; 22 percent disapprove while 20 percent are uncertain and 59 percent approve of frequenting restaurants where alcoholic beverages are sold; 24 percent disapprove while 22 percent are uncertain and 55 percent approve of renting movies for VCRs; 24 percent disapprove while 22 percent are uncertain and 54 percent approve of Christians acquiring cable TV subscriptions; and 15 percent disapprove while 12 percent are uncertain and 73 percent approve of mixed swimming.

"Uncertain" may not mean indecisiveness, for it can also mean "it all depends." Additionally, some pastors noted, "I approve, but I do not prefer." Such comments were often written in the margins of questionnaires, particularly relating to VCRs and cable TV subscriptions. The men advise discretion and discernment in these matters.

The 8 percent of respondents who identify themselves as Evangelical distinguish themselves from the majority on four practices. They are more willing to approve of attending movie theaters (39 percent compared to 4 percent for Fundamentalists), use of playing cards (64 percent to 16 percent), renting movies for VCRs (80 percent to 53 percent) and using cable TV (76 percent to 51 percent).

Conclusion

Pastors in the GARBC are a substantially homogeneous group. They are similar to each other in educational attainment, race, social class and upbringing. Undoubtedly such demographic homogeneity helps produce consensus in the pastors' views toward certain challenging lifestyle questions. GARBC pastors consider themselves philosophically conservative, and they apparently practice their philosophic convictions in the concrete experiences of everyday life.

The term "Fundamentalist" has received much negative press in recent years, but GARBC pastors are comfortable with it for the most part. A considerable majority reject the label "Evangelical," evidently because it invokes certain unacceptable symbols and ideas. Our findings indicate little or no support for the argument that GARBC pastors are becoming liberal in any social, political or theological sense of that term.

GARBC pastors are an important body of conservative Christian ministers. Their consensus attitudes help them preserve values they consider important to a dedicated spiritual walk. GARBC pastors know who they are and what they believe. Because of this, they lead their congregations with conviction and integrity.

PART TWO

Are our pastors as agreed on issues such as abortion as they are on personal lifestyle standards?

As religion and politics make headlines in the national news, Americans debate whether pastors should participate in politics or openly express their social and political views in an attempt to influence their congregations. Some pastors consider it a matter of conviction and duty to encourage church members in social and political activism, while others consciously avoid social and political statements in order to concentrate their efforts on Biblical instruction about personal spiritual life and development.

The attitudes of GARBC pastors toward social and political concerns are important. The General Association of Regular Baptist Churches is one of the largest avowedly fundamentalist associations in the United States. GARBC pastors represent a significant subgroup of the American public. The Association is a potential political force. But the GARBC is also important because it has not assumed an Association-wide politically activist stance. The questions of whether and how to participate in politics are left to individual pastors and churches. This "nonpolitical" Association posture is different from most other contemporary denominational and religious organizations.

GARBC Survey

In the April 1989 issue of the *Baptist Bulletin* we introduced the survey and reported our findings on the personal background characteristics and lifestyle standards of GARBC pastors. Now we focus on GARBC pastors' social and political attitudes. Approximately one half of the 130 survey items revealed various political views and pastors' public expression of these views. Our analysis groups the questions in three broad categories: abortion, politics in the church and selected political concerns.

Abortion

We asked GARBC pastors eight attitudinal questions concerning whether or not a pregnant woman should be able to obtain a legal abortion. GARBC pastors are unquestionably opposed to abortion-on-demand and abortion as a form of birth control. More than 99 percent disapprove of abortion simply because "the woman wants it," and more than 99 percent disapprove of abortion for a low-income family just because "they cannot afford more children." Approximately 100 percent disapprove of abortion as an option for a married woman who does not want more children.

GARBC pastors also reject abortion as a legitimate alternative to pregnancy for women who have experienced sexual attack. More than 87 percent disapprove of abortion for rape victims. Of the remaining, nearly 8 percent are uncertain while 5 percent approve of abortion for rape pregnancies. More than 86 percent disapprove, 9 percent are uncertain and 4 percent approve of abortion for incest victims. A few men suggested that a D and C be done right away.

Pastors reject abortion even if there is a "strong chance of serious defect in the baby." Ninety-six (96) percent disapprove of abortion in this instance; only 1 percent approve.

GARBC pastors differ considerably from one another in attitudes toward abortion when a "woman's own health is seriously endangered by the pregnancy." While 49 percent disapprove—a substantially lower figure than the percentages quoted for other abortion items—27 percent are uncertain and 24 percent approve. Several who approve indicated their support was for cases in which the evidence was overwhelming that the woman's life was endangered. One man asked, "How can we know whether life is endangered or not?" Other pastors contend that this scenario almost never happens.

Considering abortion as an option for protecting a mother's health creates a life-for-life tension. Some pastors noted that they disapproved of abortion to protect a mother's *health,* but approved of abortion to save a mother's *life.* In response to another question, 93 percent of our sample approved a constitutional amendment against abortion, excluding abortions performed to save a mother's life. GARBC pastors reflect majority opinion in the national pro-life movement.

It is evident that GARBC pastors are struggling with this issue. What is danger? What is health—physical, mental? For centuries Christians have permitted the taking of life by advancing a theology of self-defense. But this position generally assumed that the life taken was an adult, threatening life—not an unborn, innocent life.

Politics in the Church

GARBC pastors are virtually unanimous in their opposition to abortion, but this consensus disappeared when we asked them to share their views on a variety of "politics in the church" questions. Consider these findings:

About 84 percent believe it is appropriate to take a personal stand on a political issue, but this drops to 60 percent if the stand must be taken in the pulpit; 27 percent believe a political stance should never be assumed in the pulpit. Thirty-four (34) percent approve of personally participating in a protest march, 22 percent are uncertain and 44 percent disapprove. Only 13 percent approve of civil disobedience, while 14 percent are uncertain and 73 percent disapprove. More than 75 percent disapprove of endorsing a political candidate in the pulpit. Twenty-four (24) percent approve of personally running for public office, but 59 percent disapprove.

More than 73 percent will preach a sermon on a controversial social or political topic. Many pastors qualified their views, commenting in the survey margins: "Only when the political issue is also an ethical, Biblical issue." "Many political issues today are, in truth, moral issues, which a preacher of the Word of God is obligated to address." "I will take a strong stand against certain political issues (for example, abortion, homosexuality and pornography) because in reality these are spiritual issues."

Pastors are divided on the statement, "If enough men were brought to Christ, social ills would take care of themselves." More than 54 percent agree, but 10 percent are uncertain and 35 percent disagree. Eighty-one (81) percent agree that ministers have great potential to influence congregational political beliefs, but 97 percent disagree with the statement that the church should put less emphasis on individual sanctification and more on transforming the social in conforming with Christ's teaching.

We also asked pastors to evaluate whether "clergymen of different faiths need to cooperate more in politics, even if they can't agree in theology." About 66 percent disagree, 19 percent are uncertain and 15 percent agree with this statement. It appears that GARBC pastors are reluctant to participate in the many religious or church lobbying and interest groups organized in the past decade.

GARBC pastors concentrate their pulpit comments upon personal, family and moral concerns, tending to avoid national societal questions. Pastors demonstrated this inclination by responding to a list of 16 current issues, indicating whether they often, seldom or never mentioned them in sermons. Family problems in America, abortion, alcohol and drug abuse, pornography and obscenity, and homosexuality are often mentioned. Least likely to receive pulpit attention are United States policy in Latin America, unemployment, environmental problems, the budget deficit, national defense, civil rights, hunger and poverty, women's issues, school prayer, gambling and the Middle East.

Political Views

We asked pastors to express their opinions on a variety of public concerns. On all but three issues, a majority of the pastors assumed a position most commentators consider politically conservative. More than 35 percent disapprove, while 33 percent are uncertain and 32 percent approve that the United States should not support dictators, even those friendly to the United States; 41 percent disapprove of environmental protection as a top priority, even if it raises prices or costs jobs, while 27 percent are uncertain and 32 percent approve. Surprisingly, pastors are divided on whether Congress should pass a constitutional amendment that would permit prayer as a regular exercise in all public schools; more than 49 percent approve, but 24 percent are uncertain and 27 percent disapprove.

Pastoral views on other issues evidence more agreement. Ninety-four (94) percent reject the proposition that the United States needs an equal rights amendment; 81 percent disapprove of homosexuals having the same rights and privileges of other citizens. Many pastors insisted that homosexuals already have rights, but that they should not be considered a minority with extra rights or preferred treatment.

Sixty-three (63) percent of the pastors disapprove of the statement, "Blacks and other minorities discriminated against in the past may need special government help in achieving their rightful place in America." More than 54 percent approve of tax credits for parents of students in Christian schools, while 20 percent are uncertain and 26 percent disapprove. More than 78 percent disapprove of public policy discouraging ownership and use of handguns, and 63 percent disapprove of the United States making a nuclear arms limitation treaty with the USSR a top priority, while 21 percent are uncertain and 16 percent approve; 55 percent approve, while 27 percent are uncertain and 18 percent disapprove of the United States spending more money for the military and defense. Seventy-six (76) percent disapprove of the federal government doing more to solve problems like poverty and unemployment; in fact, 85 percent believe the government is already providing too many services. Fifty-four (54) percent believe the free enterprise system is the only economic arrangement compatible with Christian beliefs, while 22 percent are uncertain and 23 percent believe other economic systems may be compatible with Christianity.

Conclusion

GARBC pastors are socially and politically conservative. While some struggle with whether abortion is a legitimate means for protecting a mother's health or life, most pastors strongly reject abortion. GARBC pastors believe national politics should not be discussed in the church. They prefer to focus their sermons upon personal and family matters rather than upon social and political issues.

GARBC pastors are uncertain whether social ills would be solved if enough people came to Christ, yet most do not believe the church should place less emphasis upon sanctification and more on transforming the social order. They do not believe political cooperation with other clergy of differing faiths is necessary or wise. GARBC pastors prefer to exercise political influence individually, if at all.

While GARBC pastors evidence more disagreement on social and political issues than they do on lifestyle standards, they nevertheless maintain a focused commitment to conservative ideals. Their politics seem to be an extension of their theology and are clearly secondary. These pastors seek not so much to change the world as to change the people in the world and to ready them for the time to come.

PART THREE

People frequently ask pastors to sanction changing marriage and family practices and to help solve the problems these changes sometimes create.

Witness the emergence of two-income and two-career families, "commuter marriages" in which spouses spend the workweek in separate cities, rising divorce rates, single-parent families and multiple remarriages producing new terms like "serial monogamy" and "aggregate families" (meaning children by former spouses becoming half-brothers and sisters). Even the most conservative churches have faced increases of divorce among Christians, and pastors are regularly asked to remarry divorced Christians.

Churches in many denominations are reworking their constitutions, introducing "gender-inclusive" language permitting female pastoral and church staff. Some denominations are ordaining women as pastors; others are discussing allegedly sexist passages in the Scriptures.

GARBC pastors are being asked to provide a Biblical interpretation for these changes in marriage and family attitudes, and they are responding. But how? . . .

This report focuses upon pastoral responses to a series of questions about women in society, divorce and remarriage, and the role of divorced people in the work of the church. Pastors provided considerable commentary about these issues in the margins of their questionnaires. We will share some of these pastoral opinions with the survey statistics. While these statements may not be representative, they do provide clues to the subtly nuanced attitudes pastors develop on complex issues.

Women in the Family, Church and Society

A significant majority of GARBC pastors (79 percent) believe it is more important for a wife to help her husband's career than to have one herself. One pastor argued that it was *their* career, not the husband's career. Eleven (11) percent are uncertain and 10 percent disapprove of a wife yielding her career concerns to her husband. More than 86 percent of our sample believe it is much better for everyone if the man is the achiever outside the home and the woman takes care of the house and family; 7 percent are uncertain and 7 percent disagree.

More than 86 percent believe preschool children are likely to suffer when the mother works outside the home, and 63 percent insist that a working woman cannot establish just as warm a relationship with her child as a mother who does not work outside the home. One pastor stated, "I agree in theory, but it would not happen without a lot of effort." Clearly, GARBC pastors are not in favor of working mothers.

Approximately 80 percent of these men do not believe it is right for a woman to refuse to have children, even against the desires of her husband to have children; 14 percent are uncertain and 6 percent approve. GARBC pastors' attitudes about family decision-making are also revealed by the fact that 92 percent believe the husband is the ultimate authority as family head and has primary responsibility for the operation of the household. On the other hand, when it is recommended that decision-making be shared equally, 31 percent approve; 4 percent are uncertain and 65 percent disapprove.

Some pastors explain the apparent contradiction in this way: "Ultimate authority rests with the husband, but the wife should have equal input regarding matters that affect the decision, and the husband should be sensitive."

"The final responsibility is the husband's, but he is wise to follow the advice of his wife 90 percent of the time. However, he is ultimately responsible even in shared decisions or if she decides."

"If he is wise he will delegate authority to his wife, assuming she is capable."

Divorce and Remarriage

Both divorce and remarriage are increasing, and these concerns affect every segment of society. Pastors are often the first to know family problems exist, and finding resolutions to family problems is a complex task. The topics of divorce and remarriage produced as much variation in pastoral opinion as any on the entire questionnaire.

GARBC pastors are split on the divorce question between those who maintain divorce should be avoided under any circumstance (54 percent) and those who believe divorce should be avoided except in an extreme situation (46 percent). Those who checked "extreme situation" often cited repeated infidelity or desertions.

A question asking when remarriage after divorce is acceptable yielded even more disagreement. A majority of 54 percent believe that remarriage after divorce is acceptable when the former mate is dead.

Another 27 percent consider sexual unfaithfulness proper grounds for remarriage, while 11 percent authorize remarriage if reconciliation to the former mate is impossible. Slightly more than 1 percent contend remarriage after divorce is always acceptable, but 2 percent do not condone remarriage under any circumstances.

Pastors stated, "I agree with none of these options."

"Each case has to be considered individually."

"These options seem not to make provision for forgiveness."

"What about pre- and post-conversion distinctions?"

"My answer would include a repentant spirit, willingness for extensive counseling in preparation for the second marriage and a commitment to spiritual renewal."

"Remarriage after divorce is never acceptable, except to the former mate without intervening marriages."

Women, Divorce and/or Remarriage

More than 99 percent of GARBC pastors are opposed to the ordination of women, but nearly one third (32 percent) approve of women serving on a pastoral staff to exercise authority over other women. Several respondents took issue with the term "pastoral," suggesting that "church staff" would be a more appropriate designation. Others preferred descriptions like women's coordinator, counselor or minister of Christian education. Eight out of ten pastors (81 percent) disapprove of women teaching adult Sunday School classes comprised of male and female members.

Divorce and/or remarriage also raises questions relating to church service and ministry. About 94 percent of GARBC pastors disapprove of divorced individuals serving on the pastoral staff, and more than 88 percent disapprove of divorced individuals serving as deacons. GARBC pastors approve of including divorced people in the ministry in some church positions: 80 percent approve of divorced people serving as Sunday School teachers, 67 percent as youth sponsors and 98 percent as choir members.

GARBC pastors apparently make a distinction between serving in leadership positions and other roles in the church. It is interesting that more pastors accept divorced Sunday School teachers than divorced youth sponsors. Perhaps the age and discernment of the children taught make a difference in pastoral attitudes.

Conclusion

GARBC pastors hold so-called traditional attitudes toward family decision-making, working women or mothers, divorce and remarriage, and the role of women or divorced individuals in the local church. Pastors believe that husbands are responsible for family life and well-being, that divorce is wrong and that neither women nor divorced individuals should assume leadership positions in the church. Increasing educational opportunities for women and an expanding computer-based economy virtually assure more women in the work force. Pastoral responses to this development will influence family practices in the 1990s.

Approximately 100 percent of GARBC pastors reject divorce as an option for marriage partners for all but in extreme situations. GARBC pastors do not treat divorce lightly. But they do disagree. Nearly one half of our sample believe divorce is acceptable in an "extreme situation." The questions then become, What is an extreme situation? Who determines if it has occurred? Whether or not the definition of an extreme situation is broadened and extended to include more marital conflicts is an important development to watch in the future of the GARBC. If social pressures calling for a more inclusive definition continue to increase, pastoral disagreement on this issue will most likely also increase.

Two divorce-related questions present more perplexing dilemmas than any of the other 130 items on the survey. Under what, if any, circumstances is remarriage legitimate following a divorce? In what ways should divorced people be encouraged to support the ministry of a church? Divorce and remarriage, divorce and ministry—GARBC pastors would do well to discuss these family matters.

Funds for this survey were provided through a grant from the Cedarville College Faculty Development Fund. Robert G. Parr is an associate professor of sociology at Cedarville. His former colleague Rex M. Rogers served as an associate professor of political science.

Part I appeared in the Baptist Bulletin *(October 1989), pp. 14–17. Part II was published in the* Baptist Bulletin *(April 1989), pp. 10–12, 40. Part III appeared in the* Baptist Bulletin *(June 1990), pp. 12–14.*

APPENDIX H

STATISTICAL REPORT OF CHURCHES

Date	Place	Churches Received	Churches Dropped	Total
1932	Chicago, Illinois			
1933	Buffalo, New York			
1934	Gary, Indiana			
1935	Grand Rapids, Michigan			
1936	Chicago, Illinois			
1937	Johnson City, New York			76
1938	Waterloo, Iowa			105
1939	Paterson, New Jersey	18		125
1940	Erie, Pennsylvania	17		143
1941	Pontiac, Michigan	29		171
1942	Waterloo, Iowa	20	0	191
1943	Johnson City, New York	72	7	256
1944	Grand Rapids, Michigan	42	2	296
1945	Canceled	35	3	328
1946	Waterloo, Iowa	57	0	385
1947	Atlantic City, New Jersey	60	2	443
1948	Grand Rapids, Michigan	43	7	479
1949	Cleveland, Ohio	46	6	520
1950	Buffalo, New York	59	12	567
1951	Oakland, California	54	12	609
1952	Des Moines, Iowa	32	7	634
1953	Philadelphia, Pennsylvania	32	9	657
1954	Chicago, Illinois	44	11	690
1955	Kansas City, Missouri	43	7	726
1956	Seattle, Washington	44	11	760
1957	Grand Rapids, Michigan	61	12	809
1958	Columbus, Ohio	47	13	843
1959	Rochester, Minnesota	62	18	887
1960	Long Beach, California	54	7	934
1961	Winona Lake, Indiana	73	15	992
1962	Springfield, Massachusetts	52	13	1,031

Date	Place	Churches Received	Churches Dropped	Total
1963	Omaha, Nebraska	78	9	1,100
1964	Winona Lake, Indiana	68	12	1,156
1965	Des Moines, Iowa	53	9	1,200
1966	Grand Rapids, Michigan	58	14	1,244
1967	Seattle, Washington	33	13	1,264
1968	Rochester, New York	63	11	1,316
1969	Fort Wayne, Indiana	62	17	1,361
1970	Denver, Colorado	50	11	1,400
1971	Winona Lake, Indiana	37	11	1,426
1972	San Diego, California	38	21	1,443
1973	Kansas City, Missouri	46	16	1,473
1974	Ocean Grove, New Jersey	35	13	1,495
1975	Winona Lake, Indiana	26	18	1,503
1976	Seattle, Washington	49	24	1,528
1977	Des Moines, Iowa	32	18	1,542
1978	Lakeland, Florida	28	26	1,544
1979	Dayton, Ohio	35	25	1,554
1980	San Diego, California	27	24	1,557
1981	Winona Lake, Indiana	34	20	1,571
1982	Denver, Colorado	35	21	1,585
1983	Niagara Falls, New York	30	22	1,593
1984	Seattle, Washington	29	19	1,603
1985	Springfield, Illinois	22	26	1,599
1986	Grand Rapids, Michigan	22	21	1,600
1987	Ames, Iowa	12	18	1,594
1988	Anaheim, California	11	15	1,590
1989	Columbus, Ohio	18	26	1,582
1990	Niagara Falls, New York	17	25	1,574

This chart was adapted from *What a Fellowship!* by Merle R. Hull (Schaumburg, IL: Regular Baptist Press, 1981), p. 78.